PERSPECTIVES ON TRANSITIONS IN SCHOOLING AND INSTRUCTIONAL PRACTICE

Edited by Susan E. Elliott-Johns and Daniel H. Jarvis

This collection of essays by twenty-six international experts examines student transitions between major levels of schooling, teacher transitions in instructional practice, and the intersection of these two significant themes in education research. Unique in format and scope, the volume offers new insights on current pedagogical practices, obstacles to effective transitions, and proven strategies for stakeholders involved in supporting students in transition.

The book is divided into four sections, representing the four main transitions in format schooling: Early Years (Home, Preschool, and Kindergarten) to Early Elementary (Grades 1–3); Early Elementary to Late Elementary (Grades 4–8); Late Elementary to Secondary (Grades 9–12); and Secondary to Postsecondary (College and University). Combining theoretical approaches with practical examples of school-based initiatives, this book will be of interest to those dedicated to improving the student experience, both academic and emotional, and to those promoting teacher professional learning and growth.

SUSAN E. ELLIOTT-JOHNS is an associate professor in the Schulich School of Education at Nipissing University.

DANIEL H. JARVIS is a professor and Chair of Graduate Studies in Education in the Schulich School of Education at Nipissing University.

Perspectives on Transitions in Schooling and Instructional Practice

EDITED BY
SUSAN E. ELLIOTT-JOHNS
AND DANIEL H. JARVIS

UNIVERSITY OF TORONTO PRESS
Toronto Buffalo London

© University of Toronto Press 2013
Toronto Buffalo London
www.utppublishing.com
Printed in Canada

ISBN 978-1-4426-4704-6 (cloth)
ISBN 978-1-4426-1481-9 (paper)

Library and Archives Canada Cataloguing in Publication

Perspectives on transitions in schooling and instructional practice / edited by
Susan E. Elliott-Johns and Daniel H. Jarvis.

Includes bibliographical references and index.
ISBN 978-1-4426-4704-6 (bound.) – ISBN 978-1-4426-1481-9 (pbk.)

1. Articulation (Education).   2. Effective teaching.   3. Student adjustment.
4. School improvement programs.   I. Elliott-Johns, Susan, author, writer
of introduction, editor of compilation   II. Jarvis, Daniel, author, writer of
introduction, editor of compilation

LB14.7.P47 2013   371.2'1   C2013-903889-2

University of Toronto Press acknowledges the financial assistance to its
publishing program of the Canada Council for the Arts and the Ontario
Arts Council.

Canada Council   Conseil des Arts
for the Arts   du Canada

ONTARIO ARTS COUNCIL
CONSEIL DES ARTS DE L'ONTARIO

50 YEARS OF ONTARIO GOVERNMENT SUPPORT OF THE ARTS
50 ANS DE SOUTIEN DU GOUVERNEMENT DE L'ONTARIO AUX ARTS

University of Toronto Press acknowledges the financial support of the
Government of Canada through the Canada Book Fund for its publishing
activities.

Contents

Part II: Early Elementary (Grades 1–3) to Late Elementary (Grades 4–8)

Part III: Late Elementary (Grades 4–8) to Secondary (Grades 9–12)

Tables and Figures

Tables

Figures

Acknowledgments

We should like to thank all of the authors for their contributions to this text, the positive collaboration, and for assisting us, and our readers, to think deeply about these significant issues in education.

We should also like to thank the acquisition editors Brittany Lavery and Douglas Hildebrand at the University of Toronto Press for assisting us in the completion of this collective work.

We gratefully acknowledge the publication of this project was made possible through funding provided by the Schulich School of Education and Nipissing University, North Bay, Ontario.

About the Contributors

Patrick Akos is an associate professor and program coordinator for the School Counseling Program in the School of Education at the University of North Carolina at Chapel Hill. He initially trained as a teacher and subsequently worked as an elementary school, middle school, and college counsellor. He holds a Ph.D. in Counselor Education from the University of Virginia and is licensed as both a teacher and a counsellor. His research is conceptually founded on strengths-based school counselling (SBSC). In particular, his work centres on how school counsellors can promote development and build strengths in students during early adolescence–school years associated with puberty, one of the most diverse, rapid, and intense periods of human development. A primary focus of Akos's research is on school transitions (e.g., elementary to middle, middle to high school) and how school counsellors and schools can promote optimal developmental paths and strengths-enhancing environments.

Kelsey Augst Felton is a practising school counsellor at Hilburn Drive Academy in Wake County, North Carolina. She has a Master of Education in school counselling and a Master of Arts in Education in curriculum and instruction. Her research has focused upon student transitions, primarily the kindergarten transition, the transition into third grade, and the transition from elementary to middle school.

Michele Binstadt is currently a community early childhood literacy coordinator with the Ready Together – Transition to School Program (Inala to Ipswich), and she is employed by the Crèche and Kindergarten Association (C&K), Queensland, Australia. She holds a Bachelor of Psychology (Honours) from James Cook University, Townsville, North

Queensland, and a Certificate IV Training and Workplace Assessment (Bremer TAFE, Ipswich, Queensland). She has also completed the Nursery Foundation Red Seal Certificate (0–6 years) at the London Montessori Centre, England. Binstadt's research interests are in the areas of early years' literacy and transition to school. Her current role as coordinator of the Ready Together – Transition to School Program allows her to engage in action research related to the program with the results contributing to the early years' literacy and transition to school evidence base. Michele has secured diverse volunteer and paid employment in Indonesia, the United States, India, the United Kingdom, Ghana, and Turkey (1994–2002). Many of these positions involved working in the early childhood field. Binstadt's experience of working in a variety of countries contributed to her interest in cultural diversity and continues to inform her current practice.

Dawn Buzza is an associate professor and associate dean of the Faculty of Education at Wilfrid Laurier University in Waterloo, Ontario. She holds a Ph.D. in Instructional Psychology and M.A. in Education (Counselling) from Simon Fraser University. Her research interests include child and adolescent development and self-regulated learning (SRL), or how students develop expertise in how to learn. Research on SRL involves consideration of learning strategies, metacognition, and motivation. Her recent work in this area has examined pre-service and practising teachers' concepts of SRL and the ways in which teachers can support SRL in secondary school contexts. Previously, Buzza was an associate professor in the Faculty of Education at the University of Victoria, teaching undergraduate and graduate courses in learning, educational psychology, and child and adolescent development. She has published and presented her research extensively, both nationally and internationally.

Patricia Byers, Ph.D. (York University), has taught for 30 years at the college level with a focus on mathematics in business, aviation, health sciences, and technology classrooms. She has conducted sessions aimed at using technology in classroom teaching, understanding metacognition and mathematics learning, and teaching students learning strategies. Her research investigates first-year students struggling with learning mathematics with particular attention to the differences students experience between secondary and college mathematics teaching and learning. She has participated in the College Mathematics Project, at the local and provincial college levels, from its inception. Her other activities have involved projects with the Ontario Colleges Mathematics Association and the Higher Education Quality Council of Ontario. She is currently a consultant in college mathematics education.

Maria Cantalini-Williams is an associate professor in the Schulich School of Education, Nippising University, North Bay, Ontario. She has been an educator for over 30 years having worked in elementary school, university, and college settings. Cantalini-Williams has researched and written extensively in the area of early childhood education, reflecting her area of doctoral study and her focus during time spent as a board program consultant. In recent years, she has taught Bachelor and Master's of Education courses and has served in an administrative role as associate dean (interim), providing leadership over a concurrent education program for Nipissing University. Other areas of research interest include teacher education, mentorship, international teaching, and technology in education.

Jennifer Cartmel is currently a senior lecturer in child and family studies at Griffith University in Queensland, Australia. She holds a Diploma of Teaching from Mt Gravatt CAE and a Bachelor of Educational Studies from the University of Queensland. She was awarded both her Master of Education (Early Childhood) and Ph.D. from the Queensland University of Technology. Her research interests include outside hours school care; work-integrated learning; preparation of practitioners for children's services; policy, curriculum, and practice in children's services; and early childhood education and care.

Karen Choate is a middle school reading and language arts teacher and an adjunct professor of curriculum and instruction at Concordia University in Montreal. She has co-authored articles on student transitions. She received her Ed.D. in educational leadership at Roosevelt University.

Rob Graham is currently an assistant professor in the Schulich School of Education at Nipissing University, North Bay, Ontario. He holds a B.A. (Honours), a B.Ed, and M.Ed., and is currently a Ph.D. candidate at Lancaster University in England studying in the field of E-Research and Technology-Enhanced Learning. His research interests also include examining the barriers that impede the effective use of technology-enhanced learning in K–12 learning environments. Over the past 20 years

Graham has had the opportunity to teach children and adults in a broad range of varied, and sometimes exotic, settings. These have included appointments in Hawaii, Japan, a community college, a penal institution, and 13 years in an intermediate-level public school.

Susan E. Elliott-Johns is an associate professor in the Schulich School of Education at Nipissing University in North Bay, Ontario. She holds her Ph.D. and M.Ed. from McGill University and a B.Ed (Honours) from the University of London. Prior to joining the faculty at Nipissing, in 2006, she spent 25 years in public education as a teacher (K–10), literacy consultant, teacher educator, and elementary school administrator. Her current research interests include literacy teacher education and professional learning that supports and enhances effective instructional practices in contemporary classrooms.

Michael Fowler holds an Ed.D. and is currently the director of secondary accountability in the Higley Unified School District located in Gilbert, Arizona. He earned his doctorate from Northern Arizona University, and his research interests include credit-based transition programs, small learning communities, and educational leadership.

Chris Hachkowski is the principal of Aboriginal programs and an assistant professor in the Schulich School of Education at Nipissing University in North Bay, Ontario. He holds an M.Ed. from Nipissing University and is a doctoral candidate at the Ontario Institute for Studies in Education, University of Toronto. A former science teacher and principal at a First Nations–administered secondary school, his current research interests include developing culturally relevant curricula, Aboriginal teacher education, Aboriginal student success, and Aboriginal language teacher education.

Gregory M. Hauser is an associate professor of educational leadership at Roosevelt University. He has authored and co-authored book chapters, articles, and papers on technology, school leadership, and school reform. His recently published book with Dennis Koutouzos is titled *The Standards-Based Digital School Leader Portfolio: Using TaskStream, LiveText, and PowerPoint* (2010). He serves on the editorial review board for the *Journal of Scholarship and Practice, International Educational Studies*, and the *International On-line Journal of Educational Sciences*. He completed a Ph.D. in educational administration at the University of Wisconsin-Madison and was a Fulbright Scholar to Germany.

Gianna Helling has been a teacher and administrator with the Toronto Catholic District School Board for the past 20 years. She is currently the principal of Saints Cosmas and Damian Catholic Elementary School in Toronto. Helling holds a B.A. and B.Ed. from York University and an M.Ed. in Curriculum from the Ontario Institute for Studies in Education, University of Toronto. She has worked in a variety of school communities, both elementary and secondary, including inner-city and single gender schools. Helling has presented to administrators across Ontario, Canada, and internationally, on topics including Strategies for Students at Risk, Literacy at the Secondary Level, and Establishing Successful Transitions K–12. She is a member of the Toronto Catholic District School Board's New Teacher Induction Committee and the Expert Panel on Literacy, and currently, she serves as chair of the AGM Steering and Constitution Committees for the Catholic Principals Council of Ontario.

Amber Jackson is a member of sessional staff at Griffith University in Queensland, Australia. She holds her Bachelor of Human Services in Child and Family Studies with Honours from Griffith University, and is currently completing a Master of Counselling degree at the University of the Sunshine Coast. Her research interests include conducting research with children, in particular, exploring their perspectives and experiences of the transition to formal schooling; using creative research methods, such as mind maps, to engage children in research; examining different perspectives on school transition (e.g., those of children, parents, and early childhood and school educators). Jackson is also interested in exploring children's experiences of ADHD and the use of creative counselling approaches to support children with behavioural difficulties.

Daniel H. Jarvis is a professor in the Schulich School of Education at Nipissing University, North Bay, Ontario. He holds a Ph.D. in Education Studies from the University of Western Ontario, an M.Ed. and B. Ed. from Nipissing University, and a B.A. from the University of Waterloo. His background is in the areas of mathematics and visual arts, having taught both topics at the secondary level for 5 years, and at the postsecondary level for the past decade within the teacher education, continuting education, and graduate education programs. His research interests include instructional technology, integrated curricula, teacher professional learning, and educational leadership.

Anne Jordan is a professor emerita at the Ontario Institute for Studies in Education, University of Toronto, currently teaching in two Masters' programs. She previously taught in the Elementary Education Program at Queen's University in Kingston, Ontario, and in elementary schools in the United Kingdom. Her research interests have most recently taken her into over 100 Ontario elementary classrooms as part of the Supporting Effective Teachers project – an examination of inclusive teaching practices and resources. With colleagues and students, Jordan has published 27 scholarly papers, book chapters, and a textbook since 2000, based on her research. She also has written about legislation and policy in special education and its impact on school cultures and teacher beliefs and practices.

Maureen Kendrick is an associate professor in the Department of Language and Literacy Education at the University of British Columbia. Her research focuses on literacy and multimodality as social practice, family and community literacy, literacy and international development, and digital literacies. She is currently researching digital literacy practices in secondary English language classrooms in Kenya, Uganda, and Canada.

Gaye Luna holds an Ed.D. and is professor of community colleges / higher education in the College of Education at Northern Arizona University. She earned her doctorate from the University of Southern California in Los Angeles. Her research interests include mentoring, partnerships, leadership in higher education, and sex-based wage discrimination.

Callie Mady is an associate professor at Nipissing University, North Bay, Ontario, in the Schulich School of Education. She holds a Ph.D. from OISE, University of Toronto, with a focus on second language education. Her research interests include French as a second language education and multilingual language acquisition. She is the author of numerous academic articles and practical publications for educators.

Jennifer Rowsell is Canada Research Chair in Multiliteracies and an associate professor at Brock University, St. Catharines, Ontario. She received her Ph.D. from King's College, University of London, an M.A. from University College London, University of London, and an Honours B.A. from University of Toronto. Her research interests include multimodality, multiliteracies, teacher education, new literacy studies, ethnography, and Bourdieusian sociology.

Lyn Sharratt is a professor at the Ontario Institute for Studies in Education, University of Toronto, where she lectures and currently coordinates the 25-student Learning and Leadership Ed.D. Program. She is the former superintendent of curriculum and instruction services in York Region District School Board where she and her staff curriculum team analysed assessment data and developed a comprehensive literacy improvement program launched with the cooperation of senior leadership, principals, and over 8,800 teachers. She has been a curriculum consultant, an administrato, and has taught elementary grades and secondary students in inner-city and rural settings. Sharratt is lead author, with Michael Fullan, of both *Realization: The Change Imperative for Increasing District-Wide Reform* (2009) and *Putting FACES on the Data: What Great Leaders Do!* (2012). Currently an international consultant, she works with administrators, curriculum consultants, and teachers in Chile, Australia, the United States, the United Kingdom, and Canada.

Marian Small is dean emerita and professor emerita at the University of New Brunswick. Her doctoral degree was granted from the University of British Columbia, and her research interests revolve around teacher questioning, differentiating instruction, and big ideas in K–12 mathematics education. She has written over 70 student texts, teacher resources, and professional books, and her research resulted in the creation of maps describing student development in each of the five math strands.

Leslie Telfer is the principal of program–school effectiveness with the Brant Haldimand Norfolk Catholic District School Board, Ontario. She obtained a Bachelor of Arts from the University of Western Ontario, a Bachelor of Education from the University of Windsor, and a Master of Education from Nipissing University. She began her career with her current board as an elementary classroom teacher, and she has also served as a system literacy teacher, vice principal, and principal in the elementary panel. In her current role as a system support principal, she is committed to promoting continuous school improvement and success for all students. Her research interests include leadership and student achievement and effective schools.

Thomas P. Thomas is associate professor of secondary education at Roosevelt University. He has authored and co-authored book chapters, articles, encyclopedia entries, and papers on school reform, multicultural education, curriculum history, theory, and policy. He recently completed a term on the board of directors for the Society of Professors of Education. A former high school teacher, principal, and senior consultant for the Illinois State Board of Education, Thomas completed his Ph.D. in curriculum and instruction at the University of Illinois at Chicago.

Lay See Yeo is currently an assistant professor at the National Institute of Education, Nanyang Technological University in Singapore. She holds her Ph.D. (School Psychology) from the University of Iowa. Her current research interests include cognitive-behavioural therapy, child and adolescent development and psychopathology, and interventions for learning, behavioural, and developmental disabilities. Yeo is also a Nationally Certified School Psychologist (NCSP), in the United States, and a registered psychologist, in Singapore.

PERSPECTIVES ON TRANSITIONS
IN SCHOOLING AND INSTRUCTIONAL PRACTICE

Introduction

SUSAN E. ELLIOTT-JOHNS AND DANIEL H. JARVIS

This book project was conceptualized and designed with two predominant themes in mind: student transitions between major levels of schooling and teacher transitions in instructional practice, in light of contemporary reforms. We were particularly interested in how transitions in teachers' instructional practices (individual/corporate, formal/informal, mandated/voluntary) may affect student transition experiences (emotional well-being, academic achievement) throughout the schooling journey.

The book is structured according to the following four parts:

Part I: Early Years (Home/Preschool/Kindergarten) to Early Elementary (Grades 1–3)
Part II: Early Elementary (Grades 1–3) to Late Elementary (Grades 4–8)
Part III: Late Elementary (Grades 4–8) to Secondary (Grades 9–12)
Part IV: Secondary (Grades 9–12) to Postsecondary (College/University)

Based on our preliminary research into transitions literature, invitations were sent to a select number of leading experts in the field, who then agreed (as individuals or as co-author teams) to contribute a chapter relevant to one of the areas listed above. In some cases, the contents of chapters are such that they could arguably belong within two or more different sections, yet we have placed each within the particular section that seemed most appropriate.

The nineteen chapters comprise entries from four countries (Australia, Canada, Singapore, and the United States), and represent the contributions of twenty-six scholars including counsellors, coordinators, consultants, administrators, professors, and a Canada Research Chair in Multiliteracies. The collection is somewhat unique in that it brings together a group of highly informed and experienced educators, possessing very different disciplinary backgrounds and working across a wide range of contexts, all of whom are equally passionate about understanding and meaningfully addressing the needs of students and/or teachers as these relate to transitional spaces in education. The result is a rich, colourful spectrum of commentary that provides new insights into shared critical issues and related recommendations for transitional planning.

In examining transitions in schooling and instructional practice, one is invariably drawn to the history of education in terms of trying to better understand the various reform movements, political platforms, and educational manifestos that have influenced the structure of schooling and the nature of teacher practices over time and across national/cultural boundaries. Given their own backgrounds, the co-editors have become particularly interested in the major reform movements that have characterized and shaped the disciplinary areas of literacy and mathematics at all levels of formalized schooling – from early years to postsecondary education.

Specific to reading, the history of teacher education from about 1900 to the 1990s corresponds conceptually to three general trends in teacher education (Russell & Korthagen, 1995). For example, from approximately 1900 until the 1960s, the "apprenticeship" model was central to the preparation of teachers, emphasizing what teachers should learn in coursework and from their mentors. Then, from the 1960s to the early 1980s, the trend was to assist teachers in improving both their knowledge base and the application of knowledge about both content and methods; this was the basal textbook era that drove instructional practices in reading. From the mid-1980s through the 1990s, these models were challenged, and a shift occurred towards more holistic approaches emphasizing reflective teaching, journal writing, action research (Baumann, Hoffmann, Moon, & Duffy-Hester, 1998), and the development of the reader, the teacher, and the learning conditions that surround them (Paris, 2001). Recent years have seen a further shift towards balanced approaches to reading instruction in schools and classrooms, that is, incorporating integrated instructional components that promote "skills in context" and more eclectic approaches to instruction (Bomer, 2011; Routman, 2000), but as yet little is known about how the shift towards balanced literacy instruction is actually playing out in teacher education programs.

In mathematics, the past century has also featured several major shifts, or trends, in teacher education. From the beginning of formalized schooling in North America to the mid-1900s, teachers were primarily prepared to teach an agricultural-based curriculum, with an emphasis on arithmetic skills. The "race for space" following the Second World War, and Russia's launch of Sputnik, created an impetus and sense of urgency for math/science renewal in North American education. The abstract "New Math" of the 1960s, largely created by the university professoriate, was for the most part passively ignored or even actively rejected by classroom teachers who felt ill-prepared and unsupported in its implementation, and this led to bitter distrust of educational reform in mathematics. Over the next several decades, the National Council of Teachers of Mathematics (NCTM) worked diligently to encourage a more constructivist, "reform-based" approach to mathematics education, bolstering their position with research-based support. NCTM published three Standards of Practice documents in the 1980s and 1990s, culminating in their *Principles and Standards for School Mathematics* (2000), widely regarded as a global benchmark for mathematics pedagogy. The "math wars" in California (Wilson, 2003) of the 1980s and 1990s pitted reformers against "back-to-basics" proponents, in light of what was perceived by the latter group as rushed, "fuzzy," and detrimental reform implementation. The Math Program Advisory (MPA) was commissioned by the California government to study this heated public debate, and the report that this group produced in 1996 advocated for a "balanced approach" including both traditional (i.e., direct instruction, skills practice) and reform (i.e., problem-based learning, cooperative group work, manipulatives, technology, varied assessment) teaching methods in mathematics instruction. This report would have a profound effect on many North American jurisdictions and on curricula. As with literacy, recent years have seen a corresponding shift to a balanced mathematics instruction model in teacher preparation and in classrooms (Jarvis & Franks, 2011), although the definition and implementation of this approach varies greatly within faculties of education, and within elementary and secondary schools across the continent.

Thus, we have in literacy and numeracy two examples of major instructional reforms that have, over time, deeply affected the practices of teachers and the school contexts in which students learn. Equally fascinating trajectories can be researched in other major disciplines and, indeed, elements of some of these narratives are also presented here in various chapters. In preparing this text, we have continually returned to the underlying question of how transitions in instructional practice, precipitated by the above-mentioned cycles of educational reform, actually affect the lived and learning experiences of students in transition from panel to panel, and in postsecondary environments, in terms of both the cognitive and the affective domains.

This collection of chapters serves to sample interpretations of the topics under study, namely, transitions in schooling and instructional practice, and it was the direct result of a comprehensive literature search. Subsequently, this search of the literature resulted in invited contributions from significant authors and educators writing in these areas. Furthermore, the two groups included in chapter 15, "Transitioning to Being Bilingual" (Callie Mady), and in chapter 16, "Aboriginal Education: A Transition of World Views" (Chris Hachkowski), were prioritized because of their relevance to educational issues in Canada. Although we recognize the omission of other cultural and social groups relevant to central themes as a limitation of this text, the project is not intended to be a fully comprehensive treatment of these issues. Rather, as we also suggest in the Coda, the contributions presented here serve as rich and informative starting points for discussion and further research and practice.

Part I features four chapters dealing with the earliest transitions from the home or preschool contexts to formalized schooling, and from Junior/Senior Kindergarten to early elementary (Grades 1–3). In chapter 1, Maria Cantalini-Williams and Leslie Telfer document the transition in Ontario, Canada, to a new initiative involving full-day integrated early learning programs with differentiated staffing. The authors highlight the pivotal role of the school principal in ensuring a smooth transition for all stakeholders, and they underscore the importance of related professional development for school administrators. Chapter 2, by Lay See Yeo, focuses on the transition from preschool to first grade in the Singapore system, with particular attention to the challenges encountered in a "bilingual, achievement-oriented, and keenly competitive education system." In chapter 3, Amber Jackson and Jennifer Cartmel discuss the importance of friendships to young children as they start school, particularly for those living in an area of socio-economic disadvantage. The authors highlight the findings of a research study that examined the transition to school of children within such an area, noting how the provision of adequate supports helped the children to establish and maintain friendships, prior to and during the transition to school, thereby enhancing enjoyment, engagement in learning, and long-term educational outcomes. Chapter 4, by Michele Binstadt, documents an effective Ready Together – Transition to School Program in Australia, based on an ecological model with a focus on strong relationships, and also emphasizes the engagement and education of key stakeholder groups (parents, early childhood professionals, community services) for successfully supporting young children's transition to, and ongoing success in, formal schooling.

The five chapters in Part II focus on the transition from early elementary (Grades 1–3) to late elementary or middle school (Grades 4–8). In chapter 5, Patrick Akos and Kelsey Augst Felton provide an intriguing description of "the other primary transition" – that of second to third grade – which, they contend, features dramatic shifts in academic expectations and developmental milestones. In chapter 6, Susan Elliott-Johns presents and discusses findings from a qualitative research study in which Grade 5 teachers were interviewed and asked to describe their perspectives on transitions to instructional practices associated with "balanced," eclectic approaches to reading instruction in the later elementary grades. In chapter 7, Lyn Sharratt outlines her work on scaffolded literacy and professional development (PD) for teachers as critical components for student success. More specifically, Sharratt presents a PD model that she and Michael Fullan have developed known as the "13 Parameters" and that has been shown to be an effective means of supporting teacher growth and related student achievement within and across school systems.

In chapter 8, Marian Small delivers an insightful overview of the barriers and challenges faced by elementary mathematics teachers as they make the (often) discomforting move towards reform-based instructional approaches (e.g., manipulatives, technology, cooperative group work, problem-based learning). Small explains the significant differences found among early and late elementary school teachers in this regard, and she offers strategies for supporting teachers as they change practice to support both increased student learning and smoother transitions between lower and upper elementary school. In chapter 9, Anne Jordan explores inclusive classrooms in which effective and caring teachers are key to ensuring the success of all students, those with and without disabilities. Research findings are presented that indicate that the beliefs of effective teachers feature assumptions that ability, disability, and learning difficulties are temporary and malleable (rather than fixed and internal attributes of students) and that the teacher is responsible for impacting these students (rather than absolving themselves of this duty).

Chapters in Part III offer a focus on transitions in late elementary (Grades 4–8) to secondary schools (Grades 9–12). Dawn Buzza begins this section with a look at the role and importance of self-regulated learning (SRL), which is shown to involve fundamental academic skills, including the learning skills, behaviours, and motivational beliefs needed for school success. Whereas the striving for smoother transition experiences tends to be the focal point of many of our chapters, here in chapter 10, Buzza maintains that by attending to the SRL skills with adolescents we can best prepare them for the inherent stresses that are involved in any life transitions, whether it be those experienced during school years or later on in life. In chapter 11, Karen Choate, Gregory Hauser, and Thomas Thomas highlight the complex combination of developmental and environmental factors that render the transition of adolescents from middle school to high school particularly challenging. They further underscore the critical need to educate, involve, and provide support for key stakeholder groups such as parents, teachers, and students surrounding this difficult transition phenomenon.

Gianna Helling, in chapter 12, and Daniel Jarvis, in chapter 13, offer some specific examples of the kinds of constructive recommendations made by authors in the preceding chapters. Helling presents a series of Intermediate Division (Grades 7–10) transition strategies that cover four areas: cross-panel teams and professional dialogue, programming and using data, events and initiatives, and student leadership. She specifically focuses on a suite of strategies that have been effectively used in secondary schools in Toronto, Canada. Jarvis presents the findings of a case study research project in which he documented, via interviews, observations, and artefact collection, a successful "family of schools," cross-panel approach to professional development for mathematics teachers. Secondary school teachers were grouped with "feeder school" elementary teachers within professional learning communities (communities that afforded meaningful conversations around curriculum, assessment, student misconceptions, Grade 9 course/stream selection, and shared highlights of problem-based learning).

In chapter 14, Maureen Kendrick and Jennifer Rowsell explain how there is now a fundamental difference in how individuals communicate through modalities such as the visual, audio, spatial, and linguistic, and that different modalities are combined in complex ways to construct meaning. In an effort to highlight the transition from word-based literacy pedagogy and policy, to that which is visual and multimodally based, Kendrick and Rowsell present the findings of two longitudinal studies in which students express themselves using a variety of modalities. In chapter 15, Callie Mady describes how the transition to full bilingualism can be ameliorated through brief, one-week, bilingual exchanges of secondary school students. She tracks the experiences of 80 Canadian exchange students from Quebec and Ontario who were asked to keep journals of their pre-, during, and post-exchange experience. Clear benefits of the exchange program for second language acquisition are shared, as are the challenges faced by students, and related recommendations.

Chris Hachkowski provides a broad overview of the Aboriginal educational experience in Canada in chapter 16, and then narrows the focus to examine how the transition of Aboriginal students from home communities to public schools – which, historically, has been fraught with challenges and failure – can be greatly improved through the modification of teacher beliefs and practices and in light of the specific learning needs of Aboriginal students. Hachkowski calls for a radical new awareness among educators of the alternative world views that Aboriginal students bring to their classrooms, and how this might translate into different pedagogical strategies and assessment practices that lead to increased student success.

In Part IV we present three final chapters that speak to the student transition from secondary school (Grades 9–12) to postsecondary school (college/university). In chapter 17, Michael Fowler and Gaye Luna provide a detailed account of the history of the American curricular movement in high school and higher education. They then focus more specifically on credit-based transition programs between high schools and community colleges, which allow students to take college credit courses while still in high school, thereby encouraging smoother transitions and increased numbers of high school graduates that proceed to a college education. In chapter 18, Trish Byers examines the factors affecting students' ability to succeed in first-year college mathematics courses. As part of the research team that implemented the College Mathematics Project study in Ontario, Canada, Byers reports on issues that impact students as they transition into first-semester college mathematics, as well as providing recommended strategies for increasing the likelihood of success among this student population. Finally, in chapter 19, Rob Graham describes the challenges facing new teachers who may "desire to inspire" via the use of technology-enhanced learning, yet who often find themselves amid an educational landscape that is uneven and differential in terms of available technology resources. Based on his experiences as an experienced classroom teacher, but a relatively "new" university professor within a laptop-learning teacher education program, Graham contends that new teachers should be encouraged to develop a level of positive "techno-resilience" that enables them to creatively (and patiently) use whatever technology is available to increase student engagement and to constantly search out opportunities to learn from and with their students.

Following our close reading of all nineteen contributed chapters, and discussion of the various themes emerging from different perspectives shared by the twenty-six contributors, we co-authored a concluding Coda entitled "Supporting Students and Teachers within and across Transitional Spaces." This Coda underscores the varied and cyclical nature of transitions in education and the critical relationship between transitions in schooling and instructional practice. The text concludes with a brief list of recommendations that seek to promote and enhance optimal conditions for supporting student and teacher transitions in schooling and instructional practice, and a call for further research into the complexities of the many factors involved in moving successfully across transitional spaces.

REFERENCES

Baumann, J.F., Hoffmann, J.V., Moon, J., & Duffy-Hester, A.M. (1998). Where are the teachers' voices in the phonics/whole language debate? Results from a survey of U.S. elementary classroom teachers. *Reading Teacher, 51*(8), 636–650.

Bomer, R. (2011). *Building adolescent literacy in today's English classrooms.* Portsmouth, NH: Heinemann.

Jarvis, D.H., & Franks, D. (2011). "Messy time" transition to reform-based mathematics teaching and learning. *Ontario Mathematics Gazette, 49*(4), 28–34.

National Council of Teachers of Mathematics (NCTM). (2000). *Principles and standards for school mathematics.* Reston, VA: Author.

Paris, S.G. (2001). Developing readers. In R. Flippo (Ed.), *Reading researchers in search of common ground* (pp. 69–77). Newark, DE: International Reading Association.

Routman, R. (2000). *Conversations: Strategies for teaching, learning, and evaluating.* Portsmouth, NH: Heinemann.

Russell, T., & Korthagen, F. (Eds.). (1995). *Teachers who teach teachers: Reflections on teacher education.* Washington, DC: Falmer Press.

Wilson, S. (2003). *California dreaming: Reforming mathematics education.* New York: Yale University Press.

PART I

Early Years (Home/Preschool/ Kindergarten) to Early Elementary (Grades 1–3)

1 Successful Transitioning to a Full-Day Early Learning–Kindergarten Program in Ontario: The Principal Is Pivotal

MARIA CANTALINI-WILLIAMS AND LESLIE TELFER

Transitions in the field of early childhood education have been experienced historically not only by the young children who have moved between the home environment and systems of care or schooling, but also by educators and parents who have witnessed continual changes implemented in the nature and structure of programs serving children and families. This period of early childhood is especially fraught with ongoing transitions because of the significant challenges in meeting the needs of children in diverse settings and the shifting philosophies in the field. The province of Ontario, in Canada, has recently initiated a milestone transition initiative in the area of educational programming for young children with the implementation of the Full-Day Early Learning–Kindergarten Program, sometimes referred to as the Early Learning–Kindergarten Program, or EL–K. The change from the traditional half-day Junior/Senior Kindergarten programs to the new Full-Day Early Learning–Kindergarten Program has required a phase-in period including an implementation plan clearly defining the roles for the key players of this long-awaited initiative.

Principals of schools implementing EL–K have been pivotal in ensuring that the change is fully embraced and successfully implemented. These administrators are working in concert with parents, caregivers, educators, and policy makers to ensure that children experiencing the transition into formal schooling are nurtured for optimal development and learning. Principals play an important part in assuming leadership roles and championing the transition from traditional models of Kindergarten to more innovative and integrated models of early learning. Campbell, Elliott-Johns, and Wideman (2010), in describing the factors affecting change, reinforce the "importance of local leadership and decision-making in the introduction and continued growth of multi-agency initiatives as well as the importance of flexible, shared, and responsive leadership at both the local and central levels" (p. 2). The challenges associated with educational transitions are repeated in various historical periods, yet they can be addressed through effective leadership and a range of strategies to promote successful implementation.

Historical Challenges

Kindergarten has universally been a vital part of many young children's experiences since the days of Frederick Froebel, known to be the "father of Kindergarten." Likewise, the pertinent role of the school principal or headmaster in facilitating change in school systems is well documented historically. In 1944, an Ontario Ministry of Education (OMoE) document was published entitled *Programme for Junior and Senior Kindergarten and Kindergarten Primary Classes of the Public and Separate Schools* (1944). This booklet very interestingly states:

> Movements in education usually take the form of drives. In the latter half of this century, the lower age levels will receive a fair share of the consideration which is now being bestowed on the upper age brackets ... other factors quite apart from those connected with the war give impetus to this movement. The modern science of mental hygiene has definitely established the truth of the old adage that the first seven years of life are the most important. The streams of mental as well as those of physical health have here their fountains. (OMoE, 1944, p. 5)

It is notable that the Junior Kindergarten program intended for children of age 4 years began near the middle of the twentieth century in Ontario. The importance of the early years was recognized more than half a century ago and provided the rationale for educational programs serving young children today. Ideas and beliefs about the critical periods of child development are still being debated at present, even though they were already recognized in the transitional period of the 1940s:

> The most abundant educational opportunities are likely to prove of but slight advantage to the boys or girls of fourteen whose outlook on life was blighted at four. In addition, the need for more adequately providing for the physical and mental health of the child, there would seem to be a

demand in many instances that the school assume further responsibility because of recent changes in our mode of life. (OMoE, 1944, p. 6)

The responsibilities of the principal in assisting educators and parents to accept and understand new programming for young children is as important today as it was in the implementation of the Junior Kindergarten program in 1944. The principal has been known to be the decision maker at the school level. In the early days of the Junior and Senior Kindergarten programs, the principal even had the responsibility of placing the child in the grade that seemed to be most suitable for the child on school entry:

> In the Public Schools Act, the three groups are designated as follows: Junior Kindergarten comprising children between the mental ages of three and four plus; Senior Kindergarten comprising children between the mental ages of four and five plus; and, Kindergarten Primary comprising children between the mental ages of five plus and six. Nevertheless a child on first entering school should be placed in that group from which, in the opinion of the principal, he will receive the greatest benefit. (OMoE, 1944, p. 10)

Evidently, with educational change, comes a significant mandate for the school principal to be a knowledgeable, effective, and affective leader focusing on the needs of the children in the school, while attending to a successful transition process to be embraced by parents, educators, and the community.

Challenges to the Transition

When the special adviser on early learning, Charles E. Pascal released a reported titled, *With Our Best Future in Mind: Implementing Early Learning in Ontario* (Pascal, 2009), a comprehensive plan of action was provided for the implementation of the provincial government's early learning vision. Pascal's summary presents compelling research from Canadian and international sources to support the fundamental belief that early childhood development sets the foundation for lifelong learning, behaviour, and health. The resulting legislation, the Full-Day Early Learning Statute Law Amendment Act, 2010, gave school boards the legal responsibility and authority to implement full-day learning for 4- and 5-year-olds, including the extended-day programs available before and after regular school hours. This legislation helps to ensure that full-day learning programs operate under the same high quality and safety standards as other components of the education system (OMoE, 2010a).The challenges for principals of schools implementing the Full-Day Early Learning–Kindergarten Program are related to the following expectations:

• Understand the importance of early child development.
• Embrace the goals of the new initiative.
• Lead and manage the change/implementation process.
• Ensure appropriate programming and practices for young children.
• Support diverse educator teams in schools.
• Advocate for the program with parents and the community.

Assuming that principals are accepting of the evidence that high-quality early childhood learning is not just an ideal, but an essential element of the school system, the challenge remains to determine the roles, responsibilities, and effective strategies for principals as related to the smooth transition and implementation of the Early Learning–Kindergarten Program in Ontario. The timely change into an innovative initiative such as the EL–K presents challenges for principals, but also provides opportunities for personal and professional growth of these administrators of schools.

Challenge 1: Understanding Early Child Development

In any transition, principals need to be aware of the evidence related to the benefits of the new initiative and, in this case, principals need to have a solid understanding of quality, integrated early learning experiences for young children. The evidence is conclusive that appropriate early learning programs contribute to quality of life and long-term positive outcomes for young students into their later life, in addition to economic benefits for our society. The extensive research cited in the *Early Years Study: Part 2* as authored by McCain, Mustard, and Shanker (2007) describes this finding:

> The evidence is compelling and overwhelming: well-funded, integrated, child development and parenting programs improve the cognitive and social functioning of all children. Quality early learning programs are not only good for children and families; they are good for the bottom line.

Focused public spending on young children provides returns that outstrip any other type of human capital investment. (p. 135)

The imperative for action and an acknowledgment of the paramount role of the principal is grounded in this long-standing evidence that has been cited for many years. Principals need to seek and proclaim this evidence and research findings.

Challenge 2: Embracing the Goals and Purposes of the New Program

In an education-related transition to a new program, the starting point for principals includes an exploration of the Ministry of Education publications associated with the strategy to be implemented. Pascal (2009) presented guiding assumptions to structure his report. Two assumptions speak directly to the principal as leader of the instructional program and school. The assumptions are that implementation includes (1) a planned curriculum and skilled professionals to support a balance of learning-based play and academic preparation and (2) an integrated, well-managed system of early learning to achieve good results.

Challenge 3: Leading and Managing the Process
of Implementation and Change

Research findings from significant studies strongly indicate that principals who fully understand and assimilate the value of integrated early learning opportunities will develop and apply appropriate strategies to benefit the children, educators, and families in their schools. As Sergiovanni (2000) asserts, local leadership can make the difference in creating healthy, rigorous schools. By building institutional character at the school level, principals can develop an early learning system based on unified loyalties and shared accountability of all stakeholders. It is necessary that the principal have a solid understanding of the optimal curriculum for early learning and that the principal manage a system at the school that is primarily supportive of the needs of the children in the program. Strong leadership is a key component of effective early childhood programs, and appropriate training for leadership roles is a critical element in providing high-quality early childhood programs, particularly as more complex, multiprofessional teams of staff come together to deliver well-integrated programs (Siraj-Blatchford & Manni, 2007).

*Challenge 4: Ensuring Appropriate Programming
and Practices for Young Children*

The successful implementation of the Full-Day Early Learning–Kindergarten Program requires the commitment and support of principals who can articulate and operationalize the premises and practices of effective early learning. Ferrandino (2005) states that given the critical nature of learning in the first 5 years, it is imperative that school leaders are able to recognize and implement practices and a culture in schools that best reflects how children learn and develop. With respect to the role of the principal, consistent in each of the ministry's publications reviewed here is a focus on the need for sustained, focused leadership in developing appropriate policies in schools to address the nature of the young child and families served. Such practices as Kindergarten orientation workshops, active learning centres, outdoor play, and parent observation sessions are very important to the program and require principal support and involvement.

Challenge 5: Supporting Diverse Educator Teams in Schools

Another foreseeable challenge may include the development of the working relationship within the educator teams of the EL–K. As reported, a teacher and an early childhood educator will be working together with a class of about 26 students, in a program that might extend into before and after school time. A collaborative school and classroom culture will be necessary to ensure that the specific skills sets and professional experiences of both educators are acknowledged and respected. Fullan (2008) suggests, "Successful growth is accomplished when the culture of the school supports the day-to-day learning of teachers and early childhood educators engaged in improving what they do" (p. 74). It is imperative that the principal honour and nurture the various gifts of the members of the early learning team. Dufour and Marzano (2011) come to a similar conclusion stating, "Creating the conditions to help others succeed is one of the highest duties of a leader. If school and district leaders are to create the conditions that help more students, they must build the capacity of educators to function as members of high performing collaborative teams" (p. 86). If the principal, teachers, and the early childhood educators recognize that their common purpose is the optimal development of the children in their classroom, subsequently, they could consider themselves to all be "child developers" and thereby removing any barriers and, instead, build mutual respect and understanding.

Challenge 6: Advocating for the Program with
Parents and the Community

A critical part of transitioning to a new initiative is public relations and communications. Principals may need to address parent questions regarding the nature of the program and especially the readiness of their child to attend a full-day daily program because of the change from a half-day or alternate-day program. The issue that may especially be on the minds of parents enrolling young children in the early learning program is the suitability of the program for the age and development of their child, especially young children born at the end of the school year. This question of the effects of month of birth and gender on the school readiness and success of the child has been studied for many years, and consistently, the youngest males are found, on the average, to be the most challenged group entering school (Cantalini, 1987). The Full-Day Early Learning–Kindergarten Program will present a situation that may require the principal to assist parents to make decisions about school entry and to monitor the adjustment of their child to the school program. Parents will look to the principal and teachers for guidance in determining if the child is thriving in the structure of the new program. It is interesting to note that in the document published in 1944, the principal had the responsibility of determining the placement of the child in Junior Kindergarten or Kindergarten based on the "mental age and maturity" of the child.

Currently, principals can refer to school board direction and the Education Act (OMoET, 1990, c. E.2, s. 21), which allows children born between 1 September and 31 December to have a delayed entry to school to compensate for the age difference. The parents and community will expect principals to be informed and sensitive to the needs of the young children in the full-day early learning program, thereby, providing appropriate support and practices in the school to benefit all children.

Recommendations for the Transition

The challenges identified for principals inform some plausible next steps for ongoing effective implementation of the Full-Day Early Learning–Kindergarten Program. Each challenge suggests a need for building capacity through the promotion of sustained professional development of school leaders and using a variety of strategies for developing community engagement. A closer examination of the Full-Day Early Learning–Kindergarten Program (OMoE, 2010c) provides greater specificity and direction regarding the role of the principal. Embedded in this document are six fundamental principles, which guide the Full-Day Early Learning–Kindergarten Program. The role of the principal is defined in relation to the premise that knowledgeable, responsive educators are essential.

Principles for Principals of the Full-Day Early Learning–Kindergarten Program

The principal:

- Provides leadership in developing a vision and philosophy to guide pedagogy and is an integral member of the Full-Day Early Learning–Kindergarten Program team
- Supports and values the development, implementation, and evaluation of a coherent program
- Ensures that the program is based on research-informed, pedagogically sound, and developmentally appropriate practices that support all children and their families
- Builds professional learning communities that promote collaboration, reflection, and growth and that enhance teaching and learning in all areas
- Ensures that the work environment values and supports the practice of EL–K teachers and early childhood educators
- Creates a positive school climate by implementing policies and practices that respect all learners, staff, families, and community members.

From these principles, a number of specific recommendations can be developed to realize the values and goals of the Full-Day Early Learning–Kindergarten Program.

Recommendation 1: Provide Professional Development for Administrators

The special adviser's recommendation suggested that the Early Years Division of the Ministry of Education support the development of management tools and establish a provincewide in-service training plan to assist school board and municipal managers, school principals, and centre directors in the implementation of the Full-Day Early Learning–Kindergarten Program. Coherent, consistent, and collaborative professional learning is essential for the implementation of a quality Full-Day Early Learning–Kindergarten Program.

As instructional leaders, a challenge for many principals will be the expectation that they have a strong foundational knowledge of curriculum and instructional practices that foster young children's learning and development. Principals are at different points on the continuum of understanding early childhood development and pedagogy. Thus, as Pascal (2009) suggests, they might benefit from coaching by an itinerant school-board–wide mentor on early learning. Pascal also recommends that principals might benefit from a principal qualification course on early learning and development. Principals with a strong understanding of early childhood development are more effective in supporting and implementing coherent programs, making the provision of ongoing professional development essential not only for educators, but also for leaders and administrators of school systems.

Recommendation 2: Build Strong Educator Teams at the School Level

The implied need for ongoing professional growth and networking for the early learning team suggests a need for collaboration that extends beyond just developing relationships within the school. Katz, Earl, and Ben Jaafar (2009) define this type of collaboration as "intensive interaction that engages educators in opening up their beliefs and practices to investigation and debate. When colleagues engage in the dynamic process of interpretation and evaluation of practice, they enhance their own practice and that of the profession" (p. 13). Furthermore, Dufour and Marzano (2011) concur, pointing out that "shifting the focus of principals from supervising individual teachers into better performance to helping build the capacity of educators to work as members of results-oriented collaborative teams is perhaps the most powerful strategy for accomplishing this objective" (p. 62).

Recommendation 3: Showcase Evidence of Innovative Practices

Creating opportunities for collaboration involving early learning and child development specialists will support program implementation and continuous improvement. Principals are instrumental in facilitating the exchange of knowledge among professionals, practitioners, and parents. Principals can encourage the celebration of successes by providing the impetus, time, and resources for the sharing of ideas and activities. The implementation of the *Welcome to Kindergarten Program* by the Learning Partnership and its success was attributed to the active participation of the key personnel at the local level and the role of the leaders as significant catalysts (Campbell, Elliott-Johns, & Wideman, 2010). Another example of an innovative strategy to promote interchange and professional collaboration is evident in the Full-Day Early Learning–Kindergarten Program demonstration classroom at Nipissing University, Schulich School of Education, Brantford Campus. This centre has hosted several professional learning sessions for teachers of both local boards of education, from First Nations and community early years' partners. In these sessions, Kindergarten teachers, principals, early childhood educators, and child care supervisors have shared perspectives and practices. The Nipissing University classroom reflects the philosophies and practices of the Full-Day Early Learning–Kindergarten Program and provides a neutral environment for ongoing sharing, support, and research among pre-service students and educators, possibly expanding to include parents. Similar models may be available at other faculties of education and colleges to provide leadership in the field of early childhood education and development.

Recommendation 4: Engage Parents and the Community as Partners

It is widely accepted that parents and community partners are paramount for the child's smooth transition to school. The Full-Day Early Learning–Kindergarten Program promotes the belief that partnerships with parents and communities strengthen the ability of teachers to meet the needs of young children (Pascal, 2009). Principals need to provide opportunities for parents and community partners to be authentically and meaningfully involved in school activities in order to promote awareness, communication, and positive interactions. As long ago as 1944, it was known that the school and home should work together in the best interests of the child:

> The undertaking of certain phases of the child's education by the school is not to be interpreted as relieving the home entirely of responsibility but rather as ensuring a fuller partnership between teachers and parents in forwarding the child's best physical and mental interests. (OMoE, 1944, p. 5)

The principal can engage parents and community partners in such activities as open house events, observation sessions in schools, workshops, and if appropriate, teachers and community partners can visit the child's home to develop a positive rapport. The benefits to children are numerous when teachers, parents, and community service staff work together to complement their skills and knowledge. Just as secondary students are invited to go to work with their parents on Take Our Kids to Work Day as sponsored by the Learning Partnership (TLP), it would be beneficial to have at least one annual Take Your Parents to School Day with children and teachers inviting and welcoming the parents to a full day of school. Principals set the stage with these initiatives, and their leadership is the important variable affecting the outcome of any family and community engagement strategy. The TLP *Welcome to Kindergarten* initiative has been enhanced and expanded with an innovative multi-agency Family and Community Engagement Strategy (FACES) Project to engage families and community in early learning activities in three Ontario communities. Preliminary results from this pilot project indicate, again, that leadership can take on many forms that may affect sustainability:

> Complex and multiple responsibilities within contemporary leadership roles often require clarification and support, and can present challenges if not communicated effectively. Skillful leaders found ways to navigate such challenges successfully, bridging their individual efforts with partnerships that embrace the expertise/abilities and interests of their colleagues as well as available resources. (Wideman, Elliott-Johns, Black, Cantalini-Williams, & Guibert, 2012, p. 13)

When principals create a culture of community, authentically involve parents/service agencies, and utilize resources creatively, they enable smooth and successful transitions and innovations.

Conclusions

The recommendations for a successful transition to the Full-Day Early Learning–Kindergarten Program in Ontario are being acted on to varying degrees around the province. There have been some professional development opportunities provided by the Ontario Ministry of Education whereby school board teams composed of supervisory officers, coordinators, early childhood educators, teachers, and principals were invited to attend sessions to review and discuss the vision, purpose, and goals of the Full-Day Early Learning–Kindergarten Program. Information shared at these institutes, specific to the role of the principal, included a list of Top Ten Tips for Principals. This summary of practical strategies is adapted (from OMoE, 2010b) as follows:

1 Understand and value early learning as an important factor for the success of children and their families.
2 Build a vision and appreciation of the Full-Day Early Learning–Kindergarten Program with all schoolteachers and staff.
3 Support early learning teams in implementing high-quality, play-based programming and curriculum with appropriate resources.
4 Develop the relationships and the professional capacities of the early learning team by building on shared skills and knowledge.
5 Ensure strong and effective parent partnership activities (e.g., parent observation sessions) within the program.
6 Include early learning team members in staff meetings and professional development activities.
7 Create opportunities for the early learning team to discuss student needs, program content, and teaching/assessment strategies.
8 Network with early learning teams in other schools and communities.
9 Share effective strategies with other principals/administrators who are involved with the Full-Day Early Learning–Kindergarten Program.
10 Invite early years' coordinators, specialists, and researchers to work with the early learning team.

Principals shoulder significant responsibility in implementing change, and therefore, the smooth transition for schools, children, and families is dependent on the principal's knowledge, skills, and attitudes in the area of early learning. Pascal (2009) clarifies that as principals engage in the work of implementing the Full-Day Early Learning–Kindergarten Program, it is critical to recognize that the early learning team will gain new understandings during implementation. City, El-more, Fiarmen, and Teital (2009) explain, "We will learn to do the work by doing the work, not by telling other people to do the work, not by having done the work at some time in the past, and not by hiring experts who can act as proxies for our knowledge about how to do the work" (p. 17). Principals, as leaders of education systems, must proceed in the spirit of success because seamless, coordinated, and effective early learning is in the best interests of all children. Sergiovanni (2000) explicates that educational leaders need to use the "heart" in addition to the "head" in managing change. It is apparent that the role of the principal in the implementation of early learning programs is not only to be an "effective leader" but also to be an "affective leader." The principal must address the cognitive areas of curriculum, pedagogy, and instruction, but it is imperative to also address the ongoing needs of the various groups involved in the change process including children, teachers, educators, parents, and the general public. The principal needs to demonstrate a positive, caring, and affirming attitude towards all members of the school community. Informed, welcoming, collaborative, and reflective school principals are essential to the success of Ontario's transition to the Full-Day Early Learning–Kindergarten Program.

REFERENCES

Cantalini, M. (1987). *The effects of age and gender on school readiness and school success.* (Unpublished doctoral dissertation). Ontario Institute for Studies in Education, Toronto, Canada.
Campbell, T., Elliott-Johns, S., & Wideman, R. (2010). Six keys to success: Promoting early learning through authentic, shared and responsive leadership. *Journal of Authentic Leadership in Education, 1*(4), 1–8.
City, E.A., Elmore, R.F., Fiarmen, S., & Teital, L. (2009). *Instructional rounds in education: A network approach to improving teaching and learning.* Boston, MA: Harvard Education Press.
Dufour, R., & Marzano, R.J. (2011). *Leaders of learning: How district, school and classroom leaders improve student achievement.* Bloomington, IL: Solution Tree Press.
Ferrandino, V.L. (2005). Leading early childhood learning communities. *Principal, 85*(1), 72–73.
Fullan, M. (2008). *The six secrets of change: What the best leaders do to help their organizations survive and thrive.* Chicago: Wiley.
Katz, S., Earl, L.M., & Ben Jaafar, S. (2009). *Building and connecting learning communities: The power of networks for school improvement.* Thousand Oaks, CA: Corwin Press.

McCain, M.N., Mustard, J.F., & Shanker, S. (2007). *Early years study 2: Putting science into action*. Toronto: Council for Early Child Development.

Ontario Ministry of Education (OMoE). (1944). *The Programme for Junior and Senior Kindergarten and Kindergarten and Primary Classes of the Public and Separate Schools (Circular Elem. No. 1 A)*. Toronto: Government of Ontario.

Ontario Ministry of Education (OMoE). (2010a). *Backgrounder: Working together for Ontario's children*. Retrieved from http://news.ontario.ca/edu/en/2010/04/working-together-for-ontarios-children.html

Ontario Ministry of Education (OMoE). (2010b). *Full-Day Early Learning Kindergarten Program for four- and five-year-olds: A reference guide for educators #1*. Toronto: Queen's Printer.

Ontario Ministry of Education (OMoE). (2010c). *The Full-Day Early Learning–Kindergarten Program, 2010–2011 (Draft Version)*. Toronto: Queen's Printer.

Ontario Ministry of Education and Training (OMoET). (1990). Education act, R.S.O. Toronto: Queen's Printer.

Pascal, C.E. (2009). *With our best future in mind: Implementing early learning in Ontario. Report to the Premier by the Special Advisory on Early Learning*. Toronto: Queen's Printer.

Sergiovanni, T. (2000). *The lifeworld of leadership: Creating culture, community, and personal meaning in our schools*. San Francisco: Jossey-Bass.

Siraj-Blatchford, I., & Manni, L. (2007). *Effective leadership in the early years sector: The ELEYS Study*. London: Institute of Education, University of London.

Wideman, R., Elliott-Johns, S.E., Black, G., Cantalini-Williams, M., & Guibert, J. (2012, Oct.). Keys to Success in Multi-agency Partnerships: A Preliminary Report on Further Research. Paper presented at the Seventeenth Annual Conference on Values and Leadership. UCEA Centre for the Study of Leadership and Ethics, Brisbane, Australia.

2 Transition to the First Year of School in Singapore

LAY SEE YEO

Starting school is a significant milestone in development that marks the beginning of a child's journey into the world of learning. School experience in the early years is critical, and as the literature suggests, the effects are long term and forecast later achievement (Duncan et al., 2007; Entwisle & Alexander, 1995; Romano, Babchishin, Pagani, & Kohen, 2010). The quality of a child's adjustment to preschool and subsequent transition to formal schooling has a significant impact on his or her future academic success or failure. There is an incredibly large expanse of literature and research in early childhood school transition that provides myriad perspectives on school readiness – developmental (Vygotsky, 1930/1978), interactional (Meisels, 1999), and bio-ecological (Bronfenbrenner & Morris, 1998). These provide theoretical frameworks that consistently draw attention to the bi-directional interactions between the child and the environmental contexts that influence early school experiences and impact cognitive and social development.

Although much has been written on early school adjustment and school transition in the West, the literature is comparatively more reticent on these same issues in Asia. Variations in cultural contexts, values attached to education, and expectations about schooling, as well as differences in the way schools are run imply that perspectives on school readiness and transition are likely to be qualitatively different between East and West. Even much less has been written on preschool transition experiences in Singapore although we have been recognized worldwide for having one of the best education systems in the world (McKinsey & Co., 2007; Singapore Ministry of Education [SMoE], 2010a). This chapter offers an up-to-date perspective on early school transition in Singapore. First, a short description of Singapore's history and education system provides the social context for understanding early years' school transition in our country. Second, the literature on facilitators of and barriers to school transition is briefly reviewed and provides a springboard for discussing school transition experiences as reported in the limited research studies conducted in Singapore. In this, I also hope to offer a glimpse of preschool as it is perceived by our young children and the challenges that are salient in early years' school transition. Third, wherever possible, comparisons are made to transition issues and practices in other countries. Last, recommendations are made to address perceived needs in Singapore's lower primary education system.

Brief History of Singapore and Its Education System

Known as the Lion City, Singapore is a small island nation located at the southern tip of the Malay Peninsula in Southeast Asia. Its multiracial population of five million inhabitants is comprised of 74.1% Chinese, 13.4% Malay, 9.2% Indian, and 3.3% Others. Approximately one in three is a foreigner, many of whom hail from China, India, and other Asian countries. A British colony from 1819 to 1963, Singapore achieved independence in 1965. English is the official language of business and administration. English is also the language of instruction in all Singapore schools. Limited natural resources have made it imperative that a strong and enduring commitment be made towards developing our human capital in order to secure our advancement, success, and place in the world. Singapore made a remarkable and rapid transition from third world status to developed nation in just three decades (Richardson, 1995). The government invests heavily in education, to which it gives priority. Singapore prides herself on her very progressive education system where, anecdotally, the report is that there are no failing schools.

In the initial years of nation building, in the 1960s, the prime emphasis in education was literacy building to equip the Singaporean workforce, ensure economic survival, forge national identity, and foster cohesion in a culturally diverse society. From the late 1980s through the 1990s, as Singapore grew in affluence, the education system shifted gears from being survival driven to becoming efficiency driven. Attention then was directed at enhancing the social and emotional well-being of our students. At the turn of the twenty-first century, with the demands of globalization and a knowledge-based economy, the efficiency-driven educational focus made yet another shift towards an ability-driven emphasis on nurturing talent and maximizing the potential in every child. Thus, little effort is spared to ensure that the Singapore education system stays poised at the cutting edge of relevance and excellence. It is of necessity keenly competitive and based on meritocracy. Education in Singapore is highly valued as are academic qualifications. An examination- and achievement-oriented culture permeates education and the typical school-going child in Singapore sits for his or her first major examination in Primary Six (sixth grade) at about age 12. In Singapore, bilingualism "is and will remain a cornerstone of our education system" (SMoE, 2009a). To ensure that our children are well equipped to compete globally, emphasis is put on providing a strong foundation in both English and in their mother tongue. In the Singapore education context, academic achievement entails gaining proficiency in two languages: English as a first language and the mother tongue (i.e., the language spoken at home) as the second language.

A brief description of the Singapore preschool and primary (elementary) education system is warranted. The term *preschool* denotes settings (e.g., child care or kindergarten) in which young children are schooled before the first year of formal schooling (i.e., Primary One). Whereas preschool is for children from age 3 to 6, formal schooling begins in the January of the year they turn 7 years old. Education from first to twelveth grade is nationalized; however, the preschool sector is privatized. All schools from the primary to the tertiary level come directly under the purview of the Singapore Ministry of Education; however, preschools have considerable autonomy to dictate curriculum, hire teachers, and set the school fees although they must be registered with the SMoE. All teachers in Singapore in the formal education system are employees of the SMoE; all secondary school teachers and almost all primary school teachers are graduates who have completed postgraduate teacher training and are highly qualified. By contrast, preschool teachers are hired by their respective preschool centres. They have varying levels of early childhood training; however, not many have a basic degree. Hence, there is disparity in educational qualifications between teachers in the formal school system and teachers in the preschool setting. In addition, unlike in the primary and secondary schools, where there is accountability to the SMoE on all school practices (e.g., curriculum or examinations), there appears to be more flexibility in how preschools are being run. The range of preschools includes the ubiquitous but affordable PAP Community Foundation (PCF) child care centres or kindergartens, the National Trades Union Congress (NTUC) First Campus child care centres, faith-based kindergartens run by churches or mosques, and high-end expensive, private kindergartens. In 2012, there are 500 kindergartens and 950 child care centres in Singapore (Ong, 2012). However, preschools vary widely in quality depending on their teaching staff and the preschool curriculum. A landmark study commissioned by the Lien Foundation reported that, in 2012, Singapore preschools ranked 29th out of 45 countries in standards of early childhood education (Ang, 2012). In November 2010, the SMoE launched a new Singapore Pre-school Accreditation Framework (SPARK) to encourage preschool providers to strive towards excellence in the holistic development of young children (SMoE, 2010b). At present, accreditation of preschool is voluntary.

Although preschool education is not mandatory, statistics from the Singapore government in 2010 indicated a very high preschool attendance rate at close to 99% (Ang, 2012). Primary (elementary) school education has been made mandatory in Singapore since 2003. Children in Singapore complete six years of primary school: a four-year Foundation Stage from Primary One to Primary Four and a two-year Orientation Stage from Primary Five to Primary Six. Until 2008, children were streamed at the end of Primary Four according to their learning ability in order to maximize their academic potential. Streaming has since been replaced by subject-based banding. At the end of Primary Six, all children sit for the Primary School Leaving Examination (PSLE), which assesses their ability for placement in a secondary school course that matches their learning pace and aptitude.

The Singapore education system continually works at improvement to influence pedagogy, curriculum innovation, and instructional practices to enable our children to succeed in an increasingly complex, competitive, and interconnected world. In recent years, several education initiatives were introduced to strengthen the quality of lower primary education, particularly in enhancing literacy skills (e.g., building fluency in oral communication) and ensuring that learning is enjoyable and engaging. Details about these initiatives will be discussed below. In October 2008, a committee at the SMoE was convened to review the primary school education system. This culminated in the Primary Education Review and Implementation (PERI) Report (SMoE, 2009c). With the goal of providing our children with a holistic and well-rounded education in their early school years, the PERI Report recommends that schools balance the acquisition of knowledge with the development of skills and values, employ more holistic modes of assessment, pay attention to non-academic aspects within the curriculum, and invest in a quality teaching force (Silver, 2011).

Facilitators of School Adjustment

A useful framework to understand school adjustment and transition is the bio-ecological theoretical perspective (Bronfenbrenner & Morris, 1998), which views development as the interactions that occur between individuals and their multiple environments. A child's development varies as a function of his or her individual characteristics (e.g., cognitive ability and disposition) and environmental contexts (e.g., family background and quality of school environment) over time. This person-by-environment model of development situates the origin of early school adjustment in both the child and his or her interpersonal environments. Several factors have been linked to school readiness and positive adjustment. First, research indicates that the quality of children's preschool experiences is an important predictor of their readiness for school (Peisner-Feinberg et al., 2001). In a longitudinal study on a varied sample of typical community child care programs in the United States, Peisner-Feinberg et al. (2001) found that better quality preschool experiences (e.g., teacher–child closeness, classroom practices that are responsive to children's needs) led to more advanced development for children over a 5-year period. Second, research also indicated that child-centred and developmentally appropriate preschool classrooms predict positive social and emotional adjustment among children over the long haul (Perry & Weinstein, 1998). In a recent study in the United States, high-quality kindergarten preparation predicted children's socio-behavioural adjustment in the early school years over and beyond socio-economic status (SES) and child variables (Wildenger & McIntyre, 2012). Third, positive teacher–child relationships have been linked to more favourable classroom adjustment (Donelan-McCall & Dunn, 1997), and these positive relationships have also been found to serve as a protective factor in advancing learning for at-risk children (Hamre & Pianta, 2001). Pianta and Stuhlman (2004) reported that these relationships in the preschool years have significant, albeit small, effects on almost all aspects of children's academic competence in first grade. Fourth, children's ability to make friends and forge good peer relationships has been linked to a range of good adjustment outcomes not limited to academic gains (Ladd, 1990). Children who were more outgoing and friendly in preschool obtained higher scores on academic achievement (Burchinal, Peisner-Feinberg, Pianta, & Howes, 2002). In addition, preschool children who demonstrated a capacity to understand others' feelings reported more positive peer relationships in their first grade year in school (Donelan-McCall & Dunn, 1997), which is an important feature of positive school transition.

Factors That Facilitate School Transition for Young Children in Singapore

What does research in Singapore reveal about transition experiences from preschool to formal schooling in our local context? In Singapore, Yeo and Clarke (2005) and Sharpe (2002a) interviewed 6- and 7-year-old children to obtain first-hand accounts of their transition from kindergarten or child care to Primary One. The general impression was that the children were happy and well settled in Primary One, but they appeared to have adopted a very serious attitude towards learning, in which doing well academically to please teachers and parents was all-important and also a source of some anxiety. This view was reminiscent of that reported by children in Hong Kong who expressed concern about keeping up with homework, tests, and examinations (Wong, 2003). Play for children in Singapore seemed to take a back seat once formal schooling began and children had less to report about their social experiences outside of school (Sharpe, 2002a).

In a study by Yeo and Clarke (2006), which investigated teachers' perspectives of Singaporean children's adjustment to Primary One, several factors were identified as important for school transition. School adjustment was defined as the children's ability to get along with their peers, to complete work given in class, and to cope with periodic formative and summative assessments. One of the factors that facilitated adjustment in first grade for the children in Singapore was good social relationships. There was a moderate correlation (range, .56 to .62) between the children's social skills and their academic skills. Children rated by teachers to have better social skills also exhibited stronger academic grades in Primary One. Similarly, by parent report, Bangladeshi preschool children in Sydney, Australia, who enjoyed friendship with peers, particularly those who shared the same language and cultural background, also experienced positive school transition (Sanagavarapu, 2010). Consistently in the literature, the ability to form positive relationships with peers significantly predicts school adjustment

(Burchinal et al., 2002; Dockett & Perry, 1999; Ladd, 1990; Margetts, 2007), and this, too, is true in the Singapore context.

Second, proficiency in the dominant language of instruction in the classroom enables children to make the transition more smoothly into first grade (Sanagavarapu, 2010; Yeo & Clarke, 2006). This is especially pertinent in countries where children speak a different language in the home from that used in the classroom. In Singapore, where English is the medium of instruction from day one in preschool, children who come from families where English is one of the languages spoken in the home have a significant advantage over their non-English–speaking schoolmates. Singapore data suggest that speaking English at home is associated with stronger academic grades and less need for additional learning support (Yeo & Clarke, 2006). Whereas the ability to understand English seems to expeditiously unlock the door to the world of learning for Singaporean children, for Bangladeshi children in Sydney, facility in English allows entry into the dominant Australian culture (Brooker, 2002), enabling children to participate in play and learning activities, which eases the transition process.

Third, in the Singapore context, children's prerequisite academic skills at preschool most strongly impact their academic success at the end of their first year in Primary One (Yeo & Clarke, 2006). The premium attached to preschool academic readiness could be attributed to the rather exacting assessment-centred nature of the Singapore education system. The Singaporean teachers' perception of academic readiness for successful adjustment to formal schooling is contrary to that of educators in the United States, who rated social competencies, communication, independence, and motor coordination as being more important to children's first years in school (Firlik, 2001). Interestingly, in her research in Australia that examined what made a difference in children's relative success or failure in the first months of school, Comber (2000) argued that "how, whether, and to what extent children take up what teachers make available to them is inextricably connected with the repertoires of practices and knowledges that these children already possess" (p. 39). The readiness Comber (2000) referred to goes beyond academic competence to include a child's "habitus" (p. 47) or disposition towards learning. A certain repertoire of social and communicative practices is important in the classroom and necessary for early school literacy learning. A child who makes an easy transition to formal schooling demonstrates behaviours that support success, such as answering questions, participating in activities, eliciting help from teachers and able peers, and not being afraid to make mistakes when learning. Thus, what children have already learned and their disposition towards learning determine their readiness for first grade. The Primary One children in Singapore who adjusted well seemed to have acquired the "habitus" (p. 47) that supports learning.

Fourth, it is not surprising that children in Singapore who experienced a smooth transition to primary school have strong family support. Family characteristics have been found in the literature to be the best predictors of children's outcomes from early to middle childhood (Burchinal et al., 2002), as the home is undoubtedly the one consistent environment for children over time. For example, mothers' education seemed to predict children's acquisition of language and cognitive skills over the long haul (Peisner-Feinberg et al., 2001). Also, maternal control, as reflected in a more directive interaction style with children, was cited as helpful in transitioning children into preschool (Donelan-McCall & Dunn, 1997). Observation, news reports (Quah, 1999), and research in Singapore (Sharpe, 2002b) also suggest that Singaporean parents play a very significant and committed role in assisting their children to cope with the academic demands of school. Sharpe (2002b) noted that Singaporean parents explain math concepts to their children, help their children work on school math workbooks, and even learn alongside their children.

Challenges to Transition

Challenges to transition are unique to each preschool setting. In Singapore, a cohort of Primary One children interviewed in the fifth month of their first formal year in school reported being awed by the large school building, longer school hours, list of school rules, heavier school bags, the loss of nap and play times, and homework. They did not like certain subjects, especially if they could not do the work assigned, and they feared teachers who yelled at them (Yeo & Clarke, 2005). Similarly, Sharpe (2002a) noted that the Primary One children were very concerned about keeping up with schoolwork and worried about being scolded by teachers. The emotional aspect of transition (Dockett & Perry, 2003), thus, seemed to be a significant challenge for young children in Singapore. Research studies that have investigated transition experiences from the perspective of children (Einarsdottir, 2003; Potter & Briggs, 2003) were congruent in their observation that children had to cope emotionally with major shifts in daily routine (e.g., longer hours away from caregivers), orientation to often larger school premises, making new friends, and adjustment to new conventions about school. Another challenge is managing school expectations. Moving into first grade encompasses new conventions of school and expectations, which include punctuality, staying focused, observing rules, working independently, following instructions, and doing homework. In Hong Kong, primary school children similarly had to adjust to a sudden increase in schoolwork and homework (Wong, 2003). Preschools have generally tended to be caring, cozy, relaxed settings where there is more teacher attention in smaller classes. However, when formal schooling officially begins, children become quickly aware that school is hard work and they are judged on how well they perform. For the first time, there is accountability as their schoolwork is competitively evaluated (Entwisle & Alexander, 1995). This is certainly true in Singapore, as the Primary One children seemed very cognizant of academic expectations and were anxious to do well in order please both their parents and teachers (Sharpe, 2002a; Yeo & Clarke, 2005). That said, since the time these local studies were undertaken, many education initiatives to improve lower primary education have been implemented in the past 7 years and the experiences of our Primary One children may be different. The PERI Report appropriately stated, "At Primary One, there should be much less importance placed on semestral examinations to facilitate a smooth transition from preschool to primary school. At Primary 2, we could slowly ease pupils into taking examinations" (SMoE, 2009c, p. 35).

In the Singapore context, the academic realities in primary school also include the requirement to learn a second language concurrently in addition to English as a first language. Depending on the languages that are spoken at home and taught in preschool, children may experience varying levels of difficulty mastering two languages. In some preschools, it is not uncommon for a child from an Indian family to be learning Chinese as a second language, given a shortage of Tamil teachers and the lack of economies of scale to hire a Tamil teacher for less than a handful of Tamil-speaking children. Children from Tamil-speaking homes have to learn both English and Tamil concurrently in Primary One. This situation illustrates a difficulty some minority children may encounter when they are exposed for the first time in Primary One to formally learning a second language. The majority of the children from Chinese-speaking homes learn Mandarin as a second language, which in Primary One is first introduced as Hanyu Pinyin, a method of Romanized Chinese phonetic instruction. A Mandarin word in Hanyu

Pinyin uses Roman letters to represent sounds; however, these sounds do not correspond to the exact sounds in English. In other words, Pinyin does not represent English pronunciation and should not be sounded according to English conventions. This can create considerable confusion and frustration in language learning for young Chinese children, as it requires frequent switching of phonetic codes when learning to read and write in English and also in Hanyu Pinyin. Eventually, children move from Hanyu Pinyin to the logographic system, where tens of thousands of characters make up different words. One can only imagine how great a struggle this can be for the average young child and even more so for children who have reading disabilities.

Yet another challenge in early years' school transition is often thought to be the pedagogical discontinuity between preschool and first grade (Carida, 2011; Wong, 2003). To the degree that procedures are put in place to ensure educational continuity in the two school systems – preschool and primary school – children are more likely to experience a smooth transition from one level to the other. To facilitate children's development, the literature suggests a need for continuity in the curriculum and compatibility in instructional styles, classroom configuration, and management of time devoted to learning (Carida, 2011; Einarsdottir, 2007). In Hong Kong and Singapore, the pedagogical discontinuity seemed to stem from differences in teaching approaches and teacher expectations in preschool and initial years in primary school. Wong (2003) noted that whereas kindergarten teachers adopted a more flexible and less formal approach to teaching, primary school teachers focused on mastery of academics and competitive assessment. In Singapore, up until 2005, it would be fair to surmise that children experienced little continuity in curriculum and pedagogy from preschool to Primary One. As previously mentioned, even though preschool curriculum guidelines are available from the Singapore Ministry of Education, there is no standardized preschool curriculum. A concern highlighted in the Lien Foundation study is the high variability in the quality of preschool services in terms of curriculum, teaching approaches, and children's learning experience (Ang, 2012). In the primary schools, there is much greater uniformity, and the emphasis tends to be largely subject based and discrepant from the more play-based approach espoused in typical preschools. Interestingly, the pedagogical discontinuity appears to be a challenge encountered not just in Singapore but also in Hong Kong, Greece, Iceland, and the United Kingdom. For example, Icelandic preschools emphasize play, caregiving, and child-centred methods, whereas their primary schools emphasize subjects, lessons, and teaching strategies (Einarsdottir, 2006). In Northern Ireland, Walsh, McGuinness, Sproule, and Trew (2010) aptly summed up this challenge: "Tensions exist between the pedagogical traditions of preschool, which tend to adopt developmentally oriented practices, and the more formal or subject-oriented curriculum framework of primary school" (p. 53).

Good Practices to Facilitate School Transition

Some transition practices have been found to be helpful in facilitating children's move from preschool to primary school. The practice of providing an orientation program and/or a buddy system was highlighted in the literature as useful (Margetts, 2007). In Singapore, primary schools usually hold an orientation for new pupils and their parents a few weeks before the start of a new school year in January. In a typical school, the children met their Primary One teachers and had a chance to visit their classroom and tour the school building. Parents were provided information about the school (e.g., rules and regulations, curriculum, and school programs) and attended workshops on topics related to settling children into Primary One and ways parents could cooperate with the school in supporting their children's learning. In the first week of school, Primary One children in the Yeo and Clarke (2005) study were paired with their Primary Five buddies who acted as chaperones during recess. Two schools in the Wong (2003) study also had an orientation day for Primary One children and their parents, where school regulations were explained to children. In New South Wales, informational meetings with parents and children were similarly held before school started (Einarsdottir, Perry, & Dockett, 2008). A few kindergartens in Singapore organize visits for their graduating kindergarten children to the primary schools the latter will attend in the next school year. This is also a commonly used transitional practice in both New South Wales and Iceland. Teachers in New South Wales reported that, school visits aside, it was very useful for teachers to meet their new pupils and hold informational meetings with their parents (Einarsdottir et al., 2008). Apart from adjustment to the new physical environment, children also need to be supported to adapt to the new curriculum and learning expectations in the primary school environment (Ang, 2012). Hence, orientation programs are recommended to prepare children psychologically for a major school transition and to allay anxiety.

In addition, learning support for pupils who are weak in emergent literacy skills is a good transition practice. All primary schools in Singapore have a Learning Support Program (LSP) for children in the first 2 years of primary school. On school entry in Primary One, all pupils take a brief literacy-screening test in order for schools to identify and initiate early learning support for those who have weak pre-literacy skills (e.g., the ability to recognize letters of the alphabet, count to 20). Children who were identified as potentially at risk of academic difficulties were withdrawn for small-group LSP classes in English and/or math during curriculum time. These pull-out and intensive classes are typically conducted two or three times a week for about 50 minutes per session. In the LSP, a teacher who had specialist training in early literacy interventions (i.e., the learning support coordinator) slows down the pace of learning, provides attention, differentiates instruction, modifies worksheets, and if necessary, reduces the amount of work for children who need additional learning support. These children are discharged from LSP as soon as they are able to successfully follow the pace of instruction in their respective classrooms as indicated by their progress in the continual assessments. Pupils who continue to experience learning difficulties are referred to the school's educational psychologist for assessment with a view to further educational planning or remediation (Yeo & Clarke, 2006). Research undertaken by the Singapore Ministry of Education indicated that an enhanced LSP that focused specifically on teaching children basic literacy skills enabled 65% of pupils to read and write at their age level and to pass English language examinations at the end of Primary Two (SMoE, 2008a).

Another good practice for transition is the conscious effort to manage pedagogical discontinuity in primary school. Kagan (1991) advocated continuity in educational philosophy, pedagogy, and structures in preschools and primary schools as a means by which to strengthen continuity between these two school levels. Countries have responded to this barrier to transition by making changes to their education systems to safeguard pedagogical continuity. During 2007 and 2009, Greece implemented the Innovative Educational Programs (IEP) to improve the quality of full-day kindergartens and to further the kindergarten–primary school connection (Carida, 2011). Both kindergarten and primary school teachers responded positively to the transitional IEP school program and noted better management of discontinuities between preschool and primary school with benefits to the children (e.g., improvement in communication and social skills) (Carida, 2011). In 2007, Northern Ireland established the Enriched Curriculum, a play-based and developmentally appropriate curriculum in the early years of primary school, which they piloted between 2000 and 2002 (Walsh et al., 2010).

In recent years, Singapore has implemented a few education initiatives that are extremely conducive towards bridging the discontinuity between preschool and lower primary school. In about 2005, Singapore embarked on a program called Strategies for Effective Engagement and Development (SEED), a move towards adopting developmentally age-appropriate teaching strategies in Primary One and Primary Two to engage young learners as they make the transition from preschool to formal schooling (Dixon et al., 2008; SMoE, 2007). In 2009, the STELLAR (STrategies for English Language Learning And Reading) Program was introduced. It is a pedagogical approach to "strengthen both language and reading skills as well as promote a positive attitude towards reading in the foundational years through the use of well-established, learner-centered and developmentally appropriate pedagogical approaches using authentic children's literature" (SMoE, 2008b). The discussion below introduces first SEED and then STELLAR in order to elucidate the SMoE's efforts in facilitating language learning and reading in lower primary school.

SEED represented a shift in thinking about what children in Singapore need by way of environmental support for a smooth and gentle transition from play-centred learning in the kindergarten or child care centre setting to a more academically focused emphasis in primary school. Piloted with 24 schools in 2002, SEED was implemented in all Singapore primary schools in 2005. In 2005 and 2006, a policy change reduced the average class size to 30 from an average of 40 for Primary One and Primary Two classes. SEED emanated from the "Teach Less, Learn More" vision espoused by the prime minister in 2004, which encouraged better quality teacher–pupil interaction and greater learner engagement through enhancing an experiential discovery type of learning and differentiated teaching (Dixon et al., 2008).

SEED was premised on the belief that four areas of a child's development – physical, cognitive, social, and emotional – interact and need to be taken into account when helping children to learn. Each primary school was thus granted autonomy to design and implement pedagogical approaches that would engage children in learning and support their development. Teachers had a free hand to determine the needs of their pupils and to develop a curriculum that was age- and developmentally appropriate. SEED brought about visible changes to the Primary One classrooms. In place of neat rows of desks and chairs, the classroom was rearranged to accommodate the use of learning stations for small-group interactive learning. Other characteristics of SEED included a thematically integrated curriculum (akin to that adopted at the preschool level) and the use of learning journeys. The Primary One classroom environment, thus, created a learning experience for children, which was familiar and yet different from what they had encountered in the preschool classrooms.

How well did SEED assist in providing pedagogical continuity? An evaluation undertaken by Dixon et al. (2008) found that teachers had multiple and diverse understandings about SEED. That is, the conceptualization and implementation of SEED varied among schools. There was some confusion about what SEED was and how it could be implemented. The foremost concern teachers had was the perceived gap between pedagogy and assessment; teachers were anxious that the way children were assessed did not match how they were taught. The traditional test-centred culture did not support assessment of a broader scope of development (e.g., social development), which was inherent in SEED.

In 2006, refinement was made to the teaching of English in a new initiative called STELLAR. It was piloted in 2006 and implemented nationally at the Primary One level in all Singapore primary schools by 2009 (SMoE, 2009b). To cater to a diverse range of English language learners (ELLs), STELLAR seeks to develop in young children a love for reading and a strong foundation in the English language. Like SEED, STELLAR emphasizes the use of engaging and age-appropriate strategies and instructional materials. In SEED, teachers were facilitated to develop their own strategies to support engaged learning. STELLAR goes further to equip teachers with "core language teaching skills that are effective and engaging" (SMoE, 2008b) via training, teacher mentoring, and provision of instructional materials.

Unlike SEED, STELLAR provides very clear guidelines on three key strategies to support literacy development at the lower primary level. The three strategies are the following: Shared Book Approach (SBA), Modified Language Experience Approach (MLEA), and Learning Centres (LCs). In the Shared Book Approach, the teacher shares a Big Book (i.e., enlarged children's picture book with repetitive language structures) with the children, which provides a context for the children to think, speak, and write about what was being read. Teachers also focus on explicitly highlighting concepts of print, letter-sounds, vocabulary, and grammar. Drama and music are often part of SBA, which provide opportunities for children to develop oral fluency and confidence in speaking English. The second strategy is the Modified Language Experience Approach. Much scaffolding is provided as children learn to write using the context and content of the Big Book stories. Anxiety is reduced and learning made more fun when the children learn first to write as a class, then in mixed-ability groups, and finally, individually. The third strategy involves the use of Learning Centres (i.e., Reading Centre, Word Study Centre, and Listening Centre). These are activities that are differentiated according to the children's progress level. STELLAR reflects the kind of learning envisioned in the PERI Report that "learning should be engaging and enjoyable" (SMoE, 2009c, p. 29).

STELLAR is reportedly very well received by children in Primary One, which attests to its ability to engage young learners (Schoolbag.sg, 2010). There is also a report that the discharge rate from the Learning Support Program has increased since the implementation of STELLAR, which suggests that more children are making good progress in their ability to read and to follow the pace of instruction in their classroom.

Conclusion and Recommendations

Preschool and first grade are important points of transition and very critical periods of development for children. Significant adults in the child's microsystem comprising chiefly the environments in the school, classroom, and home, therefore, need to work closely together to create a child-ready school (Brostrom, 2000) as much as it is possible. Ingredients for successful transition, as suggested in the literature, point to supportive systems that manifest themselves in sensitive and nurturing relationships between teachers and pupils and between parents and their children. The importance of close collaboration between the school and home cannot be underestimated. What limited research there is on early school transition in Singapore seems to suggest that schools and parents have a genuine desire to make the first few years in school as positive and meaningful as they can be for our children. Helpful transition support structures have been implemented (e.g., LSP, SEED, and STELLAR), and these good practices are steps in the right direction. There are three areas for improvement.

First, as systems change and efforts are made to improve the contexts of learning for children, teachers need to be supported and continually updated on their professional skills. There is room for better quality training and professional development for teachers in early childhood:

"The quality of teacher training programmes needs to be better regulated to ensure that the quality of the preschool workforce is improved" (Ang, 2012, p. 12). Since 2008, the Singapore Ministry of Education has been offering scholarships to preschool teachers towards a degree in early childhood education and care so as to upgrade their teaching knowledge and skills. Primary school teachers, too, would benefit from ongoing in-service training to enlarge their repertoire of teaching strategies to facilitate hands-on learning and also to update assessment skills. Towards this end, and in striving towards a world-class education service, the Singapore Ministry of Education is developing a new Teacher Development Centre to enable teachers to "build their instructional capability, draw our pedagogical leadership from the fraternity, as well as advance continuous learning and development" (SMoE, 2009b).

Second, when pedagogy is adjusted for continuity, assessment needs to be changed accordingly. In countries like Singapore, with a traditionally strong examination-oriented culture, assessment invariably drives instruction. Thus, unless assessment is aligned to what and how pupils are being taught and unless it appropriately evaluates developmental and academic changes, teachers can be expected to feel torn between preparing children for traditional modes of assessment and embracing new pedagogies that stretch children more holistically. However, change is imminent. The PERI Report distinctly advocated a shift towards a less examination-oriented culture and a move away from a focus on examinations as an end outcome and the final indicator of achievement (SMoE, 2009c). Instead, it recommended that schools "explore the use of bite-sized forms of assessment which place more emphasis on learning rather than on grades alone" (p. 35).

Third, early childhood research in Singapore should keep pace with the changes in the preschool and primary school systems. The report issued by the Lien Foundation acknowledged the need for "a rigorous research culture whereby the impact of policy, policy development and implementation can be measured, evaluated and evidenced" (Ang, 2012, p. 11). As new pedagogical approaches are being used in the early years' classrooms, it will be informative to document best practices and identify distinctive features that advance learning. Local research should also continue to systematically evaluate shifts in pedagogical approaches (e.g., SEED and STELLAR) with a view to understanding the extent to which they are achieving the desired outcomes for our children and to fine-tune processes and improve teacher training. There is also scope for studies to examine collaborative relationships between the children's families and their schools and the unique contributions they make to children's development, both individually and collectively. Currently, the SMoE is conducting a series of longitudinal studies to evaluate children's learning and progress in STELLAR (SMoE, 2009a). Findings from these studies should be shared with teachers in school who are actively translating educational initiatives into child-centred classroom practices. It would be immensely helpful if the SMoE's research findings were made accessible to teachers and teacher-educators and published internationally to provide insight into best practices in literacy learning and development in the early years of schooling.

Finally, it cannot be emphasized enough that the first years of school are critical because they have long-term effects, in that adjustment difficulties tend to be stable (Donelan-McCall & Dunn, 1997). By the end of first grade, and maybe even kindergarten, how well children perceive they are performing academically in school has begun to influence how they feel about school in general (Valeski & Stipek, 2001). As Entwisle and Alexander (1995) put it, "Perhaps the most important way that entry into school serves as a critical period ... is that children are sorted and categorized over the first year or two of school in ways that can launch them into achievement trajectories" (p. 136). Given that learning patterns are stubborn, and habits tend to persist, it is imperative that early school adjustment be as positive as it can be so that no holds are prematurely placed on the future attainments of young children.

Postscript

At the time this chapter was "in press," the Lien Foundation released the findings of a landmark study to investigate the perspectives of leading local early childhood professionals on improving the preschool sector in Singapore. The priority areas that were highlighted included "the significant gaps in the quality, accessibility and equity of services" in preschool education (Ang, 2012, p. 11), the need to raise the status of preschool teachers, and the urgent need for well-coordinated collaboration between different ministries and agencies to strengthen the preschool sector. In response, the Singapore government is setting up a new statutory board to oversee preschool education (Ong, 2012). It will not, however, nationalize preschool. Instead, substantial resources will be committed to widening and strengthening the base of anchor preschool operators in order to raise the quality of preschool education offered by mass operators such as the PAP Community Foundation child care centres or kindergartens and the National Trades Union Congress First Campus child care centres centres. A pilot study scheme involving a few preschool centres will test new concepts in kindergarten education. These initiatives are targeted at raising the overall quality of preschool education and making good preschool education affordable for children from middle- and lower-income families and disadvantaged backgrounds (Ong, 2012). The steps taken by the government will take early childhood education in Singapore to greater heights. Our children's prospects for a successful transition from preschool to primary school have never been brighter.

AUTHOR NOTE

The perspectives offered in this chapter are the author's and should not be regarded as representative of views held by the Singapore Ministry of Education or the Singapore National Institute of Education.

REFERENCES

Ang, L. (2012). *Vital voices for vital years*. Singapore: Lien Foundation.
Bronfenbrenner, U., & Morris, P.A. (1998). The ecology of developmental processes. In W. Damon & R.M. Lerner (Eds.), *Handbook of child psychology* (Vol. 1, 5th ed., pp. 993–1028). New York: Wiley.
Brooker, L. (2002). *Starting school: Young children learning cultures*. Buckingham: Open University Press.
Brostrom, S. (2000, Aug.). Transition to school. Paper presented at the EECERA European Conference on Quality in Early Childhood Education, London.
Burchinal, M.R., Peisner-Feinberg, E., Pianta, R., & Howes, C. (2002). Development of academic skills from preschool through second grade: Family and classroom predictors of developmental trajectories. *Journal of School Psychology, 40*(5), 415–436.
Carida, H.C. (2011). Planning and implementing an educational programme for the smooth transition from kindergarten to primary school: The Greek project in all-day kindergarten. *Curriculum Journal, 22*(1), 77–92.
Comber, B. (2000). What really counts in early literacy lessons. *Language Arts, 78*, 39–49.
Dixon, M., Stinson, M., Silver, R.E., Green, N., Nie, Y., Wright, S., ... (2008). *A study on the implementation of "Strategies for Effective Engagement and Development" (SEED): Final Research Report for Project No. CRP 12/07 MD.*

Singapore: Centre for Research in Pedagogy and Practice.

Dockett, S., & Perry, B. (1999). Starting school: What do the children say? *Early Child Development and Care, 159*(1), 107–119.

Dockett, S., & Perry, B. (2003). Smoothing the way: What makes a successful school transition programme? *Education Links, 65*(1), 6–10.

Donelan-McCall, N., & Dunn, J. (1997). School work, teachers, and peers: The world of first grade. *International Journal of Behavioral Development, 21*(1), 155–178.

Duncan, G.J., Dowsett, C.J., Claessens, A., Magnuson, K., Huston, A.C., Klebanov, P., …, & Japel, C. (2007, Nov.). School readiness and later achievement. *Developmental Psychology, 43*(6), 1428–1446.

Einarsdottir, J. (2003). When the bell rings we have to go inside: Preschool children's views on the primary school. *European Early Childhood Education Research Journal Themed Monograph, 1*, 35–50.

Einarsdottir, J. (2006). From preschool to primary school: When different contexts meet. *Scandinavian Journal of Educational Research, 50*(2), 165–184.

Einarsdottir, J. (2007). Children's voices on the transition from preschool to primary school. In A.W. Dunlop & H. Fabian (Eds.), *Informing transitions in the early years* (pp. 74–91). London: Open University Press.

Einarsdottir, J., Perry, B., & Dockett, S. (2008). Transition to school practices: Comparisons from Iceland and Australia. *Early Years, 28*(1), 47–60.

Entwisle, D.R., & Alexander, K.L. (1995). A parent's economic shadow: Family structure versus family resources as influences on early school achievement. *Journal of Marriage and the Family, 57*(2), 399–409.

Firlik, R. (2001). *Honoring children's rights to quality experiences in preschool that are valued by public school kindergarten educators and administrators: Early Year's Summit*. Washington, DC: Educational Resources Information Center, U.S. Department of Education.

Hamre, B., & Pianta, R.C. (2001, Mar.). Early teacher-child relationships and children's social and academic outcomes through eighth grade. *Child Development, 72*, 625–638.

Kagan, S.L. (1991). Moving from here to there: Rethinking continuity and transitions in early care and education. In B. Spodek & O.N. Saracho (Eds.), *Issues in early childhood curriculum: Yearbook in early childhood education* (Vol. 2, pp. 132–151). New York: Teachers College Press.

Ladd, G.W. (1990, Aug). Having friends, keeping friends, making friends, and being liked by peers in the classroom: Predictors of children's early school adjustment? *Child Development, 61*(4), 1081–1100.

Margetts, K. (2007). Preparing children for school: Benefits and privileges. *Australian Journal of Early Childhood, 32*, 43–50.

McKinsey & Co (2007). *How the world's best performing schools come out on top.*

New York: Author. Retrieved from http://www.mckinseyonsociety.com/
how-the-worlds-best-performing-schools-come-out-on-top/

Meisels, S.J. (1999). A comprehensive conceptualization of school readiness.
Paper presented at the Paper presented at the biennial meeting of the
Society for Research in Child Development, Alburquerque, NM.

Ong H.H. (2012, 27 Aug.). Preschool stat board to be set up. *Straits Times.*

Peisner-Feinberg, E.S., Burchinal, M.R., Clifford, R.M., Culkin, M.L., Howes,
C., Kagan, S.L., & Yazejian, N. (2001, Sept.-Oct.). The relation of preschool
child-care quality to children's cognitive and social developmental
trajectories through second grade. *Child Development, 72*(5), 1534–1553.

Perry, K.E., & Weinstein, R.S. (1998). The social context of early schooling
and children's school adjustment. *Educational Psychologist, 33*(4), 177–194.
http://dx.doi.org/10.1207/s15326985ep3304_3

Pianta, R., & Stuhlman, M. (2004). Teacher-child relationships and children's
success in the first years of school. *School Psychology Review, 33*, 444–458.

Potter, G.K., & Briggs, F. (2003). Children talk about their early experiences
at school. *Australian Journal of Early Childhood, 28*, 44–49.

Quah, S. (1999, 19 July). Study on the family: Kid's education is no. 1 worry.
Straits Times, 4.

Richardson, J.L. (1995). *Contending liberalisms: Past and present.* Australian
National University Canberra, Australia. Retrieved from http://ips.cap
.anu.edu.au/ir/pubs/work_papers/95-10.pdf

Romano, E., Babchishin, L., Pagani, L.S., & Kohen, D. (2010, Sept.). School
readiness and later achievement: Replication and extension using a
nationwide Canadian survey. *Developmental Psychology, 46*(5), 995–1007.

Sanagavarapu, P. (2010). Children's transition to school: Voices of Bangladeshi
parents in Sydney, Australia. *Australasian Journal of Early Childhood, 35*,
21–29.

Schoolbag.sg (2010). The STELLAR way to English language learning.
Retrieved from http://www.schoolbag.sg/archives/2010/09/
the_stellar_way_to_english_lan.php

Sharpe, P. (2002a). School days in Singapore: Young children's experiences
and opportunities during a typical school day. *Childhood Education, 79*,
9–14.

Sharpe, P. (2002b). Preparing for primary school in Singapore: Aspects of
adjustment to the more formal demands of the Primary One Mathematics
syllabus. *Early Child Development and Care, 172*(4), 329–335.

Silver, R.E. (2011). Curriculum implementation in early primary schooling
in Singapore. *NIE Research Brief, 11*, 1–4.

Singapore Ministry of Education (SMoE). (2007). *Strategies for effective and engaged development of pupils in primary schools: The philosophy of SEED* (Vol. 1). Singapore: Author.bmj

Singapore Ministry of Education (SMoE). (2008a). *Enhanced learning support programme has benefitted pupils.* [Press Release]. Retreived from http://www.moe.gov.sg/media/press/2008/01/enhanced-learning-support-prog.php

Singapore Ministry of Education (SMoE). (2008b). *What is STELLAR?* Retrieved from http://www.stellarliteracy.sg/cos/o.x?c=/wbn/pagetree&func=view&rid=20031

Singapore Ministry of Education (SMoE). (2009a). *Infosheet on improving language and communication skills.* [Press Release]. Retrieved from http://www.moe.edu.sg/media/press/2009/09/improving-language-and-communi.php

Singapore Ministry of Education (SMoE). (2009b). *Teachers: The heart of quality education.* [Press Release]. Retrieved from http://www.moe.gov.sg/media/press/2009/09/teachers-the-heart-of-quality.php

Singapore Ministry of Education (SMoE). (2009c). *Report of the Primary Education Review and Implementation Committee.* Retrieved from http://www.moe.gov.sg/media/press/files/2009/04/peri-report.pdf

Singapore Ministry of Education (SMoE). (2010a). *Infosheet on Singapore highlighted in latest McKinsey report "How The World's Most Improved School Systems Keep Getting Better."* [Press Release]. Retrieved from http://www.moe.gov.sg/media/press/2010/12/singapore-highlighted-in-mckinsey-report.php

Singapore Ministry of Education (SMoE). (2010b). *Launch of Singapore Pre-school Accreditation Framework.* [Press Release]. Retrieved from http://moe.gov.sg/media/press/2010/11/launch-of-singapore-pre-school-accreditation-framework.php

Valeski, T.N., & Stipek, D.J. (2001, Jul-Aug). Young children's feelings about school. *Child Development, 72*(4), 1198–1213.

Vygotsky, L.S. (1978). *Mind in society: The development of higher mental processes.* Cambridge, MA: Harvard University Press. (Original work published 1930).

Walsh, G.M., McGuinness, C., Sproule, L., & Trew, K. (2010). Implementing a play-based and developmentally appropriate curriculum in Northern Ireland primary schools: What lessons have we learned? *Early Years, 30*(1), 53–66.

Wildenger, L.K., & McIntyre, L. (2012). Investigating the relation between kindergarten preparation and child socio-behavioral school outcomes. *Early Childhood Education Journal, 40*(3), 169–176.

Wong, N.C. (2003). A study of children's difficulties in transition to school in Hong Kong. *Early Child Development and Care, 2003,* 83–96.

Yeo, L.S., & Clarke, C. (2005). Starting school: A Singapore story told by children. *Australian Journal of Early Childhood, 30,* 1–8.

Yeo, L.S., & Clarke, C. (2006). Adjustment to the first year in school: A Singapore perspective. *European Early Childhood Education Research Journal, 14*(2), 55–68.

3 Young Children's Experience of Starting School in an Area of Socio-economic Disadvantage

AMBER JACKSON AND JENNIFER CARTMEL

Educators in early years' settings are confronted with a complex set of circumstances when providing quality transitions to school for children in early education and care settings in areas of socio-economic disadvantage. Starting school is recognized as a life transition and milestone for young children (Danby, Thompson, Theobald, & Thorpe, 2012; Dockett & Perry, 2009; Yeo & Clarke, 2007). As children undertake the transition from a flexible home or early years' setting to the structure of formal school, they encounter a period of change and adjustment, accompanied with new experiences, opportunities, and challenges (Bond & Maley, 2007). How children in low socio-economic areas experience and manage this transition can impact on their progress throughout the schooling system and their life after school.

A positive transition to school facilitates children's initial adjustment and achievement in the school environment, providing an advantage for their later attainment and enhancing the development of positive school trajectories (Dockett & Perry, 2009; Petriwskyj, Thorpe, & Tayler, 2005). Early schooling experiences also contribute to children's developing sense of self, thus, a successful start to school has a positive influence on how children view themselves as learners (Dockett & Perry, 2009). Conversely, children who are unprepared and have a negative start to school may be disadvantaged in the school setting (Centre for Community Child Health and Telethon Institute for Child Health Research [CCCH-TICHR], 2011). Poor transitions compromise children's school engagement and attendance, and they can create a negative life pathway that is difficult to alter and impacts on children's long-term outcomes (Centre for Community Child Health [CCCH], 2008a, 2008b).

Having a positive start to school is important for young children's development and lifelong learning.

Children from low-income families, including some with special learning needs, have been the focus of research that explores children's feelings about school around the transition period (Dockett et al., 2011; Hauser-Cram, Durand, & Warfield, 2007; Valeski & Stipek, 2001). Child interviews and assessments and teachers' questionnaires and classroom observations were used to understand children's early schooling experiences (Dockett et al., 2011; Hauser-Cram et al., 2007). These studies reveal that children from poorer families display less positive attitudes towards school and have reduced competence, which affects their motivation to engage and learn at school (ibid.). It is important to acknowledge children's early perceptions of school and encourage the development of positive school attitudes, particularly for children in low-income areas (Dockett, Perry, & Kearney, 2010; Hauser-Cram et al., 2007). A limitation of some studies is that they are primarily based on standardized, adult-directed assessments and measures, positioning children as objects to study rather than including them as inquirers in the research (Smith, 2010). Consequently, this provides a limited understanding of children's perspectives and experiences of starting school.

This chapter will discuss the barriers associated with undertaking the transition to school in an area of socio-economic disadvantage. It emphasizes the significant challenges that children and families face when starting school in a low socio-economic area, and the importance of considering children's experiences and perspectives to inform the development of appropriate and effective transition support programs to ensure that all children have access to a positive start to school. To highlight barriers from a child's perspective, a case study will be used. This Australian study (Jackson, 2009) used interpretive phenomenology to gain an in-depth understanding of children's lived experiences of starting school in an area of socio-economic disadvantage. The study includes recommendations for early years' educators, families, and the broader community to support all children to have a successful start to school. The chapter will conclude by exploring other related issues associated with the school transition.

Barriers

Starting school is a major life event for a young child. This transition experience varies for children and is influenced by their unique backgrounds, experiences, and opportunities prior to starting school. This section will focus on the barriers to children's successful school transition in low socio-economic areas, including the following:

- Parents' socio-economic status
- Contrasting perspectives on readiness and the transition to school
- Communication limitations between various stakeholders
- Absence of a focus on friendships.

It is important to address these barriers to ensure all children have the best possible start to their schooling experience.

Parents' Socio-economic Status

The potential consequences of living in an area of socio-economic disadvantage are numerous and complex. Parents with a low socio-economic background are susceptible to social exclusion, insufficient income or unemployment, lower levels of education, increased stress, and low self-esteem. These factors reduce parents' willingness and capacity to access services, resources, and support. Consequently, children's development and learning are affected as parents struggle to provide the necessary resources to support their children's positive development (Dockett et al., 2011; Dunlop & Fabian, 2007). Children's early experiences and relationships build a foundation for their subsequent learning and social interactions (CCCH-TICHR, 2011). When these previous experiences are stimulating, nurturing, and responsive, they facilitate young children's readiness to embrace the social and learning opportunities offered as they start school (CCCH, 2008a). Parents from low socio-economic backgrounds are less likely to be able to provide these positive early experiences, increasing their children's chances of entering school with poorer developmental outcomes that affect their readiness to learn and engage in the school environment (CCCH-TICHR, 2011; Dockett et al., 2011). Parents' low socio-economic status (SES) creates a barrier for children's positive and successful school transition because they have less access to supportive early learning experiences and resources that effectively prepare them for school.

Socio-economic disadvantage is associated with poor social/emotional, physical, and learning outcomes for young children (Edwards, 2005), because these children have an increased chance of entering school with limited language skills, as well as social, emotional, and health problems that affect their readiness to learn and effectively interact with adults and peers (CCCH, 2008a; Dockett et al., 2011). These children are at risk of having a problematic transition and difficulty adjusting, engaging, and performing well in the school environment. A negative transition to school can lead to children's reduced aspiration to engage and achieve at school, contributing to the development or continuation of a cycle of intergenerational disadvantage, which is difficult to interrupt or change (Stanley, Richardson, & Prior, 2005). Children born into areas of socio-economic disadvantage are at greater risk of having a negative transition to school, influencing their initial perception of school and long-term schooling outcomes.

Contrasting Perspectives

Perceptions of school readiness and the transition to school that contribute to conceptualizing programs and policies around this period are inconsistent. School readiness has been recently reconceptualized to provide a broader focus for understanding and supporting children's transition to school. Consequently, children's readiness for school has been reconsidered as the transition to school (Petriwskyj et al., 2005). A range of constructions of the transition to school recognize the complex, unique, and multidimensional nature of this period (Dunlop & Fabian, 2007; Petriwskyj, 2005; Petriwskyj et al., 2005). However, these constructions are limited and continue to rely on traditional constructs of childhood and school readiness, privilege adult perspectives and teachers' values, and fail to consider unequal power relations between schools, early years' services, families, and children (Petriwskyj et al., 2005). This presents a barrier for children starting school in low socio-economic areas, because children's and parents' perspectives and broader situations are not considered. Inconsistency in conceptualizing the transition to school also creates confusion around the expectations and responsibilities of the different stakeholders involved, which can have an impact on how children are prepared for school.

Reconceptualizations of school readiness and awareness of the significance of a positive start to school have prompted researchers' interest in children's transition to school throughout the world. However, children's involvement in research on the school transition has been limited. It is only recently that researchers have focused on understanding children's experiences of starting school (Danby et al., 2012; Margetts, 2007; Yeo & Clarke, 2007), or a combination of children's and adults' perceptions of this milestone (Bulkeley & Fabian, 2006; Dockett & Perry, 2009; Hauser-Cram et al., 2007). The lack of involvement of children in research and decision making around the school transition disempowers children and reduces the effectiveness of programs developed to support them through this period.

Several criticisms can be made about prior research on children's and adults' perspectives of starting school. Although the findings of these studies emphasize the importance of building collaborative partnerships between the various stakeholders in the school transition, limited consideration is given to the inequalities in power relationships between these different parties (Petriwskyj et al., 2005). This affects how accurately and extensively children's and parents' perspectives are expressed and acknowledged in research and consequent strategies aiming to support children's transition to school. Furthermore, this previous research does not place a high priority on uncovering and sharing children's perspectives of starting school separate from an adult's perspective. Combining these different perspectives may result in children's ideas and experiences being influenced and overshadowed by an adult's point of view because of the disparities in power between children and adults (Freeman & Mathison, 2009; Powell & Smith, 2009; Smith, 2010). Although the results of studies reinforce the importance of considering the perspectives of all stakeholders involved in the school transition, the perspectives of children are not the primary focus and, therefore, may be undermined by adult perspectives of the school transition.

As a result of undervaluing children's perspectives of the school transition, current programs and strategies aimed at supporting children's transition to school do not have a particularly strong focus on aspects that matter to children, such as their friendships (Jackson, 2009). Findings of the Starting School Research Project (SSRP) facilitated the development of 10 key guidelines for effective transition to school programs, which have been well accepted in Australia (Dockett & Perry, 2006). Two of these guidelines refer to the importance of building positive relationships and promoting communication and connections between the various stakeholders involved in the school transition (ibid.). Although children's friendships are included within these particular guidelines, the language used portrays an adult-based perspective of the transition to school and fails to promote the importance of friendships to children as they start school. This can lead to misinterpretation of these guidelines, as is evident in several policy briefs published by the Centre for Community Child Health that reference Dockett and

Perry's research. These policy briefs discuss key strategies for supporting children's successful school transition, including the development and continuity of positive adult–child relationships and maintaining communication and links between early years' services, schools, and families (CCCH, 2008a, 2008b). Although these factors are involved in facilitating children's positive transition to school, no consideration has been made for children's friendships, which are an integral component of children's transition, or the importance of building relationships and communication between different families thereby reinforcing these school friendships. This hinders children's successful transition because what really matters to them as they start school is not acknowledged or addressed.

Communication Limitations

Children start school with different understandings and expectations informed by their early experiences and social relationships with family, friends, and preschool carers. These expectations about school can result in children developing a positive or negative perception of and attitude towards starting school (Petriwskyj, 2005). Developing a positive attitude towards school has significant advantages for children starting school, increasing their competence, enthusiasm, and motivation to engage and participate in the school environment (Ladd, 2005; Peters, 2003). This positive attitude can serve as a protective factor for children at risk of poor achievement and disengagement at school associated with socio-economic disadvantage (Hauser-Cram et al., 2007). A lack of opportunity to explore expectations of school can increase children's anxiety and negative perception about starting school, creating a barrier to their engagement and success in the school environment.

Children experience anxiety about being alone and not knowing everyone in the new school environment, regardless of the presence of pre-existing friendships at school (Jackson, 2009). This may be related to limited communication between the various stakeholders involved in the school transition about concerns, expectations, and knowledge about school. Interaction and communication between children, parents, preschool carers, and teachers at the school is vital to ensure that everyone involved in the transition to school has a shared understanding, knowledge, and expectations about the event (Danby et al., 2012). When this open sharing of information about school does not occur, children are not able to ask questions and discuss their concerns about starting school, reducing their confidence about making the transition to Year One. Discontinuities between children's understanding and expectations of school and what it is actually like can also have a negative impact on the schooling experience, creating uncertainty, disappointment, and unnecessary concern (Petriwskyj, 2005). Without ongoing communication and collaboration between children, families, preschool carers, and school educators, a consensus understanding of the school transition cannot be achieved (Danby et al., 2012; Dockett & Perry, 2007; Petriwskyj, 2005). As a result, parents and children would not have access to valuable information about school prior to their attendance and have different expectations of the various stakeholders involved, affecting how children are prepared for school. Insufficient cooperation and communication between the children's home and school settings contributes to children's uncertainty and anxiety about what to expect at school, and reduces the consistency of attempts to support children through this transition.

Children without older siblings face additional barriers when starting school. Older siblings provide young children with valuable information about school and give them the opportunity to discuss their experiences with someone who understands what they are going through (Dockett & Perry, 2007). The support received from older siblings can reduce children's anxiety about school and help them settle into the new environment (Dockett & Perry, 2007; Dunn, 2004). The presence of older, more experienced peers who are well known to younger children starting school also enhances their sense of familiarity, safety, and confidence at school (Dockett & Perry, 2005). Children who do not have an older sibling in the school environment are less able to share their experiences and seek reassurance from someone who has already experienced the transition to school (Jackson, 2009). The absence of the familiarity and support provided by older siblings increases children's concerns of being alone as they start school and reduces opportunities to discuss these experiences. On the other hand, older siblings with negative experiences of school can contribute an additional impediment to a smooth transition to school for younger children. A lack of open communication about the transition to school can be a barrier for children from areas of socio-economic disadvantage successfully transitioning to school.

Absence of Friendships

Children who have a positive attitude towards school are more competent in their ability to succeed, increasing their motivation and enthusiasm to engage in the school environment and their sense of connectedness to school (Hauser-Cram et al., 2007; Valeski & Stipek, 2001). Ladd (2005) proposes that liking school increases children's engagement and enjoyment in the environment, enhancing their opportunity to engage in learning and achieving educational outcomes. Children from low socio-economic backgrounds are at risk of having reduced aspirations to attend, engage in, and succeed at school passed on from previous generations (Australian Government, 2009). Increased excitement and interest in attending school can disrupt this intergenerational cycle of disadvantage, enhancing the opportunity to succeed and get more out of the schooling experience. The absence of pre-established friendships during the school transition may provide a barrier to successful transition by contributing to children's negative perception and experience of starting school.

The protective factors of having friends during the early years of school are particularly beneficial for children who are vulnerable or at risk, including very shy children (Dunn, 2004). Shy children are more likely to have difficulty making and maintaining relationships with others because they may have low self-esteem, are more wary of rejection and disapproval, and are less likely to take risks in a relationship (Erwin, 1998). Difficulties associated with shyness and developing friendships can have an impact on children's schooling experience and adjustment (Ladd, 2005). Children's close friendships provide them with support and confidence when starting school and during Year One, contributing to their positive experience of school when they may have otherwise been at risk of adjustment difficulties because of their shy personality. This reinforces the negative impact of not having friends when starting school.

Children's frequent references to new and old friends in relation to the school transition are evidence of the increased social opportunities and challenges that young children are exposed to as they start school (Jackson, 2009). Moving away from the secure home environment necessitates a significant developmental task for young children, involving "the ability to engage in positive interactions with peers and develop satisfying peer relationships" (Rolfe, 2004, p. 127). Achieving this task requires good social and emotional development and well-being, a factor increasingly recognized as integral to children's readiness for school (Danby et al., 2012; Bulkeley & Fabian, 2006; Dockett & Perry, 2007; Margetts, 2007). This social and emotional development is facilitated by high-quality learning experiences, as well as caring, responsive relationships with others in the early years of life. Children from areas of socio-economic disadvantage may have less access to these stimulating early learning opportunities, and they are more likely to have limited language skills and poorer social and emotional outcomes as they start school (Australian Government, 2009; Dockett et al., 2011). Educators and policy makers must not underestimate the importance of supporting children's developing social skills and emotional well-being prior to starting school, particularly for children starting school in areas of socio-economic disadvantage.

An important context for children's social and emotional development is within their friendships, which allow them to learn more about themselves and how to effectively communicate and interact with others (Bagwell, 2004; Dunn et al., 2002). Friendships give children the opportunity to practise and enhance their social, emotional, communication, and language skills through their engagement in conversations, cooperative and pretend play, conflict, and the sharing of feelings and experiences (Dunn et al., 2002; Margetts, 2007). Through their interactions with friends, children also develop an understanding of the connections between people's thoughts and behaviour, and awareness of the feelings and perspectives of others (Danby et al., 2012). Children's confidence in the school environment is enhanced through these friendships, which provide emotional validation, support, and security on an everyday basis (Bagwell, 2004; Danby et al., 2012). Children who are not supported to establish and maintain friendships at school will have reduced communication skills and confidence, and less concern for and understanding of others' experiences and perspectives, creating difficulties in their successful transition to and engagement in the social environment at school.

As mentioned at the beginning of this chapter, interpretive phenomenology was used in an Australian study (Jackson, 2009) of children's individual lived experiences of starting school in an area of socio-economic disadvantage. Year One children attending school in a recognized area of low socio-economic disadvantage in Queensland, Australia, were invited to participate in the study. Participants were asked to share their ideas and opinions about starting school with minimal guidance from an adult's perspective. Unstructured, child-directed interviews were conducted, during which children collaboratively created mind maps with the researcher that represented their experiences of starting school. Participants were also given the opportunity to draw a picture depicting their first day at school, and their favourite thing about Year One. This study explored children's initial transition up to their first 6 months of school. The research emphasized the significance of friendships for children starting formal schooling. Early friendships matter to young children, providing support and comfort in times of stress and giving children the opportunity to experience shared pleasure and happiness at a young age (Dunn, 2004). This is particularly relevant when children are commencing school. In relation to children's friendships at the time of transition to school, the following three barriers were identified: starting school without friends, challenges making new friends, and concerns about not having friends.

Starting School without Friends

Children's illustrations and conversations revealed their concerns and about starting school without friends. Children expressed anxiety about being alone in the school environment and not being able to establish or maintain friendships at school (Jackson, 2009). A fear of being alone is common for children starting school (Peters, 2003). Children who did start school with pre-established friendships drew themselves with several friends in the school grounds on their first day of school (see Figures 3.1, 3.2, 3.3) (Jackson, 2009).

In these drawings, all the figures of children were smiling. This feature reinforces that starting Year One with friends is a positive and desirable experience for children. Pre-established friendships give children access to "immediate companionship, conversation and play" at school (Peters, 2003, p. 46). Opportunities for interacting with friends make school a more pleasurable experience and can increase children's motivation to attend school (Peters, 2003). Having old friends in the new environment provides a familiar point of interaction and enjoyment for these children (Jackson, 2009). Undergoing the transition to school without these friendships may provide a barrier to children's positive start to school. Parents, preschool carers, and schoolteachers who are unaware of the significance of children's friendships when starting school will not provide the reassurance that these friendships, where possible, will be honoured and further facilitated.

The presence of pre-established friendships reduced children's anxiety about starting school. Several children expressed their anxious thoughts and feelings about starting Year One (see Figure 3.4) (Jackson, 2009).

Starting school can be a challenging time for young children, evoking a sense of insecurity and wariness that prompts them to seek out something familiar at school (Ladd, 2005). Further on in their interviews,

Figure 3.1. "First day of school" (drawn 10.06.09; reduced from A4 size page).

Figure 3.2. "First day of school" (drawn 12.05.09; reduced from A3 size page).

Figure 3.3. "Favourite thing about Year One" (drawn 16.06.09; reduced from A4 page).

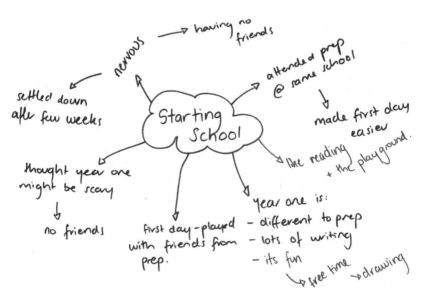

Figure 3.4. Child's mind map (drawn 20.05.09; reduced from A3 size page).

these children indicated that they overcame their concerns about starting school by interacting with their old friends: *"I played with friends from prep ... it made it not as scary"* (Jackson, 2009). Pre-existing friendships provide children with familiarity and continuity between a previous setting and the new school environment (Dunlop & Fabian, 2007). The stability, emotional support, and security gained from continuing friendships at school buffers the stress associated with this transition and helps children engage in school (Bulkeley & Fabian, 2006; Dunn, 2004). Reducing the strangeness of the school environment also makes children more comfortable, confident, and eager to engage with classroom activities and explore the learning opportunities offered (Dunlop & Fabian, 2007; Ladd, 2005). If children's concerns about commencing in a new place in Year One are not eased by the presence of old friends in the school setting, their competence and comfort in the new environment will be decreased.

Challenges Making New Friends

Entering Year One without friends means that children face a greater challenge of meeting unfamiliar children and making friends in the new environment. Being given the opportunity to choose a seat on the first day of school was significant for children in the study, and was guided by the children's intention to find friends (Jackson, 2009). The ability to make friends easily and successfully is developed and produced by context, rather than relying only on children's individual skills and personality (Peters, 2003). The structure and organization of schools can have a significant impact on children's friendships, facilitating or disrupting their access to new and old friends (Corsaro, Molinari, Hadley, & Sugioka, 2003). For one child, the significance of choosing his own desk on his first day of school was reinforced by illustrations of his first day of school and favourite thing about Year One, both of which included the classroom with numerous desks (Jackson, 2009) (see Figure 3.5).

The structure of the school environment has a significant impact on children's transition to school, and if not arranged appropriately, will hinder children's ability to develop friendships.

Concerns about Not Having Friends

The absence of friends was a key concern for children during their transition to school. Several children recalled feeling anxious on their first

Figure 3.5. "First day of school" (drawn 12.05.09; reduced from A3 size page).

day of school owing to concerns about meeting other children and making friendships in the school setting (Jackson, 2009). The following excerpt provides an example of how one child was feeling on her first day of school and the reason she attributed to this emotion: "*I was nervous … worried about having no friends*" (ibid.). The social nature of the school environment creates new opportunities and challenges for children to develop and maintain relationships with others (Dockett & Perry, 2009; Margetts, 2007). As a result, children are faced with the chance of experiencing rejection and loneliness (Dunn, 2004). Cullingford proposes that "a school's virtues derive from the pleasures of friendships; its terrors from loneliness and isolation" (1991; cited in Peters, 2003, p. 46). This statement encapsulates a common fear experienced by children starting school – a fear of being alone in the new environment (Peters, 2003). Anxiety about being alone at school and meeting unfamiliar children are frequent concerns that accompany the new social opportunities and challenges associated with starting school. Failing to acknowledge these concerns may increase children's anxiety about starting school, reducing the success and positive nature of their school transition.

The barriers to the smooth transition to school by children in areas of low socio-economic circumstances are complex. Children's social and emotional well-being is linked to their ability to make friends. This is negatively compounded if the adult stakeholders do not provide opportunities for children to develop friendships and explore their concerns about starting school through open communication, and if they fail to consider broader perspectives about learning.

Recommendations

The low socio-economic status of families and their children is a long-term issue that cannot be addressed in the scope of this chapter. However, perspectives on the transition to school and open communication about this experience can be altered in the short term with long-term gains. Critically analysing the different perspectives on children's transition to school would provide a greater foundation for challenging problematic conceptualizations of the school transition and promote genuine consideration of children's perspectives of starting school. An alternative version of the guidelines proposed by Dockett and Perry (2007) that explicitly emphasizes the importance of children's friendships during the school transition would privilege children's perspectives of this experience, and clearly identify what really matters to children as they start school in areas of socio-economic disadvantage. Furthermore, educators and parents can create better opportunities for children to establish and maintain friendships. This section will discuss these recommendations to address the barriers previously explored.

Multiple Perspectives

Contemporary research and literature identifies the multiple stakeholders involved in the transition to school, including children, parents, early years' and school practitioners, and the broader community (CCCH-TICHR, 2011; Danby et al., 2012; Dockett & Perry, 2009; Petriwskyj, 2005). As previously discussed, inconsistencies between these different perspectives and the failure to acknowledge them all create barriers for children's successful school transition. It is vital to explore the experiences and perspectives of all of these stakeholders to create a shared understanding of the school transition, promote continuity between children's different environments, and identify the strategies necessary to support children and their families through this period (Danby et al., 2012; Dockett & Perry, 2009). However, no stakeholder perspective is more important than that of young children. Understanding the transition to school from a child's perspective is crucial to produce participatory and collaborative programs, which are more effective and beneficial for children and the broader community (Powell & Smith, 2009; Sorin & Galloway, 2006). Listening to children's ideas and concerns also contributes to their sense of inclusion and empowerment in an environment, thereby facilitating their sense of well-being and engagement at school (Einarsdottir, Dockett, & Perry, 2009; Powell & Smith, 2009; Smith, 2010; Sorin & Galloway, 2006). Exploring all stakeholders' perspectives requires the use of techniques that ensure that children's perspectives are not overshadowed by adults' perceptions of the school transition.

Open Communication

Open, reciprocal communication between children, parents, preschool, and school practitioners facilitates informative discussions about school and assists children to develop accurate expectations and understanding of the school transition (Petriwskyj, 2005). Increasing the opportunities for children to share their feelings, thoughts, and concerns about starting school with other peers and adults would help reassure children and reduce their anxiety about the transition to school. The presence of open communication between educators and families also facilitates a shared understanding of the responsibilities and expectations of all involved, and increases the continuity of strategies that aim to support children starting school.

Supporting Children's Friendships

From a child's perspective, having friends at school is a positive experience (Jackson, 2009). This is reflected in children's drawings and conversations around starting school in an area of socio-economic disadvantage (ibid.). Early friendships provide opportunities for children to experience companionship as they spend time together engaging in enjoyable interactions and joint activities (Danby et al., 2012). Opportunities to interact and play with friends are often recalled by children as favourable aspects of the early schooling years (Jackson, 2009). Children associate the companionship they receive through their interactions with friends during the first year of school to their favourite thing about starting school, providing evidence of the positive and memorable nature of these experiences (ibid.). This reinforces the importance of educators and families supporting children to establish and maintain friendships before, during, and after the transition to school.

Making new friendships has a positive impact on children's perception of and attitude towards school. Establishing new friendships is an important part of starting school from a child's perspective (Margetts, 2007). The friendship-building process helps children settle into school by giving them a sense of belonging and inclusion in the new environment, and by providing a companion with whom they can share positive experiences and concerns (Danby et al., 2012; Peters, 2003). Children's concerns about being left alone by family on the first day of school are eased by the support and companionship gained from new friendships they make at school (Jackson, 2009). Building new friendships with peers increases children's self-esteem and confidence in the school environment, and plays a key supportive role during their transition to school. Even children who began the year with friends expressed individual and shared concerns about starting school (ibid.). These concerns were eased as the children developed new friendships with other children they did not already know, making them feel more confident and supported in the new environment (ibid.). Regardless of the presence of pre-existing friendships, making new friends contributes positively to children's school transition.

Children provide significant insight into how they make new friends as they start school, and the emphasis on this process demonstrates how important it is to them. In the case study, children made friends through their engagement in organized group activities in the classroom (Jackson, 2009). Adults can assist children to make friends as they start school by introducing them to others, and modelling or teaching social skills and strategies that assist children to make supportive friendships (Danby et al., 2012). The organization of classroom activities can also initiate the friendship-building process and provide the space for children to meet others and get to know them in smaller, more intimate groups (Corsaro et al., 2003). A teacher can assist children to make friends by introducing them to others and forming smaller groups in class that encourage children to form relationships with peers through their continued engagement in class activities.

Children also make friends through interactions with their peers outside of their academic learning experiences. Free playtime at school provides the opportunity for children to initiate or be invited to join in play with others (Jackson, 2009). Opportunities to engage in joint activity with peers at school provide a foundation for developing friendships (Corsaro et al., 2003). These friendships are generally formed around similar characteristics and interests, hence, engaging freely in conversations and play at school allows children to discover their similarities to and differences from others (Dunn, 2004). Children's ability to make friends at school is enhanced through the provision of time and space to engage in open social interactions with other children in the playground and classroom.

The pleasure gained from interacting with friends at school has a positive impact on children's schooling experience. "Playing with friends" was frequently related to children's favourite thing about starting school (Danby et al., 2012; Jackson, 2009). Early friendships provide the opportunity for children to spend time with one another and share positive, enjoyable experiences in the school classroom and playground (Howes, 1996). The pleasure and companionship associated with having friends increases children's motivation to attend and engage in the school environment during their first year of school (Peters, 2003). Children's ongoing achievement is facilitated by the skills, behaviour, and attitudes developed through good attendance and engagement at school (CCCH-TICHR, 2011). Engaging in play, conversation, and learning activities with friends at school is beneficial for children because being involved in the school environment facilitates their successful adjustment and performance at school. Participation and engagement at school is particularly important for children in areas of low SES because people in these areas are at risk of being stuck in a cycle of disadvantage (Australian Government, 2009). Having friends throughout the early years of school enhances children's enjoyment and involvement as they participate in a range of activities with their friends, contributing to their positive and successful schooling experience. Privileging the maintenance of these friendships is important in areas of socio-economic disadvantage where the likelihood of disengagement and school dropout is higher.

Children's enjoyment of interacting with school friends continues outside of the school environment. Children give detailed recollections of fun experiences that they have playing with friends outside of school (Jackson, 2009). Engaging with school friends outside of the school environment creates a greater connection between the school and children's home setting. Maintaining stability and continuity in children's relationships across different settings promotes children's confidence, security, and inclusion in different environments (Bulkeley & Fabian,

2006). This sense of security and belonging at school facilitates children's school adjustment and performance. Being able to interact with friends outside of the school environment is a positive consequence of having friends in the early years of school and enhances children's connection to and inclusion in the school environment. Helping children maintain and develop their friendships through interactions with friends outside of school hours contributes to their successful and positive transition to school.

Being liked by peers supports children's positive developmental outcomes in the early schooling years. Intimate, affectionate, and supportive friendships help children feel confident, secure, valued, and cared about in the school environment (Bulkeley & Fabian, 2006; Dunn, 2004). This sense of security and inclusion at school facilitates the development of children's positive sense of self, which enhances children's emotional well-being. Emotional well-being is integral to children's ability to build and maintain positive relationships and interactions and empowers them to engage in learning opportunities in the school setting (Bulkeley & Fabian, 2006). Children gain valuable support and assurance from being liked by peers and developing close, intimate friendships at school.

Children who made the transition with friends from preschool experiences were optimistic about starting school. Several children described being "*Happy*" about starting Year One and related their positive attitude towards starting school to the presence of pre-established friends (Jackson, 2009). Having friends from the Preparatory Year contributed to children's positive perception and experience of starting school because they were able to sit near and play with their old friends (ibid.). Starting school with pre-established friendships fosters children's favourable perception of school (Ladd, 2005). Promoting the continuation of children's friendships from their preschool environments would support children's successful transition to school.

Children and adults alike acknowledge the importance of schools supporting children to establish and maintain friendships during the early schooling years. Several strategies have been identified that assist teachers and schools to facilitate the friendship-building process, including the following: teaching children strategies for making friends in the new school environment; establishing buddy programs that couple new children with older peers during the early weeks of the school year; increasing children's opportunities to engage in joint activity and social interactions with others; and paying attention to the structure of the school environment and how it impacts on children's friendships (Danby et al., 2012; Dockett & Perry, 2007). By assisting children to develop friendships throughout their preschool or Preparatory Year and Year One of school, and wherever possible allowing children's friendship groups to remain together when placed in new classes enhances children's positive experience of starting school and successful adjustment to the new environment. Greater interaction, connection, and communication between children's families can also help promote the continuity of children's friendships inside and outside of the school environment.

Overall, acknowledging that friendships are important to children during the transition to school and promoting children's ability to develop and maintain positive friendships throughout this period are key recommendations for parents and practitioners to support children starting school. It is also necessary to give greater consideration to children's perspectives, without influence from an adult's point of view, to gain deeper insight into this experience for children and how they can be effectively supported throughout the school transition. Establishing open communication between early years' educators, schools, children, and families can help reduce children's concerns around this transition, and ensure that all stakeholders develop a shared understanding of the transition process and the support required to ensure that children get the best possible start to their schooling experience.

Related Issues

There are two further related issues that are intertwined with the aforementioned barriers and recommendations that have an impact on children's transition from early years' settings to school. These issues are influential to the context of the transition. One key factor is related to the early childhood workforce and the second is about juncture within the family circumstances. These systemic and structural factors seriously limit the potential of transition programs for children in early childhood education and care (ECEC) settings.

The lack of qualified, experienced, and stable teaching staff within disadvantaged communities, particularly those of low socio-economic circumstances, reduces the potential for successful transitions and transition programs. Well-qualified staff are more likely to provide consistently high-quality programs (Hilferty, Remond, & Katz, 2010). Further, the stability of the staff ensures that innovative programs targeted for low socio-economic areas are continuous and that the relationship building required with all community stakeholders is upheld (ibid.). It is now more likely that programs take the perspectives of all stakeholders into consideration and encourage frank and open dialogue between all those involved. It can be difficult to attract and retain secure qualified, experienced, and stable teaching staff within disadvantaged communities. In addition, staff turnover is significantly higher in identified disadvantaged schools than in schools in more socio-economically advantaged locations (Lamb & Teese, 2005). This is compounded in circumstances such as those in Australia where there is a national shortage of teachers both in early years' settings and in schools available to undertake such work (Productivity Commission, 2011). Hilferty et al. (2010) state that workforce issues "undermine the implementation of equity programs, and are detrimental to a quality early learning environment" (p. 28). Lack of understanding about the complexities of the social, political, and economic frameworks that surround the learning opportunities for young children reduces the intentionality of the educators to be effective in providing the time and space and other resources required to transition from one setting to the next. Suitably qualified teaching staff who are concerned about the multiple factors that impact on children's lives and, subsequently, their motivation, engagement, and ability to make a smooth transition between early childhood settings and school are critical.

For all families, especially those in socially disadvantaged circumstances, the transition from an early years' setting to school can also be a time of changeover between support services. Some families will experience a transition between programs of support, for others the transition will be from early childhood integrated services to nothing at all. Dockett et al. (2011) report on the extreme hardship for vulnerable families when children are moving into the school setting where parents and children had been heavily involved in child and family support programs prior to school, however, once the child had reached school age there was little in the way of support for parents or children.

Conclusion

Every child starts school with different ideas, emotions, knowledge, and expectations about this transition, informed by her or his unique background and experiences prior to school. Children from low socio-economic backgrounds are at risk of having a negative perception of school, resulting in a difficult transition and early disengagement from school. Acknowledging children's individual perceptions of and concerns about starting school enhances the development of effective transition support practices. Taking into account children's perspectives about school also respects children's rights, and increases children's inclusion and empowerment in the school setting. Increasing children's sense of inclusion at school and providing relevant support during the transition is particularly important for children in areas of socio-economic disadvantage. Exploring children's experiences of starting school in low socio-economic areas will enhance children's development and well-being, and contribute to knowledge of parents and educators of the support required to give children the best possible start to school.

REFERENCES

Australian Government. (2009). *Investing in the early years: A national early childhood development strategy – An initiative of the Council of Australian Governments*. Barton, A.C.T: Commonwealth of Australia.

Bagwell, C.L. (2004). Friendships, peer networks, and antisocial behaviour. In J.B. Kupersmidt & K.A. Dodge (Eds.), *Children's peer relations: From development to intervention* (pp. 37–57). Washington, DC: American Psychological Association.

Bond, T.G., & Maley, C.R. (2007). *Measuring up for big school: A role for cognitive development*. Queensland, Australia: James Cook University.

Bulkeley, J., & Fabian, H. (2006). Well-being and belonging during early educational transitions. *International Journal of Transitions in Childhood*, 2, 18–31.

Centre for Community Child Health (CCCH). (2008a). *Rethinking school readiness, policy brief: Translating early childhood research evidence to inform policy and practice* (Vol. 11). Victoria: Royal Children's Hospital.

Centre for Community Child Health (CCCH). (2008b). *Rethinking the transition to school: Linking schools and early years services, policy brief: Translating early childhood research evidence to inform policy and practice* (Vol. 11). Victoria: Royal Children's Hospital.

Centre for Community Child Health and Telethon Institute for Child Health Research (CCCH-TICHR). (2011). A snapshot of early childhood development in Australia: AEDI National Report 2009. Canberra, A. C. T.: Australian Government.

Corsaro, W.A., Molinari, L., Hadley, K.G., & Sugioka, H. (2003). Keeping and making friends: Italian children's transition from preschool to elementary school. *Social Psychology Quarterly*, 66(3), 272–292.

Danby, S., Thompson, C., Theobald, M., & Thorpe, K. (2012). Children's strategies for making friends when starting school. *Australasian Journal of Early Childhood*, 37(2), 63–71.

Dockett, S., & Perry, B. (2005). "A buddy doesn't let kids get hurt in the playground": Starting school with buddies. *International Journal of Transitions in Childhood*, 1, 22–34.

Dockett, S., & Perry, B. (2006). *Starting school: A handbook for early childhood educators*. Baulkham hills. NSW: Pademelon Press.

Dockett, S., & Perry, B. (2007). *Transitions to school: Perceptions, expectations, experiences*. Sydney, NSW: University of New South Wales Press.

Dockett, S., & Perry, B. (2009). "Readiness for school: A relational construct." *Australian Journal of Early Childhood*, 34(1), 20–26.

Dockett, S., Perry, B., & Kearney, E. (2010). School readiness: What does it mean for Indigenous children, families, schools and communities? Canberra: Closing the Gap Clearinghouse. Retrieved from http://www.aihw.gov.au/closingthegap/documents/issues_papers/ctg-ip02.pdf

Dockett, S., Perry, B., Kearney, E., Hampshire, A., Mason, J., & Schmied, V. (2011). Facilitating children's transition to school from families with complex support needs. Albury: Research Institute for Professional Practice, Learning and Education, Charles Sturt University. Retrieved from http://www.csu.edu.au/research/ripple/publications/index.htm

Dunlop, A., & Fabian, H. (2007). *Informing transitions in the early years*. London: Open University Press.

Dunn, J. (2004). *Children's friendships: The beginnings of intimacy*. London: Blackwell Publishing.

Edwards, B. (2005). Does it take a village? An investigation of neighbourhood effects on Australian children's development. *Family Matters. Australian Institute of Families*, 72, 36–43.

Einarsdottir, J., Dockett, S., & Perry, B. (2009). Making meaning: Children's perspectives expressed through drawings. *Early Child Development and Care*, 179(2), 217–232.

Erwin, P. (1998). *Friendship in childhood and adolescence*. London: Routledge.

Freeman, M., & Mathison, S. (2009). *Researching children's experiences*. New York: Guilford Press.

Hauser-Cram, P., Durand, T.M., & Warfield, M.E. (2007). Early feelings about school and later academic outcomes of children with special needs living in poverty. *Early Childhood Research Quarterly*, 22(2), 161–172.

Hilferty, F., Redmond, G., & Katz, I. (2010). The implications of poverty of children's readiness to learn. *Australasian Journal of Early Childhood*, 33(4), 63–72.

Howes, C. (1996). The earliest friendships. In W.M. Bukowski, A.F. Newcomb, & W.W. Hartup (Eds.), *The company they keep: Friendship in childhood and adolescence* (pp. 66–86). Cambridge: Cambridge University Press.

Jackson, A. (2009). *Listening to children's experience of starting year one in an area of socio-economic disadvantage.* Unpublished manuscript, School of Human Services and Social Work, Griffith University, Logan, Queensland, AU.

Ladd, G.W. (2005). *Children's peer relations and social competence: A century of progress.* New Haven, CT: Yale University Press.

Lamb, S., & Teese, R. (2005). *Equity programs for government schools in New South Wales: A review.* Report commissioned by the New South Wales Minister for Education and Training.

Margetts, K. (2007). Understanding and supporting children: Shaping transition practices. In H. Fabian & A.W. Dunlop (Eds.), *Informing transitions: Bridging research, policy and practice* (pp. 107–119). London: Open University Press.

Peters, S. (2003). "I didn't expect that I would get tons of friends ... more each day": Children's experiences of friendship during the transition to school. *Early Years: Journal of International Research and Development, 23*(1), 45–53.

Petriwskyj, A. (2005). Transition to school: Early years teachers' roles. *Journal of Australian Research in Early Childhood, 12*(2), 39–49.

Petriwskyj, A., Thorpe, K.J., & Tayler, C.P. (2005). Trends in construction of transition to school in three western regions, 1990–2004. *International Journal of Early Years Education, 13*(1), 55–69.

Powell, M.A., & Smith, A.B. (2009). Children's participation rights in research. *Childhood, 16*(1), 124–142.

Productivity Commission. (2011). *Early childhood development workforce.* Research Report, Melbourne, VIC.

Rolfe, S. (2004). *Rethinking attachment for early childhood practice: Promoting security, autonomy and resilience in young children.* Crows Nest, NSW: Allen & Unwin.

Smith, R. (2010). *A universal child?* Basingstoke, Hampshire: Palgrave Macmillan.

Sorin, R., & Galloway, G. (2006). Constructs of childhood: Constructs of self. *Children Australia, 31*(2), 12–21.

Stanley, F., Richardson, S., & Prior, M. (2005). *Children of the lucky country? How Australian society has turned its back on children and why children matter.* Sydney: Pan Macmillan Australia.

Valeski, T.N., & Stipek, D.J. (2001, July–Aug.). Young children's feelings about school. *Child Development, 72*(4), 1198–1213.

Yeo, L.S., & Clarke, C. (2007). Starting school: A Singapore story told by children. *Australian Journal of Early Childhood, 30*(3), 1–8.

4 Ready Together – Transition to School Program: Effecting Positive Outcomes for Children, Their Families, Schools, and the Community

MICHELE BINSTADT

Preparation for school, like the preparation for life, begins from conception. The early years are important in laying the foundation for a child's success in schooling and in later life (Docket & Perry, 2011; Margetts, 2012). Starting school is a significant moment for children and their families, and the changes that take place as children start school can be both exciting and challenging. A child's successful transition to school is influenced by many people, and it is the relationships and levels of communication between children, families, schools, early years' services, community services, and communities that support the process of becoming ready for school (Kagan & Rigby, 2003). Children's initial successes, both socially and academically, can be crucial to not only determining their initial adjustment to the school environment but also to their future progress and later life chances (Docket & Perry, 2011; Fabian & Dunlop, 2006). A successful transition to school can be a life-enriching experience, thus, ideally the transition to school should be a positive experience for all children and their families and a time of celebration (Kirk-Downey & Perry, 2006).

The majority of children make a smooth transition to school, but this is not always the case. For some children, it can be a time of anxiety, uncertainty, and confusion. Those children most at risk of facing challenges as they start school are children with additional needs, Indigenous children, and children from disadvantaged backgrounds (Centre for Equity & Innovation in Early Childhood [CE&IEC], 2008). The term *disadvantaged* is generally related to parents' educational experiences, the quality of the early years' home learning environment, the need for English as an additional language support, developmental problems early in life, and other factors such as socio-economic status (SES) and low income (CE&IEC, 2008).

There is worldwide interest in transition to school research, policy, and practice, and this is reflected within the Australian context. One of the most recent developments in Australia is the *Transition to School Position Statement* (Docket et al., 2011), launched by Professor Alan Hayes from the Australian Institute of Family Studies, in August 2011. This key document is based on both international and Australian understandings of the importance of transition to school. Described by the authors as an "aspirational document," the position statement reconceptualizes the transition to school in light of social justice, human rights (including children's rights), educational reform, and ethical agendas. It also considers the impact of transition to school on children's ongoing learning, development, and well-being. The document has a strengths-based approach, with the authors highlighting that the transition to school is characterized by opportunities, aspirations, expectations, and entitlements for all involved in the process (Docket et al., 2011; Docket & Perry, 2011).

It is with the recently developed *Transition to School Position Statement* in mind that the Ready Together – Transition to School Program positions itself as an example of a best practice model. Prior to providing an overview of the program, the author will provide a snapshot of Australia and the context within which the program is placed.

Located in the southern hemisphere, Australia has a population of over 20 million. Most of the population is concentrated along the east coast and the southeastern corner of the continent. Australia is one of the world's most urbanized countries, with about 70% of the population living in the 10 largest cities (About Australia, 2011). Australia is comprised of the following seven states and territories: Queensland (QLD), New South Wales (NSW), Australian Capital Territory (ACT), Victoria (VIC), Tasmania (TAS), South Australia (SA), Western Australia (WA), and the Northern Territory (NT). Each has its own autonomous education department, thus transition to school policies, practices, and programs vary across Australia.

Before the arrival of European settlers, Aboriginal and Torres Strait Islander peoples inhabited most areas of the Australian continent. Each tribe spoke its own language, and their lifestyles and cultural traditions differed according to the region in which they lived. They had complex social systems and highly developed traditions, which reflected a deep connection with the land and environment. Today, Indigenous Australians total approximately 2.2% of the population, with one-third living in rural and remote areas and two-thirds living in towns and cities (About Australia, 2011).

Australia is a culturally diverse society and present-day Australia is cosmopolitan and dynamic. Over 200 languages are spoken, with English being the common language. Four out of 10 Australians are migrants or the first-generation children of migrants, half of them from non-English–speaking backgrounds (About Australia, 2011).

The diversity of Australian society has implications for transition to school programs nationwide. To fully support the transition to school for all children and their families, it is essential that transition to school programs acknowledge, honour, and respond to the needs of these diverse groups.

Early Childhood and Transition to School Policy and Programs in Australia

Within Australia, there is recognition, at national and state government levels, of the significance of early childhood and the importance of investing in high-quality early childhood education and care (ECEC), with a view to preparing children for learning and life. There is also a strong emphasis on connecting with schools to ensure that all Australian children can make a smooth transition from ECEC to schooling (Queensland, Department of Education and Training, 2011a). Just how this is conceptualized varies across and within each Australian state and territory.

Nationally, the State of Victoria is leading the way in relation to transition to school evidence-based policy, promising practice models and transition to school program evaluation. Within Victoria, there is the Linking Schools and Early Years Project (LSEY), which is based on research conducted by the Centre for Community Child Health (Royal Children's Hospital, Melbourne, 2013). This project commenced in January 2007 and concluded in December 2012. The long-term aim of the project was that all children arrive at primary school ready to engage and continue their early learning and development. The final findings for the LSEY project are due to be released at the end of April 2013.

Victoria's Department of Education and Early Childhood Development (DEECD) has outlined policy and practices and developed resources to support children's transition to school. *Transition: A Positive Start to School Resource Kit* (Victoria, DEECD, 2010a), has been designed to help all early childhood services and schools improve the quality of transition to school planning for children and families. It details a statewide approach for children transitioning to school and highlights factors contributing to quality transition programs for children.

Welcome to Primary School (Victoria, DEECD, 2010b) has been developed to support families with children starting school.

Reform Agenda for Early Childhood Education and Care

The reform agenda involves a comprehensive plan to provide Australian families with high-quality, accessible, affordable, and integrated ECEC. The Office for Early Childhood Education and Care was established to assist in the implementation of a number of key government initiatives (Queensland, Department of Education and Care, 2012) including:

- Providing all children in the year before formal schooling with 15 hours of quality play-based early learning for a minimum of 40 weeks per year (universal access)
- The establishment of a national Early Years Learning and Development Framework (Australia, Department of Education, Employment and Workplace Relations for the Council of Australian Governments, 2009) that emphasizes play-based learning, social development, early literacy and numeracy skills
- Improvement of access to early learning for Indigenous and disadvantaged children
- Investing in the training of the early childhood workforce
- The creation of a national Early Childhood Development Index
- The establishment of national quality standards in child care and preschool.

Early Years Learning Framework for Australia:
Belonging, Being, and Becoming

The implementation of the national Early Years Learning Framework (EYLF) is part of the Council of Australian Governments (COAG) reform agenda for ECEC, and it is a key component of the Australian government's national quality framework for ECEC (Australian Children's Education and Care Quality Authority, 2011). Developed collaboratively by the Australian and state and territory governments with substantial input from the early childhood sector and early childhood academics, the EYLF underpins universal access to early childhood education. It describes the principles, practice, and outcomes essential to support and enhance young children's learning from birth to 5 years of age, as well as their transition to school. The framework has a strong emphasis on play-based learning, and it also recognizes the importance of communication and language (including early literacy and numeracy) and social and emotional development (Australia, Department of Education, Employment and Workplace Relations for the Council of Australian Governments, 2009).

Foundations for Success – Guidelines for an Early Learning Program in Aboriginal and Torres Strait Communities

Indigenous children are the most vulnerable group of children in Australia (Queensland Government, 2011), thus achieving positive educational outcomes for Aboriginal and Torres Strait Islander children is a high priority for the Australian government. Developed in 2007–08 by the then Queensland Department of Education, Training and the Arts, the Foundations for Success provides guidelines for early childhood educators working in pre-Prep settings in Aboriginal and Torres Strait Islander communities in Queensland. These part time pre-Prep education programs are for children aged 3 ½ to 4 ½ years who live across 35 discrete Aboriginal and Torres Strait Islander communities. A key focus is on building continuity of learning to lay the bases for success as children make the transition to school (Queensland, Department of Education, Training and the Arts, 2008). The guidelines highlight the need to value and build on the cultures and languages that children bring with them, promote the development of strong relationships between school and community, and work with children's families and communities to develop partnerships, creating a program that reflects local languages, cultures, and experiences (Cedric, 2011).

Australian Early Development Index

The Australian Early Development Index (AEDI) is based on the Canadian Early Development Instrument (EDI) developed by Magdalena Janus and Dan Offord (Janus & Offord, 2002). Adapted for use in Australia and funded by the Australian government, the AEDI data measure young children's development within Australia and provide a snapshot of how children have developed by the time they start school. The data are collected every 3 years and are used to influence early childhood initiatives at the community, state, and national levels. Increasing the evidence base for early childhood policy and helping governments and communities understand what is working well and what needs to be improved or developed to better support children and families is facilitated by the AEDI data (Royal Children's Hospital, 2012). Piloted between 2004 and 2008, national implementation took place in 2009, with the second round of data collection taking place in 2012.

The AEDI checklist, which is completed by teachers in the first 6 months of a child's first year of full-time school, measures the following five key areas of early childhood development (Royal Children's Hospital, 2012):

• Physical health and well-being
• Social competence
• Emotional maturity
• Language and cognitive skills (school-based)
• Communication skills and general knowledge.

Within Australia, there is a significant proportion of children, especially those from disadvantaged communities, who arrive at school developmentally vulnerable (Royal Children's Hospital, 2012). Within the Ready Together – Transition to School Program there are communities of children who are developmentally vulnerable on two or more AEDI domains (ibid.). Programs such as the Ready Together – Transition to School Program aim to build the capacity of children and their families from disadvantaged backgrounds, thereby reducing the number of children who arrive at school developmentally vulnerable. AEDI data are used to help inform the direction of the program.

Australian National Curriculum

The national curriculum is designed to "equip all young Australians with the essential skills, knowledge and capabilities to thrive and compete in a globalised world and information rich workplaces of the current century" (Australian Curriculum and Reporting Authority [ACARA], 2011). The initial phase of Australia's first National Curriculum – Foundation to Year 12 – was implemented at the beginning of 2012. Within Australia, there is no nationally consistent term for the year of schooling prior to Year 1. The term "Foundation" is used for the purpose of the Australian National Curriculum and the following terms are use in each state and territory: Kindergarten (NSW/ACT), Prep (QLD/VIC/TAS), Pre-primary (WA), Reception (SA), and Transition (NT). In Queensland, children who have turned 5 years of age by 30 June are eligible to attend Prep the following year.

Facchinetti (2011) suggests that the Australian National Curriculum could bring some commonality to the unnecessarily fragmented Australian education system, but she also notes that concerns have been raised around the increased volume of curriculum content that is expected to be covered by teachers.

Anecdotal comments made by Prep teachers based in the Ready Together – Transition to School Program region suggest that the rollout of the national curriculum will have implications related to children's transition to school. Given that many children in the region arrive at school developmentally vulnerable (Royal Children's Hospital, 2011a), and that a significant number of children and families are not prepared for school, there are concerns about the volume of the content that is expected to be taught. It has been suggested that there will be reduced time to focus on supporting children's transition to school in light of the curriculum expectations. Prep teachers are also concerned about there being less time for play-based learning given the pressure to have a greater focus on structured learning. If this is, indeed, the case then a significant number of disadvantaged children may be further marginalized due to the discontinuities they experience around learning, relationship building, and support systems. As noted by the Centre for Community Child Health (2008a, 2008b), if children do not manage the demands of the new environment then their engagement, attendance, and ultimately, their academic performance can be compromised. To support a successful transition to school there is a strong rationale for a gradual introduction to structured teacher-directed learning, but the volume of content of the national curriculum may not allow this.

The Queensland Context

Given that the Ready Together – Transition to School Program operates in the Inala to Ipswich corridor of South East Queensland, a brief overview of Queensland's commitment to the early years and the national reforms will provide further context to the program.

Since a number of significant educational reforms were initiated, there has been a change of government in Queensland and the impact that this change will have on education is yet to be determined. However, as things stand at present, education is a priority in Queensland, and during the past decade there have been a series of significant educational reforms. There is a major commitment to educating individuals about the importance of enrolling children in quality early childhood programs. In line with the Australian government's agenda, the Queensland government's *Toward Q2: Tomorrow's Queensland* focuses on the provision of access to quality early childhood education (ECE) for all children so they are ready for school (Queensland, Department of Premier and Cabinet, 2008). *A Flying Start* (Queensland, Department of Education and Training, 2010) outlines the following major reforms that will impact the future of education in Queensland:

- Getting ready for school, Objective 1: Improving children's development, well-being, and school readiness
- Getting ready for secondary school, Objective 2: Improving transitions from primary to secondary school and supporting adolescent development
- Boosting high performance for all schools, Objective 3: Improving school discipline and the quality of teaching and setting high performance standards for all schools.

In relation to Objective 1, *A Flying Start* (Queensland, Department of Education and Training, 2010) acknowledges the positive influence that parents and families have on children's school results. Although schools and teachers make a crucial difference, the more children learn at home prior to starting school, the better equipped they are to make the successful transition to school.

Queensland children lag behind their counterparts in other states in a number of areas, including language and cognitive skills (*A Flying Start*, Queensland, Department of Education and Training, 2011a). To address this issue, the state government has launched an awareness campaign to promote the importance of reading to children from an early age. *A Flying Start* supports parents and carers to assist children to acquire the necessary emergent literacy skills they need to help prepare them for school. The Ready Together – Transition to School Program, with its early years' literacy and transition to school focus, is well placed to support Objective 1 of *A Flying Start*.

A priority for the Australian government's Office for ECEC is to ensure that by 2014 all Queensland children can access a high-quality kindergarten program in the year before they start Prep. The Office is consulting with and working in partnership with stakeholders to develop and implement Queensland's plan to achieve universal access to kindergarten with up to 240 new kindergarten services being provided across the state (Queensland, Office for Early Childhood Education and Care, 2012).

Many of the new kindergarten services are located on or near school sites. Co-locating early years' services on school grounds is a way to strengthen the link between schools, early years' services, and communities and to support partnerships between home, school, and the community. With the establishment of these new kindergartens there is potential for strengthening Queensland's transition to school programs.

A significant number of new kindergartens are operated by the Crèche and Kindergarten Association (C&K), established in 1907. C&K is the strongest and most established community-based not-for-profit provider of ECEC services in Australia (C&K, 2012). C&K has a key presence across Queensland, and it is well placed to be an advocate and key player in relation to the transition to school movement.

In light of C&K's position within the early childhood sector, a transition to school project plan that uses the Ready Together – Transition to School Program as its foundation, has been submitted to the C&K Executive Management Committee. This project plan outlines how a C&K-led statewide transition to school program could operate. At the time of writing, the outcome of the project plan was not known.

The importance of facilitating a smooth transition to school is conveyed in both the *Queensland Kindergarten Learning Guideline* (QKLG) and *C&K Building Waterfalls* (C&K, 2011), with both documents highlighting the importance of this being a collaborative process.

The QKLG is based on the *Early Years Learning Framework* for Australia (Queensland Studies Authority, 2010). Although the EYLF focuses on children from birth to 5 years, the QKLG has been designed to enrich children's learning experiences specifically in the kindergarten year, which is the year before children enter the preparatory year of schooling in Queensland. The QKLG has been designed to support kindergarten teachers' professional practice. It also supports the national commitment to improving outcomes for Indigenous children.

Within the QKLG, the importance of transition to school is acknowledged, with recommendations for discussions between kindergarten staff and families to support children's transition to school being highlighted. The guideline includes reference to the importance of a collaborative summary of a child's learning. This collaborative summary is referred to as a transition statement, with information contributed by children, parents, carers, and educators. The transition statement summarizes a child's learning, "recognizing that a child's learning is fluid, particularly as they transition to a new setting" (Queensland Studies Authority, 2010, p. 37). Within the QKLG, there is a transition statement template, and the completed statement can be shared with the school by parents during discussions on entry into the Prep year.

First published in 2006, and offered by all C&K services, *C&K Building Waterfalls* is "Australia's first collaborative birth to school age curriculum created by and for educators, parents and children" (C&K, 2011b, p. 4). The second edition of *C&K Building Waterfalls* complements the EYLF and the QKLG, and it supports the national commitment to improving outcomes for Aboriginal and Torres Strait Islander children. It "communicates the right for all children to grow and learn in the spirit of peace, dignity, tolerance and equality" (C&K, 2011b, p. 10). The notion of teachers living, learning, and teaching with and alongside children, families, and communities reflects the value *C&K Building Waterfalls* places on collaboration and nurturing meaningful relationships.

C&K Building Waterfalls acknowledges the importance of children, families, teachers, and other key stakeholders planning, contributing, and collaborating as partners to support the transition to school. This collaboration is implicit in the *C&K Building Waterfalls* statement on the transition to school statement document, which is designed to reflect the views of the children, their family members, and the professionals working with them.

Conditions for a Successful Transition to School

The Centre for Equity and Innovation in Early Childhood (2008) discusses the differing perspectives that children, families, and educators have in relation to transition to school. These different views have implications in relation to judging the success of transition programs. Hence, it is important to ensure that programs are coordinated and planned collaboratively, focusing on the perspectives and needs of children, families, early childhood educators, schools, and community partners. Particular attention needs to be paid to ensuring that programs cater for the needs of children and families from Indigenous, culturally diverse, and special needs backgrounds. Ideally, individualized transition to school programs should be developed for these groups (Centre for Equity & Innovation in Early Childhood, 2008).

When considering transition to school, it is important to acknowledge that children are not merely passive recipients but rather active participants in becoming ready for learning and development in their school years. Dockett and Perry (2004) and Margetts (2009) have recorded children's perspectives on starting school and what is important to them.

One way to acknowledge and honour children as active participants in their transition journey is to support them to meaningfully take part in adding information to their transition statements. The transition statements provide children with an opportunity to share information about themselves and their feelings about starting school, including what they need to feel safe. This allows children's voices to be heard and their perspectives considered. Having access to the *Starting School* children's activity book, which has been developed as part of the Ready Together – Transition to School Program, is another way in which children can be involved in their transition journey.

Due to the considerable variety in children's development and experiences, each child's transition to school is unique. Nevertheless, there is a range of key factors impacting on children's adjustment to school and a number of key elements that are considered to be important for ensuring a successful transition to school for all children (CE&IEC, 2008; Docket & Perry, 2001; Hutton, 2011; Illawarra Children's Services, 2011; Margetts, 2012). Reference is made to best practice, or promising practice models (CE&IEC, 2008). Strategies and elements that help support the transition to school should include the following:

- Involve a range of stakeholders with families, schools, and community sharing in the leadership.
- Be inclusive of all families and their need.
- Include a focus on language and literacy, early numeracy skills, social and emotional development.
- Be strengths-based, supportive, and empower families to be actively involved in their children's learning activities.
- Involve Indigenous educators, other school staff, and Elders in the design and evaluation of transition to school programs for Indigenous children.
- Establish positive relationships between the children, parents, and educators based on mutual respect and trust.
- Involve communication and collaboration between early childhood services and schools.
- Acknowledge the impact of quality early years' education.

- Ensure continuity between preschool and school experiences with similar activities, materials, and philosophy through developmentally appropriate curricula.
- Enhance a child's independence and strengths, with each child viewed as a capable learner.
- Be long term, beginning before the school year commences.
- Provide time and resources for children and families to engage in the school environment.
- Be well planned, flexible, responsive, and effectively evaluated.
- Rely on reciprocal communication among participants.
- Take into account contextual aspects of community, individual families, and children within that community.
- Be seen as core educational business.
- Be sustainable with dedicated leaders, funds, and resources.
- Be acknowledged and valued by governments, policy makers, schools, early childhood services, communities, families, and children.
- Increase the capacity of staff in prior-to-school settings and schools to faciliate the transition by providing relevant information, training, and support.

The Ready Together – Transition to School Program has embraced the key strategies and elements outlined above. Within its coordinating role, the Program works collaboratively with all key stakeholders to increase capacity and promote the development of best practice transition to school programs that support children and families.

The Ready Together – Transition to School Program

The Ready Together – Transition to School Program is a partnership program between C&K and Mission Australia's Inala to Ipswich Communities for Children (CfC). CfC is funded by the Australian government's Department of Housing, Community Services and Indigenous Affairs under the Family Support Program, and Mission Australia is the facilitating partner for the Inala to Ipswich CfC site (Mission Australia, 2013). It is one of 52 CfC facilitating partner sites throughout Australia. This early intervention and prevention initiative supports families with children from birth to 12 years. The development of partnerships with key stakeholders and local community-based organizations is a key feature of the initiative. In the case of the Ready Together – Transition to School

Program, C&K is the community partner engaged by Mission Australia CfC to deliver the program.

The Inala to Ipswich corridor comprises extensive cultural diversity, a relatively high proportion of families experiencing economic and social adversity, and generally low levels of parental education achievement. The Mission Australia CfC site is located on the southwestern fringe of two major local government areas in Queensland (Brisbane City Council and Ipswich City Council) and two state government regional districts (Brisbane South and West Moreton). The main Queensland corrective centres for adult males, women, and youth are based within the region. Demographic socioeconomic disadvantage indicators identify this region as one of the most disadvantaged in Queensland; nevertheless, communities within the Inala to Ipswich corridor have a unique cultural heritage, and even though there are many challenges, there is a strong sense of pride, loyalty, and community spirit (Brisbane South West Neighbouring Communities, 2010). The CfC initiative aims to build on strengths identified from its consultations and engagement with the community, to provide integrated universal and targeted responses for children from birth to 12 years of age and their families.

Central to the Ready Together – Transition to School Program is the commitment to the importance of early years' literacy and the transition to school. The program includes key elements integral to facilitating the transition to school process for children and their families and is underpinned by the following two key aspects:

1 The creation of genuine and respectful relationships between home, school, early years' services, and the community, which are viewed as being the key to helping to prepare children for school
2 The importance of meeting the needs of Indigenous children, children from culturally and linguistically diverse (CALD) backgrounds, children with a disability, and children from disadvantaged backgrounds.

The Ready Together – Transition to School Program complements both the national and state early years' agenda and reforms, including the Queensland government's *A Flying Start*, which has the objective of preparing children for school by improving children's development, well-being, and school readiness. There is a particular focus on reading and early years language and literacy development. The development of the Ready Together – Transition to School Program has been informed by the following:

- The growing body of research that acknowledges the importance of supporting the transition to school for children and their families (Dockett & Perry, 2012; Margetts, 2009)
- Best practice transition to school program models (Margetts, 2012; Peters, 2011; Kirk-Downey & Perry, 2006)
- Documented, strong links between literacy, school performance, self-esteem, and life chances (Let's Read Literature Review, 2004)
- Feedback from families and other key stakeholders within the region (Mission Australia Communities for Children Inala to Goodna, 2008).

The development of the program has been an evolutionary process with additional components being added in response to the identified needs of families, children, schools, and other related services. The model operates using a strengths-based, soft-entry approach and focuses largely on increasing the capacity of children, their families, and professionals working with children and families.

Given the social and economic adversity faced by many families in the region and the culturally diverse demographic of the area, the Ready Together – Transition to School Program prioritizes supporting children and families from Indigenous and other CALD backgrounds. The aim is to empower parents to support their children's transition to school by increasing their knowledge and skills, particularly in relation to early years' language and literacy. The program also offers training and guidance to service providers to assist them to support children and families.

There are two key components of the Ready Together – Transition to School Program:

1 Ready Together, which focuses on children's early learning and literacy through engagement and education of parents and professionals by:
   - Coordinating and facilitating the delivery of tailored early years' language and literacy information sessions and workshops for a range of services catering for clients from a diverse range of backgrounds

- Coordinating professional development sessions for early childhood professionals focusing on early years language and literacy development
- Working in partnership with parents, carers, schools, ECEC professionals, and community services to deliver the Ready Together resources.

2 Transition to School, which engages the school community, early childhood services, professionals, and community services by:
- Coordinating quarterly meetings focusing on all aspects of the transition to school and using the meetings as a platform to foster and strengthen partnerships, share information, increase collaboration, and ensure the coordination of programs and activities related to the transition to school
- Supporting the development of transition to school programs across schools, early childhood services, and community services
- Coordinating professional development and community forums focusing on issues related to transition to school
- Working in partnership with schools, early childhood services, and community services to deliver the Starting School resources.

The Ready Together – Transition to School Program was developed following the conclusion of phase one (mid-2009) of the CfC initiative. At this time, the C&K was the project partner for the following two programs:

1 The Under 5s Regional Reading Campaign – Let's Read Inala to Goodna, which focused on:
- Building a regionwide awareness and commitment to early literacy and the importance of reading to children from birth to 5 years
- Recognizing and valuing traditional ways of promoting literacy within Indigenous Australian and CALD communities
- Delivering the Smith Family's *Let's Read* reading packs in partnership with schools, early childhood services, libraries, community services, and family networks.

2 The Early Childhood Partnership, which focused on:
- Linking early childhood services

- Supporting the development and strengthening of relationships between early childhood services and schools
- The development of strategies to support families and children transitioning from the early childhood and community environment to the school community.

As part of the sustainability and exit strategy of phase one, each of the above programs developed resources. The development of the Ready Together and Starting School resources was informed by feedback from a range of key stakeholders within the region, including parents, carers, and professionals. The resources were officially launched at the conclusion of phase one of the Under 5s Regional Reading Campaign and the Early Childhood Partnership in mid-2009.

The Ready Together resources (Binstadt, 2009a, 2009b) contain practical ideas and activity suggestions to assist parents, carers, and professionals facilitate the development of young children's language and literacy skills. The publications acknowledge and honour literacy across cultures, highlighting the importance of reading, storytelling, reciting rhymes, and singing to children from birth. The following books are available:

- *Ready Together* for parents and carers (English and Vietnamese)
- *Ready Together* for early childhood professionals.

These resources are delivered via Ready Together and Aussie Story Pouch information sessions and workshops, which support participants to increase their knowledge and skills in relation to early years' language and literacy. Details of the delivery method are outlined in the next section.

The Starting School resources include:

- A family and community guide, available in booklet form in English and as a talking book in four languages (English, Sudanese Arabic, Vietnamese, and Samoan). The guide provides tips and suggestions on different ways to prepare children for school and is delivered to parents and carers by either a representative of an early childhood service, a key school staff member, or a relevant service provider.
- A children's activity book that helps familiarize children with Prep and the school environment. The book is delivered to children by

either their kindergarten teacher in the year prior to the child starting school or their Prep teacher in the first week or two of school.

When the funding for phase two (2009–14) of the CfC initiative was announced by the Australian government (Australia, Department of Families, Housing, Community Services and Indigenous Affairs, 2011), Mission Australia CfC invited C&K to continue as project partner. The CfC region was extended from Goodna to Ipswich with the initiative becoming known as Mission Australia Communities for Children Inala to Ipswich.

The second round of funding has enabled the Ready Together and Starting School resources to be strategically delivered as part of the Ready Together – Transition to School Program. As per the Smith Family's *Let's Read* model, the Ready Together – Transition to School Program uses a delivery, as opposed to a distribution model (Let's Read, 2004), for both the Ready Together and Starting School resources. Delivery creates more opportunities for parents and service providers to be empowered and to develop the skills and knowledge required to support children.

Leadership and facilitation of the Ready Together – Transition to School Program sits with C&K and Mission Australia's CfC Inala to Ipswich; however, a major strength of the program is the development of collaborative partnerships with key stakeholders. These collaborative partnerships are the key to providing services that result in best outcomes for children and their families. Partnerships are also essential in promoting sustainability.

In addition to partnerships formed with a range of schools and services in the region, the Ready Together – Transition to School Program coordinator works closely with the Mission Australia CfC Schools Connect worker. The Schools Connect worker links schools with other services, offers education and training activities, supports the development of family friendly school spaces, and provides links with the CfC Family Connect worker for family support and assistance.

The Ready Together – Transition to School Program in Action

READY TOGETHER

Reading to children is the key to developing a child's future literacy skills and parent and child participation in literacy-related activities supports children's adjustment to school. Although reading is vitally important (Let's Read, 2004), songs, rhymes, and storytelling also help support early literacy learning through the development of oral language. Both the Ready Together and the Aussie Story Pouch workshops focus on early years' language and literacy with oral language development being a priority. The foundation for the delivery of theses workshops is based on Neil Griffiths' Story Sack concept (Corner to Learn, 2012), which provides both children and families with literacy-rich experiences and activities. Story Sacks are both a teaching and learning resource and are designed to help adults share books with children in a fun and interactive way. Typically, a Story Sack includes a large cloth bag containing a children's book, along with supporting materials to help make sharing the book more interesting and engaging. The workshops focus on supporting young children's language and literacy development in fun and creative ways.

The Ready Together – Transition to School Program coordinator facilitates Ready Together workshops and information sessions that are tailored to meet the needs of a wide range of services in the region. A Ready Together workshop can be a stand-alone session or it can be delivered as part of a school's transition to school program.

Ready Together workshops use the Story Sack concept to explore the information contained within the Ready Together books. A Ready Together workshop may be a "one off" session, a series of sessions over several weeks, or a number of sessions throughout the year. These workshops are conducted at various locations within the program region. Ready Together workshops include a wide range of activities, and the structure of each session differs depending on the services' client base and requirements.

Below are some examples of the Ready Together sessions in action:

• Mission Australia Pathways to Prevention Vietnamese Playgroup: This long-standing partnership was established during the first phase of the CfC initiative (2006–09). Since 2010, a number of Ready Together workshops have been facilitated each year. Parents and carers participate in a wide range of activities related to a book and create their own Story Sack. Where possible, dual language books, in English and Vietnamese, are provided. The playgroup coordinator acts as interpreter for all of these sessions.
• Mission Australia CfC Little Jarjums Indigenous Playgroup: Annual workshops have been held for Jarjums playgroup since 2010. These

workshops vary in content and are designed to cater for both the Indigenous and non-Indigenous families who attend this playgroup.

- The Home Interaction Program for Parents of Youngsters (HIPPY): Consistent with key policy issues across Australia, the HIPPY Program aims to support the transition to school process by creating a learning environment within the home that encourages the development of literacy skills and increases the chances of positive early school experience among children and parents. The program has a particular focus on Indigenous and culturally diverse families (Brotherhood of St. Lawrence, 2008). Three HIPPY Program sites operate within the Inala to Ipswich region, and the Ready Together – Transition to School Program has developed a partnership with each of these sites. The program has facilitated Ready Together workshops for the HIPPY Inala parents, tutors, and staff. The Inala HIPPY service has also delivered the Starting School family and community guide as has one of the Ipswich sites.

- Studying, Training, and Effective Parenting Program (STEPP): STEPP is a partnership between the Bremer Institute of TAFE (Technical And Further Education) and Mission Australia Inala to Ipswich CfC. It is an initiative designed to give young pregnant and parenting mothers a pathway back to education while remaining near their children (Queensland, Department of Education and Training, 2011b). Annual Ready Together workshops are offered to students accessing STEPP. To establish rapport and trust with the students, the Ready Together – Transition to School Program coordinator meets the students prior to the commencement of each Ready Together workshop. During these informal visits, students are provided with information about the workshops and are invited to select the book they would like to focus on. This approach helps to empower students by involving them in the process of guiding their own learning, with a view to further increasing the capacity of the students in relation to future employment and their roles as mothers.

- Libraries within the region: The Ready Together – Transition to School Program has been working with libraries since the first phase of the CfC initiative. Since 2010, a strong partnership has been developed with the Ipswich City Council Libraries. The libraries have offered their spaces for a variety of programs. These programs include Aussie Story Pouches and Celebrate. The Celebrate events assist the libraries to better meet the needs of the CALD groups within the program region, which is an area key library staff identified as requiring a greater focus. The Ready Together – Transition to School Program, which acknowledges and honours literacy across cultures, is well placed to support these culturally inclusive programs, which have a language and literacy focus. Celebrate events are currently held four times per year. Each event focuses on a different culture. The events include book packs for families, music, song, dance, storytelling, art, craft, literacy activities, and the sharing of food. These events are very popular and well received, particularly by members from the cultural groups that are celebrated.

Another method of delivering the Ready Together resources is via Aussie Story Pouch workshops. These workshops have been offered since November 2009 and are held four times per year. Rayner and Hingst, from the Butterfly Wings Parent Child Program team, are contracted to facilitate the Aussie Story Pouch workshops, which are open to the wider community – parents, carers, ECEC professionals, teachers, other school staff, and service providers working with children and families.

Story Pouch workshops are similar to the Ready Together Story Sack workshops; however, they are offered as a "one-off" 2-hour session. The workshop includes a theoretical component related to brain development and the importance of play, followed by a practical component where participants engage in a range of activities related to the children's storybook selected for the workshop.

They are always well attended, and feedback is overwhelmingly positive, with all participants commenting on how valuable and inspiring they find these sessions. Attempts have been made to remove all barriers to participation in these workshops:

- The workshops are free of charge.
- All resources are provided, and participants receive a copy of Ready Together, a calico bag, a quality children's book, a prop to accompany the book, workshop notes, and all materials required to complete the activities.
- Child care is provided so parents and carers are able to bring children.
- Morning tea and lunch are provided.

A number of teachers, principals, and other service providers who have attended these workshops now offer sessions for parents accessing their school or service. In addition, many participants, including parents, are making their own Story Pouches to use as a tool for engaging children in rich literacy experiences.

Service providers from the program region who have attended a workshop and are interested in independently delivering the Ready Together resources to families accessing their service are able to do so on submission and approval of a delivery plan and agreeing to the conditions outlined in the Ready Together – Transition to School Program memorandum of understanding.

TRANSITION TO SCHOOL

Schools are a natural community centre and are ideally placed to be developed as a community hub (CE&IEC, 2008). Schools also offer an excellent opportunity to access the hard-to-reach community, and they are an ideal place for playgroups and programs with a focus on the transition to school. Locating services, activities, and programs within schools often attracts the younger siblings of children already attending the school.

By working in partnership with a range of key stakeholders within the local community, there is the potential for schools to offer a range of on-site programs and community services to help familiarize children and families with the school environment and to support the transition to school. Within the Ready Together – Transition to School Program region, schools offer some or all of the following programs and activities:

- Baby clinic
- Playgroup
- Breakfast club
- Homework club
- Parent rooms
- Transition to school programs
- Information and training workshops
- Celebration and event days (e.g., open days, under 8s week celebrations).

The Starting School resources are an integral part of the Ready Together – Transition to School Program. Each stakeholder in the region who wishes to deliver the Starting School resources to children and families is requested to provide an audit of any existing activities or programs related to the transition to school and a delivery plan outlining their proposed program and associated activities for transition to school. The Starting School resources are forwarded to schools and services on submission and approval of the delivery plan and agreeing to the conditions outlined in the Ready Together – Transition to School Program memorandum of understanding.

It is acknowledged that there is no "one size fits all" model for transition to school programs; nevertheless, the Ready Together – Transition to School Program within the Inala to Ipswich area is supporting schools to develop transition to school programs that feature best practice. The following supports are available:

- Quarterly regional meetings regarding the transition to school
- Information and research related to best practice program models regarding the transition to school
- Assistance with developing a program for the transition to school
- Provision of professional development opportunities, including Koala Joeys (see below) training
- Resources to support transition to school programs, including the Ready Together and Starting School resources
- Access to information and resources from outside the region that are related to the transition to school.

Schools within the Inala to Ipswich region that are currently supported by the Ready Together – Transition to School Program include some or all of the flowing components, depending on their capacity:

- The *Starting School* family and community guide is delivered to parents/carers by key school staff at open days or at the Prep enrolment interview in the year prior to their child starting school.
- The Koala Joeys Preparing for Prep Program (Koala Joeys), which is an evidenced-based, early intervention and early literacy program developed by Rayner and Hingst (2006), is provided to parents. This parenting program is universally available to all parents and carers of children who will be registering for Prep the following year, with parents, carers, and children attending the program together. Koala Joeys has a strong oral language focus, which includes singing traditional and contemporary rhymes and songs, storytelling, and playing simple games to help both children and parents and carers as they make the transition to school. In September 2011, the Ready

Together – Transition to School Program contracted the Butterfly Wings team to facilitate a Koala Joeys training session. Staff representing 12 schools/services, both within and outside the program region, attended the training. Some of the schools implemented the program in 2011, and others have commenced in 2012.

- School-based playgroups and coffee and chat sessions for parents are offered.
- The Starting School student activity book is delivered to Prep students by their teachers in the first week or two of school.
- A Story Sack workshop or literacy event is held for children in Prep and their families. The Ready Together – Transition to School Program provides the necessary Story Sack resources. The sessions are delivered by either the program coordinator or key school staff members who have attended a Ready Together Story Sack or Aussie Story Pouch workshop. The school-based workshop begins with a session for parents focusing on language and literacy development. Parents then join their children for the Story Sack component of the session, participating in a range of activities together. Both parents and children are immersed in language and literacy, and parents have a first-hand opportunity to see how their children learn.

Feedback provided by parents who have attended these sessions is overwhelmingly positive, with parents indicating that they have a better understanding of how their children learn. Parents also noted that they enjoyed learning alongside their children.

Both the Ready Together and Starting School resources are provided free of charge to all services in the program region as part of their partnership and program agreement. There has been considerable interest in the Ready Together – Transition to School Program from services outside the region. Due to the interest from these services, and as part of the sustainability strategy, the Ready Together and Starting School resources are available for purchase by services from outside the Inala to Ipswich region. This enables groups around Australia to utilize these valuable resources to support the development of young children's language and literacy skills and the transition to school.

Although the Inala to Ipswich region is the focus of the Ready Together – Transition to School Program, the program has statewide relevance. Given that the Crèche and Kindergarten Association is the program partner, workshops have also been offered to staff from C&K services through the C&K College of Early Childhood and C&K Family

Day Care schemes. The Ready Together – Transition to School Program coordinator has also presented at the 2011 and 2012 C&K Conferences and the 2010 and 2012 C&K Parent and Community Forums.

EVALUATION

Evaluation of the Ready Together – Transition to School Program is an integral part of the program and is used to inform its future direction. Evaluation is predominately based on questionnaires and anecdotal feedback. Feedback is obtained from the following:

- Participants attending all workshops coordinated and/or facilitated by the Ready Together – Transition to School Program
- Children, families, schools, and services in relation to their experience of the Starting School resources
- Koala Joeys Preparing for Prep Programs.

Based on the feedback provided by schools about their transition to school programs, the Ready Together – Transition to School Program documents the range of program models used in the region, with a view to using this information to advocate for the adoption of a state-wide transition to school program strategy. Ideally, this strategy would support schools across Queensland to develop and operate effective transition to school programs. Should funding for the program continue beyond 2014, it is hoped that there will be the capacity to carry out a longitudinal study of the impact of the program across the region.

Barriers to Successful Transition Planning:
The Inala to Ipswich Experience

The main barrier to successful transition planning within the Inala to Ipswich region is that some school leaders have not prioritized transition to school and associated transition to school programs within their respective schools. Within Inala and the neighbouring suburb of Forest Lake, there are a total of seven state schools. Four of the seven schools are actively engaged in the Ready Together – Transition to School Program. In one of the remaining three schools, the Prep teachers have been part of the transition to school meetings, but the school they represent has not yet requested the Starting School resources. The other two schools are yet to engage, despite numerous invitations to be part of the program. Given the large number of schools in the Ipswich area, and the fact that Ipswich has formally been part of the program for a shorter period of time, partnerships with the many schools in this area are still being established. Interest is growing and additional schools have expressed that they would like to be involved in 2013.

Other barriers include the lack of knowledge about the importance of transition to school and the limited capacity of some early childhood services to be involved in the program. Key staff members from long day-care services are often not aware of how they can support children's transition to school. In addition, they find it difficult to get release time to attend meetings.

Apart from the lack of engagement by some schools and early childhood services, within the Inala area, many of the potential barriers associated with implementing transition to school programs have been minimized as a result of the culture of partnerships, collaboration, and communication initiated by the project partners during phase one of the initiative.

In addition, within the Inala area, family rooms were already established, along with school-based playgroups and playgroups catering for the range of CALD groups within the area. Thus, finding a suitable space to operate programs and activities related to the transition to school is not a barrier.

Since the CfC region has expanded, the greater Ipswich area has been part of the culture of communication and collaboration associated with the CfC initiative and its project partners. Momentum is building, and formalized partnerships are now being established in the Ipswich area. Ready Together workshops are taking place, several schools are delivering the Starting School resources, and through the Australian Early Development Index (AEDI) response group, dialogue related to supporting the transition to school has begun.

As a result of funding, and the coordinated approach to service delivery, the Ready Together – Transition to School Program has raised the profile of the development of young children's language and literacy skills and the importance of facilitating a smooth transition to school. This has occurred both within and outside the region.

Conclusion: Where to from Here?

Prior to the establishment of the Ready Together – Transition to School Program, schools in the region offered an orientation program; however, there weren't any programs dedicated to the transition to school in operation. The Ready Together – Transition to School Program has raised awareness of the importance of quality transition to school programs.

The continued focus of the Ready Together – Transition to School Program will be to elevate the importance of transition to school programs and advocate for transition to school programs to be seen as core educational business, with the necessary funds provided to ensure their sustainability. To assist in the achievement of these goals, the focus for 2013 includes the following:

- Ongoing delivery of Ready Together and Aussie Story Pouch workshops.
- The provision of information and professional development related to the transition to school. In 2010, Associate Professor Kay Margetts was invited to present a transition to school forum at two locations within the Program region. These free forums were open to parents, caregivers, school staff, early childhood educators, and other related service providers, and they were well attended. Based on the positive response to the 2010 forums, forums were held in Inala and Ipswich in mid-2012. C&K also partnered with the Ready Together – Transition to School Program, and additional forums were held in Brisbane North and Townsville, North Queensland. As part of C&K's ongoing commitment to raising awareness of the importance of transition to school programs and activities, forums will also be offered in 2013. Additioinally, in the Inala to Ipswich region, a series of transition to school "toolbox" sessions for families is planned.
- Completion of the second edition of the Starting School resources. As the program has evolved, the delivery process has been modified. The updated resources will reflect this change. The updated edition will be available for delivery at the beginning of term three, 2013.
- Further development of the evaluation of the program.
- An increased focus on facilitating the development of relationships between early years' services and schools, including the development of tools and forums to achieve this.
- Supporting schools to develop or enhance transition to school programs.
- Supporting schools and early years' services to empower families in relation to supporting their children's transition to school.
- Working in conjunction with C&K to develop a statewide transition to school program should the above-mentioned transition to school project plan be approved.

The future for the Ready Together – Transition to School Program in the Inala to Ipswich region is promising. The number of schools involved in the program is gradually increasing. The transition to school meetings in the Inala and Ipswich areas are an effective platform for keeping schools, early childhood services, and community services connected. Strong collaborative partnerships with key stakeholders will continue to be a major focus, and it is these partnerships that are the key to the success of the program, as services within the region work towards achieving ongoing positive outcomes for children and their families.

REFERENCES

About Australia. (2011). *Australia in brief.* Retrieved from http://www .about-australia.com/facts/

Australian Children's Education and Care Quality Authority. (2011). *Guide to National Quality Framework.* Retrieved from http://acecqa.gov.au/ storage/1%20Guide%20to%20the%20NQF.pdf

Australia, Department of Education, Employment and Workplace Relations for the Council of Australian Governments. (2009). *Belonging, being and becoming: The early years learning framework for Australia.* Canberra: Author.

Australia, Department of Families, Housing, Community Services and Indigenous Affairs. (2011). *Communities for children.* Retrieved from http:// www.fahcsia.gov.au/our-responsibilities/families-and-children/programs -services/family-support-program.

Australian Curriculum and Reporting Authority (ACARA). (2011). *Australian Curriculum.* Retrieved from http://www.acara.edu.au/curriculum.html

Binstadt, M. (2009a). *Ready together for early childhood professions: A resource to assist early childhood professions to facilitate the development of young children's language and literacy skills.* Brisbane, Australia: C&K.

Binstadt, M. (2009b). *Ready together for parents: A resource to assist parents and carers to develop young children's language and literacy skills.* Brisbane, Australia: Crèche and Kindergarten Association.

Brisbane South West Neighbouring Communities. (2010). *About Our Community.* Retrieved from http://www.swnc.org.au/aboutOurCommunity.php

Brotherhood of St. Lawrence (2008). *Home Interaction Program for Parents and Youngsters.* Retrieved from www.hippyaustralia.org.au

Cedric, D. (2011). Moofla and Youfla. *Presented at Living in a child's world, C&K Annual Conference 2011.*

Centre for Community Child Health (CCCH). (2008a). Policy Brief – Rethinking the transition to school: Linking schools and early years services. *Translating early childhood research evidence to inform policy and practice*. No 10.

Centre for Community Child Health (CCCH). (2008b). Policy Brief – Rethinking school readiness. *Translating early childhood research evidence to inform policy and practice*. No 10.

Centre for Equity & Innovation in Early Childhood. (2008). *Literature review – Transition: A positive start to school*. Melbourne, Australia: University of Melbourne. Retrieved from http://www.eduweb.vic.gov.au/edulibrary/public/earlychildhood/learning/transitionliteraturereview.pdf.

Corner to Learn. (2012). *About Neil Griffiths*. Retrieved from http://www.cornertolearn.co.uk/neilgriffiths.html

Crèche and Kindergarten Association (C&K). (2011). *C&K Building waterfalls: A guideline for children's learning and for teaching in kindergarten*. Brisbane, Australia: C&K.

Crèche and Kindergarten Association (C&K). (2012). *About C&K*. Retrieved from http://www.candk.asn.au/about-ck

Dockett, S., & Perry, B. (2001). Starting school: Effective transitions. *Early Childhood Research and Practice, 3*(2).

Dockett, S., & Perry, B. (2004). Starting school: Perspectives of Australian children, parents, and educators. *Journal of Early Childhood Research, 2*(2), 171–189.

Docket, S., & Perry, B. (2011). *Positioning research, policy and practice on transition to school*. Australian Research Alliance for Children and Youth webinar.

Docket, S., Dunlop, A.-W., Einarsdottir, J., Garpelin, A., Graue, B., Harrison, L., …, & Turunen, T. (2011). *Transition to school position statement*. Australia: Research Institute for Professional Practice, Learning and Education.

Fabian, H., & Dunlop, A.W. (2006). *Outcomes of good practice in transition process for children entering primary school. Paper commissioned for the EFA Global Monitoring Report 2007, Strong Foundations: Early Childhood Care and Education*. Retrieved from http://unesdoc.unesco.org/images/0014/001474/147463e.pdf

Facchinetti, A. (2011). Australia's new curriculum. *Education Today: The Magazine for Education Professionals*, (11). Retrieved from http://www.minnisjournals.com.au/educationtoday/article/Australia-346

Hutton, B. (2011). *Linking schools and the early years in the South West: Working towards children arriving at school ready to engage*. Living in a child's world, C&K Conference.

Illawarra Children's Services. (2011). *Illawarra transition to school project*. Retrieved from http://www.transitiontoschool.com.au

Janus, M., & Offord, D. (2002). The school readiness to learn project in Canada: A 2002 overview. *International Meeting on Developing Comprehensive Community-Based Early Childhood Systems*. Los Angeles, CA. Retrieved from http://www.offordcentre.com/readiness/pubs/publications.html

Kagan, S.L., & Rigby, E. (2003). *Improving the readiness of children for school: Recommendations for state policy. Policy Matters: Setting and Measuring Benchmarks for State Policy*. Washington, DC: Center for the Study of Social Policy. Retrieved from http://www.cssp.org/publications/public-policy/policy-matters-improving-the-readiness-of-children-for-school.pdf

Kirk-Downey, T., & Perry, B. (2006). Making transition to school a community event: The Wollongong Experience. *International Journal of Transitions in Childhood*. Retrieved from http://extranet.edfac.unimelb.edu.au/LED/tec/journal_vol2.shtml

Let's Read Literature Review. (2004). Prepared by Centre for Community Child Health and The Smith Family. Retrieved from http://www.letsread.com.au/About/Research/Resources/Let-s-Read-Literature-Review-PDF

Margetts, K. (2009). *'They need to know': Children's perspectives on starting school*. Victoria, AU: Department of Education and Early Childhood Development. Retrieved from http://www.eduweb.vic.gov.au/edulibrary/public/publ/research/publ/researcharticle_they_need_to_know.pdf

Margetts, K. (2012). Starting school. Presented at the Ready Together – Transition to School Program Starting School Forums, Ipswich and Inala, and the C&K Parent and Community Forums, Chermside and Townsville.

Mission Australia. (2013). Communites for Children (NSW, QLD, VIC). Retrieved from http://www.missionaustralia.com.au/community-services/families-and-children/99-ma-community-services/community-services-listing/485-communities-for-children

Peters, T. (2011). *Jumpstart Program*. South East Region, QLD: Berrinba East State School.

Queensland, Department of Education and Training. (2010). *A flying start for Queensland children*. Green Paper. Retrieved from http://flyingstart.qld.gov.au/SiteCollectionDocuments/green-paper.pdf

Queensland, Department of Education and Training. (2011a). *A flying start for Queensland children*. White Paper. Retrieved from http://flyingstart.qld.gov.au/SiteCollectionDocuments/white-paper.pdf

Queensland, Department of Education and Training. (2011b). Bremer helps young mums step back into study. Retrieved from http://www.bremer.tafe.qld.gov.au/about_us/news_events/news/bremer_helps_young_mums.html

Queensland, Department of the Premier and Cabinet. (2008). *Toward Q2: Tomorrow's Queensland*. Retrieved from http://rti.cabinet.qld.gov.au/documents/2008/sep/toward q2/attachments/Towards Q2_ Tomorrows Queensland.pdf

Queensland Office for Early Childhood Education and Care. (2012). *About Us*. Retrieved from http://deta.qld.gov.au/earlychildhood/about/index.html

Queensland Studies Authority. (2010). *Queensland kindergarten learning guideline*. Retrieved from http://www.qsa.qld.edu.au/downloads/early_middle/qklg.pdf

Rayner, G., & Hingst, L. (2006). *Koala Joeys Preparing for Prep Program*. Retrieved from http://www.butterflywingsearlyyearsconsultancy.com.au

Royal Children's Hospital (2012). *Australian early development index*. Retrieved from http://ww2.rch.org.au/aedi/schools.cfm?doc_id=13592

Royal Children's Hospital (2013). *Linking schools and early years*. Retrieved from http://www.rch.org.au/lsey/

Victoria, Department of Education and Early Childhood Development (DEECD). (2010a). *Transition: A positive start to school resource kit–Every child, every opportunity*. Victoria, Australia: Department of Education and Early Childhood Development.

Victoria, Department of Education and Early Childhood Development (DEECD). (2010b). *Welcome to primary school: A parent's guide to Victorian government schools*. Victoria, Australia: Department of Education and Early Childhood Development.

PART II

Early Elementary (Grades 1–3) to Late Elementary (Grades 4–8)

5 The Other Primary Transition: How Educators Promote Optimal Transitions during Elementary School

PATRICK AKOS AND KELSEY AUGST FELTON

Transitions are an integral part of human development. For Kindergarten to Grade 12 students, school transitions are probably the most dramatic ecological transitions that occur. Every transition has distinct phases and stages (Anderson, Goodman, & Schlossberg, 2011), and these include periods of disorganization and reorganization. The disorganization stage often creates risk and crises that are reflected in negative outcomes (e.g., grade point declines, lower school engagement). However, navigating transitions is about managing risk rather than avoiding it. Since school transitions are pre-planned (unlike surprise transitions like loss), the ability to prepare for transition can be helpful, and there is also hope and opportunity in reorganization. Part of the preparation and opportunity is to scaffold across transition contexts and promote transition self-efficacy within students. This chapter seeks to introduce the danger and opportunity in a less recognized and researched primary (elementary) school transition.

The start of formal schooling is a major milestone for students and parents alike. Scholars (Pianta, Cox, & Snow, 2007) have provided a range of reforms and interventions to enable a more successful transition. As students progress through elementary school, they experience both challenges and opportunities throughout each grade-level transition. However, the transition from second to third grade presents a dramatic academic shift for all students. In most elementary settings in the United States, rising third grade students encounter new expectations, a more challenging curriculum, and increased responsibility, while concurrently beginning their first experiences with formal standardized assessments. Sara, a third grade student, noticed these differences: "*In third grade we have to pay attention so we can learn a lot of stuff for EOGs*

(End of Grade tests). In second grade we didn't really test." Children who are able to make a smooth transition to third grade are better able to make the most of their learning opportunities (North Carolina Department of Public Instruction [NCDPI], 2007); however, very little research exists about the transition, and few articulation strategies for this shift have been recommended.

Developmentally, children in middle childhood are becoming more outgoing and confident, but they still feel anxiety in the larger community when separated from familiar people and things (Santrock, 2008). They are sensitive to criticism and will eagerly participate in tasks where they will experience success, but they tend to shy away from risks. For many students, brain development matures to where they can begin to learn the formal rules of reading, writing, and mathematics (Armstrong, 2007). Third grade students often cling to one best friend and choose to spend all of their time with a supportive peer. They also are exposed to work in cooperative learning groups and begin to use their language to clarify thinking and refine learning. Through their discussions and understandings, students in this transition are able to begin to relate the world around them to the content of their curriculum (NCDPI, 2007).

Part of this use of language allows third grade students to begin to engage in a deeper mathematical discourse. Prior to third grade, instruction tends to "focus on a limited set of cognitive abilities related to a single aspect of mathematics skill," rather than on the collection of skills (e.g., memory, reasoning, language) that fit within a more extensive cognitive framework in third grade (Fuchs et al., 2006, p. 29). Third grade mathematics can include, but is not limited to, higher demands on attention, efficient counting, memory-based retrieval, processing speed, and phonological processing (Fuchs et al.). Demands on metacognition require students to apply computational strategies (Verschaffel, Luwel, Torbeyns, & Van Dooren, 2009) in abstract ways to real-world concepts.

The focus in third grade shifts from learning to read to reading to learn, learning to write to writing in a formalized format, developing problem-solving strategies to solve multistep problems, and moving from non-standardized assessments to standardized testing (NCDPI, 2007). In fact, a lack of reading proficiency by the end of third grade has been linked to a higher rate of school dropout (Kids Count, 2010). Throughout schools, we are often hearing students exclaiming, *"I can't believe I'll have to take the End of Grade tests this year! It is going to be so hard.*" Third grade students have already heard from others about the realities of third grade and the pressure of the standardized assessments (either experienced by students themselves, or vicariously from parents and school personnel). Our experience tells us that the transition from second to third grade is an area where schools, teachers, and families must take proactive measures. We further illustrate the challenges and aim to present ideas, strategies, and best practices that can be used throughout school communities to support children through this transition.

Barriers and Obstacles to the Transition

The shift that occurs in third grade includes increased academic and social demands for students. Homework expectations increase, and teachers expect students to demonstrate basic social skills such as helping, cooperating, and negotiating (Augst & Akos, 2009). In addition, the primary curriculum moves away from basic reading instruction (Kainz & Vernon-Feagans, 2007), making the transition cognitively difficult because of the increased expectations for independent thought and mastery of more complex concepts (Marcon, 2000). School personnel expect higher levels of independence at the same time that the density of the content increases and the application of ideas to real-world concepts intensifies. While students are dealing with these new academic challenges, they are also becoming acutely aware of others' performance, particularly in standardized assessments.

Concurrently, teacher-reported instructional practices and beliefs in third grade change (File & Gullo, 2002; Fung & Chow, 2002). Although metacognition and independence are desirable, teachers often demonstrate strategies that allow students less responsibility for their own learning. Our experience also tells us that teacher–child relationships shift in third grade, possibly because of the dramatically increased expectations for students. Research has shown repeatedly that teacher–child relationships play a role in children's ability to acquire the skills necessary for success in school (Pianta & Stuhlman, 2004), making this relationship crucial for third grade students.

Risk Factors

Because of the shifts and changes in third grade curriculum and expectations, students who are already struggling in reading (e.g., reluctant readers) and math (e.g., those who struggle with addition and subtraction facts) often fall further behind (Augst & Akos, 2009). Children who have low reading levels are more likely to have further reading delays in third grade because subsequent learning in core subjects depends on independent reading (Kainz & Vernon-Feagans, 2007). The pattern of reading development becomes more difficult to disrupt over time with general classroom instruction, making the gap wider for reading development in third grade (Foster & Miller, 2007). Similarly, those students who struggle to apply simple computational skills tend to lack the ability to make connections or apply mathematical principles in novel contexts (Fuchs et al., 2003). Low achievers in mathematics tend to have lower self-confidence in third grade (Kloosterman, Raymond, & Emanaker, 1996), making them less likely to take mathematical risks and confront challenges.

Primary teachers have been able to predict and identify students who are more likely to have reading difficulties in third grade, allowing teachers to target individual students who could benefit from various interventions (Hecht & Greenfield, 2001). Hecht and Greenfield found that first grade teachers can accurately predict third grade reading attainment through the use of ratings and reading-related tests. These methods of teacher ratings and reading assessments can be used early to identify students in need of special services and early intervention, even before they reach third grade.

Recommendations for a Successful Transition

A variety of interventions, strategies, and supports can be put in place for students to make a smooth transition into third grade. Our experience has shown that when school staff collaborate, target individual students and families in need, build on student strengths, and evaluate practices, students succeed. The following school recommendations are provided under a COPE framework: Collaborate, Outreach, Promote, Evaluate (Augst & Akos, 2009). Our examples are compiled from research studies and experiences from different elementary schools in Wake County, North Carolina.

Collaboration

Collaboration among staff members is an important part of helping students to make the transition into third grade. When teachers, support staff (English as a second language [ESL] teachers, counsellors, academic coaches), intervention teachers, Special Education teachers, administrators, and parents work together, students are better supported and receive more consistent feedback.

At one school, second grade teachers collaborate at the end of the year to compile a "watch list" of students who are not meeting grade level benchmarks (Felton & Akos, 2011). They work to create a list of individualized interventions that have helped these particular students to be more successful in the classroom, as well as noting their strengths and areas of need. This list is then given to an intervention specialist, a support staff member (e.g., Title I teacher, ESL teacher) who works with the grade level professional learning team to help develop individualized interventions for students in need of support. At the start of the new school year, the intervention specialist shares this list with third grade teachers, allowing them to immediately use promising strategies and the strengths of students who are at risk for falling behind. The third grade level team and the intervention specialist work together to develop a plan for students placed on the watch list, monitor the students' progress, and evaluate the plan for effectiveness.

One student was placed on this list who had fallen below benchmarks in reading and writing, mostly because of his tendency to reverse his letters. His second grade teacher had developed an intervention that involved him checking over all of his writing assignments with an alphabet chart. Whenever he noticed a reversal, he highlighted it and corrected it. He then conferred briefly with his teacher, who helped to point out anything he may have left out. During evaluation of this intervention, the student had shown a dramatic decrease in the number of letter reversals in his writing and an improvement in his reading fluency. When he began third grade, his intervention specialist made sure to share the intervention with his new teacher. He was provided an alphabet chart and a highlighter, and he began the process again. He continued to show great improvement in his reading and writing throughout third grade (Felton & Akos, 2011). Interventions that scaffold across second to third grade like this can also target the development of reading comprehension skills and the related increased language and mathematics demands.

Another form of collaboration that has benefited students at local elementary schools are vertical grade level planning meetings (Augst & Akos, 2009) to discuss grade-specific essential learning outcomes. Second and third grade teachers work together separately to determine essential learning outcomes, or key aspects of the curriculum for their respective grade levels. An example of a second grade essential learning outcome could include mastering double-digit addition with regrouping. Both grade levels meet periodically through the year to share their essential learning outcomes and to determine similarities. Third grade teachers share with second grade teachers expectations for mastery, and both grade levels discuss ways to scaffold teacher expectations and learning goals across the transition. Similar curriculum articulation can occur within mathematics as well.

A related example of collaboration can occur with parents and teachers. A local elementary school reached out to families as part of a Parents as Learning Supporters (PALS) Program (Poovey, 2011). When students and families receive more information about the new classroom environment, they have more opportunities to make a gradual adjustment to the next grade level (Baker, 2006). A workshop was held in the spring of second grade and again in the fall of third grade for parents and students. The purpose of these workshops was to educate parents and students about the changes in third grade, curriculum expectations, and the shift into standardized testing. Staff members presented brief topics to parents including the following: curriculum changes and homework (instructional resource teacher), organization and independence (third grade teachers), social changes (school counsellor), reading and math changes (Title I teachers), and parent perspectives (third grade parent panel). The student perspective of the shift into third grade was shared with a video entitled, *A Day in the Life of a Third Grader*. This type of schoolwide collaboration is important for consistent expectations and useful to normalize transition challenges.

Outreach

These collaborative strategies allow teachers and staff members to provide outreach to targeted students and families who are already at risk for difficulties during the transition. Transition risk can be broader than simply poor academic performance. For example, students who demonstrated previous transition difficulty (e.g., into kindergarden) may deserve additional attention. Globally, those students who lack efficacy in adaptation should receive intervention beyond universal approaches. We utilize academic and behavioural struggles in second grade as data indicators for outreach in this section.

One strategy that has been implemented with successful results is a Math Masters cross-age tutoring program (Augst & Akos, 2009). This program pairs second grade students who are below benchmarks in math with fifth grade peer leaders who demonstrate high achievement. The purpose of this program is not only to boost mathematics achievement, but also to improve feelings of mathematical self-efficacy. Elementary educators need to make a pointed effort to low achievers in math to believe their efforts are worthwhile (Muis, 2004), and this program aims to do that through peer encouragement, praise, and modelling. Along with self-efficacy, the program supports the use of discourse and language development in solving complex problems through interaction with others through the problem-solving strategies.

Fifth grade students are nominated by their teachers to serve as tutors and receive three 45-minute weekly training sessions. These training sessions focus on building a relationship, giving compliments about mathematics discourse, and how to implement the structured activities that include weekly progress monitoring and math games. They provide 9 weeks of tutoring to targeted second grade students who are performing below benchmarks in math, also nominated by their teachers. These tutoring sessions take place before school and include whole group meetings, weekly progress monitoring with one-minute addition and subtraction tests, word problems, and math games that focus on one specific objective (e.g., ordering numbers, double-digit addition). This program is coordinated by the school counsellor, who works in collaboration with the second grade teachers, intervention teachers, and resource teachers. Throughout the sessions, fifth grade students support tutee strengths, help them to solve word problems through the use of problem-solving steps, and handle student frustration through encouraging words and gestures. They also write personal letters to tutees at the end of the 9 weeks, noting student strengths and areas of improvement. The purpose of these relationship-building activities is to increase student motivation through a supportive and positive relationship.

This program can provide a boost to second grade students before they even reach third grade, helping them to be further prepared for the transition. Many low achievers, who struggle with basic addition and subtraction, begin to demonstrate a decrease in confidence and a reluctance to take risks. Math Masters aims to help students to build the needed feelings of self-efficacy as they move through this transition.

Evaluations of the program have been promising over the past 3 years. Overall, approximately 70% of students who have participated in the program have shown improvement in at least one math objective, according to second grade quarterly progress reports (Felton &

Akos, 2011). Further, 25% of students who participated met or exceeded benchmarks on their second grade report card, and 33% met or exceeded benchmarks on their first report card in third grade. According to teacher surveys, 100% of students showed some improvement in feelings of math self-confidence.

Although it is important to target students who are struggling academically for various transition supports, students with behavioural concerns should also be supported. Our experience has shown that students who demonstrate high numbers of discipline referrals in second grade often have difficulty with the increased expectations of independence and responsibility in third grade. One strategy for providing support to students during this transition involves pairing targeted third grade students with a staff mentor at the beginning of the school year. This staff mentor can create a deeper relationship with the child, allowing the child to serve as a role model to the student and an adult who values the student, regardless of behavioural choices.

In our program, staff mentors spend 15 minutes per week with the student and participate in activities that include having lunch together, playing games, working on homework together, making crafts, playing basketball, or writing in a dialogue journal. Staff mentors are trained for one hour, learning and discussing ways to build relationships with students, activities to hold with mentees, and procedures for handling various student concerns. Pizza luncheons and mentor/mentee activities are held at various points in the year to further support mentor relationships. The program aims to improve students' behaviour and feelings of attachment to school through this supportive and nurturing mentor/mentee relationship.

Data from one pilot point towards the utility of the program. Of students who participated in this program, 88% reduced discipline referrals over one year, and 100% agreed that the mentoring program helped them to like school better. Further, 100% of staff mentors agreed that this program was beneficial to their mentee. Providing targeted students with an additional available and caring adult helped students to feel more connected to school and supported them through this often-difficult transition.

As academic and behavioural expectations are increasing throughout the transition into third grade, students are also experiencing social and developmental challenges. Students are expected to demonstrate basic social skills and be able to independently solve minor conflicts with peers (NCDPI, 2007). Developmentally, many students begin social comparisons at this age, building their own self-image by comparing themselves with their peers. A pilot study at a school in North Carolina aimed to help targeted students improve social skills and relations with peers throughout this key transition time (Atkins & Thompson, 2011). During the spring of second grade, all students responded to a loneliness survey. Student scores were calculated, and those students who indicated high levels of loneliness were targeted to participate in a small group program with the school counsellor. The school counsellors implemented the S.S. GRIN (Social Skills Group Intervention) program (DeRosier, 2004) with the students for eight weekly group sessions prior to third grade. This group also met again in the fall of third grade for several follow-up sessions. Loneliness data were collected again in the spring of third grade to evaluate the effectiveness of the intervention. Of students who participated in the program, 100% reported less loneliness in the third grade. Further, eight out of nine students had a good transition, as perceived by their teachers. This pilot study indicates the importance of addressing personal/social concerns as well as academic concerns throughout this transition.

Promotion of Student Strengths

Any intervention, strategy, or support should seek to promote student strengths in order to overcome weaknesses. Strategies should be provided to all students during this transition, helping not only those who are at risk, but as a universal educational practice to promote a seamless if not optimal transition.

As second grade students end their year, one school provides classroom lessons to all students to help them prepare for the third grade (Poovey, 2011). As Sara noted, the changes in third grade can be a lot to handle: "*We used to get up a lot, but in third grade we sit down more. We don't do as many centers as we used to.*" Classroom lessons can help students to have knowledge about the behavioural and academic changes in third grade. The school counsellor provides four classroom guidance lessons that focus on specific changes and expectations in third grade. Lessons include helpful homework habits, how to show responsibility and follow directions, demonstrating independence, and time management strategies. Students can be shown how to self-regulate learning where they read directions more thoroughly and identify for themselves areas where help is needed. These classroom lessons build on student strengths by eliciting examples of these capabilities they demonstrate in second grade, while also preparing them for knowledge about the shift in classroom expectations in third grade.

Third grade usually brings students' first experience with standardized tests, often invoking anxiety for many students (Felton & Akos, 2011). Students often complain about having more tests and, possibly because of a lack of experience and pressure from others, tend to have feelings of anxiety regarding them. Most third grade students are unfamiliar with the testing format (e.g., using answer sheets, following explicit directions) and can benefit from instruction in testing strategies and techniques (Boulware-Gooden, Carreker, Thornhill, & Joshi, 2011). Teachers at one school have indicated that third grade students need focused instruction on test-taking vocabulary, test format, and anxiety reduction (Felton & Akos, 2011).

One sample conducted at our school includes a strengths-based classroom guidance unit to help students succeed on third grade standardized tests (Felton & Akos, 2011). The school counsellor collaborates with third grade teachers to provide classroom guidance lessons 3 months prior to the start of testing. Students list accomplishments already achieved in third grade and discuss strengths with one another, helping them to understand that standardized tests are their opportunity to "show off" everything they have learned and accomplished in the third grade.

Lessons also focus on familiarizing students with test-taking vocabulary, such as *contrast, summarize,* and *point of view*. Schools can create testing word walls that allow students to see the words daily, helping them to recognize and understand the vocabulary. Further, lessons can focus on testing formats by providing opportunities for students to complete mock tests with example answer sheets. Students receive practice bubbling their answers, lining up the numbers on their answer sheet with their test book, and handling misalignment. Last, students can receive explicit instruction in anxiety reduction techniques, specifically positive self-talk and deep breathing.

Evaluation results from an informal survey at the start of this unit indicated that 85% of students had feelings of nervousness related to testing. Only 25% of students indicated further nervousness about the upcoming standardized assessments after the classroom lessons (Felton & Akos, 2011). Educating students about the tests helps them to prepare and instil feelings of optimism and confidence when they begin the testing process. Students who are still demonstrating anxiety and feelings of uncertainty could receive further targeted support through small group sessions with the school counsellor.

Program Evaluation

All educational programs need to be evaluated to determine their effectiveness. Program evaluation not only demonstrates the effect on students, but also provides opportunities to target potential areas for improvement in interventions. Evaluations of programs should include process data (number of students affected), perception data (how student perceptions, feelings, or thoughts change as a result of the intervention), and results data (how student outcome data change as a result of the intervention) (American School Counselor Association, 2011). Sources of perception data can include before and after surveys to students and teachers, student interviews, parent–teacher conferences, and informal observations. Results data can be found using standardized testing scores, behavioural records, report card grades, classroom assessments, weekly progress monitoring data, or attendance reports. Although a variety of evaluation strategies exist and have utility, transition interventions must ultimately be researched longitudinally with experimental designs to investigate the trajectory of developmental and academic pathways over time.

Conclusion

The transition into third grade is full of opportunities, new experiences, and increased expectations. Developmental and ecological change is clear. When educators shift expectations, students are required to reorganize and re-establish themselves in school, peer groups, and the school context. Educators can nurture students throughout this dynamic shift and help to improve student success by scaffolding across second to third grade. When school staff members collaborate, reach out to targeted students, and promote positive strengths through research-based interventions and strategies – students, teachers, and parents benefit. Although this transition into third grade can be difficult, it can also be a time of great growth and success. Attention to both preparation and support across the transition allow for hope and opportunity and the promotion of optimal developmental and academic pathways.

As one parent at our school noted, "Third grade has descended on our family, and it is a challenge. Education is a journey and we are really just at the beginning of a long, exciting road filled with responsibilities, challenges, and hopefully, a lot of fun" (Linden Fee, 2008).

REFERENCES

American School Counselor Association. (2011). *The ASCA National Model: A framework for school counseling programs* (3rd ed.). Alexandria, VA: Author.

Anderson, M., Goodman, J., & Schlossberg, N. (2011). *Counseling adults in transition: Linking Schlossberg's theory practice in a diverse world.* New York: Springer.

Armstrong, T. (2007). The curriculum superhighway. *Educational Leadership, 64*(8), 16–20.

Atkins, R., & Thompson, J. (2011). *S.S. GRIN social skills group: Support program conducted at Millbrook Elementary School.* Raleigh, NC: Wake County Schools.

Augst, K.C., & Akos, P.T. (2009). Primary transitions: How elementary school counselors promote optimal transitions. *Journal of School Counseling, 7*(3).

Baker, J. (2006). Contributions of teacher–child relationships to positive school adjustment during elementary school. *Journal of School Psychology, 44*(3), 211–229.

Boulware-Gooden, R., Carreker, S., Thornhill, A., & Joshi, R. (2007). Instruction of metacognitive strategies enhances reading comprehension and vocabulary achievement of third-grade students. *Reading Teacher, 61*(1), 70–77.

Count, K. (2010). *Early warning signs: Why reading by the end of third grade matters.* Retrieved from http://www.kidscount.org

DeRosier, M.E. (2004, Mar.). Building relationships and combating bullying: Effectiveness of a school-based social skills group intervention. *Journal of Clinical Child and Adolescent Psychology, 33*(1), 196–201.

Felton, K., & Akos, P. (2011). The transition into third grade: Helping students C.O.P.E. *Educational Leadership, 68*(7), 28–31.

File, N., & Gullo, D. (2002). A comparison of early childhood and elementary education students' beliefs about primary classroom teaching practices. *Early Childhood Research Quarterly, 17*(1), 126–137.

Foster, W.A., & Miller, M. (2007, July). Development of the literacy achievement gap: A longitudinal study of kindergarten through third grade. *Language, Speech, and Hearing Services in Schools, 38*(3), 173–181.

Fuchs, L., Fuchs, D., Compton, D., Powell, S., Seethaler, P., Capizzi, A., …, & Fletcher, J.M. (2006). The cognitive correlates of third-grade skill in arithmetic, algorithmic computation, and arithmetic word problems. *Journal of Educational Psychology, 98*(1), 29–43.

Fuchs, L.S., Fuchs, D., Prentice, K., Burch, M., Hamlett, C., Owen, R., Hosp, M., & Jancek, D. (2003). Explicitly teaching for transfer: Effects on third-grade students' mathematical problem solving. *Journal of Educational Psychology, 95*(2), 293–305.

Fung, L., & Chow, L. (2002). Congruence of student teachers' pedagogical images and actual classroom practices. *Educational Research, 44*(3), 313–321.

Hecht, S.A., & Greenfield, D.B. (2001). Comparing the predictive validity of 1st grade teacher ratings and reading related tests on 3rd grade levels of reading skills in young children exposed to poverty. *School Psychology Review, 30*(1), 50–69.

Kainz, K., & Vernon-Feagans, L. (2007). The ecology of early reading development for children in poverty. *Elementary School Journal, 107*(5), 407–427. http://dx.doi.org/10.1086/518621

Kloosterman, P., Raymond, A., & Emanaker, C. (1996). Student beliefs about mathematics: A 3-year study. *Elementary School Journal, 97*(1), 39–56.

Linden Fee, L. (2008, Sept.). How to survive the transition into third grade. Retrieved from www.examiner.com/dc-in-washington-dc/how-to-survive-the-transition-to-third-grade

Marcon, R.A. (2000). Impact of preschool model on elementary transitions from early childhood to middle childhood to and into early adolescence. Poster presented at the conference for Human Development, Memphis, TN.

Muis, K. (2004). Personal epistemology and mathematics: A critical review and synthesis of research. *Review of Educational Research, 74*(3), 317–377.

North Carolina Department of Public Instruction (NCDPI). (2007). Transition planning for 21st century schools. Raleigh, NC: Author. Retrieved from www.ncpublicschools.org/docs/curriculum-instruction/home/transitions.pdf

Pianta, R.C., Cox, M., & Snow, K. (2007). *School readiness and the transition to kindergarten in the era of accountability.* Baltimore: P.H. Brookes.

Pianta, R.C., & Stuhlman, M.W. (2004). Teacher–child relationships and children's success in the first years of school. *School Psychology Review, 33*, 444–458.

Poovey, A. (2011). *Parents as Learning Supporters (PALS) program: Transition program created and conducted at Dillard Drive Elementary School.* Raleigh, NC: Wake County Schools.

Santrock, J.W. (2008). *Life-span development.* New York: McGraw Hill.

Verschaffel, L., Luwel, K., Torbeyns, J., & Van Dooren, W. (2009). Conceptualizing, investigating, and enhancing adaptive expertise in elementary mathematics education. *European Journal of Psychology of Education, 24*(3), 335–359.

6 Teachers' Voices on Transitions in Classroom Reading Instruction

SUSAN E. ELLIOTT-JOHNS

This chapter discusses findings from qualitative research conducted with 11 Grade 5 classroom teachers in Ontario, Canada. Through questionnaires, in-depth interviews, and written reflections, the study sought to explore with teachers how their own knowledge and beliefs about reading influenced the development of classroom practices in reading instruction. Findings offered valuable insights into the teachers' thinking as they navigate transitions in current approaches to classroom reading instruction. These are illustrated in the teachers' own voices with excerpts from the data.

An overview of relevant research findings related to transitions in instructional practice in reading is followed by a discussion of teachers' perspectives on the gradual shift towards "balanced" approaches to classroom reading instruction in the later elementary grades. Excerpts portraying one teacher's thinking and experiences of implementing a strategy called *guided reading* as part of a balanced approach to instruction in her Grade 5 classroom are also presented and discussed.

Context

The field of reading research is both complex and extensive, and contemporary reading research is not neutral; rather, it continues to mirror the social and political context in which it occurs (Calfee & Drum, 1986; Lankshear & Knobel, 2006; McKeown & Kucan, 2010; Pahl & Rowsell, 2010). Studies that examine researchers' theories about the reading process from the learners' perspective have been very well documented. However, inquiries into teachers' knowledge and what teachers experience as *they* learn about the teaching of reading are more difficult to locate in the literature and often seem to represent what Shulman (1986) called the "missing paradigm." Anderson and Mitchener (1994) concluded, "The big advances in understanding about student learning have not been matched by equivalent advances in understanding about teaching" (p. 36).

Research studies into what teachers themselves know and believe about reading instruction, specifically in the later elementary grades, and including how they articulate their experiences *as* teachers of reading (as opposed, e.g., to numerous studies of "best methods"), remain underrepresented in the literature.

I have increasingly come to see the stories and details of teachers' lives as a way of knowing and understanding. Through the unique lens of my own educational background and experience, I believe that the voices of teachers must be heard more carefully and consistently in educational research if we are to be successful in mobilizing and sustaining meaningful change in reading teacher education. The conspicuous absence of teachers' voices in the literature has become a catalyst for much of my own thinking about reading teacher education and practice.

Available teacher education research reveals little about "how teachers of reading are created, how they teach, nor how they change" (Anders, Hoffman, & Duffy, 2000, p. 732). However, research does reveal the need for studies that pursue critical questions, issues, and gaps in the current literature. This is especially so if we are to better understand what is needed as transitions and changes in approaches to reading instruction occur. For example, what should be the goals of reading teacher education today? What kinds of knowledge do experienced teachers who attend in-service on reading need? How do we prepare, and sustain, teachers for meeting the multifaceted needs of the student readers they teach?

Inquiries that probe emic ("insider") perspectives and listen carefully to the voices of teachers of reading in regular classrooms significantly enrich understandings of the complexities of instructional decision making and the contexts in which teachers operate on a daily basis. Research of this nature informs reading teacher education and the design of relevant opportunities for ongoing professional development.

Overview of the Research Findings

Teachers in this study (Elliott-Johns, 2004) highlighted personal experiences, past and present, with reading as influential in their development of current instructional practices. Like Grisham (2000), I found that the construction of "personal practical" knowledge appeared to be an ongoing process for teachers, the result of complex interactions between knowledge, beliefs, and related effects on instructional practices.

A number of similar implicit beliefs and epistemological principles surfaced regarding reading, reading instructional practices, and classroom interactions (Harste & Burke, 1977; Richardson, Anders, Tidwell, & Lloyd, 1991). For example, teacher participants' descriptions of their skills-based orientation to reading instruction all referred, in one way or another, to interpretations of the need to equip students with reading skills, strategies, and positive attitudes towards reading. Students could then apply learning across the curriculum in the completion of a wide variety of assigned tasks. Participants clearly believed it was essential to explicitly model reading and share their knowledge of the processes and purposes of reading in motivating students to develop personal reading habits (Allington & Johnston, 2001; Duffy, 1982; Elliott-Johns, 2012; Gambrell, 1996; Duffy, Roehler, & Herrmann, 1988).

Research has shown that teachers' instructional decisions are often governed by the nature of instruction and classroom life (Duffy, 1977, 1982; Duffy & Anderson, 1984; Fullan & Hargreaves, 1994; Poulson, Avramidis, Fox, Medwell, & Wray, 2001) conclude that more attention needs to be given to practical concerns around how teachers can apply their theoretical beliefs within the constraints imposed by the complexities of contemporary classroom life. Currently, in Ontario, across Canada and beyond, we navigate highly politicized educational landscapes where the enactment of "evidence-based" ideas of others often seem to take precedence over teachers' own knowledge and expertise. Gallagher (2009) contends that teachers must not lose sight of authentic instruction in the long shadow of political pressures.

Findings indicated teacher participants believed that instructional decisions were inextricably linked to provincially mandated curriculum expectations and to the availability of time and appropriate resources to meet these expectations. Furthermore, teachers repeatedly voiced concerns that the "standards" movement (i.e., curriculum expectations, assessment and evaluation, and increased calls for teacher accountability) seems to have become much more than a contextual constraint, and almost *the* theory behind instructional decisions, the nature of classroom programs, and school organization. In other words, the whole standards movement (specifically, restructuring of the curriculum, assessment, and policy changes undertaken in Ontario since 1998) has become a powerful driving force behind teachers' work and the organization of life in public schools (Majhanovich, 2002). Teachers often reported feeling exhausted from coping with so many rapid changes in curriculum, assessment, and policy. Curriculum requirements were considered very rigid with little scope for modification or innovation and creativity. As reflected in many of the comments of teachers interviewed, and as Majhanovich points out, issues of power and control continue to be central to the current political climate of accountability in Ontario education:

> The legislation (Bills 160 and 74) that centralized the power for decision-making over education to the provincial Ministry of Education and Training away from school boards and teachers certainly illustrates how control over teachers and what they teach has been tightened. The rapid restructuring of the curriculum with new course outlines – all tailored to a uniform template ... the course profiles, rubrics, exemplars for standards, uniform report cards across the province, standardized testing including the Grade 10 literacy test, success in which is a requirement for graduation; all illustrate the growth of central control and de-skilling of the profession. As noted above, the new curriculum restructuring reflects a "teacher-proof" notion of education. (p. 174)

Findings were also similar to those of Baumann, Hoffman, Moon, and Duffy-Hester (1998), who surveyed elementary teachers K–5 across the United States concerning beliefs and practices related to what has been termed the "Great Debate" about the "best methods" for teaching reading (i.e., between phonics and whole language methodologies). Baumann et al.'s research found elementary school teachers tended to provide children with balanced, eclectic programs involving both reading skills instruction and immersion in rich literacy experiences, concluding that teachers in the United States were more focused on real-life classroom issues than recurring debates about best methods. Teachers' concerns with real-life classroom issues in the United States were remarkably similar to those described by the teacher participants in Canada (probably not surprising, in the light of intense political climates of "accountability" in both countries):

> How to accommodate the incredible range of students' needs and reading levels, how to deal with the frustration of not enough time to teach or

insufficient quality materials to do it well, and how to accommodate large classes of diverse learners seated before them. (p. 648)

The teacher participants provided rich descriptions of their knowledge and beliefs about reading instruction relevant to individual professional realities. Instruction in effective reading skills and strategies was considered fundamental to students' success across the curriculum. Emphases were on reading as thinking, understanding, and application of learning in practice. In fact, the teaching of thinking was synonymous with reading instruction for the majority of the teacher participants. Participants also expressed beliefs and practices consistent with (1) perceptions of reading as a process that must "make sense" and (2) approaches to reading instruction that encourage students to become self-motivated, fluent, and independent readers. Explicit skills instruction was regarded by all those interviewed to be an essential aspect of reading instruction, although their collective emphasis on purposeful and authentic reading in the context of students' lives also reflected Routman's (2000) claim that without a strong foundation of abilities to construct meaning, "basic skills" are useless.

Interview data also revealed important aspects of professional realities and related contextual constraints associated with reading instruction: Teachers considered motivation to read habitually to be an essential aspect of developing young readers, but reported that reading did not appeal to many of their students as an activity. Many students, both boys and girls – but especially boys – did not appear to enjoy reading. Reading was seen to be "in competition" for students' attention with other, more appealing pastimes (e.g., television, video games, and sports). Regular practice and frequent opportunities to read a wide range of material are critical to the development of both fluency and enjoyment in reading. Consequently, much teacher time and effort was spent seeking out appealing materials at relevant ability levels; finding creative ways to present reading in order to engage students and encourage them to read regularly.

Insufficient time was a significant contextual constraint on teachers' ability to include independent reading during class time. Three of the 11 participants said they purposely avoided scheduling "silent reading" time in class because of a lack of time, and they expected students to read regularly at home. Two other teachers maintained a priority on extended periods of reading in class; others included silent, independent reading in class whenever possible. All 11 participants reported time constraints directly related to fulfiling requirements of the mandated provincial curriculum and clearly felt these imposed between their theoretical orientation and instructional practices. Allington (2001) states,

> Everyone has heard the proverb. Practice makes perfect. In learning to read it is true that reading practice – just reading – is a powerful contributor to the development of accurate, fluent, high-comprehension reading. In fact, if I were to select a single aspect of the instructional environment to change, my first choice would be creating a schedule that supported dramatically increased quantities of reading time during the school day. (p. 24)

Although it is clearly evident that the teachers interviewed might well agree with Allington's premise, they were struggling to incorporate a minimum time for reading within the school day, and they were far from considering extensions to that time.

Creative approaches to reading instruction (i.e., as far as contextual constraints related to the provincial curriculum would allow), holistic contexts, and the integration of curriculum areas were consistently reported in current classroom programs. Explicit modelling of effective reading skills and strategies by classroom teachers and others in both the home and school settings (e.g., teacher-librarians, principal, parents, grandparents, siblings) was also directly related to the development of positive attitudes towards reading, and student recognition of reading as a "worthwhile" activity in which to engage and spend time. Teachers consistently described efforts in classroom practice to combine motivating behaviours (e.g., reading aloud to students) with modelling instructional strategies (e.g., interactive read-aloud techniques).

Wide ranges of individual needs, interests, and ability levels in their classrooms presented perpetual challenges for all teachers interviewed; the ongoing development of individualized, specific skills instruction, and small group work within a holistic context (specifically, guided reading strategies), were all regarded as key factors in promoting the success of all students in reading.

Confidence in their abilities to meet the individual needs of students in their classrooms in reading (teacher efficacy) was a significant issue, one frequently described as perceptions of their own lack of knowledge about reading instruction, and the ongoing development of their knowledge and expertise in specific skills and strategies for the teaching of reading. Teachers described doing their best with initial teacher education, teaching experiences, additional qualifications courses, and in-service sessions; most reported having participated in some form of professional development in reading since completing their pre-service program and/or continuing to read and seek out ideas and practical strategies to assist in further developing classroom practices.

The perception of a greater emphasis on reading as a discrete "subject" within elementary school language arts programs was frequently mentioned. This also appeared to be a direct result of curriculum reform in Ontario, and increased concern about the numbers of students who demonstrate difficulties in reading. These concerns appeared to be significant factors in participants' experiences as teachers of reading, and the perceived pressures not only to acquire more knowledge and expertise about effective reading instruction, but also how to assess, evaluate, and report on student progress in reading.

Towards Balanced Approaches in Reading Instruction: Teachers' Perspectives

Teachers' conceptualizations of reading and descriptions of planning for reading instruction were found to be generally consistent with a "skills" orientation, that is, where students are encouraged to use both information from the text and personal knowledge to develop meaning (Boschee, Whitehead, & Boschee, 1993). However, the teachers interviewed described balanced, eclectic approaches to reading in their classroom practice, and explicit instruction in reading skills combined with literature and language-rich activities (Allen, 2002; Appleman, 2010; Bomer, 2011; Parr & Campbell, 2012; Pressley, 2002).

Participants talked about the need to explicitly teach specific skills at the Grade 5 level that motivate and enable students to read successfully in various contexts (Gallagher, 2003). As an example, skills instruction was integrated into eclectic teaching strategies and language-rich learning experiences that promoted reading across the curriculum. To illustrate this point, excerpts from interview data in three teachers' voices follow:

HELEN: I really believe, and this may seem self-evident, that because reading is part of every facet of the curriculum it's the most important tool we can give to children. It doesn't matter what subject, we are always focusing on reading skills as a means of getting to meaning. Being able to comprehend, and use different techniques to comprehend what's on the page in different areas of the curriculum is really, really important – and equally relevant to social studies, science, and ideas in math.

LYNDA: I see reading, and this is something I've struggled with over the years, not as something taught solely during a "reading" period. Reading is taught all day long in every subject area, and especially in environmental studies, science and social studies. How can a child gain the knowledge needed if he's not able to understand the material? When I'm teaching reading, I'm making sure they understand the vocabulary, and the different ways material is presented.

JOANNE: I see it as being one of the most important areas of the curriculum for children. Reading itself is not just a skill to be isolated. It is part of everything else we do. Take, for example, the amount of communicating we do now in math. It's phenomenal! Charts, diagrams, tables and graphs … all kinds of "reading." I think there's room for teacher-centred lessons as well as more independent work, partnering, and small group work – all of those in a balanced program.

Consistent with the work of Harvey and Goudvis (2007) and Keene (2008), participants frequently described classroom practices as "embedding" the explicit teaching of comprehension skills (before, during, and after reading) in instruction, as well as including work on more sophisticated skills and strategies for reading across the curriculum (e.g., inference).

Teachers also described their rationale for explicit teaching of reading skills in Grade 5 classrooms as originating from experiences with "struggling" readers at this level. They tended to regard curriculum expectations and the pace at which it was necessary for students to complete work as increasingly challenging for those who were unable to read fluently and independently with understanding. All 11 teachers reported including specific skills instruction located in the broader contexts of their classroom program. For example, in response to the need for all students to develop skills in reading non-fiction or "content areas" of the curriculum, Kim explained:

KIM: When they don't know those aspects of print and we get to learning from non-fiction, social studies, for example, I have to look at these kinds of things: Can they look for headings? Can they use an index? How is the text organized? Otherwise, how can they even begin to try and find information when reading is already hard for them? If they don't have those strategies, I must teach them.

Guided reading, an important instructional component of balanced reading instruction in earlier grades, is also becoming increasingly common in the middle and upper elementary grades. The development of guided reading practice at the Grade 5 level and, more specifically from Kim's perspective, will be further explored with illustrative excerpts from interview data.

Guided Reading as Instruction in Later Elementary Grades

Until relatively recently, guided reading – an instructional component of balanced approaches to reading along with modelled, shared, and independent reading – was largely considered the domain of teachers in early elementary grades. However, this is changing rapidly to include upper elementary (and even secondary) grades.

Guided reading involves small-group instruction for students who read the same text. Groups are organized homogeneously with students reading at approximately the same levels, demonstrating similar reading behaviours, and sharing similar instructional needs. Students usually read silently and independently. Explicit instruction of effective strategies for processing a variety of fiction and non-fiction texts is introduced, as appropriate, by the teacher. These small groups are not static but temporary, and they change as teachers assess students' growth and needs (Fountas & Pinnell, 2001). More than half of the teachers interviewed shared experiences with beginning to implement guided reading in their classrooms.

Teacher participants felt what they knew about guided reading as a component of balanced reading instruction complemented a "skills in context" approach to reading instruction. Guided reading was also described as using a wide variety of literature and other materials that challenged students at their own personal level of reading ability. That said, efforts to implement guided reading as a component of their Grade 5 reading programs were at very different stages. Four of the teachers had attended professional development workshops provided by their district school board; five were registered to attend one shortly; and two had only just begun to learn about guided reading as an approach for teaching reading.

Challenges teachers had experienced in implementing guided reading programs were discussed in three areas: organizational and classroom management issues (e.g., small groups working together, the need for effective monitoring of a variety of activities going on in the classroom at the same time); the acquisition of sufficient and suitable resources; and increased recognition of their own need for more knowledge and expertise in reading skills and strategies. Cindy talked about her observations related to both student learning and her own learning as a new teacher:

CINDY: I have a really wide range of reading abilities, and I'm sometimes surprised how well they cooperate with the guided reading and do so well in their groups. They enjoy reading out loud to each other, even the kids that don't read as well. I was worried that they might feel singled out a bit, but they don't seem to feel like that, and most of them enjoy having the small groups. I think they like that I'm not always in their group and they can rely on other students around them to support their reading. It's working well. I've tried to encourage them: you know, "somebody is stuck on a word and you know what the word is or you know how to say it or what it means. So you can help them, but you need to give them a few minutes to try and say the word." I was quite surprised that they would ask and not feel intimidated, or perhaps not feel as smart as the others. But in this class guided reading works.

Teachers' struggles and insights related to the challenges and opportunities identified as inherent in developing guided reading as an important aspect of later elementary programs (Pinnell & Fountas, 2007) were consistently an integral feature across interview data. One teacher in particular, Kim, described developing an appealing, yet unfamiliar, classroom practice in this area. The following short excerpts are presented to capture some of the insights shared via Kim's own voice and her teacher thinking in (and on) action:

KIM: In my class now, in reading, I'm doing small group guided reading, and the class is broken into three groups: a struggling group, a mid-level group, and a higher-level group. I have two language arts periods, two fifty-minute periods a day, and there's a constant flow between. I don't tend to separate very often, this is reading, this is writing. I have an independent project going on so if they're not working with me there are a variety of things the students are doing.

Kim's classroom work emphasized the integration of reading and writing, and the rationale for organizing small, homogeneous groups became evident as she explored her own thinking and professional learning. She described regular, direct teaching and teacher interaction within small groups as well as the provision of a wide range of opportunities for application of learning about reading:

KIM: And while all that's [independent work] happening, I'm with my small groups. I will call over my lower group. I see them every day, probably 20 minutes to half an hour every single day, and we will talk about what I'd given them to read the night before. We'll do a read aloud where I will generally start the read aloud, and then I'll pick one or two of them to continue. We stop, we talk about [what we've read], even the structure of print in a novel, you know, what do the little asterisks mean at the end of one of the paragraphs? Because they don't always know. Or, another example, that the last paragraph of one chapter should lead into, or give you a clue, about what's happening next. Which they also don't always know. I found this out today. Nobody in my group had any idea that where [the story] ended in one chapter should be where it begins in the next chapter. Which is one reason why they're having difficulty because they don't even understand these, what I call, "mechanics" of what they're reading.

Conventions of print, story structure, and teaching students to expect reading to make sense were all elements woven into Kim's guided reading instruction. She considered it essential to sit with students in their small groups and hear them reading and asking questions in order to gain insights into what they already know, and what they need to learn next. Continually stressing the value of using read aloud techniques in the construction of meaning from text, Kim has observed the effects on students' understanding when they do not "read" subtle cues accurately (e.g., uses of punctuation):

KIM: A lot of what I'm doing in those guided reading groups is trying to figure out where their comprehension is breaking down and I gear my lessons towards that as much as I can. I'll go to the library or go to another teacher, any resources I can go through and think, "O.K, if I need to teach this what am I going to do? How am I going to do it?" Because if they can't decipher the words, then of course it's harder to understand what it means. I'll be reading with one group, and then I give them some comprehension questions or some vocabulary work, and then I'll call another group and they'll come over.

Kim firmly believed reading skills were essential to comprehension and the application of learning to purposeful reading in both fiction and non-fiction selections. Her practice reflects teaching that strives to assist students to make sense of what they read, and to view reading as both a source of information and enjoyment. Kim described ongoing attempts to successfully develop her professional knowledge, the organization of guided reading in her classroom, and explorations of different sources of in order to meet various students' needs:

KIM: I meet my mid-group three to four times a week in general, so not every single day, and only for about 20 minutes. We read more and they can cover more material in a given time. We're beginning to look at reasons for why is the character doing this? Or if the character says this, how do you know what they're feeling if it doesn't actually say? Or why didn't the character say when they were upset when their parents misinterpreted what they'd said, why didn't they correct their parents? What is the reason for that? How does this relate to your life? They're all reading at about grade level, and so I'm spending a lot of time focusing on relationships to what they're reading and getting them to share some of their personal stories … My higher group reads a more challenging book, and we move a lot faster and look at genre, themes, the play between protagonist, antagonist, and can they compare them to other novels [we've read] as we move through the year? It's that whole idea of taking it all one step further: What am I doing to really get them to think? I see them three times a week and that tends to be for about half an hour at a time to really get some good discussion going; then they have work to do on their own. [My ultimate goal is] to encourage them to challenge each other as the year progresses and for them to really start getting more out of what they're reading, critically.

Kim clearly makes the distinction between a student who is able to "decode" and one who "reads well." Her lessons sought to meet students at their various levels and to move them towards more sophisticated concepts involved in reading as thinking and the construction of individual interpretations:

KIM: It's working a whole lot better for me this year. I'm more structured with my time. I have a better tracking system. I do anecdotal records, almost like the primary teachers do with the yellow post-its. I make lots of notes. If we're doing a read aloud I'll pick two or three students a day who will continue to read aloud and I make notes on their fluency, or did they self-correct? It's almost like a pseudo-running record. I'm monitoring for the kinds of miscues they make. I'll also make notes if I've asked them a certain question, were they able to relate it back? Did they come up with any relation to it at all? Those things that jump out and I think, "Oh, this was really good!" or "This is something that I'm going to need to go back to and think some more about."

Kim's reference to miscue analysis and the use of running records in her classroom points to the highly analytical nature of her approach to teaching reading. It also indicates her knowledge of the strategies she has adopted for teaching and assessment of reading from colleagues in the Primary Division, and as a result of taking additional qualifications courses in reading.

Awareness of continuous improvement and the refining of her practice over time, bringing increased confidence and expertise, is reflected in Kim's comparison of her implementation of guided reading the previous year. The improved sense of satisfaction with her "tracking systems" is evident:

KIM: My tracking is much better this year as well because I'm not trying to track all five kids, every single day, all the time. That's what I tried to do before. [It was] just a ton of paper and you don't really retain everything. My groups are smaller because my class is smaller, I have three reading groups instead of four … and it's just a lot more focused. My goal with my struggling readers is to begin to figure out what they can and cannot do with their decoding, and what can I put into place to help them with that and those conventions of print.

She also made specific reference to some of the ways implementing guided reading influenced the organization and management of her classroom – for example, different instructional purposes and flexible grouping of students:

KIM: There's flux between the groups. For example, right now I have a student who is struggling in the higher group. I had pegged her as a higher reader and, I would say, for the next novel I will probably drop her down and see if that's a better place for her. You know, it comes and goes as to where they are. Where is their comfort level? And the more I get to work with them, the more I understand, one by one, what are they good at and what are their areas of need? Then I try and gear what I do within each small group to service that, to help them be better readers. To me, I don't think [their group] should be set in stone right away because that really doesn't allow for that student who suddenly makes great gains to move. Or for that student who is struggling. I think the whole purpose, in my mind, of those guided reading groups is to challenge students at their level … It's not always just the high group (working) together and they only move as a unit (either), because I really want them to work [with others] and do some of that modelling and sharing of ideas (too).

The implementation of Kim's guided reading practice is consistent with temporary, flexible groupings that change as the teacher assesses student growth and needs. Kim talked about the importance of teacher modelling, explicit teaching of skills and strategies, moving students forward in their learning, and providing a stimulating classroom and resource base. There was a constant sense of her care and concern for individual differences in planning for student success. Her own passionate (and yet very analytical) instructional practice in reading clearly resonated with guided reading as an approach to skills instruction in the context of rich language experiences.

Modelling effective reading and thinking processes, central to her teaching style, was evident throughout Kim's interview data. Beyond her own developing classroom practice, Kim described sharing her excitement about guided reading as an approach to instruction with colleagues in Grades 4 to 6 – some of whom were not yet ready to implement it in their classrooms, although others were willing to be coached. A vibrant catalyst for change in her school, Kim shared thinking about continuing her own professional learning and efforts (in the context of her leadership role, as junior lead teacher), to support and encourage others on staff to also explore their approaches to teaching reading:

KIM: Yes, and to get other teachers to share in my vision. That's what it is. There's still a place to teach reading, to teach reading, and to teach reading skills well to Junior Division students. No matter how great your novel study is I, personally, do not believe that one novel study addresses the needs of your class as well as having multilevel study groups and small group reading. I truly do not believe it. And I know it's hard to let go. I mean I know because I've had to. When you've spent all that time putting together great activities with a novel and think it's so wonderful – and it's easy: You do your lesson and everyone does the same thing. Small group work is a lot of work. It's a lot of organization, and it's keeping track of three or four novels. But I've seen the results and I can really individualize what I'm doing. I think it's pretty rare in teaching that you can really individualize what you're teaching with all students to best meet their needs. If I can help students develop those skills (reading, writing, and research), then that's something I really want other junior teachers to be doing too. I want [other teachers] to see that it's very positive and to see the results for themselves. But change takes time for students, for teachers, and for me. Definitely. And there are so many more things I know I need to learn.

In summary, teacher modelling, explicit teaching of skills and strategies, and moving students forward in their learning were central to Kim's passionate and analytical approach to navigating transitions involved in developing effective reading instruction in her Grade 5 classroom.

Discussion

Implications for future research and teaching related to a better understanding of how teachers navigate transitions in approaches to reading instruction in the middle years include (1) the importance of qualitative data and teachers' perspectives in research on teaching and (2) enriched understandings of teachers' perspectives on (a) teaching reading and (b) the nature of current transitions in classroom reading instruction in the later elementary grades.

The Importance of Qualitative Data and Teachers' Perspectives in Research on Teaching

Throughout this study it became clear that the qualitative data gathered that included teachers' perspectives in research on teaching offered rich insights and deeper understandings of teacher thinking and instructional practices.

Significant patterns and themes recurred over and again in the voices of Grade 5 teachers from their emic ("insider") perspective. There is still much to learn. Nevertheless, the findings underscore a vital role for increasing teachers' contributions to research on reading instruction.

Quantitative approaches to research on teaching appear to have dominated the field prior to the 1980s (Munby, Russell, & Martin, 2001). However, qualitative research has established a place for itself in the field of teacher education and, increasingly, studies employ mixed methods – both qualitative and quantitative. If the quality and consistency of teaching are regarded as critical factors in any attempt to improve education, it follows that there should be a continual interest in the teachers themselves. As Beattie (1995) suggests, studies that invite teachers' voices as research also have "the potential to bring new meaning to teacher education and to the continuous experiences of change, of growth, of professional development in a teacher's life" (p. 65). Teacher education research reveals very little about, "how teachers of reading are created, how they teach, nor how they change" (Anders et al., 2000, p. 732). Research does reveal that studies are needed that pursue the critical questions, issues, and gaps in the current literature on reading instruction. This is especially so if we are to better understand what is needed as transitions in approaches to reading instruction occur. For example, what should be the goals of reading teacher education today? What kinds of knowledge do experienced teachers who attend in-service on reading need? How do we prepare, and sustain, teachers for meeting the multifarious needs of the student readers they teach? Research that pursues answers to questions about the multiple demands and diverse contexts that teachers of reading encounter in contemporary classrooms can offer first-hand accounts of the complex work of teaching and may generate greater appreciation for teachers' knowledge and expertise.

Qualitative inquiries that listen carefully to the voices of teachers and re-present their perspectives on approaches to reading instruction have the potential to reveal unique and valuable insights with which to inform the fields of both teaching and teacher education. Truly, if we are to understand teaching from teachers' perspectives, we must also understand the beliefs with which they define their work (Nespor, 1987).

Enriched Understandings of Teachers' Perspectives on Transitions in Reading Instruction (Later Elementary Grades)

In-depth, qualitative interviews enabled informative discussions that delved into how, as practising teachers, participants saw their personal/ professional knowledge and beliefs influencing the ongoing development of instructional practice. Rich, illustrative examples of "reflection on action" were articulated and captured as a result.

Teachers interviewed shared their perspectives and experiences with navigating recent changes in classroom reading instruction in the mid-elementary grades, changes that have resulted in a much higher profile for "balanced" approaches to reading instruction beyond the earlier grades (K–3).

Teacher participants were gradually becoming conversant with major components of balanced reading instruction, and they talked about planning and implementing instruction in terms of incorporating phonics and meaning, explicit instruction in skills and strategies, purposeful reading, integrating different dimensions of the language arts, and the prime importance of fostering lifelong, habitual readers. They were also exploring elements of modelled, shared, guided, and independent reading in reading and language arts and across the curriculum at the Grade 5 level. The (relatively) recent developments that have seen strategic, purposeful reading instruction moving in to middle and upper elementary classrooms is a commendable transition in and of itself. However, teacher participants' comments continued to resonate with concerns about their "not really knowing how to teach reading" (e.g., because they were not "primary" teachers and had not "learned how to teach reading" at the faculty). Individuals often expressed that, although they were "doing the best they could" in the interests of their students, they were often unsure if they were "on the right track" with the teaching of reading. For example, Mark noted, "When I look back, and, especially with reading, I wish I knew more about the actual nuts and bolts of teaching reading." However, willingness to continue to learn and to articulate understandings as teachers, expanded definitions of reading and what it actually means to "teach reading," became evident.

More studies that investigate teachers' classroom lives, knowledge, and understandings of reading instruction from the teachers' perspective, even their insecurities, will better reflect and honour the voices and professional realities of contemporary classroom teachers.

Future research studies that attend to teachers' voices might also generate more enriched understandings of what is needed, in terms of pre-service and in-service teacher education in reading. Classroom instruction and practice will continue to present challenge and change in contemporary classrooms:

DONNA: I want to know what our next step is as a school in terms of junior
    reading and what's going to happen now that the focus in reading is being
    put on the juniors. Where are we going to start? How we are going to
    work through this with teachers who are at so many different places on
    a continuum of teaching reading? And don't just show me the buzz-words

like shared reading, paired reading, and guided reading. I know all the buzz-words; I've taught primary. How is this going to work in a junior class where I don't have two periods [for reading] every day? How do I do this? I'm anxious to know.

To best prepare teachers for the multiple demands and diverse contexts that they encounter in contemporary classrooms, and to facilitate successful transitions in instructional practices, evolving approaches to reading instruction must be recognized, better understood, and actively supported by those responsible for (1) designing and developing pre-service teacher education and (2) the provision of relevant and ongoing professional development opportunities for classroom teachers as these educators progress successfully along the reading teacher education continuum.

REFERENCES

Allen, J. (2002). *On the same page: Shared reading beyond the primary grades*. Portland, ME: Stenhouse.

Allington, R.L. (2001). *What really matters for struggling readers: Designing research based initiatives*. New York: Longman.

Allington, R.L., & Johnston, P.H. (2001). What do we know about effective fourth-grade teachers and their classrooms? In C.M. Roller (Ed.), *Learning to teach reading: Setting the research agenda* (pp. 150–165). Newark, DE: International Reading Association.

Anders, P.L., Hoffman, J.V., & Duffy, G.G. (2000). Teaching teachers to teach reading: Paradigm shifts, persistent problems and challenges. In M. Kamil, P.B. Mosenthal, P.D. Pearson, & R. Barr (Eds.), *Handbook of reading research* (3rd ed., pp. 719–742). Mahwah, NJ: Erlbaum.

Anderson, R.C., & Mitchener, C.M. (1994). Research on science teacher education. In D.C. Gabel (Ed.), *Handbook of research on science, teaching and learning* (pp. 3–44). New York: Macmillan.

Appleman, D. (2010). *Adolescent literacy and the teaching of reading*. Urbana, IL: National Council of Teachers of English.

Baumann, J.F., Hoffman, J.V., Moon, J., & Duffy-Hester, A.M. (1998). Where are the teachers' voices in the phonics/whole language debate? Results from a survey of U.S. elementary classroom teachers. *Reading Teacher, 51*(8), 636–650.

Beattie, M. (1995). New prospects for teacher education: Narrative ways of knowing teaching and teacher learning. *Educational Research, 37*(1), 53–70.

Bomer, R. (2011). *Building adolescent literacy in today's English classrooms.* Portsmouth, NH: Heinemann.

Boschee, F., Whitehead, B.M., & Boschee, M.A. (1993). *Effective reading programs.* Lancaster, PA: Technomic.

Calfee, R., & Drum, P. (1986). Research on teaching reading. In M.C. Wittrock (Ed.), *Handbook of research on teaching* (3rd ed., pp. 804–849). New York: Macmillan.

Duffy, G.G. (1977). A study of teacher conceptions of reading. *Paper presented at the annual meeting of the National Reading Conference,* New Orleans, LA.

Duffy, G.G. (1982). Fighting off the alligators: What research in real classrooms has to say about reading instruction. *Journal of Reading Behavior, 14,* 357–373.

Duffy, G.G., & Anderson, L. (1984). Teachers' theoretical orientations and the real classroom. *Reading Psychology, 5*(1–2), 97–104.

Duffy, G.G., Roehler, L., & Herrmann, B.A. (1988). Modeling mental processes helps poor readers become strategic readers. *Reading Teacher, 41,* 762–767.

Elliott-Johns, S.E. (2004). *Theoretical orientations to reading and instructional practices of eleven grade five teachers* (Unpublished doctoral dissertation). McGill University, Montreal.

Elliott-Johns, S.E. (2012). Literacy teacher education today and the teaching of adolescent literature: Perspectives on research and practice. In J.A. Hayn & J.S. Kaplan (Eds.), *Teaching young adult literature today: Insights, considerations, and perspectives for the classroom teacher* (pp. 41–58). New York: Rowman & Littlefield.

Fountas, I.C., & Pinnell, G.S. (2001). *Guiding readers and writers, Grades 3–6: Teaching comprehension, genre, and content literacy.* Portsmouth, NH: Heinemann.

Fullan, M., & Hargreaves, A. (1994). The teacher as a person. In A. Pollard & J. Bourne (Eds.), *Teaching and learning in the primary school* (pp. 67–72). London: Routledge.

Gallagher, K. (2003). *Reading reasons: Motivational mini-lessons for middle and high school.* Portland, ME: Stenhouse.

Gallagher, K. (2009). *Readicide: How schools are killing reading and what you can do about it.* Portland, ME: Stenhouse.

Gambrell, L.B. (1996). Creating classroom cultures that foster reading motivation. *Reading Teacher, 50,* 14–25.

Grisham, D.L. (2000). Connecting theoretical conceptions of reading to practice: A longitudinal study of elementary school teachers. *Reading Psychology, 21*(2), 145–170.

Harste, J.C., & Burke, C.L. (1977). A new hypothesis for reading teacher research: Both the teaching and learning of reading is theoretically based.

In P.D. Pearson (Ed.), *Reading: Theory, research and practice* (pp. 32–40). New York: Mason.

Harvey, S., & Goudvis, A. (2007). *Strategies that work: Teaching comprehension for understanding and engagement* (2nd ed.). Portland, ME: Stenhouse.

Keene, E.O. (2008). *To understand: New horizons in reading comprehension*. Portsmouth, NH: Heinemann.

Lankshear, C. & Knobel, M. (2006). *New Literacies: Everyday practices in classroom learning* (2nd ed.). Maidenhead, UK: Open University Press.

Majhanovich, S. (2002). Conflicting visions, competing expectations: Control and de-skilling of education – A perspective from Ontario. *McGill Journal of Education, 37*(2), 159–176.

McKeown, M.G. & Kucan, L. (Eds.). (2010). *Bringing reading research to life*. New York: Guilford Press.

Munby, H., Russell, T., & Martin, A.K. (2001). Teachers' knowledge and how it develops. In V. Richardson (Ed.), *Handbook of research on teaching* (4th ed., pp. 877–904). Washington, DC: American Educational Research Association.

Nespor, J. (1987). The role of beliefs in the practice of teaching. *Journal of Curriculum Studies, 19*(4), 317–328.

Pahl, K., & Rowsell, J. (2010). *Artifactual literacies: Every object tells a story*. New York: Teachers College Press.

Parr, M., & Campbell, T. (2012). *Balanced literacy essentials: Weaving theory into practice for successful reading, writing, and talk*. Markham, ON: Pembroke Publishers.

Pinnell, G.S., & Fountas, I.C. (2007). *The continuum of literacy learning: Behaviors and understandings to notice, teach, and support*. Portsmouth, NH: Heinemann.

Poulson, L., Avramidis, E., Fox, R., Medwell, J., & Wray, D. (2001). The theoretical beliefs of effective teachers of literacy in primary schools: An exploratory study of orientations to reading and writing. *Research Papers in Education, 16*(3), 271–292.

Pressley, M. (2002). *Reading instruction that works: The case for balanced teaching* (2nd ed.). New York: Guilford Press.

Richardson, V., Anders, P.L., Tidwell, D., & Lloyd, C. (1991). The relationship between teachers' beliefs and practices in reading comprehension instruction. *American Educational Research Journal, 28*(3), 559–586.

Routman, R. (2000). *Conversations: Strategies for teaching, learning and evaluating*. Portsmouth, NH: Heinemann.

Shulman, L.S. (1986). Paradigms and research programs in the study of teaching. In M.C. Wittrock (Ed.), *Handbook of research on teaching* (3rd ed., pp. 1–36). New York: Macmillan.

7 Scaffolded Literacy Assessment and a Model for Teachers' Professional Development

LYN SHARRATT

With standardized assessment almost universally in place, schooling is being moved away from a "one size fits all" mentality and is being driven to place the goals, aspirations, and context for each student's learning at the heart of the matter, thus, ensuring that every student matters. But little is known about how to individualize learning in systems, or how to extend the practice into schools and classrooms. My own mantra "assessment drives instruction" initially appears complex, and the chemistry of change in systems, schools, and classrooms seems a somewhat mysterious, albeit sophisticated craft. Yet, these two concepts must be grasped and integrated for professionals to develop increasing intentionality and finite precision in their classroom teaching if smooth transitions between grades and panels are to occur for all students and teachers.

Starting with the data for each learner, as we must, analyses of student achievement data provide system leaders and classroom teachers with rich sources of information, but often do not tell a complete story until administrators, principals, and teachers drill down into the relevant available data sources and put FACES (Family and Community Engagement Strategy) on the information (Sharratt & Fullan, 2012).

To focus on drilling down, and in order to get past the surfeit of information to what's really important, I have recommended literacy instruction as the theory of action in the international K–12 reform agenda and now here in the investigation of smooth, positive transitions for all. Not only does literacy narrow our focus to discuss evidence-proven instructional strategies that benefit all students, but it also focuses us on our shared vision and offers opportunities to set benchmarks and future learning goals for teaching and learning.

UNESCO (2003) states our moral imperative best: "literacy is about more than reading or writing – it is about how we communicate in society. It is about social practices and relationships, about knowledge, language and culture. Those who use literacy sometimes take it for granted – but those who cannot use it are often excluded from much communication in today's world. Indeed, it is the excluded who can best appreciate the notion of 'literacy as freedom'" (p. 1). We add to this the notion that math or numeracy is a fundamental aspect of the literate graduate in an increasingly globalized and technologically advanced world.

We start where formal education often begins – Kindergarten. Children *do* learn to read and write in Kindergarten. *If* children do not begin to learn to read, write, and do math, in an engaging Kindergarten learning environment, high school graduation rates reflect both the poor and the late start (Hanson & Farrell, 1995). These shared beliefs and understandings underscore smooth transitions for both teachers and students. Moreover, these shared beliefs and understandings (Hill & Crévola, 1999) contribute to the rigorous structure of our research-proven and highly engaging program for system reform and classroom achievement.

Self-Assessment Tool for District, School, and Classroom Improvement

Published research identifies 13 Parameters as the "nitty-gritty" of collective capacity building (Sharratt & Fullan, 2005). The Parameters are used as a self-assessment improvement tool by districts, schools, and classrooms. Think of the 13 Parameters as the specific strategies that, in combination, "cause" classroom, school, and district improvement and result in increased student achievement. Readers should note that shared beliefs and understandings comprise the number one parameter for a reason – they are not only the most important to ensure that all staff embrace them as our moral imperative, but they are also the most difficult to achieve in our work. All the other parameters are not hierarchical but must be selected after careful scrutiny of student achievement data (Sharratt & Fullan, 2005, 2006, 2009).

The 13 Parameters

These are the 13 Parameters. Parameter 1, shared beliefs and understandings, is adapted from Hill and Crévola (1999); the remaining parameters are from Sharrat and Fullan (2005, 2006).

1 Shared Beliefs and Understandings
   (a) Each student can achieve high standards given the right time and the right support.
   (b) Each teacher can teach to high standards given the right assistance.
   (c) High expectations and early and ongoing intervention are essential.
   (d) Teachers and administrators need to be able to articulate what they do and why they teach the way they do.
2 Embedded Literacy Coaches
3 Timetabled Literacy Block – focused on assessment that improves instruction
4 Principal Leadership
5 Early and Ongoing Intervention
6 Case Management Approach
7 Literacy Professional Learning at School Staff Meetings
8 In-School Grade/Subject Meetings
9 Book Rooms of Levelled Books and Resources
10 Allocation of District and School Budgets for Literacy Learning and Resources
11 Action Research Focused on Literacy
12 Parental Involvement
13 Cross-Curricular Literacy Connections

This is not esoteric, "ivory-tower stuff." Rather, it is practical, hands-on, and an "it works" type of research that has also passed the rigour of academic review. It is important to note that the 13 Parameters were the result of carefully reviewing how some schools in challenging circumstances took advantage of internal intervention resources, such as Reading Recovery teachers and literacy coaches, and succeeded in the long term in dramatically increasing student achievement and how other schools in the same situation with the same interventions and resources lost focus and were unable to raise student achievement over the same period of time.

As the Parameters are identified and stand the test of evidence and practicality, they must be adopted, implemented, monitored, refined, and then permanently embedded in every district, in every school, at every level. Rolling it out into a system or district is a process in itself and success arises from "hastening slowly." The professional learning, carefully crafted by district, school, and teacher leaders, who understand the research behind and promote opportunities to discuss the

13 Parameters, ensures that all schools increase students' achievement. Through district professional learning sessions, consultant workshops, team-based collective capacity building, and further evidence-based refinement, the Parameters have come to have a named status. Leaders throughout systems come to "walk the talk" and equally, simultaneously "talk the walk" – such as *Instructional Walks and Talks* (Sharratt, 2011) – where strategies are geared to learning about implementation during implementation. This "implementation as learning" serves to further specify the meaning of each component and its efficacy in developing collective capacity. "Implementation as learning" blurs the lines between theory and practice, further embedding successes and moving districts towards "Realization" – or full implementation (Sharratt & Fullan, 2009). With everyone using the same language in the system, having the same shared beliefs and understandings and adopting the 13 Parameters as a self-assessment tool, principals and teachers can share ideas that advance classroom practice. Furthermore, with the necessary trust developed, they can do so freely, without pressure or fear of retribution – to the benefit of the learners.

Three of the 13 Parameters (nos. 3, 6, and 13) stand out as warranting further investigation, as they strengthen smooth transitions for teachers and students, and thus are especially applicable to the discussion in this chapter.

Focus on Assessment That Informs Instruction (Parameter 3)

Assessment must drive or inform instruction daily in the classroom (Wiliam, 2011). It is this never-ending process of data today becoming instruction tomorrow that is critical to implement fully. This assessment "for" learning leads to assessment "as" learning for students who advance to be self-assessors of their leaning – the ultimate in creating independent learners – and the utopian goal of all educators. Here, I discuss three related and important ideas: learning goals, big ideas, and success criteria as the essence of formative assessment.

LEARNING GOALS

Learning goals or learning intentions are directly developed from the Ontario Curriculum Expectations. Learning goals can be several of the curriculum expectations clustered together for teaching purposes. These learning goals need to be visible in classrooms, and prominently displayed in student-friendly language so that students are clear on what they are learning.

BIG IDEAS

In our work, we define big ideas in the following way: Educational leaders are coming to understand that the notion of teaching through "big ideas" is about teaching the higher-order thinking skills of analysis, interpretation, evaluation, and synthesis of a text or curriculum unit. The term "big idea" does not mean naming a theme unit such as "Friendship" and selecting a bunch of books and activities that go along with the Friendship Theme, but rather providing students with the modelling of higher-order thinking skills and opportunities to think through text or essential questions critically, bringing them to levels of deep understanding, creativity, and new learning. "Big ideas" can be addressed through the reading of individual texts or through a unit of study but they need to cause and stretch student thinking by highlighting what is essential in the text or learning experience and connecting these ideas meaningfully to students' lives and the world. (See Melanie Greenan, Doctoral Candidate, OISE/University of Toronto, personal communication, August 2011; see also Greenan, 2011a, 2011b.)

SUCCESS CRITERIA

Success criteria for students are directly developed from the learning goal(s) and the big idea(s) and are most effective when co-constructed with the teacher. Caution here is warranted that success criteria are not developed as check lists but, rather, as purposeful, clear, and meaningful points for students to incorporate into their work in order to excel. In short, classroom charts showing success criteria work best when developed, discussed, and added to with students as their work progresses daily (Hattie, 2012).

The second parameter relevant to this chapter is using the case management approach to ensure that smooth transitions mean that all teachers embrace working with *all* students. This approach is a case-by-case approach to putting all FACES on the data.

Case Management Approach (Parameter 6)

The case management (CM) approach is used by principals and teachers who request help finding teaching strategies that work for specific students. In this type of meeting, they effectively review and use data to drive differentiated instruction and the selection of appropriate resources. Inclusive case management meetings, during the school day, bring together classroom teachers, Special Education teachers, administrators, and specialist staff to scrutinize data displayed on data walls or in tracking folders (i.e., displays indicating where all students are sequenced in the learning continuum). These meetings require creative timetabling and, for example, class coverage by teachers without classrooms and/or vice-principals. The discussion of students' work, in a case-by-case approach, enables participants at the meeting to put individual faces on data. Teachers can then discuss together what support is needed and how to provide it. This ensures that all teachers in the school have collective responsibility to "own" *all* students' achievement. I will now discuss the case management approach in two parts: case management as assessment and case management as instruction.

Part 1: Case Management as an Assessment Tool

Sometimes we have to see the trees in the context of the full forest in order to see which are developing differently. A data wall of student performance creates a visual of all students' progress enabling teachers to see the underperformers and providing a forum for rich conversation among teachers. Finding a confidential place to display the data is extremely important, as is finding time to discuss those FACES on the wall. The process of finding a common assessment tool in which to evaluate and level students' work first (see collaborative marking of students' work in this chapter) is, in itself, a high-yield first step. Once a common assessment task is agreed on and the levels of achievement determined, the next step is to place those FACES on sticky notes. Names, photos (optional), and their assessment ranking are placed on the data wall above the assessment scores. When students are levelled on the wall, below, within, and beyond their grade level, teachers can see who is lagging – who is stuck and who is succeeding. Teachers are enabled to discuss with each other what is needed to move all – each and every student – forward. Subsequently, the focused conversation becomes how can *we* move all our students forward? How can *we* extend the thinking of these high-achieving students? Once all students are placed in their levels on the data wall and the overlaps of "plummeting," "staying still," and "soaring" students are noted, and teachers stop saying "I" as it becomes a "we" challenge – this is when teachers own all of the FACES (Sharratt & Fullan, 2012).

Part 2: Case Management as an Instructional Tool

The CM forum also provides teachers with strategy support – ideas or techniques to use in working with students who teachers may not know how to move forward; thus, the focus of the CM meeting is on the next steps in instruction. To provide the greatest support and input, CM forum membership always includes the principal, the presenting classroom teacher, the instructional coach, and optionally, may include any other teachers, if available (e.g., the Special Education teacher, teacher-librarian or Reading Recovery teacher whose time may be freed up by teachers without classrooms, vice principals, or creative timetabling).

The purpose is to examine students' work, describe strengths and areas of need, and then find one or two instructional strategies that the teacher can try for 3 to 6 weeks. After that period, the forum is reconvened so the teacher can report back on the progress and the assembled group can offer new suggestions if the first recommendations are not already working. Participants provide feedback and support to the classroom teacher, and will often "walk and talk" in the class to see how suggested strategies are progressing and to offer encouragement to the teacher.

This approach ensures that all teachers in the school have a collective responsibility to "own" *all* students' achievement. The immediate beneficiaries are the teachers and the students. The longer-term benefit accrues to all participating teachers and to those who note the improved performance on the data wall. Ongoing discussions, informed by interpretations of the data, can also focus on what new techniques worked to achieve the improvement.

The third parameter I will explore, cross-curricular literacy connections, assists in ensuring smooth transitions within and across grades.

Cross-Curricular Literacy Connections (Parameter 13)

All administrators and teachers, JK–12, need to find time to discuss and demonstrate what this Parameter looks like in order to implement the teaching of literacy – and the language of the disciplines – together in the content areas across all grades and subject areas. Cross-curricular connections must be valued and used in support of literacy instruction at all grade levels (Sharratt & Fullan, 2009).

Linked to cross-curricular literacy is the twenty-first century essential skill, higher-order thinking, that engages students in inquiry, rich authentic tasks, and exploring the big ideas. It is achieved when teachers cluster curriculum expectations across the disciplines; assess students' strengths and needs; and plan to embed literacy competencies in instruction in all subject areas. For example, for students to make sense of their world, teachers make cross-curricular connections by (Sharratt & Fullan, 2012):

- Doing modelled reading (think aloud) from the current History theme (modelling what good readers are thinking as they read)
- Writing different genre in Science (teaching procedural writing)
- Making thinking visible in a Mathematical problem-solving lesson (using pictures, words, and symbols to explain the thinking)
- Using a graphic organizer in a Geography lesson (locating the main idea)
- Building a word wall in Health and Nutrition (strengthening understanding of the language of the subject).

It is especially critical for teachers in middle and high schools to find the time to discuss and demonstrate to each other what cross-curricular literacy instruction looks like and implement teaching literacy skills in the content areas across all grades and subject areas. As the integration of literacy in all subject areas is central, cross-curricular connections must be valued and used in support of literacy instruction at all grade levels.

Implications for Transitions

Three of the 13 Parameters, as discussed, present a focus for going more deeply into investigating transitions. Most districts have been seen to underinvest in capacity building or engage in a flurry of ad hoc, unfocused activity that passes for capacity building. In this model, the 13 Parameters must be intentionally reviewed to ensure *collective* capacity-building activities are strategically aligned to allow for full implementation of the 13 Parameters. The goal is consistent practice across all classrooms. Reducing the variation in practice between classrooms is essential if we believe that all students can and will learn. What does the professional development for teachers look like to achieve this goal?

**Teachers' Professional Development:
A Model to Support Transitions**

Not only does formal literacy learning begin in Kindergarten (Hanson & Farrell, 1995), it continues throughout school experience and offers support for both student transitions and teachers' development of effective instructional practices. Successful approaches to instruction can be enhanced by using the gradual release of responsibility model (Sharratt & Fullan, 2009; Vygotsky, 1934/1978) discussed here as a modelled, shared, guided, and independent approach to teaching the balanced literacy strategies. This approach becomes increasingly visible over the course of a day or a week in all classrooms: modelled (teacher does–student watches), shared (teacher does–student shares), guided (student does–teacher guides), and independent (student does–teacher observes) reading and writing are surrounded by a rich oral language program. In elementary instructional practice, there are eight essential components of a balanced literacy approach: modelled reading/think aloud, shared reading, guided reading, independent reading, modelled writing, shared/interactive writing, guided writing, and independent writing. These are powerfully connected when teachers use the gradual release model in teaching each of these components – and are carefully detailed in *A Guide to Effective Instruction in Reading* (Ontario Ministry of Education, 2003). The road to realization – every teacher and every student engaged and benefiting – is sequenced or scaffolded capacity building. *Scaffolding* is a term that refers to supported progressive learning during which knowledge is built up. New knowledge is brought into play and connected with prior knowledge. Each layer is built on a solid foundation created by previous learnings, that is, "scaffolded" (Sharratt & Fullan, 2009).

This scaffolded learning model for students is transferable to establishing the professional learning for teachers and administrators needed at all levels, in all contexts: districts, schools, and classrooms. Moreover, this progressive learning model (Joyce & Showers, 1995) results in the sustainability of increased student achievement for all or "realization." Here I define each of the four stages.

Modelled Practice

Modelled practice is the first level and it initiates the capacity-building stage. Thinking big and starting small, as a superintendent of curriculum, I worked with a small core of strong curriculum consultants to model the components of the literacy priority, articulating how the priority was formed and why it is held with unwavering passion. Learners listen attentively then self-reflect on where this fits with their current thinking, knowing, and doing. Determining how to scaffold this new, unfamiliar information onto existing learned concepts is an important step for leaders to develop.

Shared Practice

Shared practice continues the capacity building by inviting learners to participate in their own learning through dialogue and questioning in safe and supportive learning environments. It offers leader-led and -shaped learning that allows for collegiality, risk taking, and safe spaces for debate by the learners. Leaders must consider how to scaffold this sharing to help all learners reach the next level of sophisticated learning, known as guided practice.

Guided Practice

Guided practice is the transition practice that allows for the smooth passage of information between learners and deepens understanding. In turn, guided practice supports processes involved in collective capacity building and moves student learning towards interdependent practice or realization. In other words, it allows leaders to pull back and the learners to step forward and do most of the work in thinking how to apply what has been shared. As the concept is not new anymore, there should be frequent opportunities for "trying it out" and "talking it out" by learners while walking alongside their leaders. Leaders, as co-learners with teachers, for example, are in their schools and classrooms to practice.

Interdependent Practice

Interdependent practice is the ultimate practice and the target for which we have been aiming. It is often known as "independent practice" in the literature on teaching students. We have renamed it "interdependent practice" to ensure that our message is clear: each system/school/classroom must be tightly coupled, aligned, and not separated at anytime from the central focus, purpose, or shared vision. And this co-learner strategy is critical to sustainability. The organization collectively becomes as interdependent as the learners within it and approaches or surpasses the many hours required to become collectively "good" (Sharratt & Fullan, 2009).

Interdependent practice occurs when the learners have consolidated their learning and can do it alone with the leader continuing to offer minimal support. Importantly, the learning required to successfully reach this level has been carefully scaffolded. By definition, *scaffolded learning* is built layer by connecting layer – a process that is "not so fast" and results in broad-based shared experiences from the ground up. Finally, it should be noted that "leaders" can come from many different sources – literacy coaches, principals, curriculum consultants, teachers, superintendents – but how does our progressive learning model work in practice over time? Table 7.1 examines the collaborative marking of students' work – involving the gradual release of responsibility – in greater detail as an example of what it takes for teachers to move from modelled, to shared, to guided, and ultimately to interdependent practice – to provide smooth transitions for all students. This is the focus for staff professional learning.

The collaborative marking of students' work is essential at all grade levels, K–12. Cross-grade and same-grade examination of the work, based on common assessment tasks, drive the process and offer teachers invaluable data about "before, during, and after" expectations of the work.

Barriers and Obstacles to Transition

Inconsistency in instructional practice is a barrier – the looming elephant in the room – to smooth transitions for both students and teachers. The most significant variation is not from one school system to another or even from one school to another, but from one classroom to another. Meetings where teachers come together to develop a common assessment task, and then mark it together, provide places where teachers can learn and share new assessment and instructional approaches. In this way, teachers can also develop a common consistent language of practice. I emphasize that collaborative marking of students' work is a powerful process. Reeves (2011, p. 51) concurs that perhaps one of the best and most practical ways to improve accuracy (i.e., consistency) is the collaborative scoring of students' work. This is also a superb professional development experience allowing teachers to improve the quality, consistency, and timeliness of their feedback to students. Sometimes collaborative scoring occurs informally, when a teacher asks a colleague for help: "*I'm on the fence about this particular project, how would you evaluate it?*"

In more formalized collaborative marking, sometimes called *teacher moderation*, teachers come together at a scheduled time to examine a common work sample from students and, by sharing beliefs and understandings, reach consensus about the levels the students have achieved and why a certain level is the appropriate one (Sharratt & Fullan, 2012). Ben Levin (2011) believes that collaborative marking is a

Table 7.1 Collaborative Marking of Students' Work: Modelled, Shared, Guided, Interdependent

Modelled	Shared	Guided	Interdependent
Leader discusses, and teachers decide on common assessment task; timetables allocate time for marking students' work; the team reaches consensus on success criteria and levels of work (e.g., Levels 1, 2, 3, or 4).	Teachers and leader organize work to be marked and set aside common planning time to mark the work together.	Teachers organize work; leader is present for support and to learn during the process alongside the teachers.	Teachers lead, with leader part of the team; teachers and administrators determine the instructional starting points for each learn er and clearly articulate next steps in learning through the "Descriptive Feedback" to be given to each student.

great impetus for both elementary and secondary school teachers to work together on the students' achievement agenda. In a recent teacher survey the Alberta Teachers' Association notes that 76% of teachers surveyed expressed considerable or high interest in "examining student work": "When teachers work with each other to examine student work and develop curricula, resources and plans, they all benefit from the collective experience, regardless of their career stage" (Alberta Teachers' Association, 2010). This leads us to a further discussion of the conditions under which successful transitions thrive, during which I will make four recommendations.

Recommendations and Conditions for Successful Transitions

Districts contribute most powerfully to teachers' and leaders' sense of efficacy in creating smooth transitions at every level by doing the following:

• Establishing clear purposes that become widely shared
• Unambiguously awarding priority to the improvement of instruction
• Providing flexible, varied, meaningful, and just-in-time professional development for both school administrators and their staffs

- Creating productive working relationships with all the major stakeholders
- Assisting schools in the collection, interpretation, and use of data for decision making (Louis et al., 2010, p. 84).

To this list, I add my own four recommendations for ensuring smooth transitions for teachers and students:

1 Use the 13 Parameters to be precise about improvement.
2 Use collaborative marking of students' work.
3 Use writing, especially non-fiction writing, as a catalyst.
4 Use co-teaching as a way to hone the artful craft of teaching and learning.

Let me briefly elaborate on each of the four recommendations I list above.

Using 13 Parameters to Be Precise about Improvement

I have discussed this concept in the body of this chapter. Briefly restated, the 13 Parameters are a filtering tool through which we can identify, using data, the areas of improvement needed to focus our work at the district, school, and classroom levels.

Using Collaborative Marking of Students' Work

Collaborative marking of students' work (called teacher moderation in some forums) is a way to see every student's "FACE" (Sharratt & Fullan, 2012) and also engage teachers in collaborative inquiry. From developing the common assessment to deciding on the levels on which to mark the work, the marking of students' work together gives teachers a clear focus on the next steps for each student – as agreed on by colleagues sitting around a table. The results then lead to clear, intentional, descriptive feedback to each student. This process has the power to transform teaching and propel each student forward.

Using Writing, Especially Non-fiction Writing, as a Catalyst

In *Realization* (Sharratt & Fullan, 2009, pp. 22–24), we said that, at the classroom level, successful elementary and secondary school teachers use the progression of modelled, shared, and guided practice in all of their teaching approaches to ensure that students experience scaffolded learning to become independent learners – and owners of their learning. This is particularly true in using writing to increase students' literacy achievement in every discipline. From my experience, an increased emphasis on writing, in many forms for all kinds of purposes, is a critical key to improving student learning. At every turn, we need to model the moral imperative of establishing writing as the hallmark of not only a literate graduate but of a literate society. Reeves (2010, pp. 73–74) strengthens my thinking by saying that we must consider the case of non-fiction, a powerful cross-disciplinary strategy that has consistently been linked to improved student achievement in reading comprehension, mathematics, science, and social studies.

It is an established fact that a majority in the United States need improved writing skills and that our failure to respond to this evidence causes employers and colleges to spend billions of dollars to address writing deficiencies. Where has that overwhelming quantitative case led? Kiuhara, Graham, and Hawken (2009) conducted a national study on the teaching of writing to high school students and found that evidence-based teaching practices to support writing were insufficiently used with any degree of frequency and depth. The teachers in the study claimed that they had not been sufficiently trained to teach writing, with a percentage of teachers believing that they were ill prepared in this subject directly related to their failure to apply writing strategies in the classroom. In other words, teachers do not do what they do not know.

Using Co-teaching to Hone the Artful Craft of Teaching and Learning

Co-teaching is one of the most powerful ways to improve teaching practice and implement the changes in assessment and instruction that I have researched, observed, and implemented. It pushes professionals to make their practices transparent and public in order to become increasingly more skilled, reflective, and thoughtful. It allows my first three recommendations above to be tried and observed and debriefed to refine changes in practice. As seen in Figure 7.1, the co-teaching cycle includes co-planning, co-teaching, co-debriefing, and co-reflecting (Sharratt & Fullan, 2009, 2012).

Some of our co-teaching partners are now meeting with students at the end of every term to have them reflect on what worked or was challenging for them, and what changes they, as students, would make to

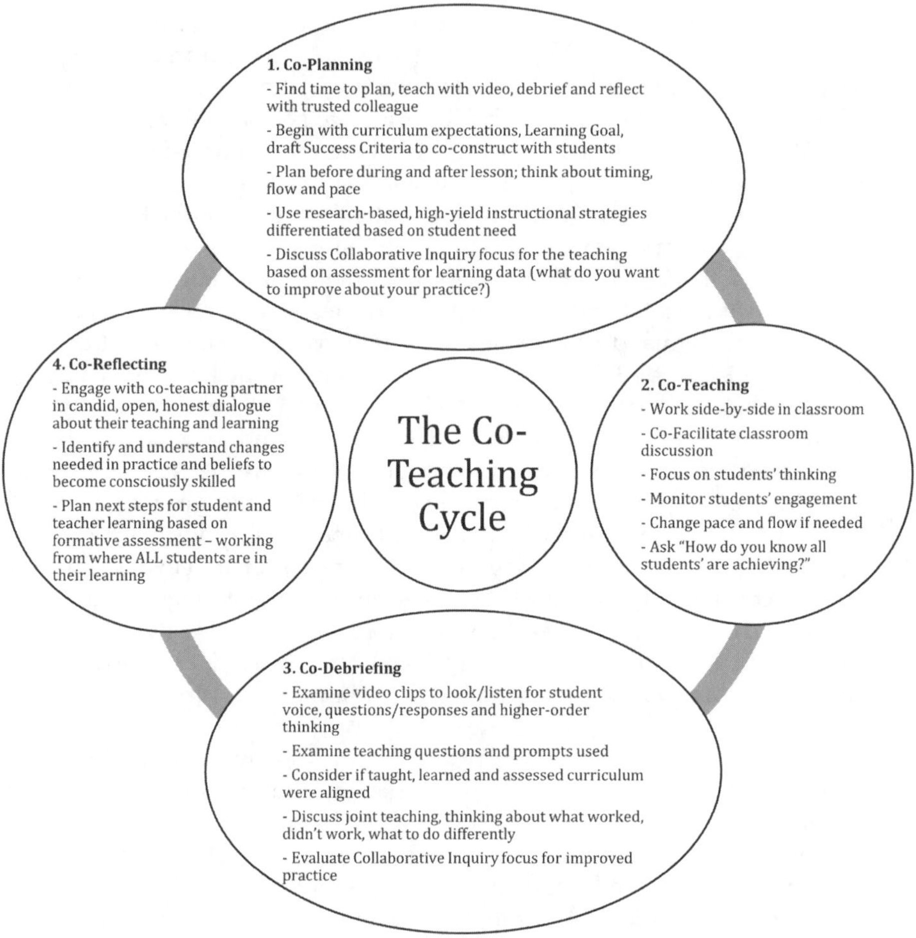

1. Co-Planning

- Find time to plan, teach with video, debrief and reflect with trusted colleague

- Begin with curriculum expectations, Learning Goal, draft Success Criteria to co-construct with students

- Plan before during and after lesson; think about timing, flow and pace

- Use research-based, high-yield instructional strategies differentiated based on student need

- Discuss Collaborative Inquiry focus for the teaching based on assessment for learning data (what do you want to improve about your practice?)

4. Co-Reflecting

- Engage with co-teaching partner in candid, open, honest dialogue about their teaching and learning

- Identify and understand changes needed in practice and beliefs to become consciously skilled

- Plan next steps for student and teacher learning based on formative assessment – working from where ALL students are in their learning

The Co-Teaching Cycle

2. Co-Teaching

- Work side-by-side in classroom

- Co-Facilitate classroom discussion

- Focus on students' thinking

- Monitor students' engagement

- Change pace and flow if needed

- Ask "How do you know all students' are achieving?"

3. Co-Debriefing

- Examine video clips to look/listen for student voice, questions/responses and higher-order thinking

- Examine teaching questions and prompts used

- Consider if taught, learned and assessed curriculum were aligned

- Discuss joint teaching, thinking about what worked, didn't work, what to do differently

- Evaluate Collaborative Inquiry focus for improved practice

Figure 7.1. The co-teaching cycle.

better meet students' needs. It has allowed teachers to be more aware of the critical importance of hearing students' voices and considering their viewpoints – thus clearly hearing from all FACES.

Discussion and Conclusion

I argue that the explicit methodology discussed here – assessment that informs instruction – is valid today and will be valid tomorrow. I believe that if sufficiently high performance or achievement standards are expected of learners and if sufficiently high quality training is available for and demanded of teachers, then twenty-first century learners will excel.

Emphatically, both of us believe that skill in *higher-order, critical thinking* is the additional foundational skill for twenty-first century teachers and students – the additional essential literacy skill that must intentionally accompany the ability to read, write, speak, listen, view, and represent (Sharratt & Fullan, 2012).

Many of us now use literacy and numeracy as our focus across all subject areas to provide a base for assessing student achievement and to provide a common language for all teachers to use in developing higher-order thinking skills within all content areas. The common language and the commonality of approaches embedded in the 13 Parameters enable and enforce the concept that every relevant bit of data shows the FACE of a student and that of his or her teacher both of whom deserve our praise and support. Furthermore, we also believe that every child can learn and every teacher can acquire new forms of instructional practice given the right support (Hill & Crévola, 1999). In *Realization* (Sharratt & Fullan, 2009) we introduced a 14th Parameter that I remind readers is equally critical for successful transitions. The 14th Parameter emphasizes the need for shared responsibility and accountability in literacy teaching and learning. As educators, we must all own the responsibility to give all of our learners the gift of literacy – a gift that will also support and enhance students' abilities to make successful transitions.

REFERENCES

Alberta Teachers' Association. (2010). *Professional learning for informed transformation: The 2010 professional development survey.* Calgary: Author.

Greenan, M. (2011a). The secret of success criteria. *Principal Connections, Ontario, 14*(3), 10–13.

Greenan, M. (2011b). *Teaching "big ideas" to little kids.* Mississauga, ON: Dufferin-Peel Catholic District School Board.

Hanson, R., & Farrell, D. (1995). The long-term effects on high school seniors of learning to read in kindergarten. *Reading Research Quarterly, 30*(4), 908–933.

Hattie, J. (2012). *Visible learning for teachers: Maximizing impact on learning.* New York: Routledge.

Hill, P.W., & Crévola, C.A. (1999). The role of standards in educational reform for the 21st century. In D.D. Marsh (Ed.), *ASCD Yearbook 1999: Preparing our schools for the 21st century* (pp. 117–142). Alexandria, VA: Association for Supervision and Curriculum Development.

Joyce, B., & Showers, B. (1995). *Student acheivement through staff development* (2nd ed.). White Plains, NY: Longman.

Kiuhara, S.A., Graham, S., & Hawken, L.S. (2009). Teaching writing to high school students: A national survey. *Journal of Educational Psychology, 101*(1), 136–160.

Levin, B. (2011). *More high school graduates: Helping more students succeed in secondary schools.* Thousand Oaks, CA: Corwin.

Louis, K.S., Leithwood, K., Wahlstrom, K., Anderson, S., Michlin, M., Mascall, B., … (2010). *Learning from districts' efforts to improve student achievement: Final report of research to the Wallace Foundation.* New York: Wallace Foundation.

Ontario Ministry of Education (OMoE). (2003). *A guide to effective instruction in reading: Kindergarten to grade 3.* Toronto: Queen's Printer.

Reeves, D.B. (2010). *Transforming professional development into student results.* Alexandria, VA: ASCD.

Reeves, D.B. (2011). *Elements of grading: A guide to effective practice.* Alexandria, VA: ASCD.

Sharratt, L. (2012). *Instructional walks and talks.* [Training Materials], Parramatta Diocese, New South Wales, Australia.

Sharratt, L., & Fullan, M. (2005). The school district that did the right things right. Annenberg Institute for School Reform, Brown University, *Voices in Urban Education*, Fall, 5–13.

Sharratt, L., & Fullan, M. (2006, Sept.). Accomplishing district wide reform. *Journal of School Leadership, 16*, 583–595.

Sharratt, L., & Fullan, M. (2009). *Realization: The change imperative for deepening district-wide reform.* Thousand Oaks, CA: Corwin.

Sharratt, L., & Fullan, M. (2012). *Putting FACES on the data: What great leaders do!* Thousand Oaks, CA: Corwin.

United Nations Educational, Scientific and Cultural Organization (UNESCO). (2003). *Literacy: A UNESCO perspective.* Retrieved from http://unesdoc .unesco.org/images/0013/001318/131817eo.pdf

Vygotsky, L.S. (1978). *Mind in society: The development of higher psychological processes.* Cambridge, MA: Harvard University Press. (Original work published 1934).

Wiliam, D. (2011). *Embedded formative assessment.* Bloomington, IN: Solution Tree.

8 Transitions in Elementary Mathematics Instruction

MARIAN SMALL

For more than 50 years, there has been increased attention in school mathematics to developing understanding rather than simply transmitting procedures (Hiebert et al., 1997) and to the use of manipulatives (Sowell, 1989; Marshall & Paul, 2008) and, more recently, to technology (Li & Ma, 2010) as important tools to support the building of mathematical understanding. This has affected mathematics instruction in the early elementary years in somewhat different ways than it has affected mathematics instruction in the later elementary years. Although primary teachers have embraced the use of manipulatives (Gilbert & Bush, 1988), manipulatives have been less welcome in many upper elementary school classrooms. Technology has, however, tended to be less common in the earlier elementary grades than in later elementary grades, although that may be changing with the use of tablet computers, which seem to suit young children as much as older ones.

In the past 30 years, the focus on teaching for understanding and the use of manipulatives and technology in mathematics learning has been accompanied by increased attention to teaching using a problem-solving approach (Hiebert et al., 1996; Lambdin, 2003; Hiebert, 2003; MacMath, Wallace, & Chi, 2009), and for the past 10 years, there has been increased attention to not only accepting, but encouraging students to create their own processes and procedures for calculating (Fuson & Burghardt, 2003; Lawson, 2007).

Again, the implementation has been somewhat different in the early elementary years as compared with the later elementary years. Although primary teachers have historically often presented fairly simple problems where students work for a short time and then discuss their thinking, upper elementary teachers have been more likely to show students how to perform some complex procedure like multiplying decimals, for example, and then assign seatwork (Handal, 2003). The change to a problem-solving approach has been a more difficult transition for upper elementary teachers.

Another difference between earlier and later elementary grades involves teacher comfort with asking students to use their own strategies rather than following teacher models. Primary teachers are more likely to encourage students to use their own approaches; upper elementary teachers are more likely to encourage standard approaches that teachers model (Carroll & Porter, 1998). Although some students seem to appreciate an environment where they can simply follow what is modelled, many students who had become accustomed to developing their own strategies in the early elementary years struggle more when alternate methods that make less sense to them are required.

The two driving forces for curriculum change and, as a result, instructional change in North American mathematics instruction have been documents produced by the National Council of Teachers of Mathematics (NCTM, 1989, 1991, 1995, 2000) and large-scale testing, particularly the Trends in International Mathematics and Science Study (TIMMS) (Olson, Martin, & Mullis, 2008), testing in which several Canadian provinces and many countries participate. The fact that the United States did not fare well internationally precipitated many changes in math education in the United States, some of which affected Canadian directions. Canada did relatively well (Education Quality and Accountability Office [EQAO], 2008), although not as well as some countries, and that has been a topic of conversation in Canadian mathematics education circles, as well.

Although many of the changes advocated in the various NCTM documents are 20 years old or more, it is truly only in the past 5–10 years when one could see the recommended approaches in a significant number of elementary school classrooms. And many teachers still struggle with these changes.

Changes in Teaching Approach

The four most significant changes in teaching approach in elementary mathematics, impacting both early and later elementary years, are the following:

- The focus on problem solving and conceptual understanding
- The focus on alternative, or personal, strategies rather than standard computational procedures
- The focus on improving students' level of mathematical communication
- The appreciation of the value of technology in mathematics instruction, even at the elementary level.

Focus on Problem Solving

As mentioned above, the focus on problem solving has been advocated for many years, but is truly just beginning to become commonplace in many classrooms. Teachers are starting to recognize the power of a student working through a problem without having been shown a model in order for that student to develop his or her own understanding of the mathematics involved (Chambers, 2002; Suurtamm & Vézina, 2008). The problems are designed to be within students' zones of proximal development (Vygotsky, 1934/1978), but requiring a cognitive stretch; after all, that's what learning really is.

For example, a problem that might be suitable for primary students might be something like:

When Keifer and Sally put together their pennies and counted them all, there were 20 pennies.
How many pennies did each have if Sally had 4 more pennies than Keifer?

Years ago, teachers might have felt the need to "start students off," for example, the teacher would have shown different combinations for 20 like 19 + 1 or 18 + 2, etc. Then the teacher would probably have suggested that students list all the possible combinations and choose the one that solves the problem. Today, teachers are more likely to provide counters and ask students to work together in pairs or small groups to solve the problem in whatever way makes sense to them. A problem suitable for upper elementary students, and one used by many teachers, is the following (see Figure 8.1):

Determine a rule for indicating the number of one-by-one tiles required to surround a square pool if you know the number of tiles

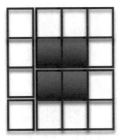

Figure 8.1. Pool and tiles problem.

on each side of the pool. The drawing provided shows that 12 tiles are required for a 2 × 2 pool.

Ten or 20 years ago, an upper elementary teacher would have not even considered presenting the pool problem until after students had been "shown" a similar problem. Today, teachers are more likely to provide square tiles and just let students work together to come up with a solution.

Part of that student learning, a part that is now considered very valuable, are missteps, situations where students make conjectures that don't work out, but where the students learn how to start over and try again (Hesketh, 1997).

For example, in the pool tile problem, seeing that 12 tiles are needed for a pool that uses 4 tiles, a student might easily assume that the number of tiles is always triple the pool size. Students learn to test that hypothesis by using a pool of a different size. They soon see, for example, using a 3 × 3 pool, that tripling does not work and then reconsider their solution. Note that there are 16 border tiles, *not* 3 × 9 = 27 border tiles (see Figure 8.2).

Notice that hand-in-hand with a focus on problem solving comes a focus on conceptual understanding (Sullivan, 2011). No longer are students just applying rules that have been given, but they are creating mathematical ideas; they are thinking about why various relationships or strategies do or do not make sense, the basis of conceptual understanding.

There seems to be an increasing interest on the part of later elementary teachers in a problem-solving approach at this point in time. One

Figure 8.2. Pool and tiles problem extended.

of the differences, though, is that at the upper elementary levels, the problems tend to be more complex, often wordier. Some upper elementary students find it hard to muster up the perseverance to work their way through a challenging problem or to provide enough detail about what they did and why they did it.

Barriers to Using This Approach and Possible Solutions

There are a number of reasons that teachers struggle with adopting a problem-solving approach, particularly teachers at the upper elementary level. Some of these reasons relate to teachers' beliefs about mathematics (Ernest, 1989; van der Sandt, 2007) and some are more about practicality. Helping teachers become aware of their beliefs might be the first step to changing them (Mewborn & Cross, 2007).

But some teachers, no matter how curricula have changed, find it difficult, if not impossible, to overcome the assumptions that underpinned their own mathematical training – the belief that children will not be able to solve mathematical problems without being shown how. They see mathematics as simply too complex for a child to "invent" on his or her own. In addition, they worry about whether they are properly preparing students for secondary mathematics instruction if they adopt a more exploratory approach.

It is likely impossible for anyone to believe that a strategy will work by just reading about it; most of us need to see it work in our own situations. Teachers have to take the risk of trying a few times to see what happens. A teacher needs to present an appropriate problem for students to solve, provide opportunities for students to work together, make available appropriate tools and manipulatives, and offer support, while visibly exhibiting confidence that students can solve the problem. Trying a few times convinces most teachers that this approach not only works but it engages students more deeply.

Many teachers are not convinced that problem solving is the focus of mathematics learning. Sometimes they observe older students with very little number sense and attribute this lack of number sense to previous teachers' problem-solving approaches, whether that is a valid assumption or not. They continue to believe that calculation is still the focus of elementary school mathematics and without a great deal of practice, students will not successfully learn to calculate; they assume that problem solving will not provide that practice time and that more dedicated practice time is required, leaving little time for a problem-solving approach. Or they believe that if students regularly solve problems that take a long time, there just won't be time left to cover the full curriculum.

Using problems that involve significant computation can help a teacher see that this is a way to practice computational skills. For example, asking students to solve the problem below not only encourages problem solving but practices computational skills.

A set of chairs is arranged in an array. Altogether, there are 144 chairs. How many rows could there have been? List as many possibilities as you can.

Transition Issues

A significant transition issue is the fact that upper elementary level students are faced with more difficult problems than primary students, often presented as a series of many, long sentences; many students just give up. A possible tactic might be the posing of problems that are suitable for a broader range of students across the elementary years. In this way, the problems are likely to be less complicated and more accessible, building student confidence.

For example, teachers in Grades 2 or 3 to Grade 7 or 8 could all agree to present the same problem to their students to solve, making students aware that this is happening. Opportunities could be provided for students at different levels to share solutions.

An example of a suitable problem might be something like this:

Lindsay had 10 coins worth $5.
What could the coins have been?

Presenting problems for upper elementary students orally or pictorially, as would be the case with primary students, rather than only in verbal form, can also encourage students who are intimidated by too many words. It makes the transition from the primary problem solver to the upper elementary problem solver easier. For example, compare the visual (see Figure 8.3) and verbal forms of the same problem.

Verbal form: *Each school day, Mike is awake for 2/3 of the time and he spends 1/4 of the time at school or on the school bus. What fraction of the day does Mike have left for other activities?*

Eventually teachers can present problems involving more text, but it would be wise to wait until students have built up a willingness to pursue problems.

Many would argue that it is important that problems be contextual to be of interest to students. It is important to remember two things:

1 A real-life context does not necessarily generate interest. It is quite possible that a context of interest to one student may not be of interest to another student.
2 There is a "puzzle" aspect to mathematics that is attractive to many students, and these puzzle-type problems can actually be more interesting to some students than contextual problems. For example, asking students to determine the values of A, B, C, and D that would make the following equation true, $4 \times ABCD = DCBA$, can be an interesting challenge for some students. Notice that many of these puzzle-type problems take little time to present to students, and have obvious starting points, making them attractive to upper elementary students.

Focus on Personal Strategies

Many adults in today's society learned mathematics in a more procedural way. They learned, for example, that there is a "best way" to add

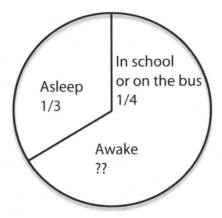

Figure 8.3. Mike's daily activities problem
(visual form).

or multiply whole numbers, a "best way" to divide fractions, etc. These beliefs are strongly held by many since they were so regularly reinforced in their mathematics instruction. For example, most people learned that the "best way" to subtract two whole numbers is to start at the right and "borrow" if necessary. For example:

$$\begin{array}{r} \overset{3\ \ 10\ \ 12}{\cancel{4}\cancel{1}\cancel{2}} \\ -\ 138 \\ \hline 274 \end{array}$$

Clearly, this gets the right answer, but who is to say it's best? In fact, if subtracting 299 from 300, this traditional approach is much, much less efficient than realizing 300 is the next number, so the difference has to be 1. Many others would even consider it more inefficient than a more additive approach to subtracting 138 from 412, wherein students might add 250 + 12 + 10 + 2, to get a total difference of 274 (see Figure 8.4).

There is now research to confirm that if students develop their own approaches to a problem, their understanding of what they did will be more meaningful to them and will make more sense (Carpenter, Fennema, Franke, Levi, & Empson, 1999; Carroll & Porter, 1997; Clarke, 2005; Hedrén, 1999). In addition, it is possible that their approach could be more efficient in certain circumstances.

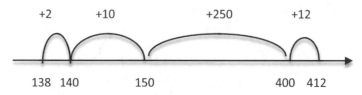

Figure 8.4. An alternative additive student approach to subtraction.

Barriers to Promoting Personal Strategies and Possible Solutions

As with adopting a problem-solving approach, some teachers are simply not confident that students will develop valuable personal strategies to share. Teachers have often seen students who passively wait to be shown how to do things, so they really don't expect students to be able to develop strategies prior to modelling.

Beliefs are difficult to change without evidence, so evidence needs to be gathered to convince teachers who are reluctant to promote personal strategies and investigation to move in that direction. There are increasing resources, both print and digital, that provide evidence that students not only can, but do enjoy developing and sharing their strategies (Fosnot & Dolk, 2001; Huinker, Freckman, & Steinmeyer, 2003). Teachers often marvel at the ingenious ideas students develop to tackle a calculation or a problem. There is also evidence that students who use standard algorithms are easily confused (Ashlock, 2006; Cobb, 1991; Nagel & Swingen, 1998; Narode, Board, & Davenport, 1993; Scharton, 2004).

Other teachers may worry about student sharing of incomplete or even incorrect strategies, or the sharing of too many strategies, thereby confusing other students. Teachers often suggest that the time required to let everyone share is simply not available.

Because time is a constraint, teachers have to learn how to decide which and how many and whose strategies are shared. One thing we know is that the quality of the strategies proposed improves if students work with one another and serve as mentors to each other. This group work not only improves the quality of what is shared, but reduces the number of strategies shared. Several educators have provided guidance on how to lead a discussion on these multiple strategies, including Fosnot and Dolk (2001), whose conception of a "math congress" involves a teacher carefully selecting certain pieces of work to bring out important ideas, and the Japanese "Bansho" approach, which has been adapted in Ontario and is currently used in many classrooms (Ontario Ministry of Education [OMoE], Literacy Numeracy Secretariat, 2010). In this latter approach, students' work is sorted in terms of similarity of strategy, posted, and discussed, again with a teacher choosing which solutions should be discussed since clearly not all solutions can be. Either of these or similar alternate approaches provide students opportunities to find strategies that suit their styles.

And some teachers worry that there really is a best strategy and they are wasting valuable teaching time by not focusing on that strategy and providing sufficient time to practise it. This is probably more common at the upper elementary levels than early elementary levels. In fact, in different countries, different algorithms, or procedures, are standard, so clearly there is no universal best strategy anyway.

Transition Issues

There seems to be a marked difference in the willingness of early elementary and later elementary teachers in acceptance of a focus on personal strategies. Early elementary teachers tend to be more willing to encourage personal strategies than upper elementary teachers. Perhaps, it is because later elementary teachers feel that exploration time is meant to be in the early years, but then it's time to "get serious." This can cause difficulty for students who had previously been encouraged and are then discouraged from forging their own approaches.

There is also a difference in the early and later years in the complexity of the mathematics. Research tells us that many upper elementary teachers themselves struggle with the content of the mathematics they are teaching, particularly with topics involving fractions and decimals (Ma, 1999). Allowing students to use their own strategies puts the teacher in the potentially uncomfortable position that she or he will have to deal with an unexpected approach in a content area in which she or he is uncomfortable; many teachers avoid this.

Depending on students' experiences, some older students virtually demand that teachers "just show me how to do it." If students have had experiences where ultimately there is a singular approach to problems, they don't want to waste their time on approaches that the teachers won't accept in the long run. This sort of attitude emerges particularly when teachers who allow multiple approaches indicate, ultimately, which solutions are unacceptable and the few (or only one) that are acceptable for use.

The most important tack a teacher can take to encourage personal strategies in the upper elementary years is to equally value all correct strategies and not label them as more or less efficient. This labelling undermines a student's willingness to share what may be viewed as inefficient.

Teachers who are reluctant to allow this type of thinking in topics where they are less comfortable benefit from removing themselves from the position of arbiter. Instead of feeling the need to evaluate the student's approach, that teacher can simply ask questions, such as:

- What did the rest of you like about [name of student]'s approach?
- What did you wonder about?
- Who else used an approach like [name of student]'s?
- Tell us why you chose that approach.

Teachers also, of course, benefit from remembering that they, too, are learners, and could and should be reading more about the alternatives students are likely to use in various mathematical situations.

Focus on Communication

Because students no longer simply perform calculations with single answers, there is a lot more to talk about in math class than there used to be. Students are likely to share their strategies, their reasoning, and their representations. Even high-stakes tests (EQAO, 2011) are requiring students to communicate mathematically. All regions of Canada have included communication as a critical math process, and some provinces and territories encourage teachers to separately assess mathematical communication.

What we value in communication should be less about using precise mathematical terms, and more about making process and reasoning clear and understandable to the reader. In current elementary school classrooms, there is a much greater tendency than in the past to have students describe their problem-solving processes and to explain their reasoning.

For example, a Grade 2 student might be asked:

What kind of picture could you draw to show whether 38 or 83 is greater?
How does your picture show this?

A Grade 6 student might be asked:

Imagine looking at a picture that somehow shows that two groups are in the ratio 3:5. What other ratios can be found in that picture? Explain your thinking.

Communication tends to be oral and pictorial in the early elementary grades and is more likely written, although sometimes still oral, in the later elementary years.

Barriers to Promoting Richer Mathematical
Communication and Possible Solutions

There are a number of barriers to richer mathematical communication. Among them are the following:

- A classroom environment where teachers do a lot of the talking and really don't leave space for students to say that much
- A lack of modelling of what good communication looks like
- Mixed signals about what good communication sounds like (e.g., sometimes teachers accept oral answers that they do not accept in writing or vice versa, so students are confused about what is or is not acceptable)
- A culture where risk taking is not encouraged or is frequently met with criticism, so that students are nervous about taking the chance of saying something wrong
- An undue focus on the format/structure/punctuation, etc. of the communication
- A lack of appropriate tasks where communication makes sense
- A teacher's fear that the direction of the conversation may veer to a place where she or he does not have the required knowledge to bring to bear.

There is a fair bit of literature on the creation of what are typically called *rich math talk learning communities*. This term is used to describe a classroom culture where it is common for students to confidently converse about their mathematical thinking. For example, Hufferd-Ackles, Fuson, and Sherin (2004) documented the steps to building a math talk learning community. They point to the key role questioning plays, where teachers move from questions that seek answers to questions that seek the thinking behind the answers, and where teachers encourage students to ask each other questions. They point to increased attention to asking students to explain their thinking and a greater likelihood that the development of the content flows from student ideas.

Richer communication cannot evolve unless teachers choose to speak less, leaving space for students to speak more. But teachers could choose to model what good communication looks like. They might, for example, indicate what is good about the way a student chose to explain something; they might describe a theoretical solution of their own, in student voice, to help students hear how it would be explained, or they might take an incompletely explained idea and show students what questions they might ask themselves to improve their communication.

Teachers can revoice a student response, clarifying it a bit, could have one student repeat what another says, could ask students to add on to other responses, and, most importantly, could provide wait time so students have time to think about their responses (Chapin & O'Connor, 2007).

Without being overly critical, teachers need to question responses that are really not clear. For example, suppose a teacher asks students: *Why doesn't it matter in which order you multiply numbers?* and a student responds, *4 × 3 is 12 and so is 3 × 4*. It is critical that the teacher keeps probing, e.g., *Can you be sure it will be true with other numbers? How?* or, *How many more examples would you need to try before you're pretty sure it's always true? Are you sure that's enough?*

Teachers can physically rearrange their classrooms so that students are sitting with one, two, or three other students (Dowling, 2009). In this way, students are first communicating in a smaller, safer environment, making it more comfortable to share with a larger group later. Using a document camera to focus on students' work so that it can be shown and shared can also create much more math dialogue.

Most importantly, teachers have to take risks; they have to be willing to allow a mathematical conversation to go into uncharted territory. To make it somewhat less uncomfortable, teachers can do a few things. One is to work at gaining more knowledge of mathematics for teaching so that they become more comfortable with the content. Another is to trust that students are true partners and that it may be the students, not the teacher, who will make the ideas become clear. For example, if one student says something a teacher is not sure about, she or he can ask the student to explain her or his thinking or can ask other students their opinion on what has been said. Often the ideas are completely clarified in this conversation.

To attain a rich math talk learning community, students also have to take risks, and this only becomes likely in an environment where students know that errors are not treated as mistakes, but as steps towards success. For example, sometimes students make a statement and a teacher will ask others if they agree or disagree, and why. Students learn that it is completely okay if others disagree and that, through the conversation, ideas are clarified. Teachers learn to question answers, whether they are correct or incorrect, to probe more deeply, so students realize that they are treated the same way whether their responses are on target or not.

Transition Issues

Often, primary teachers encourage primarily oral communication. This is often safer for students, who can use the teacher's reaction to each statement to help him or her adjust what is said. Upper elementary teachers generally require written communication of responses either instead of or in addition to oral communication. This is more difficult for students, and so they sometimes say as little as possible in their written responses. Teachers can focus more on oral communication and, if they wish a more permanent record, can either allow students to record their oral responses or encourage pictorial representations instead of verbal responses as a transition. This may encourage more students to attempt to "say" more.

Teachers in the upper elementary years also tend to attach grades to a greater proportion of the work students do (as will be discussed below). Again, this tends to inhibit communication; students say as little as they can to avoid saying anything wrong that will lower their grade. Providing opportunities to communicate mathematically that are more risk free, as is often the case in the primary years, is a helpful transition for many students.

Acceptance and Appreciation of the Value of Manipulatives and Technology in School Mathematics

For the past 40 years, there has been encouragement to teach mathematics with the use of manipulatives (Sowell, 1989; Marshall & Paul, 2008). Tools as simple as counters, or as deliberately constructed as base 10 blocks, rekenreks, and pattern blocks are used to help students embody the abstract concepts of mathematics concretely.

Many teachers, particularly primary teachers, regularly use counters or other materials; however, use of manipulatives in upper elementary grades is mixed. Embraced by some teachers, many teachers do not see the value of manipulatives or worry that using manipulatives may make it more difficult for students to adapt to secondary instruction. Upper elementary teachers often will allow students to use the materials, but suggest that they are more suitable for students who are struggling with math, and not for others.

Technology, however, is viewed in a very different way. One of the major changes in the twenty-first century has been the prevalence of very powerful technology and young people's comfort with it. Many of the topics we learned, and the way we learned them, are relatively irrelevant in this day and age. For example, years ago, our grandparents learned how to divide very large numbers by large numbers (e.g., 4,214 ÷ 23) by hand. This skill seems irrelevant now, since calculators are available virtually everywhere and to all. It still is important, though, that students understand in what situation this calculation is important and what a reasonable estimate might be.

Other digital tools allow students to measure geometric shapes, perform geometric transformations and constructions, tile spaces with pattern blocks, use virtual base 10 blocks to model numbers, and instantly create equivalent fractions, etc. Still other tools allow a teacher to randomly generate as many "practice" questions as he or she might wish. Rather than banning these devices, more and more teachers are embracing them and using them to pose more interesting and meaningful problems for students (Moyer, Niezgoda, & Stanley, 2005).

"Clickers" allow students to respond to teacher questions anonymously, but still allow the teacher to see the class profile. A teacher can use this technology to minimize risk to individual students while gathering diagnostic information about what students know.

The use of interactive white boards has had a dramatic effect on mathematics instruction. These tools offer both visual and tactile gratification – students see, in bright and clear colours, the objects or words being discussed, but they can also touch the board and physically move objects around to work through mathematical concepts. From a more practical point of view, they allow teachers to save the work of a lesson for students who miss a class and post it on the Internet, as well as record the mathematical conversations students have as they stand near the board.

There is a wonderful immediacy when using interactive white boards. If, for example, one wants to see how a diagram is affected by changing the scale, it can be shown instantly. If one wants to have enough base 10 thousand cubes to model a big number like 23412, it is easy to "clone" a cube and show the number (few classrooms have enough cubes to do this).

Technology also has the power of allowing students and teachers to interact over long distances and share teaching ideas in ways that were not possible before. For example, in some jurisdictions, classes are connected by technology and two teachers in different locations co-teach a lesson to both rooms. The students talk to each other, ask each other questions, and each teacher learns from the other teacher.

Web-based technology and interactive white boards are used in both early elementary and late elementary school classrooms, although often calculators are reserved for late elementary school classrooms, if used at all.

Barriers to Acceptance and Appreciation of the Value of Manipulatives and Technology in School Mathematics and Possible Solutions

Tools are most useful to students when those tools are readily accessible and when there are choices about what tool to use. If students have to go to another location to get manipulatives, or if only a limited number are provided, students are less likely to use them. Clearly, one solution to this problem is to provide a variety of materials in small bins readily accessible to students. Another solution is to use virtual manipulatives, manipulatives on a computer screen. These can be accessed at home as well as in school, and in a classroom with a fair bit of technology, they can be accessed by many students without a great financial outlay and without storage issues.

Some teachers have had relatively little experience with manipulatives, and they are hesitant to use them since they are not sure how they are best used and feel that they cannot appropriately model for students. There are many on-line videos as well as written materials showing how such tools are used. Teachers can, and should, also allow free exploration time when new manipulatives are introduced; many times, students figure out, on their own, how the tools work.

It is interesting that although many teachers are embracing some technologies, for example, interactive white boards, they are still reluctant to allow the use of calculators in their classrooms (Houssart, 2000). Some indicate that they have seen children go through elementary school not becoming proficient at calculations and blame the availability of calculators for creating what they see as a serious deficiency.

There exists a fair bit of research that shows that performance of students is not harmed when calculators are used in classrooms appropriately (Pomerantz, 1997). This begs the question for some about what appropriate use is; generally, the notion is that calculators are used for exploration or calculators are used when the focus is on a real-life problem with "difficult" numbers.

Calculators might be used for straightforward calculations, but normally, not for students who are just learning these procedures, unless those students have particular learning disabilities that require them. Often procedures are taught more to build and exercise number sense than for their own sake, so the ultimate goal is not to develop high levels of proficiency with complicated paper and pencil calculations.

It is helpful if teachers read the relevant research, but teachers can make judicious decisions about when to use calculators and see for themselves the excitement students have in solving a real problem they could not solve without a calculator, for example, how many hours old they are.

Some teachers worry about equity: what if some students cannot have access to technology, should anyone? As technology becomes less expensive and more accessible, equity becomes somewhat less of an issue. A large proportion of students have access to technology even at home or in public libraries. More and more school districts are purchasing sets of tablets or netbooks to make them useful to all students.

Some teachers are uncomfortable that their students may be more proficient with the technology than they are, and that they may not look professional or knowledgeable enough to their students. Although some teachers worry about whether they will not seem proficient enough with technology to their students, others take just the opposite approach; they welcome the opportunity to empower their students to be the leaders, even sometimes the instructors, in a classroom.

Still other teachers wonder whether the scarce dollars sometimes available to an education system are best spent on technology as compared with other things, such as smaller class size or more professional development for teachers. Teacher concern about dollars spent on technology may well be valid, but given that the money is likely going to be spent anyway, it makes sense to make the most of it rather than treat it as an impediment to the use of that technology.

Transition Issues

Primary teachers are generally likely to provide support of manipulatives in their mathematics instruction; however, this is not as prevalent in upper elementary grades. This lack of support can negatively impact many of these upper elementary students. Ideally, staff at a school might work together to consider how the same purchased manipulatives could be used as students move up the grades. Students would then be comfortable with those manipulatives without a lot of additional instruction, although new manipulatives could certainly also be introduced for new topics.

Placing manipulatives in a readily accessible location in a classroom where a student can unobtrusively choose to use or not use them is a good way to encourage the use of manipulatives, whether during instruction or during assessment. Teachers modelling with manipulatives will make it clear that manipulatives are valued. What is most important is ensuring that the impression is not given that manipulatives are only used as a last resort.

As mentioned above, there is definitely an increased tolerance for use of calculators in the upper elementary grades. Some students become so excited that they can use their calculators, they use them for everything, but this is really not good and can actually inhibit the development of number sense. It is critical that teachers at the upper elementary levels take the time to discuss when calculators are appropriate and when not.

For example, for the vast majority of students, it is not ideal to use a calculator to determine 4 × 3, but is very appropriate to use them in calculations when numbers are big. But students need to know why, and teachers need to explain this. It is valuable to have conversations about when calculators are useful and when it is better to use mental math.

Changes in Resources

Elementary school teachers in the past, particularly at the upper elementary level, were likely to use a textbook as their main teaching resource; now, however, many more teachers are using the sample problems provided in curriculum documents or shared in school districts as a main teaching resource.

In the early elementary years, this is not a dramatic change. For a long time, primary teachers have used teacher resource materials to help them shape lessons, but they did not necessarily follow the lessons literally, nor use student texts. Teachers who did follow textbooks more closely tended to struggle more as officials began to ask them to take more initiative and use textbooks to get ideas, but not to follow page by page.

Barriers to Acceptance of Less Reliance on Texts and Possible Solutions

A number of teachers are reluctant to rely less on texts because of the security the text affords them. They assume, as might be reasonable, that they are not experts in math, that the authors probably are, and that they are doing their students a service by delivering lessons based on the experts' materials.

They also struggle with having the time to create lessons from scratch each day. Elementary school teachers usually have to prepare to teach many subjects in a day, and they simply do not feel they have adequate time to devote long hours to each preparation. A textbook is seen to do some of the prep for them.

One solution is to use the ideas they might find in a text lesson, but adapt them and deliver them in a more personal style. That may actually feel more authentic to their students.

Another solution is to collaborate with colleagues, thereby sharing the planning. Many teachers have found that this is a very valuable way to plan lessons.

With the availability of so much material on the Internet (although some of it is not, of course, vetted), teachers have much more choice for locating teaching materials that might appeal to themselves and their students. That is just as true at the upper elementary level as in the early elementary years.

Transition Issues

As mentioned above, teachers of younger grades tend to be less text dependent. They recognize that many children at that age respond better to oral presentation than having to wade through written text. Teachers of older elementary students, however, tend to feel that the content gets complicated enough that texts – particularly ones that "tell students what to do" – provide appropriate and even necessary reference for students. These teachers, particularly, may benefit by working with colleagues to create lessons.

Because texts are often introduced at the Grade 3 level, many Grade 3 teachers notice that students struggle in moving back and forth between questions in a text to answering the questions in a notebook. This has motivated some of these teachers to stop using texts and to create their own approaches to the lesson.

Changes in Assessment

The nature of assessment in mathematics has changed significantly over the past 10 years. One of the biggest changes has been a move from norm-referenced reporting to criterion-referenced reporting. In other words, rather than comparing students with one another and ranking them within a class, teachers are asked to compare the performance of each student against teaching expectations and/or outcomes; in this scenario, a very successful classroom could have all high marks since all students would have met the criteria.

There is much more attention to assessment for learning and assessment as learning and not just assessment of learning (Brookhart, Moss, & Long, 2008; Chappuis & Chappuis, 2008; Clark, 2010; Ginsburg, 2009; Western and Northern Canadian Protocol [WNCP], 2006). Teachers use information gathered while watching and listening to students to help them make informed decisions about what their students know and what is still out of reach (Black & Wiliam, 1998; Shafer & Romberg, 1999). There is also much more use of constructive feedback in assessment, rather than just grades (Boaler, 2009).

Increasingly, there is attention to assessing process knowledge and higher-level thinking (Kulm, 1990) rather than simply factual knowledge or low-level applications. As a result, because it is fairly difficult to pin down extremely fine differences in the ability to reason, problem solve, communicate, etc., there is a much greater willingness to use rubrics based on performance on significant tasks rather than percent marks on tests and quizzes (Liliburn & Clurak, 2010).

Barriers to Changes in Assessment Practice and Possible Solutions

Parents and the community at large often value what is more familiar. Some parents would rather know their child's mark is 85% or 87% and how that compares with other students rather than specifically what their child can or cannot do. They are not really familiar with the notion that it is performance against criteria and not a comparison with other students that is being measured. This is not that surprising in the competitive society in which we live, but serves to make it difficult for a teacher who has recognized that it might be more instructive, and more fair, to measure students' performance against what was being taught.

One solution is to remind parents of what is being measured and why. Teachers can help parents see that knowing that a student is performing at or above expectation is what should matter most.

Many teachers believe that virtually every piece of work a student does should be graded; their focus is on assessment of learning. Conversations with other teachers and personal experience are often helpful to show that fewer pieces of work need to be graded to have reliable information and to realize that grading fewer pieces actually frees students to take more risks and learn more. Teachers can study student responses together and discuss what those responses tell them about those students' thinking and how that could impact their instructional directions with those students.

Many teachers who are uncomfortable with the change to rubrics from percent marks cite the fact that students will be faced with percent marks later, so why not get used to them. They also often feel that marks should be based on "objective" criteria and so feel that questions should be tight enough that points can be assigned. It helps to realize that a student with a mark of 90% on a test could easily have had a mark of 92% had one question been changed, but a student with a level 4 (above expectation) performance on one task would almost certainly have had that level on a similar task; in other words, rubric marks are more reliable. This actually might be seen as making them more objective.

It is also important to realize that percent marks for processes like communication or reasoning are not terribly meaningful. What is the difference between an 84% and an 87% on communication anyway?

Transition Issues

Teachers in the early elementary years tend to provide anecdotal feedback to students rather than "marks." This sort of feedback helps students to re-focus their learning efforts. When students are given marks, they tend to focus on the number received, not what they understood or didn't understand. This can be fairly devastating for some students whose marks are low and even a student with high marks tends to focus on what he or she did wrong, and not celebrate what was done well.

A longer transition from anecdotal comments to marks might serve the interests of students in all of the elementary years, as would feedback that probes rather than evaluates. For example, if a student responds to a question about whether prime numbers are even or odd by saying they are odd, instead of pointing out that they forgot about the number 2, more constructive feedback might be: *How did you decide they were odd? How many and which primes did you think about?* This puts the onus back on the student to do more thinking rather than just looking at how many points he or she got for the answer.

Increased Attention to Differentiated Instruction

It is certainly not new that teachers face classrooms where students differ significantly in their academic readiness for what is being taught. What is different is that there is greater pressure on teachers than there used to be to deal with that reality by actually providing varied instruction, depending on students needs. This is often referred to as differentiating instruction. It normally does not mean individualized instruction, where 25 students are doing 25 different things, but might well mean that teachers adapt tasks to better suit the different types of students they have.

Although differentiating instruction has been, until fairly recently, more popular in other subjects than in math, lately, there has been more attention to differentiating instruction in math. Initially, the attention was on differentiating based on learning styles, but increasingly, the differentiation is based on complexity of task.

I have been one of the people doing a fair bit of work on what are called "open questions" and "parallel tasks" to accomplish this differentiation in a manageable way (Small, 2009) in math, something an increasing number of teachers in North America are doing. The idea is that teachers ask questions that are open enough to be addressed by students at many different readiness levels or provide two similar, but differentially complex, tasks as a choice. For example, an open question related to multiplication for a Grade 5 student might be: *Choose two numbers to multiply. Create a story problem that is solved by doing that multiplication.* Students can use whatever numbers are more comfortable for them, but they would all still be dealing with what multiplication means.

Two parallel tasks might be offered, instead, where students have a choice of creating a story to match the calculation 8 × 10 or to match the calculation 22 × 34. This is an alternate way to address student differences. One might worry that it is not "fair" that some students end up doing what is generally perceived to be an easier question, but if the focus is not on the actual calculation, but when multiplication is used, these tasks really both fit the bill. The value of posing both tasks is that although all students get to see that the same meanings of multiplication are attached to both smaller and larger numbers, the struggling students are not intimidated by the numbers involved in their selected task.

Barriers to Differentiating Instruction and Some Solutions

A number of teachers shy away from differentiating instruction because they feel they cannot manage many "small" lessons within the limited amount of time they have with their students and because they worry that some students will be off-task if they are not being monitored as the teacher works with other students. One solution to this is using the more open-ended type of question or using parallel tasks so that the teacher is interacting with all students at the same time, but also addressing the needs of subgroups of students in the classroom. Another solution is to set up a problem-solving environment where students are more accustomed to working with peers reasonably independently, with only some interaction with the teacher, as the teacher works with other students.

Some teachers shy away from differentiation because they feel bound by a set of curriculum expectations or outcomes that significantly limit what they feel is appropriate to present to their students. Although, of course, teachers are legally responsible to teach their provincial or territorial curriculum, if a student is not ready for what is expected, it makes more sense to build a solid foundation so that eventually those ideas can be taught meaningfully rather than to deliver something that means nothing to the student anyway.

Still other teachers feel that it is not fair to allow students to do different tasks. For these teachers, open tasks might be more suitable than parallel tasks; all students are doing the same thing.

Transition Issues

Although early elementary students arrive at school with different levels of readiness for what they are to learn in math, the differences between students' academic readiness in math seems to grow and grow. In a Grade 6 class, a teacher typically has students operating anywhere from what might be termed a Grade 2 to a Grade 8 level. Ignoring those differences between students becomes much more of a struggle the higher the grade level. It is even more important, then, that teachers of upper elementary students adopt differentiation strategies to better serve the needs of their students.

One related and significant issue is that as the mathematics content becomes more complex, for example, involving fractions and decimals, teachers worry more and more about using open questions. Their concern is that the content is uncomfortable for them too, and students might go in directions for which they are not prepared. This was discussed above, in terms of how important it is for teachers to take risks.

Furthermore, students who enter school in Kindergarten or Grade 1 have no preconceived notions about what school should be like. But as students go through the system, some become uncomfortable if teachers start behaving differently from what they expect. For example, if students are accustomed to very straightforward questions, they are not sure how to handle differentiated questions that are more open and may, as a result, demonstrate resistance or off-task behaviour. Teachers of upper elementary grades might have to work harder to reassure students that they truly will accept and actually welcome a variety of responses before students become comfortable enough to respond.

Summary

This chapter has focused on how mathematics instruction has changed in the elementary years, barriers for teachers in adapting to these changes, and how those changes create transition problems for both students and teachers. Topics addressed include calls for changes in teaching approach, particularly a focus on conceptual teaching and on teaching through problem solving, calls for the encouragement of diverse approaches rather than uniformity from students, a recognition of the much more significant role of communication in mathematics, and a recognition of the increased role of technology in mathematics and the resulting influence on pedagogy. Also discussed were changes in the nature of resources accessible to teachers, changes in the education culture's beliefs about what we should assess and how we should assess it, and a much stronger societal requirement that the needs of all students, even struggling ones, need to be addressed.

All of these changes and calls for change impact what we see in class-rooms and what we hear discussed in staff rooms, although perhaps none as much as the focus on differentiated instruction and the encour-agement of diversity, rather than uniformity, in our approaches to mathematics instruction.

That said, one thing has not changed: teachers make a significant dif-ference in student success in math (Marzano, 2003). Teachers must be supported and encouraged in order to help our children. It is clear from the earlier sections that the changes that we want require teachers' pro-fessional commitment to developing their knowledge of mathematics for teaching and require that education systems provide opportunities for teachers to do so.

REFERENCES

Ashlock, R.B. (2006). *Error patterns in computation: Using error patterns to improve instruction* (9th ed.). Upper Saddle River, NJ: Pearson.
Black, P., & Wiliam, D. (1998). Inside the black box: Raising standards through classroom assessment. *Phi Delta Kappan, 80*, 139–148.
Boaler, J. (2009). *What's math got to do with it?* New York: Viking.
Brookhart, S., Moss, C., & Long, B. (2008). Formative assessment that empow-ers. *Educational Leadership, 66*, 52–57.
Carpenter, T.P., Fennema, E., Franke, M.L., Levi, L., & Empson, S.B. (1999). *Children's mathematics: Cognitively guided instruction.* Portsmouth, NH: Heinemann.
Carroll, W.M., & Porter, D. (1997). Invented algorithms can develop meaning-ful mathematical procedures. *Teaching Children Mathematics, 37*, 370–374.
Carroll, W.M., & Porter, D. (1998). Alternative algorithms for whole-number operations. In L.J. Morrow & M.J. Kenney (Eds.), *The teaching and learning of algorithms in school mathematics* (pp. 106–114). Reston, VA: National Council of Teachers of Mathematics.
Chambers, D.L. (2002). Direct modeling and invented procedures: Building on students' informal strategies. In D.L. Chambers (Ed.), *Putting research into practice in the elementary grades* (pp. 12–15). Reston, VA: National Council of Teachers of Mathematics.
Chapin, S.H., & O'Connor, C. (2007). Academically productive talk: Support-ing students' learning in mathematics. In W.G. Martin, M.E. Strutchens, & P.C. Elliott (Eds.), *The learning of mathematics* (pp. 113–128). Reston, VA: National Council of Teachers of Mathematics.

Chappuis, S., & Chappuis, J. (2008). The best value in formative assessment. *Educational Leadership, 65*, 14–18.

Clark, I. (2010). Formative assessment: "There is nothing so practical as a good theory." *Australian Journal of Education, 54*, 341–352.

Clarke, D. (2005). Written algorithms in the primary years: Undoing the "good work"? Presented at Making Mathematics Vital: Proceedings of the Twentieth Biennial Conference of the Australian Association of Mathematics Teachers. Retrieved from http://morelandnumeracyaiznetwork .wikispaces.com/file/view/Using+Algorithms+in+the+classroom+Doug +Clarke.pdf

Cobb, P. (1991). Reconstructing elementary school mathematics. *Focus on Learning Problems in Mathematics, 13*, 3–32.

Dowling, D. (2009). Reading (articles), writing (reflections), and a-risk-metric: Working to improve my practice. In B. Herbel-Eisenmann & M. Cirillo (Eds.), *Promoting purposeful discourse* (pp. 57–70). Reston, VA: National Council of Teachers of Mathematics.

Education Quality and Accountability Office (EQAO). (2008). *Trends in International Mathematics and Science Study (TIMSS), 2007: Ontario results report.* Toronto: Author.

Education Quality and Accountability Office (EQAO). (2011). *Grade 6 Assessment of Reading, Writing and Math: Junior division.* Toronto: Author. Retrieved from http://www.eqao.com/pdf_e/09/6e_Math_web_0609.pdf

Ernest, P. (Ed.). (1989). *Mathematics teaching: The state of the art.* London: Falmer Press.

Fosnot, C.T., & Dolk, M. (2001). *Young mathematicians at work: Constructing multiplication and division.* Portsmouth, NH: Heinemann.

Fuson, K.C., & Burghardt, B.H. (2003). Multidigit addition and subtraction methods invented in small groups and teacher support of problem solving and reflection. In A.J. Baroody & A. Dowker (Eds.), *The development of arithmetic concepts and skills* (pp. 267–304). Mahwah, NJ: Erlbaum.

Gilbert, R.K., & Bush, W.S. (1988). Familiarity, availability, and use of manipulative devices in mathematics at the primary level. *School Science and Mathematics, 88*(6), 459–469.

Ginsburg, H. (2009). The challenge of formative assessment in mathematics education: Children's minds, teacher's minds. *Human Development, 52*(2), 109–128.

Handal, B. (2003). Teachers' mathematical beliefs: A review. *Mathematics Educator, 13*, 47–57.

Hedrén, R. (1999). The teaching of traditional standard algorithms for the four arithmetic operations versus the use of pupils' methods. In I. Schwank

(Ed.), *European research in mathematics education I*. Retrieved from http://www.fmd.uni-osnabrueck.de/ebooks/erme/cerme1-proceedings/cerme1-proceedings-1-v1-0-2.pdf

Hesketh, B. (1997). Dilemmas in training for transfer and retention. *Applied Psychology: An International Review, 46,* 317–339.

Hiebert, J. (2003). Signposts for teaching mathematics through problem-solving. In F. Lester, Jr., (Ed.), *Teaching mathematics through problem solving: Prekindergarten–Grade 6* (pp. 53–66). Reston, VA: National Council of Teachers of Mathematics.

Hiebert, J., Carpenter, T.P., Fennema, E., Fuson, K., Human, P., Murray, H., …, & Wearne, D. (1996). Problem solving as a basis for reform in curriculum and instruction: The case of mathematics. *Educational Researcher, 25,* 12–21.

Hiebert, J., Carpenter, T.P., Fennema, E., Fuson, K.C., Wearne, D., Murray, H., …, & Human, P. (1997). *Making sense: Teaching and learning mathematics with understanding*. Portsmouth, NH: Heinemann.

Houssart, J. (2000). I haven't used them yet: Primary teachers talk about calculators. *Micromath, 16,* 14–17.

Hufferd-Ackles, K., Fuson, K.C., & Sherin, M.G. (2004). Describing levels and components of a math-talk learning community. *Journal for Research in Mathematics Education, 35*(2), 81–116. http://dx.doi.org/10.2307/30034933

Huinker, D., Freckman, J.L., & Steinmeyer, M.B. (2003). Subtraction strategies from children's thinking: Moving toward fluency with greater numbers. *Teaching Children Mathematics, 9,* 347–353.

Kulm, G. (Ed.). (1990). *Assessing higher order thinking in mathematics*. Washington, DC: American Association for the Advancement of Science.

Lambdin, D.V. (2003). Benefits of teaching through problem solving. In F. Lester, Jr., (Ed.), *Teaching mathematics through problem solving: Prekindergarten–Grade 6* (pp. 3–14). Reston, VA: National Council of Teachers of Mathematics.

Lawon, A. (2007). Learning mathematics vs. following rules: The value of student-generated methods. *What works? Research into practice*. Toronto: Literacy and Numeracy Secretariat, Ontario Ministry of Education.

Li, Q., & Ma, X. (2010). A meta-analysis of the effects of computer technology on school students' mathematical learning. *Educational Psychology Review, 22*(3), 215–243.

Liliburn, P., & Clurak, A. (2010). *Investigations, tasks and rubrics to teach and assess math, Grades 1–6*. Sausalito, CA: Math Solutions.

Ma, L. (1999). *Knowing and teaching elementary mathematics*. Mahwah, NJ: Erlbaum.

MacMath, S., Wallace, J., & Chi, X. (2009). Problem-based learning in mathematics: A tool for developing students' conceptual knowledge. *What works? Research into Practice Research Monograph #2.* Toronto: Literacy and Numeracy Secretariat, Ontario Ministry of Education, and the Ontario Association of Deans of Education.

Marshall, L., & Paul, S. (2008). Exploring the use of mathematics manipulative materials: Is it what we think it is? Retrieved from http://ro.ecu.edu.au/cgi/viewcontent.cgi?article=1032&context=ceducom

Marzano, R.J. (2003). *What works in schools: Translating research into action.* Alexandria, VA: Association for Supervision and Curriculum Development.

Mewborn, D.S., & Cross, D.J. (2007). Mathematics teachers' beliefs about mathematics and links to student learning. In W.G. Martin, M.E. Strutchens, & P.C. Elliott (Eds.), *The learning of mathematics* (pp. 259–270). Reston, VA: National Council of Teachers of Mathematics.

Moyer, P.S., Niezgoda, D., & Stanley, J. (2005). Young children's use of virtual manipulatives and other forms of mathematical representations. In W.J. Masalki & P.C. Elliott (Eds.), *Technology-supported mathematics learning environments* (pp. 17–34). Reston, VA: National Council of Teachers of Mathematics.

Nagel, N., & Swingen, C.C. (1998). Students' explanations of place value in addition and subtraction. *Teaching Children Mathematics, 5,* 164–170.

Narode, R., Board, J., & Davenport, L. (1993). Algorithms supplant understanding: Case studies of primary students' strategies for double-digit addition and subtraction. In J.R. Becker & B.J. Preece (Eds.), *Proceedings of the 15th Annual Meeting of the North American chapter of the International Group for the Psychology of Mathematics Education* (Vol. 1, pp. 254–260). San Jose, CA: Center for Mathematics and Computer Science Education, San Jose State University.

National Council of Teachers of Mathematics (NCTM). (1980). *Agenda for action.* Reston, VA: Author.

National Council of Teachers of Mathematics (NCTM). (1989). *Curriculum and evaluation standards.* Reston, VA: Author.

National Council of Teachers of Mathematics (NCTM). (1991). *Professional standards for teaching mathematics.* Reston, VA: Author.

National Council of Teachers of Mathematics (NCTM). (1995). *Assessment standards for school mathematics.* Reston, VA: Author.

National Council of Teachers of Mathematics (NCTM). (2000). *Principles and standards for school mathematics.* Reston, VA: Author.

Olson, J.F., Martin, M.O., & Mullis, L.V.S. (Eds.). (2008). *TIMSS 2007 technical report.* Chestnut Hill, MA: TIMMS & PIRLS International Study Center, Boston College.

Ontario Ministry of Education (OMoE), Literacy and Numeracy Secretariat. (2010). *Communication in the mathematics classroom: Capacity building series.* Toronto: Author.

Pomerantz, H. (1997). *The role of calculators in math education.* Retreived from http://education.ti.com/sites/US/downloads/pdf/therole.pdf

Scharton, S. (2004). "I did it my way": Opportunites for students to create, explain and analyze computation procedures. *Teaching Children Mathematics, 10,* 278–283.

Shafer, M.C., & Romberg, T.A. (1999). Assessment in classrooms that promote understanding. In E. Fennema & T.A. Romberg (Eds.), *Mathematics classrooms that promote understanding* (pp. 159–184). Mahwah, NJ: Erlbaum.

Small, M. (2009). *Good questions: Great ways to differentiate mathematics instruction.* New York: Teachers College Press.

Sowell, E. (1989). Effects of manipulative materials in mathematics instruction. *Journal for Research in Mathematics Education, 20*(5), 498–505. http://dx.doi.org/10.2307/749423

Sullivan, P. (2011). *Teaching mathematics: Using research-informed strategies.* Camberwell, Victoria: Australian Council for Educational Research.

Suurtamm, C., & Vézina, N. (2008). Transforming pedagogical practice in mathematics: Moving from telling to listening. *International Journal for Mathematics Teaching and Learning.* Retrieved from http://tsg.icme11.org/document/get/188

van der Sandt, S. (2007). Research framework on mathematics teacher behaviour: Koehler and Grouws' framework revisited. *Eurasia Journal of Mathematics, Science & Technology Education, 34,* 343–350.

Vygotsky, L.S. (1978). *Mind in society: The development of higher psychological processes.* Cambridge, MA: Harvard University Press. (Original work published 1934).

Western and Northern Canadian Protocol (WNCP). (2006). *Rethinking classroom assessment with purpose in mind.* Edmonton, AB: WNCP.

9 Fostering the Transition to Effective Teaching Practices in Inclusive Classrooms

ANNE JORDAN

As the research on resilient children shows us (Reicher, 2010; Seligman, Ernst, Gillham, Reivich, & Linkins, 2009), a single year's experience with a caring and effective teacher can establish a child on a positive track for the remainder of his or her school career. Conversely, a negative experience may well set that child back for the remainder of his or her life. Students with disabilities[1] and those who are underachieving in their elementary school years are more at risk than their normally achieving peers of further losing ground as they make the transition through higher grades (King, Warren, Boyer, & Chin, 2005). They are perhaps more likely than successful students to need the attention of an effective teacher in order to establish a base of self-confidence and resilience that can carry them through to their secondary and postsecondary careers. As Artiles, Kozleski, Dorn, and Christensen (2006) claim, this calls for effective inclusive schooling since inclusive education is based on a school culture that offers *all* students, regardless of their current achievement, (1) increased access to learning, (2) acceptance from the school personnel and peers, (3) participation in various domains of activity, and (4) increased achievement.

There is a popular belief in the teaching profession that inclusion is not an appropriate policy for regular classroom and subject teachers. Complaints about the policy include the following: students with disabilities detract from teachers' instructional time with students who are more likely to achieve, teaching students with special needs requires specialized skills beyond the repertoire of a classroom teacher, and teachers are not trained to deliver the specialized instruction that students with special education needs require.

Despite these complaints, the literature suggests the contrary. Booth, Ainscow, Black-Hawkins, Vaughan, and Shaw (2000) and Kalambouka,

Farrell, Dyson, and Kaplan (2005) show that students with disabilities included in the general education classroom consistently benefit from such settings compared with students in segregated and withdrawal settings. In a study of 11,000 students in the United States, Blackorby et al. (2005) report that students with disabilities who spend more time in regular classrooms have higher scores on achievement tests, are absent less, and perform closer to grade level than their peers who are withdrawn for instruction. At the secondary school level, Blackorby et al. (2005) corroborate the findings of Wagner, Newman, Cameto, and Levine (2003) that students in inclusive settings perform closer to grade level on standards-based achievement tests than their more segregated peers.

Overall, students with disabilities performed less well on achievement tests than those without disabilities. Some subgroups of students and, in particular, those with learning and sensory disabilities, mental retardation, and autism cluster at the low end of the achievement spectrum. Even so, students with disabilities in inclusive settings outperformed their segregated peers with disabilities.

In this chapter, three broad questions are raised: Is there any evidence for the popular claims that inclusion at the elementary level is not effective in enhancing the learning experiences of students both with and without disabilities and difficulties? What are the characteristics of teachers who are successful in including a diversity of learning needs in their regular classrooms? How can teachers, particularly those in teacher training programs, be assisted to transform their practices to reflect success in inclusive settings? The Supporting Effective Teaching (SET) Project has investigated the classroom practices of elementary school teachers in regular classrooms in Ontario schools. The project extends from 1992 to the present and is reported in multiple studies. The studies have centred around a model of teacher characteristics and school-related factors that predict differences in regular elementary school teachers' classroom practices with students with and without disabilities included in their classrooms. Figure 9.1 illustrates the components of the model.

Three constructs are central to the model: teachers' practices in elementary school core subjects in their classrooms, as observed using the Classroom Observation Scale (COS) of effective teaching strategies and teacher practices in accommodating students with special education needs and those at risk of school failure (Jordan, Glenn, & McGhie-Richmond, 2010; McGhie-Richmond, Underwood, & Jordan, 2007);

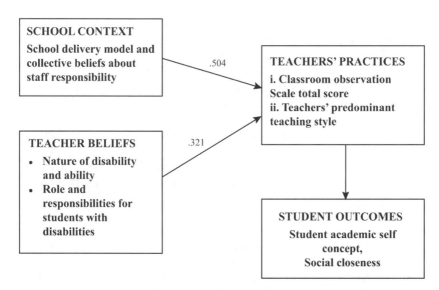

Figure 9.1. Elements of the model of teachers' characteristics for effective inclusion, 1992 to 1998. Simultaneous regression Beta weights predicting teachers' practices are indicated. See Stanovich (1994) and Stanovich and Jordan (1998, 2002).

teachers' beliefs about disability and about their roles with and responsibilities for students with disabilities (Jordan et al., 2010; Stanovich & Jordan, 1998); and the influence of the school norm, that is, the beliefs of the administrators and staff in the school about how services should be delivered to students with exceptionalities in the school (Stanovich, 1994; Stanovich & Jordan, 1998, 2002). The fourth construct, student outcomes, is represented empirically (Jordan & Stanovich, 2001; Stanovich, Jordan, & Perot, 1998), but will be tangential to this chapter. Since 2002, we have focused on the development of the teachers' beliefs and practices variables, and this phase of the project will be presented here. We address the following questions:

1 Effective Teachers' Practices in Inclusive Classrooms
  What are teachers with highly effective teaching practices *doing* when they are working in inclusive classroom settings, with students both with and without disabilities? How do the practices of less-effective teachers differ? In differences in the effectiveness of

teaching practices with students as a whole, are there also differences in how teachers instruct students with disabilities and learning difficulties, and are these related?

2 Teachers' Beliefs about Roles and Responsibilities
What do teachers believe about their roles and responsibilities for students with disabilities and those at risk of underachieving in inclusive elementary school classrooms? What assumptions do they make about the nature of disability and how students with disabilities learn?

3 Relationships between Patterns of Beliefs and Effective Practices
(a) Do differences in teachers' practices correlate with patterns of beliefs about their roles and responsibilities, and with assumptions about the nature of disability?
(b) Are differences in beliefs about disabilities related to beliefs about a broader underlying epistemological belief system about ability and how learning proceeds?
(c) Are any differences in teachers' epistemological beliefs related to their teaching styles, as indicated by their preferences for how to deliver instruction (e.g., for teacher- or student-centred learning methods, for intrinsic or extrinsic forms of motivation)?

4 Length of Experience and Other Antecedents to Beliefs and Practices
Is there any evidence that the beliefs and practices of teachers change over time as a result of teaching in an inclusive school context? Are there any other antecedents to successful inclusive practices that emerge from the data, such as training and/or prior work with people with disabilities?

5 Implications of the Findings for Fostering the Transition of Teacher Practices towards More Effective Inclusion
(a) What can we infer about what teachers need to believe, know, and be able to do in order to be effective in inclusive classrooms?
(b) What are the implications of the findings for teacher preparation at both the pre-service and in-service levels?

1 Effective Teaching Practices in Inclusive Classrooms

Our primary tool is the Classroom Observation Scale (Stanovich 1994). The scale is made up of four parts: (1) total COS score, (2) predominant teaching style, (3) interaction with a student with a disability, and (4) interaction with a student at risk.

Total COS Score

Trained observers rate teachers on 32 items based on Englert, Tarrant, and Mariage's (1992) self-rating checklist of effective teaching practices in inclusive classrooms. The items cover time management, classroom management, and lesson presentation. Most items are derived from process-product research; there are, however, items that address constructivist teaching and scaffolding instruction.

COS total scores range from 23 to 64, with a mean total COS score of 49.33 (SD = 10.63), which is consistent with other studies using the COS (McGee, 2001, 2004).

Predominant Teaching Style

A 7-point scale is used to score each teacher's practices on extent of teacher–student interaction with members of the class during the seatwork part of a lesson. The lowest score on the scale is "no observed interaction" with the students. Midpoints include "teacher checks student work and moves on" and "teacher transmits" instructions or comments. At the top rating, teachers interact one-on-one with individuals and small groups, engaging students in dialogue that "extends cognitive engagement" by challenging the students' thinking. The 7-point rating scale is described more fully below.

Interaction with a Student with a Disability

Prior to the observation session, the teacher rates all the members of the class on three scales. The scales reflect whether each student is above, at, or below the class average on academic performance, need for accommodations and/or modifications, and behaviour. Observers pick one student who has either been formally designated as having an exceptionality or who is rated by the teacher as being in the lowest quartile of the class.

Observers rate the teacher's interaction with this student with a disability. At the observation, the teacher is not told which student is being monitored. The same 7-point scale is used as in Predominant Teaching

Style, this time focusing on the teacher's one-on-one interactions specifically with this student. This scale is a measure of the extent to which a student receives instruction geared to his or her needs. A high rating indicates that the teacher takes time to work one-on-one with this student and at high levels of student engagement geared to the student's learning needs.

Interaction with a Student at Risk

Again, this scale uses the same 7-point scale as Predominant Teaching Style. The student observed, however, is one who has been designated by the teacher as being below the class average on the rating scale but not yet formally designated as exceptional. Again, the teacher is not aware which student is being monitored. This measure indicates the extent to which the student at risk is receiving one-on-one instructional interaction with the teacher and at what level geared to his or her needs. It may, therefore, be a proxy for the extent to which the teacher attends to the needs of those students whose slide into difficulties might be prevented.

There was a possible score range of 0 to 7 for Predominant Teaching Style, and observations of teacher interactions with students who were exceptional or at risk. The scores for Predominant Teaching Style ranged from 2 to 7, with a mean score of 5.44 (SD = 1.32). The mean score derived from the observations of teacher interactions with exceptional students was moderate ($M = 4.71$, SD = 1.87), as was the mean score from the observations of teachers with students who are at risk ($M = 4.36$, SD = 1.88).

Observers undergo extensive training in using the COS, including an apprenticeship as a third observer in classrooms with two experienced observers. The COS observation system is used by two trained observers simultaneously during a half-day of core lessons (language arts, math, science) in the regular classroom when students with disabilities are present (i.e., not withdrawn). The observers have a seating plan and are able to identify the students that they have selected to observe from the teachers' ratings.

In a study that analysed the composition of observed skills that distinguished high-scoring from low-scoring teachers, McGhie-Richmond et al. (2007) report that the inter-rater reliability between the two observers for 63 teacher observations on the three rating scales was 94% agreement. Using a canonical discriminant functions analysis, a set of COS items distinguishing effective from less-effective teachers was identified. The sequence of instructional practices appears to be cumulative rather than differentiated, and five items contributed to a factor, termed *student engagement*, that distinguished the most-effective teachers from their colleagues. These five items all related to keeping students informed about lesson expectations, such as stating seatwork expectations in advance, gaining and maintaining student attention, monitoring transitions, and maintaining high student response rates during large group activities.

It appears, therefore, that the Classroom Observation Scale may be a good indicator of effective teaching. Not surprisingly, there is a strong positive correlation between total COS score and Predominant Teaching Style (+.77, $p < .01$, see Table 9.1), suggesting that teachers who are effective on the process-product criteria of the COS are also engaging their students in extended dialogues and one-on-one instruction during seatwork.

This leads to the question of whether teachers who are effective with students overall are also more likely to engage their students with disabilities and at-risk students during seatwork dialogues and one-on-one instruction. That is, do the observations of the level of instructional interaction between the teacher and students designated as exceptional and students designated as at risk, correlate with their overall COS scores, and with their Predominant Teaching Style score? As seen in Table 9.1, there is, indeed, a correlation between teachers' COS scores and their interaction scores with students with disabilities ($r = .372$, $p < .05$), and between teachers' Predominant Teaching Style score and their interaction scores with students with disabilities ($r = .44$, $p < .01$). However, there is no significant correlation between teachers' interaction scores with students at risk with either their COS scores or their Predominant Teaching Style scores.

These findings suggest that teachers who are effective overall in engaging students in learning, and who promote extended cognitive engagement with their students during seatwork activities, are also more effective in interacting with their students with disabilities. Unfortunately, the same is nor true for students at risk who are underachieving and below the class average, but who have not been formally designated as exceptional. These "at-risk learners" may not be benefiting from one-on-one instructional interactions with their teachers compared with other students.

We have claimed (Stanovich & Jordan, 2002) that good teaching in inclusive classrooms is good teaching for all. Certainly, we have shown

Table 9.1 Correlations between Classroom Observation Scale, Teaching Style, and Teachers' Interactions with Exceptional and At-Risk Students (*N* = 36)

Factor	Classroom Observation Scale	Predominant Teaching Style	Teachers' Interactions with Exceptional Students
Classroom Observation Scale	1.000		
Predominant Teaching Style	.766**	1.000	
Interactions with Exceptional Students	.372*	.441**	1.000
Interactions with At-Risk Students	.101	.209	.516**

Source: Glenn (2007).
* *p* < .05.
** *p* < .01.

that effective teachers allocate copious amounts of instructional time and use it to engage in higher levels of instructional interactions with both their regularly achieving students and those with disabilities (Jordan, Lindsay, & Stanovich, 1997). The at-risk students, however, may still fall between the cracks even with the most effective teachers.

So, what is the evidence for claims that including students with disabilities in the regular classroom detracts from the time and attention that a teacher requires to meet the needs of students who are normally achieving? Our research has established that some teachers are more effective than others, and that those who are effective are able to engage students both with and without disabilities. Indeed, effective teachers are able to allocate almost double the amount of instructional time compared with less-effective teachers (Jordan et al., 1997), in part, because they are skilled at classroom and time management, are effective designers of large group lessons and small group work, and are unlikely to be sidetracked by non-instructional activities such as behaviour management and housekeeping. They use their time to work with individuals and small groups of students, interacting with them on the lesson materials and challenging them in ways that engage them with the lesson.

The finding that effective teachers are excellent technicians is not new (Wayne & Youngs, 2003), but it is interesting to note that students with disabilities benefit from these teachers, as do students who are normally achieving. Using the Ontario Education Quality and Accountability Office (EQAO) scores of students in Grade 3, Demeris, Childs, and Jordan (2007) reported that the number of students with disabilities included in Grade 3 classrooms, and the size of the class had no negative influence on the test achievement scores of the students without disabilities and may, indeed, have contributed to a slight increase in their scores on reading and mathematics. In effect, those Ontario teachers who were effective, as indicated by the achievement scores of their Grade 3 students, were also likely to have more of their students with disabilities represented in the tests.

The evidence of the Supporting Effective Teaching Project points to effective teaching as a variable in determining the opportunity to learn provided to students both with and without disabilities. Far from detracting from teacher time and attention with normally achieving students, effective teachers are better overall in offering a rich and challenging instructional experience, calibrated to their students' various needs.

2 Teachers' Beliefs about Roles and Responsibilities

If it is the case that some teachers are more effective with students both with and without disabilities in their classrooms, what are the characteristics that distinguish them from other teachers? One attribute that we have studied intensively is teachers' beliefs about their roles and responsibilities for students with disabilities and those at risk of underachieving in inclusive elementary school classrooms. In personal interviews, we ask what beliefs they hold about their responsibility to teach children with disabilities, and to what they attribute student learning difficulties and how students with disabilities learn.

The Pathognomonic-Interventionist Interview

We have developed an interview that avoids the transparency of standard paper-and-pencil measures of attitude and belief (Kagan, 1992). When asked to focus on a specific student who has difficulty learning, teachers are able to explain the steps that they have taken to work with the student over a school year in a chronological sequence, in the manner of a narrative story (Engel, 1993). Teachers describe their recalled experiences, reporting their perceptions of the student's characteristics, the decisions they made, their instructional intentions, their reasons for why they chose to act in the ways they describe, and their judgments about the results. This narrative is interpreted in relation to teachers' understanding of their roles and responsibilities in meeting the needs of their students with disabilities.

The interview is conducted as a narrative of the teachers' experiences over the previous school year, usually with a student with a disability included in the class, and with a student whom the teacher considers to be at risk of academic failure. In the manner of an informant approach (Powney & Watts, 1987), the interviewer uses a set of probe questions to guide, but not to lead the teachers' descriptions so that, by the end of the interview, five topics have been covered in whatever sequence they arose in the dialogue. The interviewers are trained to use probes that elicit teachers' rationalizations and attributions, their judgments and reasons for the decisions they made. Probes include "Why did you do that?" "What did you think might happen?" "What did you hope would be the result?" and "If you'd had a choice, what would you have chosen to do, and why?"

The topics are the following:

1 The teacher's initial concerns about and assessments of the student, as he or she enters the teacher's class (collecting data and observations, gathering information from previous teachers, school records, and parents, and conducting informal assessment)
2 Instructional programming (modifying curriculum, making accommodations in instructional and evaluation techniques)
3 Monitoring and reviewing student progress (provisions for formative evaluation, working with the in-school team)
4 Communication with staff (whether and for what purpose the teacher collaborates with colleagues and resource staff about the student, whether programs are coordinated with those offered by resource and support personnel)
5 Communication with parents (how often and for what purpose the teacher communicates with/reports to the student's parents).

The confidential interviews are conducted individually with teachers in a private room in the school, and take between 40 and 70 minutes. The interviews are tape recorded and later transcribed for coding. The scoring system is then applied to respondent statements in the transcripts to yield a numerical score of between 1 and 3 for each of 20 criteria (see Appendix to this chapter for examples). The summed score reflects a bipolar dimension of beliefs about the characteristics of disability and about a teacher's roles and responsibilities in working with such students. At low scores, the belief system is defined by assumptions that the disability is a structural, organic, or neurological condition, which is internal to the students. We used the term *pathognomonic* or *P-beliefs* for this belief system to indicate that teachers who hold it understand that the disability condition is a pathological attribute of the learner, can be reliably named and identified by traditional standardized assessment instruments, and is within the domain of special education interventions. General education teachers who express P-beliefs do not see themselves as responsible for intervening in the student's instruction, since specialists with training are assumed to take responsibility for that role. The pathognomonic perspective reflects a traditional set of beliefs that have been variously termed *medical, deficit or pathology based, clinical* (Kalyanpur & Harry, 1999), or *norm referenced* (Gartner & Lipsky, 1987). Some time ago, Sarason and Doris (1979) denounced the "search for pathology" that characterizes the actions of people who hold this set of assumptions about disability.

On the other end of the continuum is the *interventionist* set of beliefs, the *I-beliefs*. These are characterized by the understanding that the teacher is responsible for all students and that all students can profit from learning and instructional opportunities, irrespective of their individual differences. Disability is understood to be an attribute of the student that may give rise to barriers in the teacher's communication of instruction and/or to the student's communication of his or her learning. In any case, learning difficulties are understood to be amenable to instructional accommodations for which the teacher is responsible. This view of disability is termed the *social perspective* (Oliver, 1990; Rioux, 1997; Slee, 1997) and *socio-cultural perspective* (Kalyanpur & Harry, 1999). Disabilities are assumed to result from socially constructed barriers to individual access that were designed for the convenience of the larger society (Booth et al., 2000). Kalyanpur and Harry refer to traditions outside of Western medical culture in which the community takes responsibility for accepting and supporting the child with the disability. In the context of schools, it is the responsibility of teachers, in collaboration with parents and professionals, to find ways to circumvent the barriers to communication and learning that result when the child is included in the community.

The teachers' pathognomonic-interventionist (P-I) interview narratives are analysed to identify the statements that represent their attributions of the students' characteristics, the decisions the teachers made and their justifications for making them, their intentions and their reasons for doing so, and their judgments about the results. These statements are then rated by third-party raters on a 3-point scale on each of 20 pairs of criteria. One point represents a pathognomonic belief and three points represents an interventionist belief. Statements that are composites of both criteria, or that vacillate between the two, are given a midpoint (M) belief score of 2. Examples of the pairs of contrasting criteria that are used for the P-I scoring procedure are presented in the Appendix.

Glenn (2007) reports that among a sample of 36 teachers, the P-I scores ranged from 1.40 to 3.00, with a group mean P-I score of 2.46 (SD = .50). This suggests teachers' belief scores are skewed towards the interventionist end of the range and is consistent with other samples using the P-I measure (McGee, 2001, 2004). However, in our early studies conducted in the 1990s, about 25% of general education classroom teachers held pathognomonic beliefs, while 20% held interventionist beliefs (Jordan et al., 1997). The remaining teachers held beliefs that tended to vacillate between the P and I criteria termed "mid-range" beliefs. These may have been indicative of teachers' struggles to resolve the paradoxes caused by policies that seem to contradict each other, such as the mandate to include students with disabilities in regular programs, but also to label disabilities by category.

In addition to the total P-I score, two holistic ratings are given to each interview transcript.

Responsibility: a holistic rating (with a range 1 to 5) of the teacher's involvement and responsibility in providing instruction to students. Teachers who receive a lower rating on this measure are those who tend to use a student's exceptionality to justify his or her exemption from responsibility for that student's instruction. Such teachers assume that resource teachers, the student himself or herself, or even the parents are responsible for undertaking instruction and implementing accommodations. Teachers who receive a higher rating are those who tend to describe efforts to understand the student's disability and how it impacts other aspects of learning. During the interview process, these teachers describe taking a personal initiative in generating interventions and seeking services to meet students' individual academic needs. In Glenn's study (2007), scores ranged from 1.50 to 5.50, with a mean score of 4.22 (SD = 1.15).

Attribution: a holistic rating (with a range of 1 to 5) of to what the teacher most often attributes the student's learning difficulties during the interview. Teachers who tend to attribute a student's learning difficulties to characteristics internal to the student (e.g., ability, IQ, or exceptionality) receive a lower rating on this measure. Teachers who tend to attribute students' learning difficulties to previous or current instructional factors receive a higher rating. According to Glenn (2007), scores in a previous study of 83 teachers had a range of 1.50 to 4.50, with a mean score of 2.82 (SD = .87).

Evidently, teachers vary widely in their beliefs about their roles and responsibilities for students with disabilities and learning difficulties included in their classrooms, and they attribute the struggles of these learners to a variety of sources, such as their lack of effort, low intelligence, or poor family support (pathognomonic attributions) or to lack of opportunity to learn, previous gaps in instruction, and individual learning styles that require accommodation (interventionist attributions).

3 Relationships between Patterns of Beliefs and Effective Practices

The next question asks whether this array of teachers' differing assumptions, beliefs, and attributions are linked to the differences in their practices observed in the Classroom Observation Scale. Do differences in teachers' practices correlate with patterns of beliefs about their roles and responsibilities and with assumptions about the nature of disability? If we can demonstrate that teachers who are more effective in inclusive classrooms, as indicated by the COS, Predominant Teaching Style and interactions with students with disabilities are also more likely to hold interventionist views (I-beliefs) about their students with disabilities, then assumptions and beliefs about disability may possibly be determinants of teachers' practices.

In Table 9.2, some tentative evidence for this relationship is found. Working with 36 elementary school teachers, Glenn found no correlation between overall effective teaching as measured by the COS and beliefs on the P-I scale. There were, however, significant correlations between the P-I interview ratings of Responsibility and the COS ($r = .44$, $p < .05$) and between Responsibility and Predominant Teaching Style ($r = .43$, $p < .05$). The P-I Attribution score also correlated with teachers' Predominant Teaching Style ($r = .36$, $p < .05$) and with Interactions with Exceptional Students (Students with Disabilities) ($r = .38$, $p < .05$).

Table 9.2 Correlations between Classroom Observation Scale, Pathognomonic-Interventionist (P-I) Interview, Responsibility, Attribution, Entity-Increment Beliefs, Teaching Style, and Teachers' Interactions with Exceptional and At-Risk Students (*N* = 36)

Factor	Pathognomonic-Interventionist	Responsibility	Attribution	Entity-Increment
Classroom Observation Scale Total	.077	.440*	.304	.261
Predominant Teaching Style	.280	.428*	.361*	.284
Interactions with Exceptional Students	.178	.318	.378*	.189
Interactions with At-Risk Students	.054	.045	.205	.346*

Source: Glenn (2007).
* *p* < .05.
** *p* < .01.

Teachers who describe efforts to understand students' disabilities and learning difficulties, and who take responsibility for designing instruction and accommodations for such students tend to have higher overall scores on the COS measure of effective teaching. Teachers who attribute students' learning difficulties, in part, to instructional and environmental factors also tend to spend more instructional time with students with disabilities, engaging them in the lesson materials.

Epistemological Beliefs

We then asked whether the P-I beliefs of teachers were related to a larger set of epistemological beliefs about the nature of ability as well as disability. Are P-I beliefs about disabilities related to beliefs about ability and how learning proceeds?

Jordan, Washington, Schwartz, and Ahmed (2005) developed a questionnaire that we dubbed the Beliefs about Teaching and Learning Questionnaire (BTLQ). The BTLQ is a measure of teachers' beliefs about the nature of ability and about their preferences for teaching core subjects (e.g., math, language arts, and science). Completion of the measure required teachers to rate their agreement with 57 statements using a 6-point Likert-type scale, from "strongly disagree" to "strongly agree." To explore the factor structure of the new instrument, data were collected in a pilot study of 77 general education classroom teachers and subjected to a factor analysis. Using principal axis factoring with varimax rotation, the results yielded three interpretable factors.

Items that loaded on the second factor reflected teachers' epistemological theories about ability on a dimension from "Entity" (which reflects the belief that ability is a fixed trait) to "Increment" (which reflects the belief that ability is developed in relation to stimuli from one's environment). Examples of entity beliefs are "The ability to learn is something that remains relatively fixed throughout a person's life," and "I can improve my learning skills, but I can't change my basic ability." In their preliminary work with the BTLQ, Jordan et al. (2005) found a relationship among a small sample of six teachers that suggested teachers who viewed *disability* as a pathognomonic or fixed internal characteristic of the student (as measured by the P-I interview) also viewed *ability* as a fixed trait (as measured by these items of the BTLQ), that is, not amenable to teaching or learning. Their responses reflected the belief that students with disabilities require specialized intervention, and they did not view themselves as responsible for the teaching of those students. Teachers who held these beliefs also perceived themselves as the authority in the classroom. That is, they viewed themselves as being in control of their students' learning (Jordan et al., 2005). Conversely, those teachers who held interventionist or I-beliefs about disability as being malleable and responsive to instruction appeared to view ability in the same way. Jordan et al. found that these teachers rated themselves as more student-centred in their teaching, allowing students the freedom to participate in the construction of their own learning.

Glenn (2007) administered the Beliefs about Teaching and Learning Questionnaire to 66 classroom teachers and 120 teacher candidates. She reduced the item pool to 44 items with Cronbach alpha co-efficients greater than .79, and performed a factor analysis using the maximum likelihoods procedure with oblique rotation of the resulting items. Four factors emerged (statistical details are in Jordan et al., 2010):

- Factor 1: Teacher-Led Instruction
- Factor 2: Entity-Increment Beliefs (E-I)

- Factor 3: Student-Centred Instruction
- Factor 4: Extrinsic Motivation

In Table 9.3 the correlations between teachers' scores on the P-I interview and responsibility and attribution are shown with those of the four BTLQ factors. Looking at the correlations between the P-I variables and the Entity-Increment factor, one sees that there is quite a strong relationship between them, particularly between teachers' beliefs that ability is fixed or fluid and their views of their own responsibilities for and attributions about students with disabilities.

It appears that some teachers hold the belief that both ability and disability are fixed and permanent characteristics of learners, caused by factors internal to the learner and, therefore, unlikely to be affected by their efforts as teachers. They, therefore, take less responsibility for working with these students and see the responsibility as lying with others (e.g., special education teachers, health care professionals, parents) rather than with themselves. Conversely, other teachers hold the beliefs that both ability and disability are fluid, subject to change as a result of opportunities to learn, caused by factors in the environment, including prior and current learning experiences, and are, therefore, a central part of their responsibility as teachers.

Relationships between Teachers' Epistemological Beliefs and Their Teaching Practices

To close the loop, we need to establish that not only beliefs about disability but also about ability have an impact on how teachers teach. In her doctoral study, Schwartz (2008; see also Jordan et al., 2009; Schwartz & Jordan, 2011) analysed in depth the statements of 12 teachers derived from the P-I interview, mapping their comments onto theoretical models of epistemological beliefs developed by Baxter Magolda (2002), Hofer (2001), Hofer and Pintrich (1997), Schommer-Aikins (2004), and Schraw and Olafson (2002). Schwartz discovered that clusters of beliefs not only validate the dimension of P-I, but also reflect the diversity and complexity of teachers' understanding of the nature of knowing, knowledge, and learning, and about the relationship of teachers' beliefs to differences in their preferred styles of teaching, setting assignments, and motivating learning. Schwartz posits clusters of beliefs that either focus on the fixed, universal nature of knowledge or on the fluid, relative nature of knowledge, and whether knowing is seen to be a collective or

Table 9.3 Correlations between Pathognomonic-Interventionist (P-I) Interview, Responsibility, Attribution, and the Beliefs about Teaching and Learning Questionnaire ($N = 36$)

Factor	P-I	Responsi-bility	Attribution	Entity-Increment	Teacher-Controlled Instruction	Student-Centred Instruction
Responsi-bility	.662**	1.000				
Attribution	.287	.553**	1.000			
Entity-Increment	.372*	.539**	.479**	1.000		
Teacher-Controlled Instruction	−.087	−.339	−.347	−.692**	1.000	
Student-Centred Instruction	.438*	.463**	−.011	−.251	−.369	1.000
Attaining Standards	−.541**	−.571**	−.545**	−.368	−.525**	−.042

Source: Glenn (2007).
* $p < .05$.
** $p < .01$.

personal attribute. Teachers' described instructional styles flow from these distinctions. Schwartz showed that teachers' descriptions of the decisions they make, the steps they take to seek support for students, and the extent to which they accommodate learning difficulties are aligned with differences in their profiles of epistemological beliefs.

4 Length of Experience and Other Antecedents to Beliefs and Practices

Can we predict which teachers will hold which set of beliefs from their profiles of training and experiences? We are frequently asked whether there is any evidence that the beliefs and practices of teachers change over time as a result of teaching in an inclusive school context. Are there any other antecedents to successful inclusive practices that emerge from the data, such as the amount of training they have received or their prior exposure to people with disabilities?

Our data suggest that length of teaching experience has no relationship with differences in either beliefs or practices. In all our analyses, length of experience has not correlated with any other measures. Experience with people with disabilities may, however, be a contributor to beliefs. Although the evidence is anecdotal, teachers who were identified as outstanding practitioners often remarked during their interviews that they had a relative with a disability or had worked with people with disabilities in the community.

5 Supporting Transition in Teachers' Beliefs: Implications for Pre-service and In-service Teacher Training

Effective teachers design and implement instruction that accommodates learner differences. They actively draw on resources to assist their struggling learners, and they adapt their instructional routines to reach a broad range of student needs (Robinson, 2007; White, 2007). Both Glenn's (2007) and White's studies and our earlier work indicate that teachers who are less effective, spend little or no time with their students with disabilities seldom consult their Individual Program Plans (Individual Educational Programs, or IEPs), which they view as unhelpful, and seldom draw on the resources available in the school and parents to assist them to accommodate these students.

How can we impact teachers' beliefs especially at the pre-service and in-service levels to assist them to make the transition to becoming more effective teachers overall, and more inclusive in their practices?

White (2007) examined the beliefs and practices of five elementary school teachers who were part of the Supporting Effective Teaching Project in 1999 and continued to participate in 2004. Her analysis of the changes in thinking of teachers over the intervening time period was largely dependent on the beliefs with which they entered the project. One teacher, the mother of three children with learning disabilities, commenced the project with strong interventionist views, and completed the exit P-I interview and Classroom Observation Scale observation with considerably more confidence and a broader repertoire of accommodative and differentiated teaching skills. The same cannot be said for three other teachers who, in 1999, expressed doubts about inclusion, were rated as holding pathognomonic beliefs because they blamed the students with disabilities for not working harder, assigned parents to undertake instruction at home, and failed to draw on readily available resources to assist them to meet the requirements of the students' IEPs and their classroom needs. None of these teachers had personal experience with disability except in their classrooms. Five years later, even in a school system with a strong focus on inclusive practices, and after in-service exposure to techniques for diversifying instruction, these three teachers had barely moved in either P-I beliefs or COS practices.

Our preliminary evidence, therefore, is that length of experience, in-service training, and the influence of policies in the school system have little effect on those teachers who hold pathognomonic views and who attribute ability to learn to factors that they do not control. Something more is needed. This might include greater exposure of teachers to people with disabilities, either through practicum experiences in special education settings or in agencies that deliver service to people with disabilities. We have only anecdotal evidence of this, but it has emerged as a characteristic of effective teachers in several studies, including those by White (2007) and Robinson (2007).

Giangreco, Dennis, Cloninger, Edelman, and Schattman (1993) reported a landmark description of how the beliefs and practices of 17 of 19 teachers made the transition from exclusion to inclusion during their year of including a student with a disability. Such studies suggest that experience with disabilities can be transformative. It behooves us, therefore, to find ways to challenge the beliefs of teachers during their pre-service as well as in-service training to enable them to undertake the transition to inclusive practices.

There are major challenges in preparing teachers at the pre-service level to be effective with all their students. Pajares (1992) and Wiebe Berry (2006, 2008) reflect White's (2007) conclusion that teacher beliefs about inclusion are related to other beliefs about equity and fairness and are relatively hard to change. Our findings that beliefs about disability and ability share a common understanding, in general, and are based on differing perspectives of how learning occurs suggest that teachers may need a broader understanding of learning and how knowledge is acquired before they are able to shift their perspectives about their practices.

White (2000) notes that pre-service teachers' beliefs appear to be little affected by their teacher education programs. The majority of pre-service teachers in White's study believed that how best to deal with problematic classroom situations, and what knowledge might inform the solution, is a matter of opinion. Most of them lacked an understanding of the nature of learning and knowing that would have enabled them to make judgments that were defensible. They fell back on making judgments on the basis of their own experiences and prior understandings. White suggests that changing this mindset requires that teachers acquire the "disposition to seek and assess critically and honestly all available information and to reason dialogically with that information, all the while refraining from rushing to conclusions" (p. 302).

The development of pedagogical skill in the interactive aspects of teaching is left almost entirely to field experiences, the component of professional education over which we have little control. Feiman-Nemser (2001) contends that schools are not organized for teachers to work together on teacher inquiry or experimentation in serious or sustained ways. The challenge for teacher educators is to ensure that pre-service teachers may need to engage in challenging dialogues that question their assumptions and beliefs and that expose them to their own attributions of and understandings about ability and disability.

Although exposure to students with disabilities may also be an important part of pre-service training, few programs require that the practicum experiences of teachers in training include a special education component. At present, we do not know how such an experience, for how long, and with which students might foster the transition of the beliefs and practices of teachers in training, but this is, surely, an important next step in our understanding of training teachers.

The importance of training in special education has not been recognized in the programs accredited in the province of Ontario, since the same pathognomonic assumptions that absolve teachers of working with disabilities have led politicians and policy makers to view special education as an "add-on" program, to be learned through additional courses after candidates have qualified as classroom teachers. Yet, the very diversity of our classrooms suggests that this is ill-conceived – that diversifying to accommodate learner differences in abilities and disabilities is at the heart of learning how to become an effective teacher. And we now know that effective teaching practices are effective for all students.

The schools themselves may also play a part in influencing the synergy between beliefs and practices of teachers, particularly in terms of the administration's vision of learning and how that is communicated (Stanovich & Jordan, 1998). Dyson, Farrell, Polat, Hutcheson, and Gallannaugh (2004, p. 104) note how fragile this synergy may be:

Where schools have relatively high proportions of [special education needs] pupils, there appears to be a delicate balance between the resources they can bring to bear on the task of teaching and the demands which the presence of these children create. Through good policies, good leadership, and the skills and energies of teachers, this balance is often maintained.

However, the balance is delicate and subject to falling apart when fiscal and staffing shortfalls occur. The transition to inclusive beliefs and practices may, therefore, be fragile and in need of long-term fiscal and human supports.

The challenges of training teachers to become effective in working with students with disabilities goes far beyond special education. Effective teachers are not those who create separate and specialized programs for their included students with disabilities, but rather, they engage in diversifying instruction for all their students, using principles of universal design in making their pedagogical and curriculum choices. Such skills are built on their beliefs about their own responsibilities and on the impact that their teaching has on all their students. In turn, this in part depends on how teachers view their roles as teachers, and how they cope with seemingly competing professional demands and variable resources in order to succeed in meeting high achievement standards for all their students. For the most part, effective teachers are self-taught, individually "reinventing the wheel" to calibrate their practices with their beliefs. We need to have a deeper understanding of how these exceptional teachers have made the transition in their beliefs and practices, so that we might foster it in others.

Teacher training is a notoriously short and fragmented period in the lives of teachers. Solutions to fostering the transition of teacher beliefs, and hence practices, will be as complex as challenging and will require career-long commitments and resources. Yet, the potential investment in teacher training could make the difference in the school careers of so many students, particularly those who will need to develop resilience and a belief in their own self-worth as they make the transitions through the grades and into adult life.

Appendix: Examples of Pathognomonic-Interventionist Interview Rating Criteria

I ENTRY TO CLASS

1 Information about the individual student: The teacher's priority for finding out about a new student with a disability:

1 The teacher does not familiarize himself or herself with the characteristics of the incoming student on entry to the class.

2 The teacher reads/examines information routinely delivered to him or her (e.g., IEP, summary of information from previous grade).

3 The teacher actively investigates the characteristics of the incoming student (e.g., Ontario School Record (OSR), IEP, previous teachers, parents, Resource teacher).

2 Formal assessment

1 The teacher understands the purpose of formal assessment (psycho-educational, normative) to be to *confirm* the student's disability category.

2 The teacher vacillates between understanding assessment as confirmatory of disability and as instructionally useful.

3 The teacher expects formal assessments to uncover information that is useful for instructional planning and adaptation (e.g., learning characteristics and preferences, entry-level skills).

3 Grade level vs. functional level

1 The teacher does not identify the individual student's entry point for learning but uses curriculum expectations set for the grade level.

2 The teacher relies on information in the OSR or IEP or regularly scheduled boardwide tests to identify the student's entry point for learning (grade-level identifiers).

3 The teacher relies on her or his own and/or Resource teacher's informal assessments and individual observations with formal assessment and IEP data to identify the student's entry points for learning.

...

II COLLABORATION WITH STAFF

1 Individual vs. collaboration with Resource teacher, colleagues

1 The teacher sees resource/special education (if the student is part-time in class) teacher as primarily responsible for working directly with the student. The teacher does not integrate her or his own program with others.

2 The teacher values collaboration with resource/special education teacher as useful and informative but does not integrate her or his own program and expectations for this student with others.

3 The teacher values collaboration, uses it to share common expectations, uses resources to increase opportunity for the student to achieve in class.

2 Tracking progress

1 The teacher assumes the resource teacher and/or others are keeping track of the student's progress in their respective pieces of the student's program.

2 The teacher assumes the resource teacher and/or others are keeping track of the student's progress in their respective pieces of the student's program, and that checking in with each other is needed occasionally.

3 The teacher values frequent conferencing and planning with resource and other teachers and expects that resource will support student learning objectives in the classroom (e.g., pre-teaching vocabulary, concepts, scribing, helping with accommodations).

NOTE

1 The term "student with disabilities" is used to indicate a student who has formally been identified as exceptional by a committee, or who has been deemed to require an IEP. In other sources, the terms "exceptional student" and "exceptional pupil" are used, and the terms are generally interchangeable. "Student at risk" indicates a student who is struggling to achieve but who has not been formally identified nor has been given an IEP.

REFERENCES

Artiles, A.J., Kozleski, E.B., Dorn, S., & Christensen, C. (2006). Learning in inclusive education research: Re-mediating theory and methods with a transformative agenda. *Review of Research in Education*, *30*(1), 65–108.

Baxter Magolda, M. (2002). Epistemological reflection: The evolution of epistemological assumptions from age 18 to 30. In B. Hofer & P. Pintrich (Eds.), *Personal epistemology: The psychology of beliefs about knowledge and knowing* (pp. 89–102). Mahwah, NJ: Erlbaum.

Blackorby, J., Wagner, M., Cameto, R., Davies, L., Levine, P., & Newman, L. (2005). *Engagement, academics, social adjustment, and independence*. Palo Alto, CA: SRI.

Booth, T., Ainscow, M., Black-Hawkins, K., Vaughn, M., & Shaw, L. (2000). *Index for inclusion: Developing learning and participation in schools*. Bristol: Centre for Studies on Inclusive Education.

Demeris, H., Childs, R., & Jordan, A. (2007). The influence of students with special needs included in grade 3 classrooms on the large-scale achievement scores of students without special needs. *Canadian Journal of Education, 30*(3), 609–627.

Dyson, A., Farrell, P., Polat, F., Hutcheson, G., & Gallannaugh, F. (2004). *Inclusion and pupil achievement* (Research Rep. No. RR578). London: Department for Education and Skills. Retrieved from http://www.dfes.gov.uk/research/data/uploadfiles/ACFC9F.pdf

Engel, D.M. (1993). Origin myths: Narratives of authority, resistance, disability and law. *Law & Society Review, 27*(4), 785–826.

Englert, C.S., Tarrant, K.L., & Mariage, T.V. (1992). Defining and redefining instructional practices in special education: Perspectives on good teaching. *Teacher Education and Special Education, 15*(2), 62–86.

Feiman-Nemser, S. (2001). Helping novices learn to teach: Lessons learned from an exemplary support teacher. *Journal of Teacher Education, 52*(1), 17–30.

Gartner, A., & Lipsky, D.K. (1987). Beyond special education: Toward a quality system for all students. *Harvard Educational Review, 57*, 367–395.

Giangreco, M.F., Dennis, R., Cloninger, C., Edelman, S., & Schattman, R. (1993, Feb.). "I've counted Jon": Transformational experiences of teachers educating students with disabilities. *Exceptional Children, 59*(4), 359–372.

Glenn, C. (2007). *The impact of teachers' epistemological beliefs and their beliefs about disability on their teaching practices in inclusive classrooms*. Unpublished Ph.D. dissertation, University of Toronto.

Hofer, B. (2001). Personal epistemological research implications for learning and teaching. *Educational Psychology Review, 13*(4), 353–383.

Hofer, B., & Pintrich, P. (1997). The development of epistemological theories: Beliefs about knowledge and knowing and their relation to learning. *Review of Educational Research, 67*(1), 88–140.

Jordan, A., Glenn, C., & McGhie-Richmond, D. (2010). The Supporting Effective Teaching (SET) Project: The relationship of inclusive teaching practices to teachers' beliefs about disability and ability, and about their roles as teachers. *Teaching and Teacher Education, 26*(2), 259–266.

Jordan, A., Lindsay, L., & Stanovich, P. (1997). Classroom teachers' interactions with students who are exceptional, at risk, and typically achieving. *Remedial and Special Education, 18*(2), 82–93.

Jordan, A., Schwartz, E., & McGhie-Richmond, D. (2009). Preparing teachers for inclusive classrooms. *Teaching and Teacher Education, 25*(4), 535–542.

Jordan, A., & Stanovich, P. (2001). Patterns of teacher-student interaction in inclusive elementary classrooms and correlates with student self-concept. *International Journal of Disability Development and Education, 48*(1), 33–52.

Jordan, A., & Stanovich, P. (2004). The beliefs and practices of Canadian teachers about including students with special needs in their regular elementary classrooms. *Exceptionality Education Canada, 14*(2–3), 25–46.

Jordan, A., Washington, D., Schwartz, E., & Ahmed, Q. (2005, May). Effective teaching in inclusive classrooms. *Symposium presented at the Canadian Society for Studies in Education*, London, Ontario.

Kagan, D.M. (1992). Implications of research on teacher belief. *Educational Psychologist, 27*(1), 65–90.

Kalambouka, A., Farrell, P., Dyson, A., & Kaplan, I. (2005). The impact of population inclusivity in schools on student outcomes. London: University of London, Centre for Evidence-Informed Policy and Practice in Education. Retrieved from http://eppi.ioe.ac.uk/cms/Default.aspx?tabid=287

Kalyanpur, M., & Harry, B. (1999). *Culture in special education: Building reciprocal family-professional relationships*. Baltimore: P.H. Brookes.

King, A.J.C., Warren, W.K., Boyer, J.C., & Chin, P. (2005). *Double cohort study: Phase 4 report*. Ontario Ministry of Education. Retrieved from http://www.edu.gov.on.ca/eng/document/reports/phase4/index.html

McGee, M.R. (2001). *Measuring effective teaching in inclusive classrooms*. (Unpublished master's thesis). University of Toronto.

McGee, M.R. (2004). *Teacher and school variables associated with the social and academic outcomes of students with special needs in general education classrooms*. (Unpublished Ph.D. dissertation). University of Toronto.

McGhie-Richmond, D., Underwood, K., & Jordan, A. (2007). Developing effective instructional strategies for teaching in inclusive classrooms. *Exceptionality Education Canada, 17*(1–2), 27–52.

Oliver, M. (1990). *The politics of disablement*. Basingstoke, UK: MacMillan.

Pajares, F. (1992). Teachers' beliefs and educational research: Cleaning up a messy construct. *Review of Educational Research, 62*(3), 307–332.

Powney, J., & Watts, M. (1987). *Interviewing in educational research*. London: Routledge & Kegan Paul.

Reicher, H. (2010). Building inclusive education on social and emotional learning: Challenges and perspectives – A review. *International Journal of Inclusive Education, 14*(3), 213–246.

Rioux, M.H. (1997, Apr.). Disability: The place of judgement in a world of fact. *Journal of Intellectual Disability Research, 41*(2), 102–111.

Robinson, P. (2007). *The characteristics of teacher expertise in elementary school inclusive classrooms*. (Unpublished Ed.D. dissertation). University of Toronto.

Sarason, S., & Doris, J. (1979). *Educational handicap, public policy, and social history*. New York: Free Press.

Schommer-Aikins, M. (2004). Explaining the epistemological belief system: Introducing the embedded systemic model and coordinated research approach. *Educational Psychologist, 39*(1), 19–29.

Schraw, G., & Olafson, L. (2002). Teachers' epistemological worldviews and educational practices. *Issues in Education, 8*(2), 99–149.

Schwartz, E. (2008). *Elementary classroom teachers' epistemological beliefs and their practices with students with disabilities and at-risk*. (Unpublished Ed.D. dissertation). University of Toronto.

Schwartz, E., & Jordan, A. (2011). Teachers' epistemological beliefs and practices with students with disabilities and at-risk in inclusive classrooms: Implications for teacher development. In J. Brownlee (Ed.), *Personal epistemology in teacher education* (pp. 210–226). London: Routledge Falmer.

Seligman, M.E.P., Ernst, R.M., Gillham, J., Reivich, K., & Linkins, M. (2009). Positive education: Positive psychology and classroom interventions. *Oxford Review of Education, 35*(3), 293–311.

Slee, R. (1997). Imported or important theory? Sociological interrogations of disablement and special education. *British Journal of Sociology of Education, 18*(3), 407–419.

Stanovich, P.J. (1994). *Teachers' sense of efficacy, beliefs about practice, and teaching behaviours as predictors of effective inclusion of exceptional and at risk pupils*. (Unpublished doctoral dissertation). University of Toronto.

Stanovich, P., & Jordan, A. (1998). Canadian teachers' and principals' beliefs about inclusive education as predictors of effective teaching in heterogeneous classrooms. *Elementary School Journal, 98*(3), 221–238.

Stanovich, P., & Jordan, A. (2002). Preparing general educators to teach in inclusive classrooms: Some food for thought. *Teacher Educator, 37*(3), 173–185.

Stanovich, P.J., Jordan, A.B., & Perot, J. (1998). Relative differences in academic self-concept and peer acceptance among students in inclusive classrooms. *Remedial and Special Education, 19*(2), 120–126.

Wagner, M., Newman, L., Cameto, R., & Levine, P. (2003). *Changes over time in the early post-school outcomes of youth with disabilities.* A report from the National Longitudinal Transition Study-2 (NLTS2). Menlo Park, CA: SRI International. Retrieved from http://www.nlts2.org/reports/2005_06/nlts2_report_2005_06_execsum.pdf

Wayne, A.J., & Youngs, P. (2003). Teacher characteristics and student achievement gains: A review. *Review of Educational Research, 73*(1), 89–122. http://dx.doi.org/10.3102/00346543073001089

Wiebe Berry, R.A. (2006, Jan.–Feb.). Beyond strategies: Teacher beliefs and writing instruction in two primary inclusion classrooms. *Journal of Learning Disabilities, 39*(1), 11–24.

Wiebe Berry, R.A. (2008). Novice teachers' conceptions of fairness in inclusion classrooms. *Teaching and Teacher Education, 24*(5), 1149–1159.

White, B. (2000). Pre-service teachers' epistemology viewed through perspectives on problematic classroom situations. *Journal of Education for Teaching, 26*(3), 279–305.

White, R. (2007). *Characteristics of classroom teachers which contribute to their professional growth in implementing their inclusive classroom practices.* (Unpublished master's thesis). University of Toronto.

PART III

Late Elementary (Grades 4–8)
to Secondary (Grades 9–12)

10 Supporting Students in the Transition to High School: The Role of Self-Regulated Learning

DAWN BUZZA

This chapter addresses key issues for learners as they transition from elementary school to high school. Consideration is given to how teachers and schools can assist all students, including those who are at risk for failure, by supporting the development of effective motivational beliefs and self-regulated learning (SRL) during this critical transition. As an illustrative case, a schoolwide inititative in which secondary school teachers provide SRL support across curriculum and instructional settings is described.

Although there are many students for whom the transition to high school is relatively smooth and even positive, a substantial number experience a decline in attendance and academic achievement (including standardized test scores and grades), increased perceived isolation, alienation from school and behavioural problems, and decreases in other aspects of social and emotional well-being (Hauser, Choate, & Thomas, 2009; National Centre for Education Statistics, 1992) There is growing evidence indicating that getting off-track academically in Grade 9 has both academic and social consequences far beyond the transition to high school, including a greater likelihood of dropping out before graduating (Allensworth & Easton, 2005; Cohen & Smerdon, 2009; Roderick, 1993; Roderick & Camburn, 1996; Stevenson, Schiller, & Schneider, 1994; Weiss & Bearman, 2007). For instance, many students surveyed in the Canadian Youth in Transition Survey (Statistics Canada, 2005) who dropped out of high school by age 17 were disengaged from school by the time they were 15. The 15-year-olds who did eventually drop out were not necessarily struggling academically, nor did they necessarily have a low self-image. However, school-related reasons, including being bored or not interested in school, problems with schoolwork and with teachers, or being "kicked out of" school were cited by nearly half of those who dropped out by the age of 17. At age 15, 49% of later drop-outs (compared with 34% of those who stayed in school beyond 17) felt that discipline was not handled fairly in their school, that students were not respected and that their school was not a friendly place.

Even though academic difficulties and alienation from school do not always result in dropping out, these challenges, nonetheless, have important implications for students' development and their future personal, social, and career success. Given that adolescents spend more of their waking hours in school than in any other setting, the experiences they have there and their social and academic engagement in school will have a major influence on their psychological, social, and emotional adjustment and well-being (Eccles & Roeser, 2011).

Explaining the Challenges in the Transition to High School

A number of possible explanations have been suggested to elucidate why the transition to high school is so challenging for many youngsters. Drawing on district-based statistical evidence as well as published research, Neild (2009) examined four possible theoretical explanations for the academic difficulties experienced by students during the first year of high school. The first kind of theory attributes transition problems to life-course and developmental changes in learners. Most of this argument is based on social and parenting changes at this time in a teen's life, as he or she experiences increases in both independence and peer influence. Although there is some evidence of difficulty in high school that can be attributed to social factors such as changes in parental supervision, romantic relationships, and risk-taking behaviour, these changes do not appear to influence students' getting off-track in Grade 9, once other explanations are accounted for.

A second theory attributes transition difficulties to changing schools at Grade 9, which occurs in about 80% of cases in the United States. The evidence that Neild reports (2009) does not support school change as a major source of students' high school difficulties; in fact, a change in schools can often be a fresh start, and thus a positive factor in students' adjustment and ultimate success in high school, especially for students who were alienated from school in Grade 8 (Neild, 2009; Weiss & Bearman, 2007).

The third explanation is based around indications that many students are inadequately prepared for high school, particularly in terms of academic skills and fundamental content knowledge in mathematics and literacy. Interestingly, it appears that learning skills and not just content knowledge are important. Neild's investigation showed that Grade 8 course grades were better predictors of academic difficulty in Grade 9 than were math and literacy standardized test scores (Neild, 2009, p. 60): "The stronger effect of course grades relative to test scores provides indirect evidence that, in addition to math and reading skills, academic attitudes, behaviours, and coping strategies developed before high school have an effect on ninth-grade outcomes." Specifically, course grades are more likely to be based on learning behaviours and coping strategies as well as content knowledge, although standardized tests are designed to assess only content knowledge and skills.

The fourth kind of explanation attributes Grade 9 students' difficulties to aspects of high school organization and climate. Neild (2009) suggests that three school organization and climate features that appear to be particularly important for the academic success of students are the following: (1) staff who share responsibilities, decision making, and a commitment to common goals; (2) an emphasis on trusting, personal teacher–student relationships; and (3) teachers who hold high expectations for students to work hard, stay in school, and have high aspirations for the future.

In summary, inadequate preparation of students for high school and the organization and climate of high schools were the major sources of difficulty in students' transition to Grade 9. It is important to note that Neild's analysis focused only on academic difficulties during Grade 9 that might impact progression and graduation, without consideration of social and emotional outcomes. However, even with academic success as the outcome variable of interest, the relationship between student-perceived school climate factors and student outcomes was important. For instance, Allensworth and Easton (2005) found that fewer Grade 9 course failures occurred at schools where there was a high level of student–teacher trust and where teachers offered more personal attention in class, held higher expectations for students, and offered more help with personal problems.

School and Classroom Effects on Student Motivation and Engagement

The effects of school- and classroom-climate factors on the experience of many students as they transition to Grade 9 have been studied extensively. Research shows that declines in school-related motivation and engagement observed when students move into high school can be attributed, in large part, to developmentally inappropriate changes in the school environment and instructional practices. Eccles and Roeser (2011) reviewed evidence related to several aspects of curriculum and instruction, teacher beliefs, and school policy that are important to the motivation and engagement of adolescents. Choosing curriculum materials and instructional activities that are developmentally appropriate in terms of both topical interest and cognitive requirements is important in making schoolwork meaningful, yet it may not be occurring in many high schools. In addition, the efficacy beliefs of teachers in terms of their ability to teach all of their students, belief in their students' ability to master challenging material, and trust in students and their parents, referred to as *academic optimism* (Beard, Hoy, & Woolfolk Hoy, 2010), may be lower in high school than in the elementary grades (Eccles & Roeser, 2011). Beard et al. (2010) argue that teachers' academic optimism is a key motivational construct that underlies effective teaching and effective teacher–student relationships.

A related set of teaching and classroom environment variables that are important for adolescents' motivation and engagement are captured in the research on classroom goal structures and on both teachers' and students' beliefs about the nature of ability. There is a wealth of research literature on achievement-goal theory and its implications for teaching practices and achievement motivation (e.g., Dweck, 2006; Meece, Anderman, & Anderman, 2006; Midgley, 2002; Roseth, Johnson, & Johnson, 2008). One study, by Roeser, Eccles, and Sameroff (2000), found that students most at risk for school failure were those who were highly aware of a competitive and "relative-ability" goal orientation in their school, where the goal of learning was seen as having students demonstrate their abilities relative to others, rather than mastery. A mastery-goal orientation, on the other hand, involves teachers emphasizing student mastery of material, their investment of effort, self-improvement, progressive skill development, and collaboration, based on the belief that ability is incremental rather than fixed (Dweck, 2006; Midgley, 2002). Eccles and Roeser (2011) point out that the greater emphasis on performance-oriented/relative-ability instructional practices in secondary, compared with elementary school classrooms render these environments less motivating and supportive for all but the highest achievers.

In their theoretical work on self-determination theory, Ryan and Deci (2009) identified the psychological needs for autonomy, competence, and relatedness as critical to adolescents' development and maintenance of intrinsic motivation. In earlier research (Deci, Schwartz, Sheinman, & Ryan, 1981), these authors found that students were more intrinsically motivated and had higher self-esteem and perceived competence when their teachers were oriented toward supporting student autonomy and self-regulation through offering choice and supportive feedback, compared with students in classrooms where teachers used extrinsic rewards and evaluations to control behaviour. A large body of research since that time has found similar results across international contexts and at every level of education (Ryan & Deci, 2009). At a period in their development when parental control is decreasing and students are expected to become more independent, they may be especially in need of relatedness in their school environment. Classroom contexts that support relatedness and autonomy require trusting student-teacher relationships, which are more difficult to forge in rotary systems where teachers encounter five to eight different classes each day. This contention is supported by the considerable empirical evidence of a decline in adolescents' perceptions of teacher emotional support and a sense of belonging in their classrooms between elementary school and high school (Burchinal, Roberts, Zeisel, & Rowley, 2008; Eccles & Roeser, 2011; Wigfield, Eccles, Schiefele, Roeser, & Davis-Kean, 2006). Moreover, research related to self-determination theory shows that school environments that are controlling and unsupportive of autonomy contribute to academic failure and dropout (e.g., Ryan & LaGuardia, 1999; Statistics Canada, 2005; Vallerand, Fortier, & Guay, 1997).

School and Classroom Environments and At-Risk Students

The negative effects of environments where goal structures are competitive and performance based and where instructional practices are based on teachers' beliefs that ability is fixed are exacerbated in academically at-risk student populations and in groups traditionally targeted with stereotypes of intellectual inferiority (Eccles & Roeser, 2011; Lane & Carter, 2006). For instance, Roeser, Urdan, and Stephens (2009) proposed a model of school effects on motivation and achievement that posits perceptions of school culture and motivational processes as mediating variables between student characteristics and educational outcomes. One important implication of this model is the notion that student background characteristics such as race, ethnicity, and social class interact with school culture and climate, such that students' beliefs, goals, values, and well-being are likely to influence their subjective perceptions of the school environment.

In experiencing exaggerated challenges as they transition into high school, students from ethnic and cultural minority groups are joined by (and also overlap with) student populations designated as in need of special education services. These groups include students for whom English is not their first language and students with learning disabilities, autism spectrum disorder, emotional-behaviour disorders, and numerous others. Historically, considerable resources have been provided for elementary-level programs to support the social and academic needs of students identified and designated as in need of special education; however, many of these programs are unavailable at the secondary level (Lane & Carter, 2006).

Student Academic Preparation for High School

As noted above, another major explanation for many students getting off track in Grade 9 is inadequate academic preparation for the rigours of high school. It is important, however, to unpack what is meant by "academic preparation" before making assumptions about potentially effective remediation approaches. For instance, since course grades in math and litreacy, along with academic skills and attitudes appear to be better predictors of Grade 9 difficulties than are standardized test scores (Neild, 2009, p. 60), support in developing both content knowledge and more general academic skills and behaviours is called for. There are some examples of remedial or "catch-up" math and literacy courses supplementary to the regular curriculum, as well as summer "bridge" programs aimed at the same objectives for students entering Grade 9. However, Cohen and Smerdon (2009) reported that, although summer courses for students who need extra support prior to entering high school may be successful in lowering course failures and dropout rates, few of these programs allow adaptation to specific student needs. Also, evaluations of these programs, while providing some evidence of their effectiveness, are limited in that they typically are not based on randomized samples (Neild, 2009). As such, the positive outcomes shown for these programs may, in part, be the result of self-selection factors such as higher levels of student motivation, less pressure to engage in part-time employment during the summer, and so forth, compared with students who did not attend these courses and programs.

Self-Regulated Learning Support

Another potentially useful focus for academic support for students making the transition to high school is to help them develop effective strategies and behaviours that will enable them to manage their academic work and also their emotions and motivational responses related to schoolwork. Interventions designed to support students' development of self-regulation and self-motivation skills are examples of these kinds of efforts. Research has shown consistently that achievement, both in and outside school, is influenced positively by students' use of self-regulated learning (SRL) skills and behaviours to manage learning situations effectively, regardless of the learners' ability levels (Boekaerts, Pintrich, & Zeidner, 2000; Schunk, 2005).

There are varying models of SRL in the education literature. Most theoretical formulations, however, hold that when learners self-regulate they manage their abilities and capacities (e.g., thoughts, emotions, and behaviours) and their social and contextual surroundings to reach their goals for learning and achievement (Reeve, Ryan, Deci, & Jang, 2008). Self-regulated learners are seen to have internalized self-motivational beliefs, such as self-efficacy and intrinsic interest in their academic work. Intrinsic motivation for learning involves strong self-efficacy beliefs, a focus on personal progress and deep understanding, and a tendency to attribute outcomes to factors the learner can control. Self-efficacy beliefs have been found to influence students' academic goal setting and also their achievement of those goals (Zimmerman, Bandura, & Martinez-Pons, 1992). Metacognitive skills, such as being aware of one's strengths and weaknesses as a learner and an ability to apply strategies effectively to manage challenging tasks, are also key aspects of self-regulation (Winne & Perry, 2000).

In academic contexts, SRL is often defined from a social-cognitive theoretical perspective as a recursive or cyclical process involving goal setting, strategic learning behaviours, and use of cognitive and affective feedback to reassess and adjust both behaviours and goals (Winne & Hadwin, 2008; Zimmerman, 2000; Zimmerman et al., 1992). In these models of SRL, the adaptive processes that are key to successful self-regulation can be viewed from the perspective of how learners proceed through a single task and also across many tasks over time, such as occurs in school (Cleary & Zimmerman, 2004; Winne & Hadwin, 2008; Zimmerman, 2008). A volitional component is also integrated into the cognitive and motivational aspects of SRL, taking into account the importance of students planning for and protecting their efforts to reach their goals by managing their work environments, avoiding distractions, or self-reinforcing persistence on tasks (Corno, 2008; Schunk & Zimmerman, 2006). Students who are able to control their use of self-regulation to accomplish academic work are developing effective work habits that, in turn, are likely to result in higher levels of motivation, achievement, and satisfaction.

Giving students the opportunity to evaluate their own learning processes and products provides them with feedback on how they are managing their learning and can contribute to their development of metacognitive knowledge. More importantly, with effective modelling and coaching, students can be empowered to use their self-evaluation feedback to enhance future learning. Zimmerman (2008) describes effective self-regulated learners as being *proactive* in their use of goal setting, task analysis, and awareness of their motivational beliefs and expectations, as well as in their task strategies such as time management and organization. *Reactive* learners, on the other hand, tend to self-regulate less effectively because they rely only on self-reflection and self-evaluation processes following work on a task to improve their performance. Thus, it is not only the knowledge of how to self-regulate in approaching academic tasks, nor one's attention to self-evaluative feedback, but also the planning for and enacting of goal-protective behaviours that enables learners to succeed, even when facing obstacles and difficulties.

Although the positive effects of SRL are well documented (Boekaerts et al., 2000; Perry, 1998; Perry, Phillips, & Dowler, 2004), we also know that many learners across wide range of ages and learning contexts are not self-regulating effectively (Howard-Rose & Rose, 1994; Perry, 1998; Winne & Hadwin, 2008). Research has shown that low achievers can improve academic performance if they are given instruction in SRL, and if they are supported in developing autonomy or personal agency (Ryan & Deci, 2009).

When Perry and VandeKamp (2000) asked teachers about their goals for students, most indicated that they want to help students become more independent and effective learners, but were not sure about how much support their students needed, or what kinds of support would be most helpful. Indeed, many students are not taught the strategies that could help them to manage their learning, or how to choose and apply them effectively in the right situations. Even if learning strategies are taught explicitly, students need to become proactive in their approach to learning tasks, so that they are equipped to identify the right strategies for the situation they are in, and enact them in an adaptive way.

How Can Teachers Provide SRL Support?

Self-regulated learners can adapt effectively to changes in tasks, situations, surroundings, and self. By helping students to develop more effective strategies, including volitional strategies, they will be in a stronger position to cope with the multiple changes they face as they move into the challenging high school curriculum and social context.

Teachers can support students' development of self-regulated learning by providing explicit instruction in the use of various cognitive and metacognitive strategies and by offering frequent opportunities to participate in open-ended, challenging tasks, discuss their progress, and practice newly acquired SRL skills (Perry et al., 2004). These authors described practices of teachers who provided high levels of SRL support by:

> Ensuring students acquire the curricular and strategy knowledge they need to operate independently, make appropriate choices, and expand their abilities by attempting challenging tasks. Also, these teachers use nonthreatening evaluation practices that encourage students to focus on personal progress (vs. besting peers or impressing the teacher) and view errors as opportunities to learn. (p. 1856)

These teachers were thus promoting the motivational beliefs that are associated with SRL by providing students with autonomy support and helping them to develop academic self-efficacy. Although this particular study was conducted in elementary school classrooms, the literature on motivation and SRL clearly demonstrates the importance of supporting older students' SRL development through similar kinds of practices.

The three-phase cyclical model of self-regulation described above (Zimmerman, 2000) has been applied through a Self-Regulation Empowerment Program (SREP) (Cleary & Zimmerman, 2004). This program has shown promise in helping at-risk middle school and high school students to develop self-regulated and self-motivated beliefs and behaviours, while empowering them to take responsibility for their improved academic performance (Cleary & Chen, 2009; Cleary, Platten,

& Nelson, 2008; Cleary & Zimmerman, 2004). The SREP is based on the three cyclical phases of *forethought* (i.e., processes that precede any effort to act), *performance control* (i.e., processes occurring during learning efforts), and *self-reflection* (i.e., processes occurring after learning or performance) (Cleary & Zimmerman, 2004, p. 538).

In the SREP intervention a self-regulated learning coach (SRC) works with one or several students to conduct a diagnostic assessment followed by a self-regulated learning development component. The diagnostic assessment begins with collecting data at a general level (e.g., to discover in which classes the student struggles and on which grading criteria he performs poorly) and becomes gradually more specific (e.g., through student self-report, interviews and reviewing study materials, finding out what strategies he uses to perform well in this class). Finally, a highly specific, microanalytic assessment involving think-alouds and interviews provides details of *how* the student selects, uses, and regulates specific strategies within that class and task situation. Once the student's motivational and strategic weaknesses are identified through this assessment, the SRC implements three specific steps aimed at changing these weaknesses into strengths. The first step involves having students keep track of their strategy use and their performance outcomes (e.g., test grades or assignment marks), thus empowering students by helping cultivate the belief that academic success is under the their own control. The second step involves teaching specific learning and study strategies using cognitive modelling and guided practice. Third, students are taught to use graphing for goal setting and planning and for monitoring performance outcomes and processes. The SRC guides them in the use of this performance feedback to evaluate goal attainment and then to make strategic attributions and inferences about future learning behaviour.

Along similar lines, but with a less prescriptive approach, Butler (2002) developed an intervention to promote SRL called *strategic content learning* (SCL). This teacher-led intervention has been evaluated with secondary and postsecondary students with learning disabilities and in the context of individual, small group, and whole class instruction (Butler, 1995, 1998; Butler, Beckingham, & Lauscher, 2005). The implementation of SCL is not focused specifically on a single type of performance evaluation or learning task; it takes the form of teacher–student interactions intended to help students to view learning and performance tasks as problems to be solved. In the context of regular instruction, students are assisted to interpret task criteria, select, adapt, and implement strategies to achieve task goals, assess outcomes against task criteria, and then revise their learning approach as needed (Butler et al., 2005). Some SCL techniques are similar to those used in the SREP intervention, such as the use of cumulative "strategy sheets" in which students keep track of the strategies they are using for particular learning or performance evaluation tasks; however, a significant difference between the two approaches is that teachers using SCL assist students in their own construction or adaptation of strategies rather than providing explicit instruction in teacher-specified strategies.

The work of Cleary and Zimmerman and of Butler and her colleagues has shown that the development of SRL can be nurtured through intensive, targeted interventions that engage students in cycles of self-regulation. Both of these types of interventions are aimed at supporting the development of SRL in the context of regular curriculum and instruction (Butler et al., 2005; Cleary & Zimmerman, 2004). It is interesting to note that the Grade 9 students in Cleary et al.'s 2008 study, who were struggling to keep up in an honours-level science course, had arrived there with proficient or higher scores on standardized science tests. Their initial difficulty in Grade 9 science and their later success in terms of classroom test performance and SRL behaviours resulting from this intervention supports Neild's (2009) contention that helping transitioning students with general academic skills and motivational beliefs as a means of supporting their subject area learning may be a key determinant of whether or not they stay on track in high school.

From these examples, it can be shown that classroom instructional strategies that provide support for student's development of SRL can help them achieve success academically and become more engaged in their schoolwork by developing self-empowering performance attributions and higher academic self-efficacy. These teaching practices involve providing structured opportunities for goal setting, monitoring, and analysing one's efforts toward those goals, and coaching toward developing and selecting effective learning and problem-solving strategies – all of which can be incorporated into the completion of existing and ongoing curriculum objectives. In fact, some research has shown that embedding SRL instruction and support into regular curriculum shows better outcomes in terms of both strategy use and achievement than providing SRL instruction separately (Butler, 2002; Butler et al., 2005). However, so far, there is limited evidence of the effectiveness of SRL interventions in the context of whole-class instruction. This and other challenges for secondary school teachers and schools in providing SRL support to their at-risk students will be addressed next.

Opportunities and Challenges in Providing SRL Support

Whole-Class Instruction and SRL Support

As with most kinds of skill learning, SRL strategy instruction is more effective in raising student achievement if it offers students many practice opportunities over time and provides specific feedback in terms of performance results (Cleary & Zimmerman, 2004; Dignath & Buttner, 2008; Miller, Heafner, & Massey, 2009). Given the individualization involved in the SREP and SCL interventions described above, applying the principles of cyclic self-regulation development in teaching a whole class may be quite challenging. Nonetheless, it is not impossible to imagine a classroom in which many of the steps in the SREP intervention are completed through whole-class instruction along with individual student activities, while other interactive steps are conducted in small groups, as often occurs when teachers implement small-group conferencing activities for other purposes. Butler (2002) provides clear and practical guidelines for adapting instruction for strategic content learning to individuals, small groups, or a whole class. A key advantage of whole-class instruction compared with pull-out settings, as she points out, is that it is the teacher who designs tasks and assignments for students and prescribes performance criteria (Butler, 2002, p. 90). Teachers can, thus, assign students subtasks as part of regular assignments that are opportunities to promote SRL. These subtasks might include things like developing performance criteria for a writing assignment and then discussing these in class, allowing for diagnosis of problems in understanding the task or expectations before assignments are completed. Similarly, students can be asked to write reflections on the feedback they receive after an assignment is marked, so that they can make optimal use of teacher feedback in the next assignment or performance opportunity (e.g., on an exam). In this way, individual analysis and reflection can be combined with discussion, in dyads, small groups, or the whole class to scaffold students' task understanding to help them articulate their current and future approaches to task completion.

Teachers' Collaborative Professional Learning

It is often not possible for secondary school teachers to provide long-term interventions that would allow for multiple practice–feedback cycles. Nevertheless, students' development of SRL may be facilitated through schoolwide efforts in which teachers work in concert toward the same SRL support goals. Through collaborating in the development of instructional practices and assessment tools across courses and subject areas, teachers may be better able to provide the instructional supports that best suit their individual contexts, while promoting a common understanding about SRL to students. Perry and VandeKamp (2000) described a 3-year teacher development effort in which they worked collaboratively with five elementary school teachers using a community-of-practice framework (Lave & Wenger, 1991; Palincsar, Magnusson, Morano, Ford, & Brown, 1998), aimed at developing SRL-supportive teaching practices. These kinds of professional learning communities, in which teachers are encouraged to create, share, and test out novel curricular and instructional practices, and where researchers provide appropriate theory and models in support of their efforts, allow for what Randi and Corno (2000) call "Collaborative Innovation." These authors describe several examples of researcher-teacher collaborations in which teachers combine and/or adapt instructional models or interventions found in the literature to their own curricular objectives and classroom contexts, where, for instance, they may have found some aspects of the original models ineffective or difficult to implement as prescribed. Given the iterative ways in which teachers typically plan instruction, in which student cues about their ongoing understanding and interest play an important feedback role (Randi & Corno, 2000, p. 664), these teacher-generated innovations might often involve teaching students strategies, such as aspects of SRL, in the context of regular content instruction, as was the case in Butler's teacher–researcher collaborations (Butler, 2002; Butler et al., 2005).

Although this approach shows promise, teacher engagement in professional learning communities in which they collaborate toward common SRL-supportive practices will not occur without some challenges. As demonstrated in the literature on teacher professional development and conceptual change (e.g., Fullan, 2007), teachers may not always be motivated to try out and continue using new strategies. Gregoire (2003) proposed that teachers' conceptual change depends in part on whether they perceive professional learning opportunities as a threat to their efficacy or a challenge that can enhance their efficacy. Teacher efficacy beliefs are their expectations about their ability to help students learn and, in particular, to do so by implementing specific instructional strategies or approaches (Wigfield et al., 2006). Teacher efficacy is said to buffer the stress associated with trying out new instructional practices, but other necessary conditions for teachers to be willing participants in the change process include adequate time for professional learning, supportive colleagues, and adequate subject knowledge with which to approach the challenge.

By implication, teachers' efficacy beliefs may also reflect either static or incremental beliefs about students' ability. For instance, in their study of changing teacher practices during a year-long professional development project, Turner, Warzon, and Christensen (2011) noted that it is common for teachers to believe that both mathematics ability and student motivation are fixed rather than malleable. Their study demonstrated a number of obstacles to changing teachers' beliefs and their practices, including an unwillingness to accept responsibility for student motivation or learning because of thir fixed beliefs about students, their low self-efficacy for teaching in general, or for teaching math in particular, and limitations in their subject matter knowledge (Turner et al., 2011).

Importance of School Culture

A third factor that will likely influence how readily teachers can support students' development of SRL as they enter and navigate high school is the broader school culture. Recent literature has identified several characteristics of "successful" public high schools in the United States (i.e., schools with higher average levels of academic achievement and fewer socio-economic status and fewer race/ethnic differences in academic achievement). These characteristics were a high value placed on learning, high expectations that all students can learn and master a core curriculum, and the belief that though the business of school is learning, each person has inherent value and dignity and is a valued member of a social community (Hattie, 2009; Lee & Smith, 2001; Stewart, 2007).

The concept of *academic optimism* described earlier in relation to teacher beliefs can also be viewed at the school level. As a property of schools that includes teachers' collective efficacy beliefs, trust in students and their parents, and an academic emphasis, academic optimism has been linked to student achievement in several studies (Hoy & Miskel, 2008; Hoy & Smith, 2007; McGuigan & Hoy, 2006). Hoy and Miskel also describe "enabling school structures" as hierarchies that support or enable teachers' work through shared authority within established roles, two-way communication, respecting differences, engendering trust, seeing problems as opportunities, learning from mistakes, and welcoming the unexpected. These features of enabling school structures have been shown to predict academic optimism (Beard et al., 2010).

Research has begun to demonstrate the importance of academic optimism to the creation of effective communities of practice (e.g., Hord, Roussen, & Sommers, 2010). Teachers' professional learning communities rely on open communication and sharing among teachers, shared goals and ongoing collaboration, and a climate of trust in which all views are valued and the cost of errors is small (Lave & Wenger, 1991). Given these features, it would be anticipated that enabling school structures and a "communal" school organization and culture where teachers share decision making, responsibility, and a common set of goals (Neild, 2009) may facilitate teachers' efforts to learn and try out new practices, such as SRL-supportive instruction, through collaborative and self-reflective professional learning.

One School's Professional Learning about SRL

This section presents a case study illustrating how staff at one school collaborated in learning about SRL and trying out SRL-supportive practices across subject areas, programs, and grade levels. The secondary school that is the focus of this case study draws 1,150 students from across a medium-sized urban region. Typical of a downtown core high school, their student body represents a broad range of socio-economic, ethnic, and educational backgrounds. Teachers at the school describe it as having a large number of high needs and at-risk learners. This school is seen as an integral part of the downtown community and the region and is recognized as a school that welcomes students from all walks of life. The culture and academic policies at the school encourage teachers to collaborate toward common goals, to share decision making, and to take risks in trying out new instructional strategies. It could, thus, be characterized as a "communal" school that supports teachers' development of a community of practice.

Professional learning in the district and at the school had been focused on "assessment *for* and *as* learning"; the staff decided to address this focus through SRL support, which they also viewed as a way to increase student engagement and success. In a year-long professional learning cycle, a group of about 40 teachers, including department heads, had worked together to develop, implement, refine, and reflect on unit plans that included opportunities for students to develop SRL strategies. The identified SRL strategies included articulating individual learning goals, tracking progress toward their goals and analysing their effectiveness, and self- and peer assessment. At the end of the first year of collaboration, the group met to share and reflect on their results, both in terms of student outcomes and their own professional learning. Students in their classes represented varying achievement levels, including those with identified special learning needs.

As teachers from across the school community shared their experiences, several themes emerged, and a range of SRL support strategies were described. Many teachers made use of students' voices in articulating clearly defined success criteria and exemplars to help guide student goal setting and monitoring. Many of them focused their efforts on metacognitive skills development – teaching students to become more aware of *how* they learn and helping them make choices that support their learning styles and needs. They described efforts to enhance metacognitive skills in terms of *assessment as learning*. Another common theme was the use of "high-yield instructional tools" such as graphic organizers, anchor charts, open-ended critical questions, and exemplars used to promote self-assessment and cognitive monitoring. Student self- and peer assessment were commonly articulated as part of classroom assessment practices aimed at learning skills development. Finally, students were often taught help-seeking strategies and were supported in advocating for their learning needs. An overarching theme appeared to be one of academic optimism, as described earlier (Beard et al., 2010) – teachers shared openly their challenges, doubts, and areas of confusion, as well as their successes. Most notably, however, they expressed great pride in their students' efforts and achievements in response to the SRL strategies they had implemented.

Examples of SRL Support Strategies

Individual interviews were conducted with four teachers who had participated in the professional learning cycle and also with two other teachers at the school. The following two examples from this group of six participants illustrate how SRL support can occur in the context of differing subjects and instructional contexts.

French Immersion – Grade 9 Geography and Grade 11 Literacy

Collette[1] described several ways in which she guided students in goal setting and analysis as a focus for helping them develop SRL skills. In

Grade 10 and Grade 11 French immersion literacy classes, students kept a Daily Learning Journal in which they used a teacher-provided template to articulate daily learning goals, evaluate their goals, identify current understandings and things that required clarification, and then to specify the next day's goal. A key purpose of this goal analysis process was for students to reflect on how realistic their goals were and to analyse and critique them. The template offered five possible judgments about each day's goal: (1) too simple, (2) simple, (3) reasonable, (4) complicated, and (5) too complicated. A similar template was used to analyse assignments after they were marked and returned to students. This template included sections for students to assess what they did well, what they needed to improve, and how they planned to reach their improvement goals. The individual goal analysis and reflection on assignment feedback, combined with class discussions to identify and share strategies for task completion used by Collette are well aligned with the approach suggested by Butler (2002) for promoting self-regulation in whole-class settings.

In describing her impressions of how students responded to these activities, Collette noted that they seemed to take more ownership of their work in the class than they did before. In this course, most students were high achievers, yet many of them struggled with time management due to many commitments and activities outside of school. She introduced the Daily Learning Journal as follows:

> I feel the need for this and the aim is to get you better organized because we have issues – even with just my calendar, you don't follow it. I know you don't follow it because on the day that it said you should have read chapter 3 for example, I did a surprise quiz and half of you had not read the thing, so, how can we have a fruitful discussion when you don't know what we're talking about?

Altough she imposed the journal at first, her plan for the next class group was to involve students in establishing the goal-analysis process from the beginning by inviting them, for instance, to help decide whether daily or weekly journal entries would be more useful. She hoped to encourage more ownership and responsibility on their part, so that they would be motivated to place priority on their learning goals and strategies.

Collette also described her Grade 11 learners as much more metacognitively aware and more strategic than those in Grade 9:

When they arrive in Grade 9, I find that they don't have a lot of strategies regarding how to tackle something, how to get it started. So we work on all the possible strategies, from brainstorming together out loud, and I scribe things, or some kids scribe things. Or they start doing a graphic organizer, whichever shape they want, the spiderweb thing or whatever – or lists of pros and cons.

She also worked with her Grade 9 students to help them learn to make better choices about how they arranged their learning conditions and environment. For instance, at first she allowed students to sit wherever they wanted to, with the understanding that the seating plan would change every 2 weeks:

So the first 2 weeks, you can sit wherever you want, to get yourself accustomed to the school. But in 2 weeks we're going to change. My first change is, since I don't know you, the computer's going to choose. So it's random … The second change, you get a chance to sit with whomever you want. So they do. But we're going to talk about your choice afterwards – we're going to see if that worked. Did I have to talk to you too often about not paying attention? Did you share nicely? [etc.]

Collette noticed a considerable difference in these students over the semester, especially with respect to their willingness to take responsibility for their learning. For example, if they came to class unprepared, they accepted their own role in the situation, rather than making excuses and blaming others or circumstances beyond their control.

Promoting SRL in the School Library

The library proved to be a hub for supporting and assessing SRL skills throughout the school community. Marlene, the head librarian, described the development of strategies to help students become more goal directed and strategic in their use of teachers, peers, and library resources to meet their learning needs. She first presented at school assemblies to give students common messages and instruction about what "good" (i.e., effective) goals are, as well as why and how to assess progress toward goals. Students were then required to write down a goal for every visit to the library, on an "MSIP pass." This is a "multi-subject instructional period" travel pass that allows students to use school time to visit the library, get extra help in specific subjects, work in a computer lab, or study independently in a designated classroom. In Marlene's words:

> So what has happened is we have created a situation where you take a little bit of time from each of the courses they're taking and you put it into this chunk of time. So that they can work on assignments and get things done. So a teacher can say, as part of my course requirement, "This is something that you need to get done during MSIP." And that's kind of the expectation; that you're not losing those 15 minutes, you're putting it somewhere else, basically.

When using their MSIP pass to visit the library, students were required to articulate a specific goal and to explain that goal to a librarian when asked. Over time, Marlene began to ask students for more specific goals, and she adapted these requirements to meet the needs of different learners:

> [So the] kids dutifully would write something. It might just say "English," or it might say "Math." And then I realized, "That's not enough." English and Math are too undefined. So we started to do a lot of work with getting to write a good goal, a specific goal, an achievable goal, a measurable goal. So, when I introduced that, we have whiteboards at the front of the library and I would explain it on there. I would talk to kids individually if they didn't have what I considered to be a goal. And then I started giving stickers on the bottom, if they gave me a good goal, I would just throw a sticker down. And they liked the stickers, so we kept giving stickers! And then they would ask the question, "Well why didn't I get a sticker?" And I would get to say, "Well because you don't have a specific goal and you need to have [one]." ... And again, what I expect sometimes from the academic student, compared to what I'll expect from a Fast Forward[2] student in terms of their goal setting, can be two entirely different things. With the academic student, I might say, "Well which questions? Is it questions 10–20 on quadratic equations?" You know, you can't just say math homework. But with a Fast Forward kid, if he's saying "Math homework, Chapter 20," Whoa! We've just won a huge victory with that kid. If they say their Geography summative, that's a huge thing. I don't need that kid to say, "I'm going to write the first introductory paragraph and two body paragraphs," but I would expect that from the academic kid. So again ... with the Fast Forward kids, [it's] incremental growth.

The library's initiatives to promote goal setting in conjunction with the MSIP program allowed students to manage their time and their learning environment strategically – to be in charge of where and how they allocated their MSIP time to complete their assignments, taking advantage of the school resources they had determined they would need. When in the library, they were able to decide whether to work alone in a cubicle, collaborate with peers, or ask for librarians' help in finding and using books, computer programs and databases, or other available resources.

In her role as librarian, Marlene also was well situated to scaffold students' strategic knowledge in the context of working in groups:

> I would say there are some kids who are excellent at recognizing good group work strategies and keeping on task, and asking question/answer back and forth. And there are others who will pretend that they are studying together but haven't got any effective strategies for studying together. So again, that's where sometimes I'll intervene and I'll say "Maybe, a way of testing each other would be to do x, y or z." Or if I see kids who are doing it, I'll say "Wow. That's really excellent. I like the way you are asking each other these questions so that you are testing your knowledge." And you say it in a way that then, three other people have heard you and they think, "Oh, we should be doing it."

Because students often used their MSIP time in the library to work on group eassignments, there were many opportunities such as this to assess and support their developing collaboration skills.

Next Steps

As they completed their year-long professional learning cycle, we asked teachers to participate with us in a research project to study the processes and outcomes of their efforts more formally. We asked teachers who had participated in the first-year learning cycle to work with us and also to help identify others in their departments who had not yet begun to experiment with SRL supportive teaching and assessment practices, but who would like to join in this collaboration.

Participating teachers will first read and talk about SRL and how it has been instantiated in various instructional contexts. They then will describe the kinds of challenges they see their students facing in a particular class and identify ways in which SRL support might help them.

Next, they will collaborate together in developing, refining, and testing strategies and tools for student learning and assessment of SRL. Although SRL-supportive teaching and assessment methods from research literature will be provided, teachers will be encouraged to select from, combine, and adapt these practices and tools for their own purposes within their subjects and teaching situations. Key to this investigation will be teachers' innovative design of academic tasks, classroom structures and interactions, and ongoing assessments to help students acquire SRL skills and motivational beliefs. Building measures of student demonstrations of SRL into existing content area performance evaluations (rather than using separate, stand-alone assessments) will be critical to their usefulness in regular, ongoing classroom practice (Cleary & Zimmerman, 2004; Randi & Corno, 2000; Zimmerman, 2000). We plan to collect data from both teachers' and students' perspectives and to follow initial participant groups over time to observe the incremental development of teacher knowledge and practices as well as students' SRL.

Summary and Conclusions

This chapter began with consideration of the importance of the transition to high school and why it is so challenging for many young adolescents. Although a variety of possible explanations have been suggested for the difficulties that students experience, research findings generally point to two major causes. One is lack of academic preparation for the independence and rigour of high school, especially in terms of learning skills (as opposed to knowledge measured through standardized achievement tests). The other identifies environmental variables, such as academic policies and school and classroom culture, as primary influences on student motivation, engagement, and success. The importance of developmentally appropriate curriculum and instruction, as well as emotional and social support for young adolescents at this critical time in their lives (Eccles & Roeser, 2011) has been emphasized in literature on the transition from elementary to secondary school.

Self-regulated learning (SRL) was described from a social-cognitive perspective as a strategic, goal-directed approach to learning in which students define their learning goals, monitor their progress toward goals, and use effective strategies for managing task-related activities, emotions, and the environment. SRL behaviours and associated motivational skills and beliefs have been shown to enhance academic success for learners at all levels of achievement and ability. Classrooms that promote the development of SRL are those in which student choice, personal agency, and connectedness are supported; these classrooms are characterized by cooperative goal structures in which increased learning and competence are valued, rather than outperforming peers. SRL development can be promoted through individual and whole-class instructional practices, but several factors were identified that can influence these efforts, either positively or negatively. Drawing from research on educational change, the importance of teacher efficacy was highlighted in terms of how teachers' beliefs in their own ability to help students learn can influence their ability and willingness to try out new approaches and practices.

Enabling school structures, in which teachers are encouraged to collaborate toward common goals and to take risks in trying out new and innovative practices, seem to support academic efficacy beliefs and create opportunities for the kind of collaborative innovation that can lead to SRL-supportive instruction. Potential affordances for innovations of this kind were shown in a case study of the professional community of practice at one secondary school. Through effective schoolwide collaborative professional learning it will be possible to increase students' likelihood of success in negotiating the challenges of the transition to high school, socially, academically, and motivationally.

NOTES

1 To ensure confidentiality, psuedonyms have been used for all teacher participants.
2 Fast Forward is a special program for students who are not working at grade level and who plan to move directly from secondary school to the workplace but wish to earn an Ontario Secondary School Diploma in 4 to 5 years.

REFERENCES

Allensworth, E., & Easton, J. (2005). *The On-Track Indicator as a predictor of high school graduation*. Chicago: Consortium on Chicago School Research.
Beard, K.S., Hoy, W.K., & Woolfolk Hoy, A. (2010). Academic optimism

of individual teachers: Confirming a new construct. *Teaching and Teacher Education*, 26(5), 1136–1144.

Boekaerts, M., Pintrich, P.R., & Zeidner, M. (Eds.). (2000). *Handbook of self-regulation*. San Diego, CA: Academic Press.

Burchinal, M.R., Roberts, J.E., Zeisel, S.A., & Rowley, S.J. (2008). Social risk and protective factors for African American children's academic achievement and adjustment during the transition to middle school. *Developmental Psychology*, 44(1), 286–292.

Butler, D.L. (1995). Promoting strategic learning by postsecondary students with learning disabilities. *Journal of Learning Disabilities*, 28(3), 170–190.

Butler, D.L. (1998). The strategic content learning approach to promoting self-regulated learning: A report of three studies. *Journal of Educational Psychology*, 90(4), 682–697.

Butler, D.L. (2002). Individualizing instruction in self-regulated learning. *Theory into Practice*, 41(2), 81–92.

Butler, D.L., Beckingham, B., & Lauscher, H.J.N. (2005). Promoting strategic learning by eighth-grade students struggling in mathematics: A report of three case studies. *Learning Disabilities Practice*, 20(3), 156–174.

Cleary, T.J., & Chen, P.P. (2009). Self-regulation, motivation, and math achievement in middle school: Variations across grade level and math context. *Journal of School Psychology*, 47(5), 291–314.

Cleary, T.J., Platten, P., & Nelson, A. (2008). Effectiveness of the self-regulation empowerment program with urban high school students. *Journal of Advanced Academics*, 20, 70–107.

Cleary, T.J., & Zimmerman, B.J. (2004). Self-Regulation Empowerment Program: A school-based program to enhance self-regulated and self-otivated cycles of student learning. *Psychology in the Schools*, 41(5), 537–550.

Cohen, J.S., & Smerdon, B.A. (2009). Tightening the dropout tourniquet: Easing the transition from middle school to high school. *Preventing School Failure*, 53(3), 177–184.

Corno, L. (2008). Work habits and self-regulated learning: Helping students find a "will" from a "way." In D.H. Schunk & B.J. Zimmerman (Eds.), *Motivation and self-regulated learning: Theory, research and applications* (pp. 197–222). New York: Erlbaum.

Deci, E.L., Schwartz, A.J., Sheinman, L., & Ryan, R.M. (1981). An instrument to assess adults' orientation toward control vs. autonomy with children: Reflections on intrinsic motivation and perceived competence. *Journal of Educational Psychology*, 74, 642–650.

Dignath, C., & Buttner, G. (2008). Components of fostering self-regulated learning among students: A meta-analysis on intervention studies at primary and secondary school level. *Metacognition and Learning*, 3(3), 231–264.

Dweck, C.S. (2006). *Mindset*. New York: Random House.

Eccles, J.S., & Roeser, R.W. (2011). Schools as developmental contexts during adolescence. *Journal of Research on Adolescence*, 21(1), 225–241.

Fullan, M. (2007). *The new meaning of educational change*. New York: Teachers College Press.

Gregoire, M. (2003). Is it a challenge or a threat? A dual-rocess model of teachers' cognition and appraisal processes during conceptual change. *Educational Psychology Review*, 15(2), 147–179.

Hattie, J. (2009). *Visible learning*. New York: Routledge.

Hauser, G.M., Choate, K., & Thomas, T.P. (2009). A two-year study of stake-holder perceptions associated with the transition from 8th grade to high school. *International Journal of Learning*, 16(3), 315–326.

Hord, S.M., Roussen, J.L., & Sommers, W.A. (2010). *Guiding professional learning communities: Inspiration, challenge, surprise, and meaning*. Thousand Oaks, CA: Corwin Press.

Howard-Rose, D., & Rose, C. (1994). Students' adaptations to task environments in resource room and regular class settings. *Journal of Special Education*, 28(1), 3–26.

Hoy, W.K., & Miskel, C.G. (2008). *Educational administration: Theory, research and practice* (8th ed.). New York: McGraw-Hill.

Hoy, W.K., & Smith, C.W. (2007). Influence: A key to successful leadership. *International Journal of Educational Management*, 21(2), 158–167.

Lane, K.L., & Carter, E.W. (2006). Supporting transition-age youth with and at risk for emotional and behavioral disorders at the secondary level: A need for further inquiry. *Journal of Emotional and Behavioral Disorders*, 14(2), 66–70.

Lave, J., & Wenger, E. (1991). *Situated learning: Legitimate peripheral participation*. Cambridge: Cambridge University Press.

Lee, V.E., & Smith, J. (2001). *Restructuring high schools for equity and excellence: What works?* New York: Teachers College Press.

McGuigan, L., & Hoy, W.K. (2006). Principal leadership: Creating a culture of academic optimism to improve achievement for all students. *Leadership and Policy in Schools*, 5(3), 203–229.

Meece, J.L., Anderman, E.M., & Anderman, L.H. (2006). Classroom goal structure, student motivation, and academic achievement. *Annual Review of Psychology*, 57(1), 487–503.

Midgley, C. (2002). *Goals, goal structures, and patterns of adaptive learning.* Mahwah, NJ: Erlbaum.

Miller, S., Heafner, T., & Massey, D. (2009). High-school teachers' attempts to promote self-regulated learning: "I may learn from you, yet how do I do it?" *Urban Review, 41*(2), 121–140.

National Centre for Education Statistics (NCES). (1992). *Statistics in brief: Eighth to tenth grade dropouts (NCES 92–006).*

Neild, R.C. (2009, Spring). Falling off track during the transition to high school: What we know and what can be done. *Future of Children, 19*(1), 53–76.

Palincsar, A.S., Magnusson, S.J., Morano, N., Ford, D., & Brown, N. (1998). Designing a community of practice: Principles and practices of the GIsML Community. *Teaching and Teacher Education, 14*(1), 5–19.

Perry, N.E. (1998). Young children's self-regulated learning and the contexts that support it. *Journal of Educational Psychology, 90*(4), 715–729.

Perry, N.E., Phillips, L., & Dowler, J. (2004). Examining features of tasks and their potential to promote self-regulated learning. *Teachers College Record, 106*(9), 1854–1878.

Perry, N.E., & VandeKamp, K.J.O. (2000). Creating classroom contexts that support young children's development of self-regulated learning. *International Journal of Educational Research, 33*(7-8), 821–843.

Randi, J., & Corno, L. (2000). Teacher innovations in self-regulated learning. In M. Boekaerts, P. Pintrich, & M. Zeidner (Eds.), *Handbook of self-regulation* (pp. 651–685). Orlando, FL: Academic Press.

Reeve, J., Ryan, R., Deci, E.L., & Jang, H. (2008). Understanding and promoting autonomous self-regulation. In D.H. Schunk & B.J. Zimmerman (Eds.), *Motivation and self-regulated learning: Theory, research, and applications* (pp. 223–244). New York: Erlbaum.

Roderick, M. (1993). *The path to dropping out: Evidence for intervention.* Westport, CT: Auburn House.

Roderick, M., & Camburn, E. (1996). *Academic difficulty during the high school transition.* Chicago: Consortium on Chicago School Research.

Roeser, R.W., Eccles, J.S., & Sameroff, A.J. (2000). School as a context of early adolescents' academic and social-emotional development: A summary of research findings. *Elementary School Journal, 100*(5), 443–471.

Roeser, R.W., Urdan, T.C., & Stephens, J.M. (2009). School as a context of student motivation and achievement. In K.R. Wentzel & A. Wigfield (Eds.), *Handbook of motivation at school* (pp. 381–410). New York: Routledge.

Roseth, C.J., Johnson, D.W., & Johnson, R.T. (2008). Promoting early adolescents' achievement and peer relationships: The effects of cooperative, competitive, and individualistic goal structures. *Psychological Bulletin*, *134*(2), 223–246.

Ryan, R.M., & Deci, E.L. (2009). Promoting self-determined school engagement: Motivation, learning and well-being. In K.R. Wentzel & A. Wigfield (Eds.), *Handbook of motivation at school* (pp. 171–196). New York: Routledge.

Ryan, R.M., & LaGuardia, J.G. (1999). Achievement motivation within a pressured society: Intrinsic and extrinsic motivations to learn and the politics of school reform. In T. Urdan (Ed.), *Advances in motivation and achievement* (Vol. 11, pp. 45–85). Greenwich, CT: JAI.

Schunk, D.H. (2005). Commentary on self-regulation in school contexts. *Learning and Instruction*, *15*(2), 173–177.

Schunk, D.H., & Zimmerman, B.J. (2006). Competence and control beliefs: Distinguishing the means and ends. In P.A. Alexander & P.H. Winne (Eds.), *Handbook of educational psychology* (2nd ed., pp. 349–367). New York: Taylor & Francis.

Statistics Canada. (2005). Early indicators of students at risk of dropping out of high school. Retrieved from http://www.statcan.gc.ca/pub/81-004 -x/2004006/7781-eng.htm

Stevenson, D.L., Schiller, K.S., & Schneider, B. (1994). Sequences of opportunities for learning. *Sociology of Education*, *67*(3), 184–198.

Stewart, E.B. (2007). School structural characteristics, student effort, peer associations, and parental involvement. *Education and Urban Society*, *40*(2), 179–204.

Talbert, J.E., & McLaughlin, M.W. (1994). Teacher professionalism in local school contexts. *American Journal of Education*, *102*(2), 123–153.

Turner, J.C., Warzon, K.B., & Christensen, A. (2011). Motivating mathematics learning: Changes in teachers' practices and beliefs during a nine-month collaboration. *American Educational Research Journal*, *48*(3), 718–762.

Vallerand, R.J., Fortier, M.S., & Guay, F. (1997). Self-determination and persistence in a real-life setting: Toward a motivational model of high school dropout. *Journal of Personality and Social Psychology*, *72*(5), 1161–1176.

Weiss, C.C., & Bearman, P.S. (2007). Fresh starts: Reinvestigating the effects of the transition to high school on student outcomes. *American Journal of Education*, *113*(3), 395–421.

Wigfield, A., Eccles, J.S., Schiefele, U., Roeser, R., & Davis-Kean, P. (Eds.). (2006). *Motivation* (6th ed., Vol. 3). New York: Wiley.

Winne, P.H., & Hadwin, A. (2008). The weave of motivation and self-regulated learning. In D.H. Schunk & B.J. Zimmerman (Eds.), *Motivation and self-regulated learning* (pp. 297–314). New York: Erlbaum.

Winne, P.H., & Perry, N.E. (2000). Measuring self-regulated learning. In M. Boekaerts, P. Pintrich, & M. Zeidner (Eds.), *Handbook of self-regulation* (pp. 531–566). Orlando, FL: Academic Press.

Zimmerman, B.J. (2000). Attaining self-regulation: A social-cognitive perspective. In M. Boekaerts, P. Pintrich, & M. Zeidner (Eds.), *Handbook of self-regulation* (pp. 13–39). San Diego, CA: Academic Press.

Zimmerman, B.J. (2008). Goal-setting: A key proactive source of academic self-regulation. In D.H. Schunk & B.J. Zimmerman (Eds.), *Motivation and self-regulated learning: Theory, research and applications* (pp. 267–295). New York: Erlbaum.

Zimmerman, B.J., Bandura, A., & Martinez-Pons, M. (1992). Self-motivation for academic attainment: The role of self-efficacy beliefs and personal goal-setting. *American Educational Research Journal, 29,* 663–676.

11 Stakeholder Perceptions Associated with the Transition of Students from Eighth Grade to High School

KAREN CHOATE, GREGORY M. HAUSER,
AND THOMAS P. THOMAS

The successful transition from one educational level to another is increasingly being recognized as important to the realization of a number of educationally prized outcomes including higher academic achievement (Akos, 2004; Smith, 2006), increased graduation rates (Akos, 2004; Chapman & Sawyer, 2001; Rourke, 2001; Smith, 2006), and better social and emotional adjustment (Akos, 2004; Rourke, 2001; Smith, 2006). Regardless of the age of the learner or the institutional change, each transition holds unique difficulties for students.

A growing body of literature focuses on various aspects of these discrete transitions, namely, from home to preschool or kindergarten (Riley, 2000; Schulting, Malone, & Dodge, 2005; Stormont, Beckner, Mitchell, & Richter, 2005), from elementary to middle school (Espinoza & Juvonen, 2011; Potter, Schliskey, & Stevenson, 2001; Theriot & Dupper, 2010), from middle school to high school (Akos, 2004; Chapman & Sawyer, 2001; Choate, 2009; Cohen & Smerdon, 2009; Hauser, Choate, & Thomas, 2009a, 2009b; Rourke, 2001; Smith, 2006), and from high school to postsecondary institutions or work (Bozick & DeLuca, 2005; Larose, Bernier, & Tarabulsy, 2005; Mounts, Valentiner, Anderson, & Bosswell, 2005). The transition from middle school to high school is particularly difficult because of the complex combination of developmental and environmental factors. The developmental factors are particularly acute for middle school students as they experience the social, intellectual, and physical changes that come with adolescence. The transition from the middle school environment to the high school environment is further complicated by differences in educational philosophy and pedagogy, organization and structure, culture, climate, and stakeholder perceptions. This chapter is organized in four parts. Following this introduction, relevant scholarship on the barriers and obstacles related to the transition from junior high and middle school to high school in the United States is reviewed with particular focus on literature on stakeholder perceptions on the transition to secondary schooling. Recommended strategies for teachers, school administrators, districts, and states to facilitate a successful transition from middle school to high school comprise the third part of this chapter. This is followed by a discussion and conclusion offering three summary recommendations with emphasis on the need to conduct inquiry on student, parent, and teacher perceptions related to the transition to secondary school.

Barriers and Obstacles in the Transition to High School

The research and literature on student transition from one educational level to another is clustered by educational levels (e.g., middle school to high school) and by three dependent variables, namely, academic, behavioural, and affective challenges. The academic dimension related to the transition to high school is well evidenced in scholarship and school practice. More students fail ninth grade than any other grade (Herlihy, 2007), and even previously high-achieving students may experience lower grades and/or fail courses during the freshman year of high school (Akos, 2004; McCallumore & Sparapani, 2010; Smith, 2006). Whether a student drops out of high school is not strictly based on his or her high school experience but instead starts much earlier (Reyes, Gillock, Kobus, & Sanchez, 2000). Grossman and Cooney (2009) found that students who graduate from high school and those who drop out tend to show differences even before the high school transition. Successful ninth graders typically had high grade point averages and attendance records in middle school, demonstrating effective time-management and study skills. Students who had the greatest difficulty in ninth grade were those students who had GPAs in the lowest quartile and were judged as not academically prepared (Cauley & Jovanovich, 2006). Students with a low GPA in middle school were more likely to drop out in high school (Grossman & Cooney, 2009). Therefore, how well the middle school prepares a student for the transition to ninth grade can factor into whether he or she graduates (Reyes et al., 2000). These pre-transition differences indicate that academic preparation plays a significant role in a successful transition to high school.

Important behavioural consequences can result from difficulties in the transition from middle school to high school with increased absences, suspensions, and expulsions (Smith, 2006), decreased involvement in school activities (Akos, 2004; Smith, 2006), students not reaching their full academic and social potential, or ultimately, students failing or dropping out of school (Frey, Ruchkin, Martin, & Schwab-Stone, 2009; Heck & Mahoe, 2006; McCallumore & Sparapani, 2010; Weiss & Bearman, 2007). This is especially true for students from low-income families and students from traditional socially marginalized populations (Rourke, 2001). Studies indicate that students who have a difficult first year in high school are at a greater risk of dropping out (Chapman & Sawyer, 2001; Herlihy, 2007; Oakes & Waite, 2009).

In the transition from middle school or junior high school to high school, there are particular challenges that can impede student success. Research has suggested these obstacles can arise from personal, institutional, and/or social perceptual factors.

Individual Challenges

A complex mix of developmental and environmental issues make the transition from junior high or middle school to secondary school a personal challenge for many adolescents. As adolescents mature, they go through a wide variety of intellectual, physical, emotional, and social changes (Frey et al., 2009; Potter et al., 2001). Intellectually, many adolescents are undergoing changes in thinking centred on the emergent sense of individuality, including reconceptualizing the world around them, the questions they pose, and self-reflection on personal experiences. Relationships with adults often change as adolescents experiment with greater self-direction. Physical and emotional changes prompted by puberty inevitably impact social relationships as young people begin to view others through a lens of sexual attraction. Also, adolescents' emotional maturation affects their self-perceptions and often their status and social relationships with both peers and adults. With a desire for peer acceptance, adolescents often switch allegiance from family to peers at a time when adult input in their decisions is critical (National Middle School Association, 2010). Adolescents also experience changes in self-esteem and self-concept along with value formation and social-group identification (Booth & Curran, 2010). Although they do not go through all of these changes at the same time, the developmental nature of adolescents should be considered when developing appropriate transition programs in middle school.

The success of transition to high school may also depend on a student's expectations, motivation, and feelings of belonging. Those adolescents who reported liking school and feeling suported demonstrated increased motivation to achieve (Frey et al., 2009; Wilkins & Kuperminc, 2010). Benner and Graham (2007) examined students' school-related affect by measuring their "school liking, and feelings of belonging" (p. 208). They found that the transition from one school to the next level impacted students' feelings of community inclusion and support. In addition, Barber and Olsen (2004) found that students' reports of liking school declined as they transitioned from eighth grade to high school. This was especially true of African-American students and more often with boys than with girls.

Institutional Challenges

As students deal with the quest for independence and identity and self-esteem issues, they are often required to navigate a new environment, form new relationships with peers and teachers, succeed with more difficult academic challenges, and assume greater responsibility for their social and academic lives (Rourke, 2001). The environmental factors associated with the transition to high school are sometimes based on the philosophical differences evident between middle school and high school personnel and the attendant differences in the organization and structure of the school. Middle school teachers are encouraged in teacher preparation and by administrators to collaborate as teams that address the needs and aspirations of the "whole child" (National Middle School Association, 2010). High school teachers, on the other hand, are most often certified as academic subject specialists and their collaboration usually centres on the curriculum in a school subject rather than on addressing the needs of an identified group of adolescents. A given teacher might have freshman students one period and seniors for their next class, sometimes leading to ninth grade teachers who are not disposed to the primary responsibility to address the social and emotional needs of 14-year-old boys and girls (Hertzog, 2006). Furthermore, there are significant differences in the organization and structure of the typical middle school versus the typical high school. High schools tend to be larger and more bureaucratic, have classes with students from different grades, have no advisory period where teacher/student bonds are formed, and high schools are often a more socially comparative and more academically competitive environment.

Social Perceptions

In contrast to the abundant research documenting the importance of the transition from middle school to high school regarding educational outcomes, there is limited inquiry related to stakeholder perceptions associated with this phenomenon (Akos, 2004; Choate, 2009; Hauser, Choate, & Thomas, 2009a). Research to date, however, suggests two important findings: There are often important differences in perceptions among these stakeholders and eliciting and addressing these perceptions can be an important tool in the development of effective transition programming. A recent case study conducted at a middle school and high school in a suburban district outside a large city in the Midwestern United States documents the important differences in parent, teacher, and student perceptions associated with positive and negative aspects of the transition to high school (Choate, 2009; Hauser, Choate, & Thomas, 2009b). The study investigated the perceptions of all three stakeholders at the end of eighth grade and then again at the end of ninth grade. Parents anticipated many positive outcomes from the transition to high school. The majority of eighth grade parents identified one or more possible positive academic outcomes such as getting good grades and being able to choose classes. They also identified positive social factors for their child such as having more freedom, making new friends, and being involved in more activities such as sports and clubs. Some parents indicated that they were looking forward to further personal growth for their child, including becoming more responsible and independent. By the end of ninth grade, these same parents still reported choosing classes and participating in sports and clubs as positive aspects of the transition, but far fewer indicated that getting good grades and having more freedom were positive aspects.

In this same study, students in eighth grade stated positive expectations for high school that were similar to the perceptions of their parents. Positive aspects of the transition included meeting new people and making friends, participating in sports and clubs, and having new teachers (Choate, 2009). By the end of ninth grade, these same students, when asked what they perceived as positive features of the transition to high school, responded in ways that were largely consistent with their expectations. Even more students said they were happy about being in a larger school and having new teachers, but fewer were positive about attending school events and receiving good grades.

Eighth grade teachers in the study also supported the expectation for greater autonomy for the students, with students able to choose some of their classes, make new friends, and get involved in more school activities (Choate, 2009; Hauser, Choate, & Thomas, 2009a). All ninth grade teachers involved claimed that making new friends and participating in school activities were the most positive aspects of the transition for students.

A comparison of all eighth grade parent, student, and teacher responses from the study showed that students perceived aspects of the social environment as the most frequently identified positive aspect of the transition to high school (Choate, 2009; Hauser, Choate, & Thomas, 2009b). Teachers and parents, however, viewed the academic benefits of high school as more significant than the social benefits.

Comparing student responses from eighth grade to the end of ninth grade, perceptions of the benefits of high school remained relatively constant except more students by the end of ninth grade chose being in a larger school and having new teachers as positive responses. The biggest changes in parent perceptions from the end of eighth grade to the end of ninth grade occurred in three areas: getting good grades decreased by almost 30% as a positive aspect of high school; more freedom increased as a positive aspect by over 35%; and although 32% of the eighth grade parents felt that having new teachers would be a positive aspect for their children, no parents in the survey reported this as a benefit by the end of ninth grade.

The student and parent populations for both years of the study were from the same group; however, the eighth grade teachers were a different group of stakeholders than the ninth grade teachers. The areas with the largest difference between the two groups were the perception of ninth grade teachers that more freedom and opportunity to participate in sports and clubs was the most positive aspect of the transition.

Stakeholders were also asked about the concerns they had regarding the transition to high school. The most frequently identified concerns about student transition were related to academics, with over three-quarters of the students expressing concern about having too much homework and about navigating the larger institution. More than half of the students were also concerned about hard classes and unfriendly teachers. Parents, like students, most frequently identified academic expectations as their foremost concern for students. More than half of the parents had concerns about the amount of homework, getting good grades, and pressure to do well, while a third were concerned with hard classes, unfriendly teachers, and peer pressure. Teachers identified aspects of the social environment, such as fitting in, making new friends, and peer pressure, as their most frequently identified concerns. Less than half of the teachers identified academic expectations, such as the pressure to do well and hard classes, as concerns.

At the end of ninth grade, stakeholders continued to differ in their concerns regarding the transition to high school. Although most students stated that hard classes or unfriendly teachers were the most difficult aspect sof the transition, parents felt that getting good grades and the amount of homework were the most difficult aspects for their children. Ninth grade teachers felt that the students had the most difficult time with the amount of homework and fitting in.

Recommendations and Conditions for Successful Transition

Strategies adopted by school personnel have been shown to help students successfully make the transition to high school. Schools with fully operational transition programs have substantially decreased dropout rates (Herlihy, 2007). Research by the Center for Equity and Excellence in Education at George Washington University recommends that transition programs include aligned curriculum standards, a focus on rigorous academics including strong literacy development, well-prepared teachers, and communication among all stakeholders (Oakes & Waite, 2009). Cauley and Jovanovich (2006) suggest that transition programs should address four areas of student preparedness: academic success, independent work habits, conformity to adult standards, and coping mechanisms. Thus, common elements in promoting an effective transition require attention to academics and adjusting the institutions to ensure individual fit to the new social setting.

Academic Support

Horwitz and Snipes (2008) recommend that teachers can increase a student's academic preparation by focusing on literacy. Explicit literacy instruction, which includes direct instruction in vocabulary acquisition and reading comprehension strategies, are promoted as a major focus in all academic areas in middle school. Without solid comprehension strategies or knowledge of academic vocabulary, students are unable to construct meaning from academic texts. Literacy instruction must be the focus throughout a student's day in all curricular areas. The more practice in reading comprehension strategies a student gets, the better. Block scheduling or doubling the amount of time a student spends in reading class is one strategy.

Combined with a recommended emphasis on literacy, middle school teachers should work with high school personnel to align curriculum in each content area with a focus of increased rigour at both the middle school and high school levels. The coursework that students take during middle school and high school is one of the most influential factors in later obtaining a college degree (Huber, Huidor, Malagon, Sanchez, & Solorzano, 2006). One approach to promoting this alignment can be seen in the 45 states in the United States where they are adopting the recommendations of the Common Core State Standards Initiative (CCSSI, 2010). These evidence-based math and English language arts standards cover Kindergarten through Grade 12 and are aligned with college and work expectations. Middle school teachers, along with school leaders and district officials, need to prepare curricula to match these core standards, ensuring that academic demands are rigorous and challenging in order to prepare students for higher expectations in high school and to give students confidence about learning.

Within the eighth grade classroom, teachers can address many of the questions students have about the rigour of the high school curriculum. Some of these questions include: How hard is it at the high school? What is a credit? What is College Prep? How much homework do they assign? (Morgan & Hertzog, 2001). Besides visits to the high school, which is a common transition activity, middle school personnel can invite high school students, teachers, or counsellors to speak at the middle school. Middle school teachers can also obtain a sample syllabus, sample homework assignments, and even a sample test for eighth graders to examine. Textbooks used during ninth grade can also be made available in the middle school library so that students can become familiar with the level of difficulty of the texts.

School leaders can help teachers by implementing a systemwide focus on literacy instruction and adding it to the School Learning Improvement Plan (SLIP). Schools can also implement monitoring systems in order to identify at-risk students before they fall too far behind. This, of course, should start at the Pre-K level and continue through high school. Identifying at-risk students before they fall too far off-track in

the transition to high school is critical. A school in Philadelphia con-
tended it can identify 50% of eventual dropouts as early as eighth grade,
and 80% by ninth grade using a student data system that tracks attendance, behaviour, and failing grades; a similar monitoring system in
Chicago predicts with 85% accuracy which ninth graders will not graduate (Horwitz & Snipes, 2008). Monitoring systems can be used not
only to identify at-risk students, but they should also be used to target
literacy instruction and interventions to keep students on track.

Comprehensive interventions designed to help students through the
transition to high school need to be formally supported by the school
district. This means that teachers should be given the release time to
meet with the high school teachers and to visit the high school on a
regular basis, as well as formal districtwide curricular alignment from
pre-Kindergarten through Grade 12.

About 30 states have some form of "P–16 initiative," aligning curriculum from Pre-K through the senior year of college (Chamberlin &
Plucker, 2008). The goals of P–16 systems include reducing achievement gaps, aligning curriculum and standards at all levels of education,
and smoothing transitions between the academic levels (ibid.). States
should also support schools by providing statewide monitoring systems and incentives for schools and districts who undertake programs
that support successful transitions. The National High School Center
(Herlihy, 2007) provides the following 10-item checklist for the state to
help support smooth transitions to high school:

1 Identify readiness indicators for high school–level coursework.
2 Require districts and schools to report annually the percentage of
  students completing algebra and Freshman English by the end of
  freshman year.
3 Track whether schools are offering more rigorous courses to more
  ninth grade students each year.
4 Communicate to families what ninth graders are expected to know
  and be able to do to succeed in high school.
5 Require one-on-one planning sessions for all students and their
  parents for the purpose of planning a rigorous high school program.
6 Require high schools to inform middle grades feeder schools of the
  percentage of students who completed 2 years of College-Prep
  English, Math, and Science by the end of tenth grade.
7 Provide guidelines on how middle schools and high schools can
  work together to prepare students for high school.

8 Require and fund high schools to identify eighth graders who
  are not ready to take College-Prep English and Math in Grade 9
  and provide a rich summer school experience.
9 Provide guidance on how to offer double doses of remedial
  courses – courses that are designed to help students meet
  the demands of more rigorous high school work, specifically
  Algebra and English, when necessary – in the first semester
  of high school and enroll them in high school work by the
  second semester.
10 Require districts to report on the outcomes of their transition
  programs.

With support from school leadership, districts, and states, teachers
can implement strong transition programs. Each eighth grade class is
unique, of course, and transition programs must, therefore, suit the
needs of each particular group of students and their parents. Surveying
middle school students and their parents to find out what they are most
concerned about regarding the transition to high school is important in
order for teachers and administrators to build transition programs
unique for each group of students.

Fitting the School to the Student

Preparing students during middle school for high school goes beyond
rigorous academics and information about high school curriculum; it
also involves preparing students socially and emotionally as well as
quelling their fears about the high school environment and procedures
in general.

As noted previously, moving to high school often involves a shift
from teaching and nurturing the whole child to an environment that is
more socially comparative and competitive (Herlihy, 2007). High
schools are usually larger and more bureaucratic which can lead to a
sense of depersonalization (ibid.). One developmental challenge ninth
graders face is finding their place, or sense of belonging, in the midst of
environmental and social changes (Tilleczek, 2010). Counsellors are
usually the personnel who deal with the social and emotional well-
being of students. However, some middle schools do not have counsellors. Even when they are available, students have indicated that
counsellors are not always helpful in preparing students for the transition to high school (Choate, 2009). Here, again, middle school teachers

can be an integral part of the facilitation of the transition to high school by working closely with high school teachers and counsellors.

Differences in philosophy between high school and middle school personnel need to be bridged. The case study by the authors (Choate, 2009; Hauser, Choate, & Thomas, 2009a) revealed that eighth grade teachers perceived challenges in high school to be principally social rather than academic; in contrast, high school teachers cited an academic issue (workload) as a principal concern. Both parents and students also had limited awareness of the challenges related to academic issues in high school. By forging a relationship with high school personnel, middle school teachers can work closely with high school teachers in implementing strategies that will make ninth grade a more personal experience for the students and teachers and foster greater awareness of academic challenges that students may encounter in freshman year. One strategy is to form ninth grade teacher teams responsible for a group of students throughout the year better enabling students and teachers to form relationships. A Philadelphia high school has had success with ninth grade teacher teams citing that if a student is having difficulty all the team members support one another in order to support the child (Smith, 2007). Another innovation is to allow ninth graders to take fewer but longer classes during the freshman year instead of the typical one-fourth of all classes required for graduation. Extended time in classes allows teachers to reinforce learning as well as form relationships, an asset towards a smooth transition (Tilleczek, 2010). Both eighth and ninth grade teachers should also be given time to meet together and discuss the incoming ninth grade students so ninth grade teachers are aware of specific students' learning styles and their strengths and weaknesses.

Middle school teachers and high school teachers can work together to help students form a sense of belonging and responsibility to the school and surrounding community through service learning as a transition tool. Service learning has also been shown to help students find intrinsic motivation (Dedmond & Kestler, 2010). By providing service learning opportunities within the high school and community that involve eighth and ninth grade students and their teachers, students engage in projects that address transition needs by forming relationships with high school students and teachers in a safe environment outside of school, as well as addressing the needs of the school or community (ibid.). One example is Montana's Troy County recycling project. One company is working with students in Grades 7–12 to recycle mine waste into marketable materials (ibid.). According to Dedmond and Kestler, there are several benefits of service learning that facilitate a successful transition including an increase in self-efficacy, resiliency, and self-confidence; a higher attendance rate and higher grades; an increase in knowledge of civic and ethical responsibility; and, a greater awareness of the connection between academics and work. In a survey of high school students who dropped out, 47% cited being bored or disengaged (Herlihy, 2007) as influencing their withdrawal from school. Service learning projects can help students see the purpose of academics as well as increase their excitement about school because they are working on something that interests them, therefore avoiding the feeling of disengagement or boredom. When students feel a sense of belonging and attachment, they fare much better academically, socially, and emotionally (Grossman & Cooney, 2009).

Besides changes in academic expectations and teacher relationships, students also face changes in school size, climate, and procedures. Many students fear getting lost, being late to class, and not knowing what to expect from teachers (Choate, 2009). The most common transition activities that address these procedural concerns are high school tours and counsellor appointments (Cauley & Jovanovich, 2006; Horwitz & Snipes, 2008). Larger reforms that address this transition issue include complete structural changes to the ninth grade environment such as freshman or ninth grade academies – a school-within-in-a-school with interdisciplinary teacher teams specifically designed to help ninth graders effect a smooth transition (Kemple & Herlihy, 2004). Research has found that the large size of many high schools is commonly associated with lower levels of achievement (Horwitz & Snipes, 2008). Freshman academies address this problem by physically grouping ninth grade students together and providing more personalized attention (Herlihy, 2007). Although there are more than 125 freshman academies in U.S. high schools (Kemple & Herlihy, 2004), this remains a limited strategy for easing the transition.

Middle school teachers can offer other activities that can help ease the anxiety eighth grade students have about the size and procedures of the high school. Teachers can allow time for students to browse the high school's website to gain familiarity with the course offerings, school schedules and maps, teacher blogs, the discipline code, the school newspaper, and activities pages. Using simple learning activities such as webpage scavenger hunts can help students find information that is useful to them. If possible, a forum supervised by a middle or high school teacher can be set up for eighth graders and ninth graders to dialogue throughout the year. Or, similar to many college websites, a student blog page can be set up on the high school website where several high school freshmen record their experiences throughout the school year. Other activities, such as visiting the high school for sports programs, dances, cultural performances, and shadow days can increase an eighth grader's confidence regarding the physical aspect of the high school. For middle schools that do not use lockers, high school is often the first time a student will use a combination lock. Students can be given a combination lock to practice using. Once a student has his or her schedule, visiting the high school and finding all his or her classrooms and locker before the first day of school, or having a freshman only first day, can also ease anxiety.

Teachers can arrange for parent discussion groups during regularly scheduled open houses. Inviting parents of the previous eighth grade class to answer current eighth grade parents' questions is an informal way for parents to get information about the high school. Both the high school and middle school can offer monthly or quarterly meetings for parents to address concerns about the transition with teachers, counselors, and/or administrators.

Discussion and Conclusion

There is sufficient evidence that the successful transition of students from middle school to high school can promote various positive educational outcomes. The authors contend that to maximize the potential for success, the above-cited strategies should be considered as options for implementation contingent on the character of the school communities. Overall, preparing middle school students for the transition to high school is more likely to be successful when attention is given to the following three recommended practices: (1) focused, formal, and sustained collaboration between middle school or junior high school personnel and the high school's administration and ninth grade teachers; (2) formal and systematic programming contoured to the character of the school communities to prepare students and parents for the transition; and (3) stakeholder perception studies conducted at the local level on a regular basis to gain insight into how students, parents, and teachers are "reading" the transition, thus guiding decisions in both communication and programming.

The need for communication between institutional personnel regarding both academic and environmental continuity is well established in the above-cited literature on the transition to high school. This communication should be a formal and regular part of the school year for school-site level administration, counsellors, and faculty directly working with the eighth and ninth grade students, established by the administration to be effective in establishing wide, comfortable bridges in practice and expectations. Thus, rather than informal chats and inconsequential electronic forums, the communications should result in a formal action plan that is practical, capable of implementation, and addresses continuity in curriculum, instruction, and achievement reporting as well as environmental changes that can ease the transition for students. The focus on curriculum can establish common assumptions on what knowledge and skills are to be mastered by the time the student enters high school. Redundancies in topics and skills can be eliminated, and sequencing of the curriculum can be mapped. Instructional approaches can be informed and realistic, introducing common instructional approaches used in the high school in feeder the middle school rather than acting on the often-presumed adage that there will be more lecturing and less engaged learning in high school. Reporting systems should be reviewed to ensure that there is clarity and that the level of academic pressure is not a dramatic shift, usually in increased but sometimes decreased expectations for the students.

This communication can also inform staff of identified students who are at risk of not being successful in the transition either academically or behaviourally and coordinate a plan of attention to better provide resources and accommodations to maximize opportunity for success. Given the research that establishes that profiles of students in middle school can be a good predictor of whether a student will complete high school (Grossman & Cooney, 2009; Reyes et al., 2000), this coordination can be a service to students who otherwise will leave high school without a diploma. The formal communication between personnel can also foster a sense of shared vision and purpose, enhancing the compatibility of the institutions in setting goals and expectations and directing initiatives, perhaps shared between institutions, towards improved student learning.

A second recommendation is to develop a formal program that prepares students and their families for the transition to the high school. The various options discussed above are options for constructing this formal program, ranging from shadow visiting and practice with school lockers to meetings with parents and students where the issue of transition is specifically addressed and common misconceptions, problems, and opportunities are frankly discussed by participants. This range of formal activities differs contingent on the character of the community served and the institutional profile, thus emphasizing the need to gather meaningful data from key participants in this transition (parents, students, and their teachers). Informal opportunities to bring middle school students into the high school environment should accompany the formal transition program. The high school can take the lead in sponsoring science fairs, math competitions, public speaking and theatre events, and music and art presentations by and for elementary school students, thus fostering a sense of familiarity with the high school environment in settings that are more natural and interactive than the conventional transition activities (shadow days or tours) that can prove less about insight and more about promotion.

Whether developing communication channels between institutions or implementing a set of formal and informal interactions between middle school and high school students, teachers, administrators, and parents, stakeholders' perceptions of this transition can be a valuable insight into the level of commitment needed and the kinds of activities to be developed. Assessing these perceptions is an essential tool to inform program planning, implementation, and evaluation.

In investigating stakeholder perceptions, school and district policies and procedures associated with conducting research need to be reviewed. It is essential to have the support of district and school administrators as well as the assistance of the relevant teaching staff. It is also essential that all stakeholders have a clear understanding for the purpose of the study. A commonly shared understanding facilitates effective data collection and ultimately, acceptance of the findings. The various purposes of the study should be carefully explained to the school community. Failure to clearly outline the purposes of the study could lead to stakeholder resistance, and this could adversely affect data collection and the integrity of the study.

Given the potentially sensitive nature of the findings related to teachers, staff members, and programs, careful consideration should be given to whom, when, and how the results will be disseminated. To illustrate the point, assume that eighth grade school counsellors are identified by students as not being particularly helpful in addressing their transition concerns. How, when, and the manner in which the results of these findings are communicated to the eighth grade counsellors may affect the acceptance of the findings by personnel as well as the likelihood of making desired improvements.

If the study is being conducted in collaboration with a higher educational institution, identifying and responding to both the shared and unique needs of the practitioners and college or university faculty members alike is essential to the creation of synergistic collaboration. On the one hand, school and district personnel are most commonly consumers, rather than producers of research. On the other hand, college and university faculty members are most often producers rather than consumers of research. Practitioners in the field and college and university faculty members each bring to a potential research study unique and special skills and abilities. Practitioners provide access to the school community and the means and the methods of collecting the data. College and university faculty members can provide a wide array of technical supports including assistance with the research design, methodology, data analysis, and perhaps most importantly, serving as critical friends to practitioners in the field.

These perceptions serve two important functions. First, they provide information related to potential issues and concerns related to each constituency as well as areas of difference in perception. These perceptions, in turn, can help ensure that the transition program is tailored to meet the unique and special needs of local stakeholder populations and institutional contexts. The results of the study can serve as a substantial starting point for conversations and actions by personnel and for calling parents and students together to learn the results of the study and elicit recommendations based on the findings. The results may also serve as a valued foundation for confronting common "myths" that parents, students, and even teachers may have about their high school and hold conversations on the origins of these suppositions. The role of popular media in misrepresenting the high school experience can be matched against these perceptions as well as a subject of conversation.

Second, stakeholder perceptions measured at the end of the transition period, for example, at the end of the ninth grade, can serve as a component in evaluating the success of the transition program. Setting a series of common goals on what school personnel hope to see in a successful transition and then placing them against this data can serve to highlight aspects that have been successfully accomplished and areas for further labour. Understanding, the needs, expectations, and concerns of various stakeholders assists educators in personalizing the program to each local school and community context. Obviously, data about grades, standardized test scores, attendance, and student participation in sports, clubs, and other school-sponsored activities are good indicators that a transition program is successful, but data regarding stakeholder perceptions are additional important indicators of a successful transition. To the extent possible, the potential programmatic, personnel, and budgetary implications that may emerge as a result of expected and unexpected findings should be considered.

REFERENCES

Akos, P. (2004). Middle and high school transitions as viewed by students, parents, and teachers. *Professional School Counseling*, 7(4), 212–221.

Barber, B.K., & Olsen, J.A. (2004). Assessing the transitions to middle and high school. *Journal of Adolescent Research*, 19(1), 3–30.

Benner, A.D., & Graham, S. (2007). Navigating the transition to multi-ethnic urban high schools: Changing ethnic congruence and adolescents' school-related affect. *Journal of Research on Adolescence*, 17(1), 207–220.

Booth, M., & Curran, E. (2010). "I feel so confused": A longitudinal study of young adolescents' change in self-esteem. *Online Submission*. (ED510386).

Bozick, R., & DeLuca, S. (2005). Better late than never? Delayed enrollment in the high school to college transition. *Social Forces*, 84(1), 531–550.

Cauley, K., & Jovanovich, D. (2006). Developing an effective transition program for students entering middle school or high school. *Clearing House (Menasha, Wis.)*, 80(1), 15–25.

Chamberlin, M., & Plucker, J. (2008). P-16 education: Where are we going? Where have we been? *Education Digest*, 74(2), 25–33.

Chapman, M., & Sawyer, J. (2001). Bridging the gap for students at risk of school failure: A social work-initiated middle to high school transition program. *Children & Schools*, 23(4), 235–240.

Choate, K. (2009). Student, parent, and teacher perceptions of the transition between middle school and high school. *Dissertation Abstracts International*, UMI No. 3349766.

Cohen, J.S., & Smerdon, B.A. (2009). Tightening the dropout tourniquet: Easing the transition from middle to high school. *Preventing School Failure*, 53(3), 177–184.

Common Core State Standards Initiative (CCSSI). (2010). Retrieved from http://www.corestandards.org

Dedmond, R., & Kestler, E. (2010). Making a meaningful connection: Freshman transition and service learning. *Techniques: Connecting Education and Careers*, 85(4), 30–32.

Espinoza, G., & Juvonen, J. (2011). Perceptions of the school social context across the transition to middle school: Heightened sensitivity among Latino students? *Journal of Educational Psychology*, 103(3), 749–758.

Frey, A., Ruchkin, V., Martin, A., & Schwab-Stone, M. (2009, Mar.). Adolescents in transition: School and family characteristics in the development of violent behaviors entering high school. *Child Psychiatry and Human Development, 40*(1), 1–13.

Grossman, J., & Cooney, S. (2009). Paving the way for success in high school and beyond: The importance of preparing middle school students for the transition to ninth grade. New York: Public/Private Ventures. Retrieved from http://www.ppv.org

Hauser, G.M., Choate, K., & Thomas, T.P. (2009a). A two-year study of stakeholder perceptions associated with the transition from eighth grade to high school. *International Journal of Learning, 16*(3), 315–326.

Hauser, G.M., Choate, K., & Thomas, T.P. (2009b). A research model for practitioners investigating the transition of eighth grade students to high school. *Paper presented at the Hawaii International Conference on Education,* Honolulu.

Heck, R.H., & Mahoe, R. (2006). Student transition to high school and persistence: Highlighting the influences of social divisions and school contingencies. *American Journal of Education, 112*(3), 418–446.

Herlihy, C. (2007). *Toward ensuring a smooth transition into high school.* Washington, DC: National High School Center.

Hertzog, J. (2006). *Planning for the transition to high school.* Retrieved from http://www.naesp.org

Horwitz, A., & Snipes, J. (2008). *Supporting successful transitions to high school.* Research Brief. Washington, DC: Council of the Great City Schools.

Huber, L., Huidor, O., Malagon, M., Sanchez, G., & Solorzano, D. (2006). *Falling through the cracks: Critical transitions in the Latina/o educational pipeline.* Los Angeles: Chicano Studies Research Center, UCLA.

Kemple, J., & Herlihy, C. (2004). The talent development high school model. In J. Kemple, C. Herlihy, & T. Smith, *Making progress toward graduation: Evidence for the Talent Development High School Model.* Retrieved from http://www.mdrc.org/talent-development-high-school-model.

Larose, S., Bernier, A., & Tarabulsy, G.M. (2005, Jan.). Attachment state of mind, learning dispositions, and academic performance during the college transition. *Developmental Psychology, 41*(1), 281–289.

McCallumore, K.M., & Sparapani, E.F. (2010). The importance of the ninth grade on high school graduation rates and student success in high school. *Education, 130*(3), 447–456.

Morgan, L.P., & Hertzog, C. (2001). Designing comprehensive transitions. *Principal Leadership, 1*(7), 10–18.

Mounts, N.S., Valentiner, D.P., Anderson, K.L., & Bosswell, M.K. (2005). Shyness, sociability, and parental support for the college transition: Relation to adolescents' adjustment. *Journal of Youth and Adolescence, 35*(1), 71–80.

National Middle School Association. (2010). *This we believe: Keys to educating young adolescents.* Westerville, OH: Author.

Oakes, A., & Waite, W. (2009). *Middle-to-high-school transition: Practical strategies to consider.* Center for Comprehensive School Reform and Improvement. Retrieved from http://centerforscri.org

Potter, L., Schliskey, S., & Stevenson, D. (2001). The transition years: When it's time to change. *Principal Leadership, 1*(7), 52–55.

Reyes, O., Gillock, K.L., Kobus, K., & Sanchez, B. (2000, Aug.). A longitudinal examination of the transition into senior high school for adolescents from urban, low-income status, and predominantly minority backgrounds. *American Journal of Community Psychology, 28*(4), 519–544.

Riley, R.W. (2000, Sept.). *Speech given at the National Press Club.* Washington, DC. (ED445794).

Rourke, J.R. (2001). The ninth grade experiment. *Principal Leadership, 1*(7), 26–30.

Schulting, A.B., Malone, P.S., & Dodge, K.A. (2005, Nov.). The effect of school-based kindergarten transition policies and practices on child academic outcomes. *Developmental Psychology, 41*(6), 860–871.

Smith, J.S. (2006). Examining the long-term impact of achievement loss during the transition to high school. *Journal of Secondary Gifted Education, 17*(4), 211–221.

Smith, T. (2007). Managing the transition to ninth grade in a comprehensive urban high school. Washington, DC: National High School Center. (ED501072)

Stormont, M., Beckner, R., Mitchell, B., & Richter, M. (2005). Supporting successful transition to kindergarten. *Psychology in the Schools, 42*(8), 765–778.

Theriot, M.T., & Dupper, D.R. (2010). Student discipline problems and the transition from elementary to middle school. *Education and Urban Society, 42*(2), 205–222.

Tilleczek, K. (2010). Building bridges: Transitions from elementary to secondary school. *Education Canada, 48*(1), 68–71.

Weiss, C.C., & Bearman, P.S. (2007). Fresh starts: Reinvestigating the effects of the transition to high school on student outcomes. *American Journal of Education, 113*(3), 395–421.

Wilkins, N., & Kuperminc, G. (2010). Why try? Achievement motivation and perceived academic climate among Latino youth. *Journal of Early Adolescence, 30*(2), 246–276.

12 Establishing Successful Transitions for Intermediate Students

GIANNA HELLING

This chapter describes some intermediate-level transition initiatives developed by the Toronto Catholic District School Board (TCDSB). The programs, resources, and initiatives described are from "Establishing Successful Transitions for Intermediate Students," and they fall into the following four areas:

• Cross-panel teams and professional dialogue
• Programming and using data
• Events and initiatives
• Student leadership.

The strategies and interventions that support students transitioning from an elementary school to a high school are described in detail. Further, a comprehensive and successful transition initiative at one particular high school – Jean Vanier Catholic Secondary School in Toronto – will be highlighted.

Background

The Toronto Catholic District School Board is a publicly funded Catholic school board in Ontario, Canada. The school board currently serves approximately 61,000 elementary (Kindergarten to Grade 8) and 30,625 secondary (Grades 9 to 12) students throughout the City of Toronto. The board employs almost 6,000 teachers, 356 principals and vice principals, approximately 2,800 support and academic staff, and over 200 employees in administration. The TCDSB educates more than 90,000 students from diverse cultures and language backgrounds in its 201 Catholic elementary and secondary schools, and serves 474,876 Catholic school supporters across the city (www.tcdsb.org). The following section describes the programs and supports developed by the TCDSB and their use within a family of schools surrounding Jean Vanier Catholic Secondary School. This chapter was developed from a presentation written by Bianca Auciello and Gianna Helling for the International Confederation of Principals in Toronto, in 2011.

Part of the TCDSB, Jean Vanier is a publicly funded Catholic secondary school in Toronto's east-end neighbourhood of Scarborough. During the time of the transition initiative being described here, Bianca Auciello and I, Gianna Helling, were both vice principals at the school.

Jean Vanier has approximately 1,100 students. Before the initiative began in 2006, however, the school was suffering from declining enrolment, with a population of under 700 students. New students bring new staff and new ideas. Jean Vanier is benefiting from the diversity, energy, and substantial expertise of the teachers, with their varied levels of experience, now on staff. The teachers and support staff who organized and planned many of the activities described here represent a team of extremely dedicated, professional, and knowledgeable people. They embraced the belief that every child can succeed. They also enjoyed the support of the Student Success Department, resource teachers, research department, coordinators, and superintendents within the TCDSB.

Barriers and Obstacles to Transition

Currently, Toronto's southeast end is seeing a significant influx of new Canadians. Many of the students described herein were English language learners (ELLs) fully literate in their first language. A number of students move homes and schools often as they become established in their new country. Many attend more than one elementary school and more than one secondary school before graduating from high school. The area is surrounded by many apartment complexes. Prior to the transition initiatives described below, many Vanier students did not meet provincial standards on the provincial literacy assessments – their scores have since exceeded the provincial standard and represent some of the most improved results in the province. Convincing students from the local Catholic elementary schools to attend Jean Vanier Catholic Secondary School was a major obstacle that needed to be overcome.

Recommendations and Conditions for Successful Transition

The programs, resources, and initiatives described in this chapter fall into the following four areas, as outlined above:

1 Cross-panel teams and professional dialogue, which includes
   • Student success learning networks (SSLNs)
   • Kindergarten to Grade 12 principal's meetings
   • Student success conference
   • Central resource staff and support.

2 Programming and using data, which includes
   • Exchange of information between elementary and secondary school staff
   • Use of data to make informed decisions for student programs and curriculum delivery
   • Purposeful timetabling and differentiated instruction
   • Purposeful planning for locally organized summer schools for incoming Grade 9 students
   • Curriculum nights for parents of students entering Grade 9.

3 Events and initiatives, which includes
   • Local summer school programs for Grade 8s transitioning to Grade 9
   • Take Our Kids to High School event
   • Family math night
   • Community involvement documents
   • Parent and student transition guides, including special services documents
   • Assigning a caring adult to students transitioning to Grade 9
   • Northern Spirit Games.

4 Student leadership, which includes
   • Students' role in organizing and leading community events
   • Transition assemblies for students in the Intermediate Division
   • Mentors and peer buddies.

These transition initiatives were introduced and supported by the TCDSB central staff including the Student Success Department, the

Curriculum and Accountability Department, the Special Education Department, and the field superintendents who supported and facilitated the dialogue between the schools. These programs and initiatives will be explained in detail in the following pages.

Cross-Panel Teams and Professional Dialogue

One important initiative implemented by the TCDSB is the area principal meetings organized to facilitate cross-panel dialogue. According to the Ontario Ministry of Education (OMoE), "Building capacity, trust and respect through collaborative work is essential to progressing along the trajectory from great to excellent" (OMoE, 2011). This belief undergirds the Kindergarten to Grade 12 principals' meetings. These meetings are organized by the TCDSB's superintendency. Elementary and secondary school principals meet in teams with their local area superintendent twice per month. These semi-monthly meetings allow for common messaging and discussion for, and between, elementary and secondary panels. These meetings are aligned with the Ontario School Effectiveness Framework (SEF), the District Effectiveness Framework (DEF), and the Ontario Leadership Framework (OLF). These provincial frameworks were developed by the Ontario Ministry of Education as part of the Ontario Leadership Strategy (OLS). The Ontario School Effectiveness Framework is a support for school improvement and student success, and includes the use of indicators, or evidence of student success. The Ontario Leadership Framework (OMoE, 2011) is a tool for thinking, talking, and learning about educational leadership. The core of this framework is student achievement. These meetings help align the school learning and improvement plans with the board learning and improvement plan. The focus of the K–12 principal meetings is professional development and building instructional leadership capacity. Figure 12.1 depicts the *K–12 School Effectiveness Framework: A Support for School Improvement and Student Success* (OMoE, n.d.) which supports K–12 dialogue and promotes a collaborative learning culture.

Another TCDSB initiative supporting cross-panel dialogue is the Student Success Learning Networks, made up of one high school and five elementary schools. SSLN meetings are centrally supported by the TCDSB but locally driven. Time is carved out of each Kindergarten to Grade 12 regular meeting for principals' to meet in their SSLNs. Schools work together to select the annual focus of the meetings: "Elementary and Secondary Principals collaborate to determine possible focus/foci

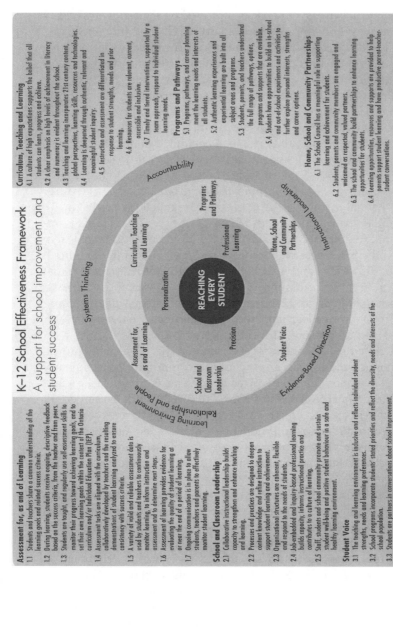

Figure 12.1. K–12 School Effectiveness Framework, Literacy and Numeracy Secretariat, Ontario Ministry of Education (n.d.).

based on a mutual area(s) of need, as indicated on their individual SLIP [School Learning and Improvement Plan]" (TCDSB, Student Success Team [SST], 2011). Release days for teachers are included in this initiative to support cross-panel dialogue and planning. The focus for the SSLNs is based on the professional learning cycle and includes the following topics: differentiated instruction, the teaching learning critical pathway (a professional learning cycle for literacy), using data to promote student achievement, the numeracy assessment for learning cycle, student engagement–student voice, pathways, teen health (social-emotional focus including mental health issues), assessments for learning, and cross-curricular literacy. Moderated marking between panels is encouraged. Students' work is used to inform our teaching practices. Next steps for improved student learning are discussed and planned for as a team.

According to the framework for SSLNs (TCDSB, SST, 2011a), it is important that the school team (elementary and secondary school teachers) to lead the SSLN session: "In order for true collaboration and rich cross-panel discussion and learning to take place, it is important that both elementary and secondary (Grades 7–10) classroom teachers attend the sessions." Figure 12.2 demonstrates the professional learning cycle and collaborative learning culture that guides the framework for the TCDSB's Student Success Learning Networks.

Facilitated by the superintendents of schools, this cross-panel professional dialogue among teachers within the community of elementary schools that surround Jean Vanier was invaluable. Inviting teachers and administrators from the elementary panel to co-plan with the secondary school, changed the perception of the school. These professional dialogue, program planning, and moderated marking activities created a supportive, collaborative environment between the schools. The relationships between staff members in the elementary and secondary panels supported the welcome, safe, and caring environment that Jean Vanier was fostering. Following the lead of the superintendent, the high school hosted principals' and vice-principals'meetings, professional development for teachers, community masses, and a number of community events. Teachers planned together to meet the needs of their students, supporting students' academic, social, and emotional development as they transitioned from Grade 8 in their elementary school to Grade 9 in the high school. Elementary and secondary school teachers worked together to support the unique and individual needs of each student.

Another opportunity to bring intermediate teachers together for planning is the annual TCDSB Student Success Conference for teachers

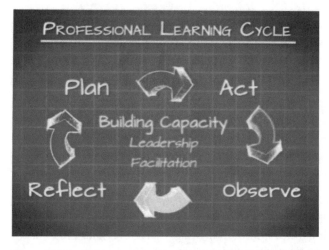

Figure 12.2. Framework for Toronto Catholic District School Board's Student Success Learning Networks (TCDSB, STT, 2011).

and administrators from Grades 7 to 12. This 2-day event includes internationally acclaimed speakers as well as presentations supporting best practices. The theme, speakers, and presentations are aligned with the TCDSB's Learning and Improvement Plan. This conference allows teachers and administrators from the Intermediate and Senior divisions (Grades 7–12) to dialogue and plan for student success for students transitioning to high school. The topics and presentations help support the efforts of the elementary and secondary schools.

The central resource staff at the TCDSB support the teachers in their planning and professional learning cycles. The focus of their support is collaboration and co-planning. This central staff includes central literacy, numeracy, community, culture and caring, and pathways teams. The teams provide professional development workshops and plan events such as Family Math Night. They work with the elementary and secondary school teachers and administrators in the schools. They model co-teaching and learning in the schools. Their work includes supporting cross-panel transitional work in curriculum and programming, and developing resources such as the "Transition Guide for Parents: The Complete Picture – Your Child's Future Secondary School and Beyond"

(TCDSB, 2010a) and the "Transition Guide for Students: Your Future –
One Piece at a Time" (TCDSB, 2010b).

The TCDSB's "Transition Guide for Parents" (2010a) covers the following topics:

- Program pathways
- The high school application process including specialized programs
  within the TCDSB
- Students with special needs
- Terms and definitions
- Decoding a course code
- Decoding a timetable
- Earning an Ontario Secondary School Diploma (OSSD)
- Selecting a level of study
- Selecting a destination pathway with a level planning chart
- Assisting your child in transition
- Learning skills and your child
- Experiential learning
- Career program pathways and apprenticeship programs
- Ontario colleges
- Ontario universities
- The workplace
- Career exploration and the Internet
- Student success initiatives
- Helpful hints
- Student destination planning form
- Individual school websites.

This guide, as a best practice, invites parents and their children to
take increasing responsibility for the learning and choices as they transition from an elementary to a secondary school.

The "Transition Guide for Students" (TCDSB, 2010b) includes the
same sections as the guide for parents, but is simplified and includes
many graphics and charts to help students. Figure 12.3 shows an example of the page from the guide entitled: "How Do I Apply to High
School?"

The central resource staff also support student transitions for students with special needs. This includes the development of the following resources: "Transition to Secondary School Service for students
with Autism Spectrum Disorders (ASD): A Parent's Guide" (TCDSB,

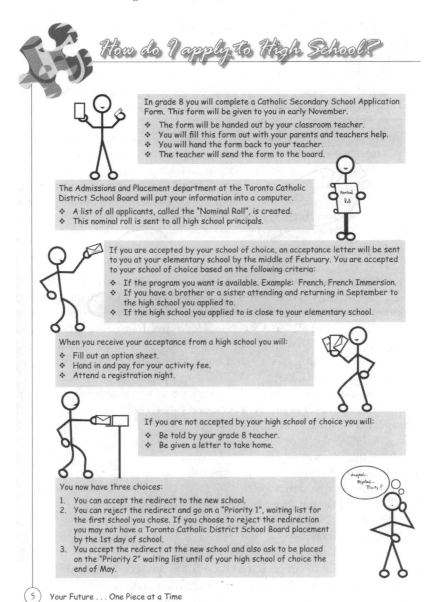

In grade 8 you will complete a Catholic Secondary School Application Form. This form will be given to you in early November.

❖ The form will be handed out by your classroom teacher.
❖ You will fill this form out with your parents and teachers help.
❖ You will hand the form back to your teacher.
❖ The teacher will send the form to the board.

The Admissions and Placement department at the Toronto Catholic District School Board will put your information into a computer.

❖ A list of all applicants, called the "Nominal Roll", is created.
❖ This nominal roll is sent to all high school principals.

If you are accepted by your school of choice, an acceptance letter will be sent to you at your elementary school by the middle of February. You are accepted to your school of choice based on the following criteria:

❖ If the program you want is available. Example: French, French Immersion.
❖ If you have a brother or a sister attending and returning in September to the high school you applied to.
❖ If the high school you applied to is close to your elementary school.

When you receive your acceptance from a high school you will:

❖ Fill out an option sheet.
❖ Hand in and pay for your activity fee.
❖ Attend a registration night.

If you are not accepted by your high school of choice you will:

❖ Be told by your grade 8 teacher.
❖ Be given a letter to take home.

You now have three choices:

1. You can accept the redirect to the new school.
2. You can reject the redirect and go on a "Priority 1", waiting list for the first school you chose. If you choose to reject the redirection you may not have a Toronto Catholic District School Board placement by the 1st day of school.
3. You accept the redirect at the new school and also ask to be placed on the "Priority 2" waiting list until of your high school of choice the end of May.

5 Your Future . . . One Piece at a Time

Figure 12.3. How Do I Apply to High School? Transition Guide for Students, Toronto Catholic District School Board (2010b).

2010c). They have also produced a video entitled "Transition to Secondary School for Students with Autism Spectrum Disorders" and a video that includes pictures from each secondary school within the TCDSB and a book to help students prepare for their new learning environment (TDSCB, 2010d, 2010e, 2010f). An OMoE memorandum (2007) introducing these materials states:

> Transition planning is an important process for all students, but especially for students with ASD. Principals are required to ensure that a plan for transition is in place for students with ASD. Transitions may include: entry to school; transition between activities and sittings or classrooms; transitions between grades; moving from school to school or from an outside agency to a school; transition from elementary to secondary school; transition from secondary school to postsecondary destinations and/or the workplace.

A program developed by the TCDSB's central special education staff in response to the Ontario Ministry of Education's 2007 memorandum, includes transition visits where students with special needs can meet with staff and students in a supportive environment. Students are encouraged to familiarize themselves with the new high school before they begin, alleviating anxiety and helping students through the transition process. The TCDSB's "Welcome to High School Profile Book" (2010e) suggests that before September, special education staff at the elementary school help Grade 8 students to transition to their new high school by introducing them to the following:

- Where their locker will be
- Their schedule
- Who their teachers may be
- List of Professional Activity days, assemblies, etc.
- Where their classes are
- Their homeroom
- A designated area if the student needs a break
- How to handle or prepare the student for changes in their routine (e.g., fire drills, mass assembly, seating changes).

This resource includes photographs and brief descriptions of the main areas of each of the high schools in the TCDSB and can be customized for the student depending on the high school she or he will be attending within the board. At the bottom of this resource there is a cut-out section. This section becomes a mini-information booklet that is small enough to slip into the student's pencil case, wallet, or pocket. The booklet contains useful information such as emergency phone numbers and locker combination. Teachers are encouraged to fill out the information booklet with their students. Some students might want to keep the booklet with them at all times – especially for their first few weeks of high school. Other suggestions from the book include:

- Assign a peer buddy to review the "Welcome to High School" book (TDCSB, 2010e) with the student. The peer buddy can give the student tips on how to enjoy and make the most of the high school experience.
- Think about the student's interests (e.g., if the student likes music, include a photo of the music room).
- Clearly explain expectations of the new places (e.g., the library, hallway, and cafeteria).
- When giving directions to get somewhere in the school use visual landmarks.
- Encourage students to join clubs that relate to their special interests.

It is especially important for elementary and secondary school staff to work together on behalf of the student with Autism Spectrum Disorders and/or other special needs students to provide the necessary supports during the transition period. This cooperation helps to lessen the students' anxieties and provides a foundation for student success (TCDSB, 2010d).

Programming and Using Data

The Ontario Leadership Framework (OMoE, 2011a) identifies five core leadership capacities. Number four is using data:

- To inform school improvement plans
- To build staff confidence around the effective use of data
- To foster a school culture in which staff have high expectations for student achievement, assess student performance, modify practice based on findings, and take ownership for the results (Education Quality and Accountability Office [EQAO], 2011, Sept.).

The use of data to program for student success includes using the following types of student data: the standardized, provincial assessments developed and implemented by the EQAO for Grade 3 and Grade 6 (reading, writing, mathematics), Grade 9 (mathematics), and Grade 10 (Ontario Secondary School Literacy Test [OSSLT]); assessments developed by the Canadian Test Centre such as the Canadian Achievement Test (CAT 3 and 4); classroom assessments such as report cards and running reading records; credit accumulation data in high school; attendance records; and, Safe School survey results. This precision planning enables teachers to address the gaps in prior learning, assess prior knowledge, and plan academic as well as social/emotional supports. The data inform the professional learning cycles in literacy and numeracy. These data also inform the School Learning and Improvement Plan (SLIP). Superintendents meet with the school learning and improvement teams in each elementary and secondary school. For example, currently, the field Superintendent in Area 3 of the TCDSB looks after 21 elementary schools and 4 high schools. The superintendent meets with each school's Learning and Improvement Team at least twice per year to discuss what specific evidence or data will inform the local SLIP for the year. Questions for discussion during the meeting usually include the following:

1 As a result of the examination of your data/evidence of strengths and needs, what have you determined are your school's areas of greatest need?
2 Are the "strategies" precise and sufficiently clear so that all stakeholders can understand what is needed for effective implementation?
3 How has the SEF data guided your School Improvement Team (SIT) discussions in the development of the SMART Goals (Specific, Measurable, Attainable, Relevant, Time Bound)? What is your SEF focus for this year and how will you use that focus to monitor your progress?
4 What communication and collaboration strategies have your SIT used to inform and involve all stakeholders about the multi-year School LIP?
5 How were equity issues addressed with SIT/SST during the analysis of data? (specific subpopulations)

(TCDSB SLIP Visit 1, Fall 2011)

The supportive role of the superintendent, in co-planning for student success, enables school learning and improvement teams to use assessment data to effectively plan for each student's success. The SLIP is aligned with the TCDSB's learning and improvement plan and is focused on student achievement and well-being.

The student data above also inform the exchange of information process between the elementary and secondary panels. This cross-panel dialogue is centrally supported through the use of teacher release days. Teachers from the elementary schools discuss the following topics listed below with the Guidance Department, child and youth workers, special education teachers and student success teachers at the secondary school. The information on the Exchange of Information Form includes student strengths, student challenges, and interventions to date and suggested future classroom interventions. Standardized assessment information in reading, writing, and mathematics is also included as well as special education and English language learning (ELL) programming information. Figure 12.4 denotes the TCDSB Student Success–Exchange of Information Form.

The data listed above are available to the administration, student success, special education, and guidance staff to help program for student success. At Jean Vanier Catholic Secondary School, this includes the use of data to purposefully timetable students for success. The first purposeful timetabling is for the incoming Grade 9 summer school program.

A local summer school program occurs in 15 high schools in the TCDSB. The program is centrally funded through the Continuing Education Department, but organized locally by each high school. All incoming Grade 9 students are encouraged to attend their new high school through July. This enables students not only to earn a high school credit, but more importantly, to become familiar and comfortable with their new high school. Students are introduced to each other, to the school, and to the teachers and support staff.

The data accumulated through the exchange of information as well as the assessments and surveys conducted in elementary school are organized and available to teaching staff through the TCDSB's Data Integration Platform (DIP). This electronic database is updated by teachers and maintained by the TCDSB Research Department. It can be accessed by teachers and the administration to plan and program for student success. The information is organized according to cohort, student, assessment, or other and can be transferred to different file formats for

CONFIDENTIAL

STUDENT SUCCESS- EXCHANGE OF INFORMATION FORM
(To be completed by grade the 8 Teachers for all students.
For identified students, proceed to Principal's Report after completing top portion.)

Student Name:	Elementary School:	High School:
Student D.O.B: (year/month/day)		Exchange of Information Date:

Grade 6 EQAO Level:	Grade 7 CAT 3 Stanine:	IPRC: YES ☐ NO ☐
Reading ____	Overall Math:	(If yes, please proceed to the Principal's Report in preparation for Exchange of Information Meeting)
Writing ____	Overall Language:	
Math ____	Overall Reading:	E.S.L. YES ☐ NO ☐

STUDENT'S STRENGTHS	STUDENT'S CHALLENGES	INTERVENTIONS TO DATE	SUGGESTED FUTURE *SCHOOL* INTERVENTIONS	SUGGESTED FUTURE *CLASSROOM* INTERVENTIONS
☐ Attendance/punctuality	☐ Attendance/punctuality	☐ Attendance Counsellor	☐ Attendance Counsellor	☐ Class seating and arrangement
☐ Submitting assignments	☐ Submitting assignments	☐ Parent conferences	☐ Parent conferences	☐ Set and post clear expectations
☐ Homework completion	☐ Homework completion	☐ Remedial support	☐ Remedial support	☐ Monitor notes/ homework/assignments
☐ General learning skills	☐ General learning skills	☐ Peer mentor/buddy	☐ Peer mentor/buddy	☐ Have student use agenda each day
☐ Test performance	☐ Test performance	☐ Board services support	☐ Board services support	☐ Keep student engaged in lesson
☐ Conduct/attitude	☐ Conduct/attitude	☐ Community agency support	☐ Community agency support	☐ "Chunk" larger assignments
☐ Focus and attention	☐ Focus and attention	☐ Program accommodations	☐ Program accommodations	☐ Use a variety of teaching strategies
☐ Co-curricular activities	☐ "At Risk" activities	☐ ESL Support	☐ ESL Support	☐ Restrict out of class time
☐ Social relationships	☐ Social relationships	☐ In-class support	☐ Review student schedule	☐ Notify parents about meetings/progress
☐ EQAO/ Report Results	☐ Anxiety/stress	☐ Guidance	☐ Alternative education	☐ Provide ongoing praise/feedback
☐ Literacy skills	☐ Motivation	☐ School Psychologist	☐ Guidance support	☐ Arrange in-class peer support
☐ Math skills	☐ EQAO/ Report Results	☐ School Social Worker	☐ Review course selection	☐ Connect curriculum to life experiences
☐ Other	☐ Literacy skills (Level 1)	☐ PHAST	☐ Substitution/deferral	☐ Use a variety of assess/eval strategies
	☐ Math skills (Level 1 & 2)		☐ Peer/class placement	☐ Other
	☐ Grade 9 course selections		☐ Student Success Support Team	
	☐ Other		☐ Other	

Copies to: Student Success Teacher ☐   E.S. Principal Signature: _____   Date: _____

Parent ☐   OSR ☐

Figure 12.4. Toronto Catholic District School Board Student Success – Exchange of Information Form.

easy use. At Jean Vanier, the information was used to plan students' summer school classes. The summer school provided enrichment for each student, in the arts or support for literacy or numeracy depending on the information received. In partnership with Immigration Canada (n.d.), the Settlement Workers in the Schools Program, and the high school provided a further week of enrichment for new Canadians. This program included community building for new Canadians and was open to any grade. Students were paired with a peer mentor to help ease the transition throughout their first year at an Ontario high school. At Jean Vanier, the summer school programs helped to ease the social/ emotional stress of joining a new school by introducing students to each other, the staff, and the facility. It also provided an opportunity to ensure that student needs in literacy and numeracy were addressed before their first year of high school.

The TCDSB's Data Integration Platform was accessed by the special education, student success, and guidance teachers to purposefully timetable students to address any gaps in prior learning. Students' timetables were individualized to support their unique learning profiles including student supports for social and emotional concerns, special education, and English language learners.

Curriculum night at Jean Vanier Catholic Secondary School involved sessions explaining the high school credit system in Ontario, the role of guidance, various pathways, including apprenticeship programs and graduation requirements, including the Ontario Secondary School Literacy Test. Breakout sessions in Tagalog, Spanish, Tamil, and Portuguese enabled parents to ask questions and receive resources in their own language. Including parents as partners in their children's education is important to a successful transition to high school. Parents are encouraged to take part in school activities that will increase their familiarity with the high school and the supports available for their teen.

Events and Initiatives

Events and initiatives to support students transitioning from elementary to high school enable students in the high school to take on leadership and mentoring roles. The elementary students, in turn, (1) are given the opportunity to experience high school, (2) get a taste for the high school curriculum, (3) are introduced to the rotary system, (4) familiarize themselves with the facility, and (5) meet friends before entering school in September. Events include a summer school program run by the individual high school for incoming Grade 9s. Take Our Kids to High School is a one-day event that invites Grade 8 students from the local elementary school to experience a day in the high school. The following description of the event is taken from an article first published in the spring 2009 edition of the Catholic Principals' Council of Ontario magazine entitled *Principal Connections*.

Take Our Kids to High School Day
at Jean Vanier Catholic Secondary School

Jean Vanier Catholic Secondary School in Scarborough hosted 450 students from local elementary schools for Take Our Kids to High School Day. As the high school said goodbye to the Grade 9 students, for the provincially sponsored Take Our Kids to Work Day, staff and remaining students focused their talents on organizing and welcoming Grade 7 and Grade 8 students to a unique "day in the life experience."

Students from eight elementary schools in Scarborough had a chance to get to know each other, the school facility, and Jean Vanier staff and students. This exciting day was intended to facilitate the transition from elementary to high school. Although not all of the 450 students who attended Take Our Kids to High School Day, attended Jean Vanier in the fall, each student benefited from the experience.

Students began their day in the gymnasium with a welcoming prayer and a series of interactive get-to-know-you games hosted by the leadership students. When students arrived, they were separated into eight teams. They were given a Jean Vanier "toolkit" for the day that included a timetable, pencil, and a healthy snack in a specially monogrammed knapsack. These specially monogrammed backpacks also helped to identify visiting students in the school, and they were great souvenirs for the participants.

Jean Vanier student leaders accompanied each team of elementary school students as they rotated through their four one-hour class blocks mimicking a typical high school day, including a self-serve lunch from the cafeteria. The curriculum for the day was designed with fun and learning in mind. Students experienced a science lab with digital microscopes, examining pond water for signs of life, as well as exploding gummy bears in the chemistry lab. Photoshop was their passport around the world, as they superimposed digital photos of themselves onto famous international landmarks. Leadership students led participants on a schoolwide scavenger hunt where they discovered the school'sspecialty programs including fine arts and auto mechanics. A lesson on communication and public speaking allowed them to hone their improvisational skills.

Preparing for this day was truly a team effort. The Student Success Team, comprised of administrators, guidance counsellors, teachers, and staff, began by identifying the key components to planning a meaningful day. A resource binder provided by the TCDSB's central SST helped frame priorities and protocols for the day. Guidance was responsible for identifying and inviting Grade 7 and Grade 8 classes. It was imperative to the success of this project for the Guidance Department to foster positive relationships with the elementary school principals and classroom teachers. The Guidance Department was able to support the Grade 8 teachers in preparing permission forms, coordinating transportation, and other details such as money and orders for the cafeteria lunch. Participating departments were responsible for creating the curriculum for the day and organizing the staff to teach the lessons.

Student Leadership

Student council and student volunteers were an integral part of the day. They were responsible for ensuring the success of the classroom rotations, leading the groups of students from one activity to the next, and ensuring participation by all the students. They also organized and ran the student scavenger hunt. Departments selected student volunteers to help facilitate the classroom lessons, showcasing the many talents of the community.

Professional Dialogue

Since the students and staff were looking after the Grade 7 and Grade 8 visitors, the Intermediate Division teachers from both the elementary and secondary schools were free to dialogue and participate in professional development opportunities. Teachers shared ideas and best practices on topics such as technology in the classroom – including the use of SMARTBoards, literacy, and numeracy development, and they also enjoyed a discussion around pathways for success led by the Guidance Department. The opportunity to share a cup of coffee and great conversation with colleagues was valued by all involved.

Overall, the day was a huge success. After the event, the team met to reflect on the experience, debrief, and read the many thank you letters from the Grade 8 teachers and students who participated in the event. The following are examples of the feedback from the Grade 7 and Grade 8 students, demonstrating that the event was valued by the participants:

- "It felt very real going to different classes. I think I will be less nervous when it comes to my first day of high school."
- "Although many students think high school is scary, there is nothing to worry about. You get to make new friends and … the teachers were welcoming."
- "I learned to just be yourself. People help you out with difficulties."
- "My favourite part of the day was the whole day!"
- "Take Our Kids to High School Day was a really fun and educational experience!"

Post-event activities were provided for teachers through the TCDSB's centrally developed resource binder, as were the following tips to start planning your own Take Our Kids to High School Day.

- Set regular times for your team starting in September.
- Decide how many Grade 8 students you can accommodate.
- Designate which rooms will be used.
- Determine how best to use senior students.
- Establish how lunch will occur for this day.
- Establish how students will be transported to and from the high school.
- Determine how you will assign each student a timetable.
- Determine how you will distribute the timetables.
- Communicate the plans to the rest of your staff.

Family Math Night

Family Math Night was an event organized through the TCDSB's Numeracy Department. The event focused on one strategy or game to support numeracy in the Primary, Junior, and Intermediate divisions. This event was hosted at St. Maria Goretti Catholic Elementary School. At this event, Jean Vanier students came back to their elementary school to teach the game and lead the Math Night. This leadership event for high school students, with the neighbouring elementary school, helped nurture the relationship between the intermediate students. Intermediate elementary school students became friends with their high school buddies while they were playing math games. The organizing of events, such as Family Math Night with the local high school, continued through the next year, along with other events. Students at Jean Vanier continued to plan events with St. Maria Goretti organizing, in partnership with the parent council, an event to support Healthy Active Living and Girls' Self-Esteem. Below is a summary of an article published in *Principal*

Connections (Helling, Spring 2011), explaining one Family Math Night, using the oldest board game in the world, Oware.

Game of Oware

Oware is an ancient board game that originated in Africa around 1400 B.C., and it is still played today in Ghana, Malawi, the Caribbean, South America, Sri Lanka, Indonesia, Malaysia, and the Philippines. There are many different versions and names for this game, depending on what country you are from. Mancala is one name – Sungka, Bao, and Oware are other names. Because of its wide appeal, many of the students in our schools know the game and have played it.

Oware can be played by students in all grade levels. The level of complexity is entirely dependent on the players. Oware boards are sold in Canada by MACPRI, an organization committed to supporting Africa's development through the promotion and marketing of "Made in Africa" art. Their website is http://www.macpri.com. Students can also learn to play on-line, on a SMARTBoard, or using an egg carton and 48 buttons, seeds, marbles, beads, beans, etc. Although a representative of MACPRI came to sell Oware boards from Ghana, many staff, students, and parents learned to play with their own Oware board (e.g., using an egg carton and 48 buttons).

As part of the African Heritage Month celebrations, the students at Saints Cosmas and Damian Catholic School were taught how to play Oware. Using a presentation developed by the TCDSB's Curriculum and Accountability Department, two mathematics resource teachers were able to teach eight classes how to play Oware. A lunch and learn was organized for primary and specialty teachers. Intermediate students were asked to take on leadership roles and to help teach younger students. They also acted as student ambassadors for our Family Math Night. Further to this event, students in Grades 4–8 from across Toronto could participate in an Oware tournament, organized at St. Jean De Brebeuf School in Scarborough.

Family Math Night is a fun event for students and their parents to experience math beyond the curriculum. Although students were at first reluctant participants, they soon learned that math is fun! Students enjoyed playing Oware with their classmates and were excited to play the game with their siblings, parents, and friends. Families filled the gymnasium, the hallways, and the classrooms. Parents and children competed for prizes that included Oware games from Ghana. Although the TCDSB's Mathematics Department brought about 40 games for the evening, and parents purchased games through MACPRI, other students simply made their own Oware game with egg cartons and buttons.

Why Have a Family Math Night?

• Family Math Night introduces math topics to students in a different way. This appeals to students' different learning styles.
• Multicultural games and activities such as Oware provide a context that makes mathematics significant and meaningful for all Canadians.
• The host school models positive attitudes towards mathematics by encouraging families to engage in mathematical activities beyond the classroom and engaging students in positive mathematics activities.
• Children do better in school when parents are involved in their learning. Family Math Night emphasizes that parental support will benefit children's attitudes, self-esteem, and potential to understand mathematics.
• Community Building: Family Math Night gives busy parents, teachers, and students one more chance to connect with each other. In one community, high school students helped to teach elementary students how to play Oware as part of their transition and community building.

Family Math Night shows students and parent that math is fun. It offers an opportunity for children and their parents to learn mathematics together and have fun.

Northern Spirit Games

Students from TCDSB elementary schools are given an opportunity to participate in the annual Northern Spirit Games each February (see TDCSB, 2010i). The athletic, cultural, and spiritual celebrations welcome 300 students at five high schools across Toronto. Students participate in 10 indoor and outdoor activities based on traditional Inuit and First Nations games. Each day's activities are run by trained leaders from the hosting school.

Staff and students partake in traditional cultural pastimes such as art, music, and time-honoured games and activities that focus on physical strength, agility, and endurance. The games emphasize teamwork and introduce students to sports and activities still enjoyed in northern communities. These activities include snowshoeing, rope skipping, and the spear throw.

The Northern Spirit Games Day kicks off with an opening ceremony led by students from one of the participating elementary schools. The opening ceremonies are based on the teaching of the Medicine Wheel and honour the gifts of Mother Earth, reminding students of their sacred connection to nature. Students pray and sing together and are treated to a drum performance. Guest speakers from First Nations groups, including storytellers, Elders, musicians, and cultural leaders, address the children before the athletic activities begin (see TCDSB, 2010j).

The Northern Spirit games are part of the TCDSB's First Nations, Metis, and Inuit Initiatives, including curriculum development, teacher workshops, and twinning with northern communities. The TCDSB Northern Spirit Games (formerly, Arctic Games) arose from the twinning initiative established by former Lieutenant Governor of Ontario James Bartleman to honour Canada's Inuit and Aboriginal populations (TDCSB, 2010i).

Table 12.1 desribes the games and how to organize them.

The TCDSB's Northern Spirit Games Day offers elementary school students a unique athletic, cultural, and spiritual experience. Through this event, elementary school students have a chance to build community with their teachers, their schoolmates, students from other elementary schools, and with the high school leaders who run the event. The ability to familiarize themselves with the high school facility, the teachers, and especially the high school students helps ease the transition from elementary to high school.

The TCDSB's transition plan was first launched in June 2006. As part of this initiative, Grade 9 students were encouraged to pair themselves with a "caring adult." Student Success Teams were established at every high school to provide extra attention and support for students in need. This "caring adult" is especially important if the student has special needs. The TCDSB and the School Support Program published the following pamphlet entitled "Looking Ahead ... Together: Transitioning the Young Adult from High School to the Community" (TDCSB, 2010g). The resource encourages the student to establish a staff member at the high school as a safe person to support the student through the transition to high school. Parents are encouraged to develop a plan with school personnel supporting the student and monitoring her or his progress both academically and socially. This connection to a "caring adult" at school will help students both academically and socially as they transition from elementary to secondary school.

Table 12.1 Northern Games: Names and Descriptions

	Activity	Equipment	Description	Special Notes
A	Snow Shoe Relay Kaska, Koyukon, Dogrib, Slavey, Gwich'in, Ahtna, Dena'ina, Sahtu, Chipewayan & Han Peoples (Alaska, B.C., NWT, Nunavut, Yukon, Saskatchewan, Manitoba)	– 4 pairs of medium snow shoes – 10 pylons (5 for each line)	Teams form 2 lines. Students must put on snowshoes and then run through the slalom course and back towards their team. Once they have completed their run, the students take off the snowshoes, give them to the next participant on their team, and then proceed to the end of the line.	Please set up 2 parallel courses in such a way that racers cannot run into each other as they run around pylon.Help students put on the snowshoes. Warn students to be careful they do not pinch their fingers when putting on the snowshoes.
B	Seal Crawl	– 4 pylons – 10 rubber fish	Teams form 2 lines. The first student in each line lies on the ground, crosses his or her legs to simulate a seal's back flipper, then uses arms only to crawl to the pylon, retrieve the rubber fish, and then return to the team. Then the studentgets up on knees and claps hands like a seal before the next student may proceed.	Place one pylon as a starting point and the other about 5 metres away to mark the boundary of the relay. Place five rubber fish at one end of each course.Students cannot carry the fish in their mouth. They can use any other method to carry the fish. Replenish the fish as needed.
C	Tug-of-War Nunavut	– 2 long ropes at each station – gloves	Each team will be divided into 2 even groups. Each half-team will work cooperatively to pull its side of the rope across a line marked on the ground. Best 4 out of 7 pulls will be made.	The 2 ropes are crossed in the centre to create a 4-way pull.Caution students to make sure they remain standing during the pull. No one is to just let go of the rope until the end of the pull.

Table 12.1 Northern Games: Names and Descriptions (*Continued*)

	Activity	Equipment	Description	Special Notes
D	Kick Ball Game Nunavut	– 2 high jump standards – 2 tether balls – high jump pole – tape	Each person will attempt to kick the tetherball by standing on one foot and jumping in air, kicking the ball with the same foot, and landing on both feet. After each person has taken his or her turn, the ball will be raised to 75 cm, and each person will take another turn at this new height. If time permits, raise the ball to 90 cm.	Set up 2 high jump standards with a high jump bar set at 4 feet high. Tape the high jump pole to the standards. Tie a tetherball to the pole with the tetherball dangling about 60 cm off the ground to start.
E	Rope Skipping Pangnirtung, Nunavut	– long skipping rope – 5–10 loofa sponges (approx. 20–30 feet of cord and sash rope)	One member for each team grasps the ends of the rope. Two competitors (1 from each team) begin in the middle of the rope. They stand with their backs to the rope, facing opposite directions. The rope is swung back and forth without passing overhead. The jumpers compete against one another to see who is able to jump the longest without touching the sponges (caribou skin). One point is awarded to the team whose jumper lasts the longest. When finished, jumpers return to the end of the line.	Thread loofa sponges onto the rope. The persons swinging the rope become the next jumpers.

Table 12.1 Northern Games: Names and Descriptions (*Continued*)

	Activity	Equipment	Description	Special Notes
F	Blanket Toss Nunavut	– 2 12 foot diameter parachutes – 2 balls	Each team gathers around their parachute with the ball in the middle. On the count of 3, the ball is to be tossed in the air. One point is awarded to the team that has the highest toss. Each team will have 10 tosses against one another.	Make sure teams are far enough apart that they do not interfere with each other. The ball must remain on the parachute for a toss to be considered a success.
G	Backpack Relay Slavey Peoples (NWT, B.C., Alberta, Nunavut)	– 2 backpacks-survival gear (e.g., boots, coat, hat, gloves, blanket) – 4 pylons – 2 hula hoops	Teams form 2 lines. Students must pack their bags with the survival gear, put on the backpack, and run around the pylon once, and then run back towards their team. The student who is completing his or her run must take off the backpack, unpack the bag, placing all the survival gear in the hula hoop, and then proceed to the end of the line. Once the bag is unpacked, the next person in line can begin to pack the bag and continue on with the race.	At the start of the race, the survival gear is placed so it is piled inside a hula hoop.
I	Stick Throw Sahtu & Chipewayan Peoples (NWT, Nunavut, Alberta, Manitoba, Saskatchewan)	– 30 relay batons – 2 hula hoops	Teams form 2 lines. Each student is given a baton. One after the other, the students will try and toss their baton into the hula hoop. Once all the students have tossed their batons, the team captain will retrieve the batons not in the hula hoop and bring them back to be thrown again at the target. One round is complete when all the batons end up inside the hula hoop.	Place the hula hoops approx. 3 metres away from the tossing line. Make sure all students are behind the tossing line. A toss is successful if any part of the baton is inside the hula hoop. No batons are removed from the hula hoop until the end of a round. If a baton is knocked out of the hula hoop, it must be rethrown. The team with the most successful rounds is the winner.

Table 12.1 Northern Games: Names and Descriptions (*Concluded*)

	Activity	Equipment	Description	Special Notes
J	Rest Station	– liquid refreshment	Team's line up for liquid refreshment and a well-deserved break.	
L	Spear Throw Sahtu, Dogrib, & Dena'ina Peoples (NWT, Nunavut, Alaska)	– 2 soft spears – 2 hula hoops – 2 high jump standards – tape	Place the hula hoop on the snow embankments approx. 3 metres away from the tossing line. Teams form 2 lines. One after the other, the students will try and throw their spear through the hula hoop. For each successful toss, one point is awarded to the team. Once the student has tossed the spear, he or she must retrieve it and give it to the next person in line.	Tape hula hoop to one of the high jump standards so that students can throw spear through the hoop. Make sure all students stay behind the throwing line except when retrieving spear. The spear must go completely through the hula hoop.

Source: TCDSB (2010j), Northern Games 2010 Information Package.

An important component in creating a foundation for student success is fostering positive communication between parents and the school. As such, it is important for parents and teachers to work together on behalf of students to provide the necessary supports during the transition period. This cooperation will help lessen students' anxieties and provide a foundation for students' success. The TCDSB transition booklets mentioned above, including the "Transition Guide for Parents" (TCDSB, 2010a), "Transition Guide for Students" (2010b), "Transition to Secondary School Service for Students with Autism Spectrum Disorders (ASD)" (TCDSB, 2010c, 2010d, 2010e, 2010f), and "Looking Ahead ... Together (TCDSB, 2010g), as well as school-developed resources, all help to foster the partnership between home and school for the student transitioning from elementary to secondary school.

Transition events such as high school information evenings for Grade 8 parents and students, high school open house events, and locally run transition assemblies for Grade 7 and Grade 8 students, also help ease student and parent anxiety over transitioning from elementary to secondary school. The TCDSB welcomes students and parents to both locally organized and board-organized events. Intermediate students and parents of Grade 8 students transitioning to high school are encouraged to attend a general information evening on high schools within the TCDSB. Topics addressed include the following:

- How do I apply for high school?
- What is the credit system?
- Specialized high school programs
- Credit levels
- Cooperative education
- Timetables
- Lockers
- Exams
- Accessing high school information.

Local events, such as high school open houses, will include many of the previous stated topics, but will focus on the individual flavour of the specific high school that is presenting. It will include presentations by student leaders outlining the extracurricular activities and clubs as well as any special programs within the school. High schools will also host assemblies for incoming Grade 8 students. Jean Vanier Catholic Secondary School student leaders hosted an assembly on dispelling the myths of high school. It included a play and presentation by student leaders. This event afforded an opportunity for incoming Grade 9s to experience the high school and its students in a supportive, fun way.

Student Leadership

At Jean Vanier Catholic Secondary School, students are paired from their first visit with a Jean Vanier mentor. The Jean Vanier mentor is a student leader whose purpose is to make the transition to high school as successful as possible. The Jean Vanier mentors help lead many transition events such as the Northern Spirit Games, the Take Our Kids to High School event, Family Math Nights in the elementary schools, transition assemblies for Grade 8 students, the open house for Grade 8 students, and the Grade 9 orientation day. Throughout the first few weeks, the mentors (identified by their t-shirts) will be available to help the Grade 9 students. The mentors also meet the Grade 9 students within the first week of school, in small groups, to share their strategies for success at Jean Vanier Catholic Secondary School.

The Transition to Secondary School Service for Students with Autism Spectrum Disorders suggests that a peer buddy arrangement be made for students transitioning to high school. The parent guide (TDCSB, 2010c) encourages the development of friendships with a peer that could be a buddy for the teen. This peer can help the student with autism record classwork, move classrooms, help with communication, and in turn, reduce stress for the student during the first few months of high school. Organizing a peer buddy is just one of the strategies suggested in the information booklet and is among the various resources and initiatives that have been undertaken by the TCDSB to support a more successful transition to high school for students with autism and their families.

Community involvement within the TCDSB goes beyond a graduation requirement. The stated purpose of the student community involvement requirement, according to the document entitled "Student Community Involvement TCDSB" (TDCSB, 2011) is to encourage students to:

- Grow in the Christian calling to service and reflection, develop a generous and compassionate response to the local community and to the world
- Foster an awareness and understanding of social and civic responsibility

- Experience and celebrate the contributions they can make in supporting and strengthening their communities.

School community service may include service within the school community that provides benefit to others that takes place outside the regular school day. The TCDSB community involvement documents foster participation and community involvement in the school, parish, and larger community. This participation helps foster a feeling of belonging, helping students as they transition from one panel to another. It also promotes student leadership.

Student leadership in all of the events and initiatives listed above is integral to creating a supportive environment that fosters a sense of belonging for all students. Student leadership is essential in the following domains:

- Transition events
- Mentors and peer buddies
- Visits to elementary schools
- Social justice initiatives and community involvement
- Student government and leadership in clubs and activities.

This contribution to the school community is invaluable for the student leader who gains valuable skills and provides opportunities that increase self-esteem but also for the transitioning students who, in turn, have a peer support system that enables them to feel more comfortable in their new school setting.

Related Issues

Students preparing for a transition of any sort need time to adjust to the new expectations and environment that they will be experiencing. Planning and talking about the transition enables students to work through their fears and anxieties about moving to a new school. The programs listed above enable teachers to help prepare students for their move to a new school. As with any transition, students need people to help them adjust to the realities of their new learning environment. Positive transition programs can help teachers support students as they adjust to the change. Planning and talking about the students' new school helps to ease the concerns and worry inevitably associated with a new school. The process of transitioning from an elementary to a secondary school should not occur overnight. This is especially true for students with special needs. A transition team is important for all students, but is especially important for students who require academic, social, and/or emotional support. The Student Success Learning Networks can help all students find their way in the "larger" school environment that most students face when transitioning to high school. The support of a transition team that includes the special education staff at both the elementary school and the receiving secondary school is especially important for the student with special needs. A deliberate transition program should be established, enabling students to overcome their fears and anxieties and to establish the supports they need to succeed academically, socially, and emotionally.

Conclusion

Change is an inevitable part of life. When students are changing classrooms, schools, teachers, and friends, they should not be left to transition alone. They require teacher, parental, and peer support. Often, the adults in a child's life are concerned about the student's transition to a new learning environment, but they are not completely sure how to support them. A deliberate transition program gives parents, schools, and students a template for developing programs to help students overcome their fears and anxieties, and to succeed both academically and socially in their new school. The program should offer a template of supports, but the template needs to be flexible enough to meet the diverse needs of each individual community. The way one community supports students as they transition is not necessarily the way another school community might find success. However, considering a student's academic and social/emotional needs will inevitably ease parent and student anxiety, leading to a more successful transition for all students. Although the examples from the TCDSB and the Jean Vanier Catholic Secondary School community may provide some ideas to educators who are building a transition program for intermediate students, they will need to consider the specific geography and the student/parent demographics that form their individual school communities. Considering the needs and interests of parents, students, and communities is imperative to the success of any transition initiative. Establishing strong relationships between the elementary and secondary staff members will support students as they transition to their new school. Nurturing strong transition teams and professional dialogue are essential to students' academic success, as are mentoring student leadership and supporting a focus on active student participation in school communities. Possible highlights of a transition program include cross-panel team building, transition events, academic programming using professional learning cycles, and support for student success including data-driven dialogue.

Personal Remarks

The Toronto Catholic District School Board transition documents referred to in this chapter are used with permission from the school board. I would like to thank the TCDSB for sharing these documents. I would also like to thank the many TCDSB members who co-planned the initiatives and resources mentioned in this chapter. This list would include the following: Superintendent of Schools Doug Yack; Superintendent of Schools Geoff Grant; Superintendent of Student Success Patrick Keyes; Superintendent of Curriculum and Accountability Josie Di Giovanni; Superintendent of Schools Loretta Notten; Superintendent of Special Education Frank Piddisi, and the resource teachers and program coordinators for special education; Chief Speech–Language Pathologist and the Autism Support Team Susan Menary; Program Coordinator, Student Success, Pathways Programs, Guidance and Counselling Carmela Giardini; the Literacy Resource Team at the TCDSB; Coordinator of Literacy and Library Services K–12 Teresa Paoli; the Mathematics Resource Team at the TCDSB and their Coordinator Gina Iuliano Marrello; the Research Team at the TCDSB; the Catholic Principals' Council of Ontario; the staff at Saints Cosmas and Damian Catholic School; the staff at Jean Vanier Catholic Secondary School; Peter Aguiar, former principal at Jean Vanier and coordinator for Academic Information and Computer Technology; and Literacy and Student Success Program Coordinator Bianca Auciello.

REFERENCES

Education Quality and Accountability Office (EQAO). (2011, Sept.). The Power of Good Information: Using Data for School Improvement Planning. EQAO Regional Workshop: School Support and Outreach Team.
Helling, G. (2011, Spring). Oware and Family Math Night. *Principal Connections, 14*(3), 40–41.

Ontario Ministry of Education (OMoE), Literacy and Numeracy Secretariat. (n.d.). *K-12 School effectiveness framework: A support for school improvement and student success.* Toronto: Queen's Printer. Retrieved from http://www.edu .gov.on.ca/eng/literacynumeracy/framework.html

Ontario Ministry of Education (OMoE). (2007, 17 May). *Incorporating Methods of Applied Behaviour Analysis (ABA) into Programs for Students with Autism Spectrum Disorders (ASD).* Policy/Program Memorandum No. 140.

Ontario Ministry of Education (OMoE). (2011, 17 Aug.). How we're doing it in Ontario: From great to excellent – Leveraging leadership research, policy and practice. *Presentation delivered at the International Confederation of Principals,* Toronto.

Toronto Catholic District School Board (TCDSB), Student Success Team. (2011a, Sept.). *A framework for Toronto Catholic District School Board's Student Success Learning Networks.*

Toronto Catholic District School Board (TCDSB). (2011b, Jan.). *Elementary guidance counsellors present: "Transition to high school"–An information evening for parents.* [Poster]

Toronto Catholic District School Board (TCDSB). (2011c). *Student community involvement TCDSB: A secondary school graduation requirement–Information manual for Toronto Catholic District School Board students and families.*

Toronto Catholic District School Board (TCDSB). (2010a). *Transition guide for parents: The complete picture – Your child's future secondary school and beyond.*

Toronto Catholic District School Board (TCDSB). (2010b). *Transition guide for students: Your future – One piece at a time.*

Toronto Catholic District School Board (TCDSB). (2010c). *Transition to secondary school service for students with Autism Spectrum Disorders (ASD) Information Package.* Support service for students with autism, Surrey Place Centre (SPC), School Support Program (SSP).

Toronto Catholic District School Board (TCDSB). (2010d). *Transition to secondary school service for students with Autism Spectrum Disorders (ASD): A parent's guide.* Support service for students with Autism, Surrey Place Centre (SPC), School Support Program (SSP).

Toronto Catholic District School Board (TCDSB). (2010e). *Transition to secondary school service for students with Autism Spectrum Disorders (ASD): Welcome to high school profile book.* Support service for students with Autism, Surrey Place Centre (SPC), School Support Program (SSP).

Toronto Catholic District School Board (TCDSB). (2010f). *Transition to secondary school service for students with Autism Spectrum Disorders (ASD): Student support package.* Support service for students with Autism, Surrey Place Centre (SPC), School Support Program (SSP).

Toronto Catholic District School Board (TCDSB). (2010g). *Transition to secondary school service for students with Autism Spectrum Disorders (ASD): Looking ahead, together–Transitioning the young adult from high school to the community.* Support service for students with Autism, Surrey Place Centre (SPC), School Support Program (SSP).

Toronto Catholic District School Board (TCDSB). (2010h). *Transition to secondary school for students with an ASG: Asperger Syndrome Workbooks.* Support service for students with Autism, Surrey Place Centre (SPC), School Support Program (SSP).

Toronto Catholic District School Board (TCDSB), Communications Department. (2010i, 8 Feb.). *News Release: TCDSB Northern Spirit Games.*

Toronto Catholic District School Board (TCDSB). (2010j). *Northern Spirit Games 2010 information package.*

13 Exploring a "Family of Schools" Model for Cross-Panel Mathematics Teacher Professional Development

DANIEL H. JARVIS

In an era of reform-based mathematics education (National Council of Teachers of Mathematics [NCTM], 2000; Ontario Ministry of Education [OMoE], 2005a, 2005b, 2007), in which key elements such as problem-based learning (PBL), cooperative group work, manipulatives, technology, and varied assessment are being emphasized, it is not difficult to understand why teaching K–12 mathematics represents a complex undertaking. The tweny-first-century mathematics educator must possess the following four overlapping areas of specialized knowledge and competencies (see Figure 13.1):

- She or he must have a thorough understanding of the *mathematics content* (e.g., Ontario curriculum expectations as listed/described within the five mathematics strands).
- She or he must also master, and be able to implement with confidence, an ever-expanding range of *mathematics resources for teaching* such as manipulatives (e.g., linking cubes, GeoBoards, Pattern Blocks, Algebra Tiles) and technologies (e.g., graphing/CAS calculators, computer software, Internet web resources, Interactive Whiteboards).
- She or he must develop what Deborah Ball and colleagues (Ball & Bass, 2000; Thames & Ball, 2010) have described as unique mathematics knowledge for teaching (MKT), or a pedagogical awareness of how mathematical topics are connected, and how students acquire, organize, and communicate their mathematical thinking (including an awareness of common student misconceptions and alternative solution strategies).

Figure 13.1. Four components of effective reform-based mathematics teaching.

- She or he must incorporate *balanced instructional planning*, featuring both the more traditional methods of memorization and practice (e.g., making 10, multiplication facts), combined with regular opportunities for rich, interactive problem-based learning.

Professional development (PD) models that offer teachers elements of *choice* (i.e., selection of topics, research questions, number/length of days), *voice* (i.e., participation in the preparation/implementation/debriefing cycles of professional development), and *ongoing support* (i.e., over time, often involving classroom-embedded activities and/or observations) have been shown to be effective in further equipping mathematics educators for the challenging profession in which they are engaged (Jarvis, 2009; Loucks-Horsley, Hewson, Love, & Stiles, 1998; Stein, Smith, Henningsen, & Silver, 2000). Many elementary school teachers are generalists who may possess relatively weak skills in mathematics, thus rendering the mastery of content, pedagogy, and technology all the more challenging for them. Further, not only do the grade-based divisions of many school buildings found within much of the North American system lead to a geographical "great divide" between elementary (Grades 1–8) and secondary (Grade 9–12) facilities, but there is often a philosophical (i.e., teacher beliefs about mathematics) divide as well.

One model of professional development that has shown some promise in its attempt to bridge this elementary/secondary gap is that of cross-panel, "family of schools" professional learning communities (PLCs). Cross-panel initiatives can be difficult to organize and implement in terms of logistics (i.e., often across town or within a large geographical region), curriculum content focus (i.e., what topics should form the shared core of the professional development?), and general communication between colleagues (i.e., avoiding defensive positions and potential finger pointing).

As Suurtamm and Graves (2007) reported, in their study of provincial curriculum implementation in Intermediate Division mathematics classrooms in Ontario, cross-panel professional development initiatives can reveal inconsistent views of mathematics curriculum and pedagogy:

> The mathematics leaders reported that when groups of teachers from different panels have the opportunity to get together, there are often very different views of teaching and learning expressed. In addition, their discussions revealed that the positions of elementary and secondary teachers are not necessarily consistent within each panel. In one group, the elementary teachers were noted as being more traditional than the secondary, whereas another group of mathematics leaders described the secondary teachers as more traditional. (p. 22)

In 2008, Jarvis followed the progress of a mathematics coordinator as she continued to implement an existing "family of schools" approach to professional development and learning within a district school board in north-central Ontario, Canada. To better understand this Grades 7–10 initiative, interviews were conducted with the original coordinator (Rick[1]) who had set in motion the first "family of schools" groupings (i.e., secondary school mathematics teachers meeting with their elementary "feeder school" counterparts), the coordinator (Carole) who was responsible for scaling up the initiative within the board in subsequent years, and three teacher leaders in the project (two elementary school teachers, Alex and Linda; and one secondary school mathematics teacher, Rob). The researcher also attended the closing event for the year-long series of "family of schools" meetings, a day in which the various groups shared their progress, analysed elementary/secondary students' work samples together, and debriefed on the entire experience in both their cross-panel groups and also with the whole group of teachers involved within the board. This chapter will highlight the findings of the case study research, first describing the initiative and the research method, and then presenting a summary of perceived affordances, challenges, outcomes, and a brief discussion of some related issues.

Description of the Professional Development Model

In the research interviews, the local coordinator explained how the "family of schools" approach involved the selection of a "lead teacher" for each teacher team, a shared problem-solving focus, lesson planning/analysis, and perhaps most importantly, cross-panel observation.

Structure and Shared Leadership

The "family of schools" professional development model involved seven "families" of secondary mathematics teachers (Grade 9 and Grade 10) and "feeder school" elementary teachers of mathematics (Grades 7 and 8; most of whom taught mathematics along with the other core subjects, but some of whom were strictly specialist "math teachers" within a rotary style elementary school context). There were approximately 75 teachers involved altogether in the initiative. Wanting to incorporate a *shared leadership* approach, the coordinator invited seven "lead teachers" (some elementary, some secondary school teachers) to act as organizers and key contacts for their respective teacher teams. These lead teachers received five "training days" in preparation for the facilitation work they would be asked to do within their respective teacher teams throughout the initiative. The coordinator shares thoughts on the "lead teacher" role:

CAROLE: In varying degrees, some [lead teachers] took on more responsibility than others. We co-facilitated when it came to the meetings. We would often discuss what part would I do and what part would they do. The elementary teachers were very nervous about speaking to the secondary teachers at first. They needed that support of me as a secondary lead being there with them ... Although they teach all the time, not all teachers are comfortable with teaching other teachers, or being in that facilitator role. It's a lack of confidence for a lot of them, or feeling they don't have a lot to share ... I wanted this to be about collaboration and discussion.

A secondary school lead teacher underscored the importance of administrative support:

ROB: It was important to have [facilitator training] and ... I think it has to be an initiative where the administration is supporting it, because it doesn't occur on its own. We're all busy and without it – to be honest with you, I can find a thousand projects to do if the transitions are not going to occur – I can find things to do in my own school. So really to get outside of that mindset of being so centralist ... that initiative has to come from the administration and allow the time for the interaction to occur. It doesn't occur naturally.

The decision to focus on the "transition years" was partly motivated by senior administrators at the board level who wanted to address the lack of achievement in mathematics in both the Grade 9 and Grade 10 Applied[2] level courses throughout the board. The provincial resource (print/digital) known as *Targeted Implementation and Planning Strategies for Revised Mathematics* (TIPS4RM) already existed in Ontario and was freely available to mathematics teachers. This resource focused heavily on the use of problem-based learning, technology, and manipulatives – areas in which, according to the coordinator, their existed great interest among these teachers, but relatively few opportunities for professional growth.

Six half-days of "family of schools" meetings were planned throughout the 2007–08 school year. The first 3 half-days occurred with only one "family of schools" team, as a form of pilot project, involving four teachers/classrooms within a Grades 7–12 school context. These sessions were based on a (textbook publisher's) program, which involved an "expert" representative being brought in (from that publisher) to the board to help teachers prepare to plan, teach, and analyse lessons. During these 4 months, teachers were able to observe each other's classrooms as part of their new learning. In the winter term, when the new coordinator took over the role of Grades 7–12 numeracy, she planned to continue with the initiative and use the remaining funding, but decided to expand the professional development to involve six other teacher teams from across the board. The fourth half-day involved early discussions around selecting and co-planning a mathematics lesson (i.e., based on a TIPS4RM lesson), anticipated student responses, and, appropriate strategies and questioning. Teachers were afforded the opportunity to observe lessons being taught within the other panel (e.g., elementary school teachers were able to observe their secondary counterparts teaching a similar, but more advanced, version of the shared lesson). The fifth day was meant for sharing reflections on how the lesson was implemented, student responses and sample work, ideas for refinement, etc. The sixth, and final, half-day was planned as a district-wide meeting of all seven teams together, during which they shared their findings and insights, first, with their own family of schools group and, then later, with the larger group.

Perceived Affordances and Benefits

When asked about her perceptions of benefits stemming from the "family of schools" initiative, the coordinator emphasized communication among teachers from the different panels, and the shared and self-selected focus on problem-based learning, which involved the use of manipulatives:

CAROLE: One of the key things was the opportunity to work with the two different panels, getting to work together and talking about what the kids need to learn or know, what skills, what concepts are being taught, what concepts have to follow through from Grade 7, 8 and 9 ... The other thing that came through was the impact on their teaching – the importance of the problem solving and letting the kids struggle, and using rich activities where the kids really had to get a deeper conceptual understanding ... The use of manipulatives came out really big too.

In the following section, we will look more closely at some of the perceived affordances, or benefits, of this particular "family of schools" approach to professional development: increased communication between panels, meaningful mathematics content review, an empowering choice of curricular focus, and classroom-based lesson study with cross-panel observations.

COMMUNICATION BETWEEN PANELS

Various terms have been popularized in describing professional development models for teachers. McGraw, Arbaugh, Lynch, and Brown (2003) discuss "communities of practice"; DuFour (2004) has promoted his "professional learning communities" approach; and, more specific to mathematics education, Hufferd-Ackles, Fuson, and Sherin (2004) refer to "math talk learning communities." The organized and board-funded opportunity for elementary school teachers to communicate with colleagues from other local elementary schools, and with math teachers from local secondary schools, to which many of their students ultimately are sent, was described by those interviewed in this small case study as being very beneficial for a number of reasons. First, the coordinator draws attention to the isolation that teachers often experience in their daily work:

CAROLE: Maybe I'm biased, but math I find at the secondary level – we're all in our classrooms … We're in different parts of the school – it's not like you have departments anymore – so a lot of math teachers do work in isolation, and it is a closed-door kind of thing … Having teachers allow other teachers to come in, that was positive, and sharing ideas … So, this was a good thing to get to meet other people – they've exchanged emails … The biggest one probably was the elementary teachers getting to see what [secondary school teachers] are teaching – where it's leading; and the secondary seeing where [elementary school teachers] are coming from.

The former numeracy coordinator also felt strongly that moderate "discomfort" can actually be quite productive and instructive, in terms of the teacher team groupings that took place:

RICK: One of the benefits is that changing the social grouping adds a dynamic that breaks down some barriers. So, if you've got people who are used to working together in a Math Department in a secondary school or in a division in a middle school, they fall into pretty set ways of working together, and how their social arrangements will work. They probably don't talk an awful lot about professional development, or some of these deeper questions. So, I think there's just a group dynamic thing that's very valuable to put people together in a broader, less comfortable setting where they're going to have to negotiate rules.

An elementary lead teacher shares how the networking aspect of the "family of schools" approach was very productive, despite how awkward some of the original conversations may have felt:

ALEX: Networking is one of the benefits. You get to know the high school teachers at your family of schools. They get to know you. So, the teachers are sometimes more comfortable because they're just discussing students ... "This is what our Grade 8s are doing ..." and, "This specific student is ..." and, "This is how we can help them for this coming year ..." As a Grade 8 teacher, I now have a little more insight into what they're looking for, and what they do in Grade 9. The Grade 9 teachers have a better idea of what we do in Grade 7 and 8 – so, we're trying to help with that transition ... When we first started – I think it's natural – all the high school teachers were sitting together and all the elementary teachers were sitting together. As it evolved over time it became a lot more – we were working together ... It's the people you have involved. If the people are willing to participate, then everything goes along quite well.

Part of the communication experienced among teachers in the "family of schools" groups centred on the specifics of mathematics content from the *Ontario Curriculum: Mathematics (Revised)* (Ontario Ministry of Education, 2005).

MATHEMATICS CONTENT REVIEW

Although elementary and secondary school teachers in Ontario are required to cover curricular expectations as outlined in the Ministry of Education curriculum documents, many seem to be more inclined to follow a commercial textbook package (textbook, sometimes a workbook, and teacher's manual; albeit tailored to the provincial curriculum and often co-authored and reviewed by participating Ontario teachers on contract with the publishers) rather than regularly referring to the curriculum itself for their planning/teaching. So, beyond being relatively unfamiliar with the expectations for their own assigned grade level, teachers are even less familiar with the curriculum from the "other" panel. For example, an average Grade 8 teacher is not likely to know what the Grade 9 Academic or Applied level curriculum entails (or vice versa), not having any reason, other than perhaps a personal interest, to become aware of their counterparts' mathematics course content. Further, since standardized provincial assessment in mathematics takes place at the Grade 3, 6, and 9 levels in Ontario, the Grade 7 and Grade 8 teachers are also often unaware of what the Grade 9 assessment involves, how it relates to the provincial curriculum, or how to best prepare students for the assessment. In the "family of schools" approach to professional development, teachers from both panels (elementary and secondary) had occasion to examine each other's curriculum expectations and to discuss mathematical content. The coordinator notes:

CAROLE: Remember too that the elementary levels are not all math teachers. They're very textbook-driven because that's their main support, right? Especially if you're in a small school and you're the only Grade 8 teacher. It was good for them to have the conversation back and forth and take a look at what the Grade 9s had to teach ... The Grade 7s and 8s ... have absolutely no idea about EQAO[3] [Education Quality and Accountability Office] ... They do EQAO in Grade 6, but the Grade 7 and 8 teachers have absolutely nothing to do with it. That's one of the things that I did, I developed the resource binders for each of the elementary schools. It's got the formula sheets, the key words, sample tests, and we talked about the format of the questions.

One of the elementary school teachers corroborates this focus on EQAO, both for math and literacy, and indicates that she, as an elementary generalist, appreciated the input from the secondary school teachers:

LINDA: We looked at the EQAO, we looked at the Grade 9 numeracy, Grade 10 literacy test depending on what professional development group we were in, so we did have an idea of what that is, and trying to get that continuum because certainly at the elementary level we're trying to work on a continuum. So, we know from Kindergarten to Grade 8 what we're supposed to be doing, but then there's that big jump to the high school ... The math teachers at the high school are saying, "We've noticed that there's a strength here, but a weakness here," or, "We're teaching this – please make sure your kids are good in this area." – whether its fractions or algebra. That would be a real strength. It gives us some focus on where they want the kids to be when they go there. I think that's a real strength.

Another elementary school teacher described how, in the teacher team meetings that he facilitated, participants did spend time analysing the ministry curriculum documents, and textbooks, from both panels: "We actually brought in textbooks from Grades 7, 8 and 9, so we could familiarize ourselves with the layout, and looked at the curriculum documents. It was nice to see that there is somewhat of a progression from K–8 ... and so let's take it one step further [to Grade 9]."

As generalists, elementary school teachers are often asked to teach mathematics as one of several/many topics, and this is often not their area of strength or undergraduate background focus. As noted by an elementary school teacher, the sessions were informative for secondary school teachers in this regard:

ALEX: There were some of our elementary teachers that weren't as comfort-able, certainly, with math. One of our math teachers had been teaching Grade 1 for a number of years, and then she moved into Intermediate – she wasn't having difficulty with the concepts, it was how to teach the concepts. So, a lot of the discussion – she was discussing with the other elementary teachers and with the high school teachers. I think that was quite valuable for her, and I think that was also an eye-opener for some of our secondary mathematics teachers, that they could see that not all of our Grade 7 and 8 teachers in the schools necessarily have a math background. When we are in elementary we tend to be generalists, as opposed to having a specific area.

The shared review of mathematical content and curriculum documents was clearly shown to be beneficial for teachers from both the elemen-tary and the secondary school levels.

THE CHOICE OF PROBLEM SOLVING AS A SHARED FOCAL POINT

Beyond the advantages of communicating with cross-panel colleagues, discussing specificities of curricular content, and benefiting from inher-ent accountability of classroom observations, another significant affor-dance of the "family of schools" approach implemented within the board was that of teacher choice concerning the shared curricular focus. Elementary and secondary school teachers within the seven teams were not required to focus on a certain mathematical topic or strand during their sessions, but rather were left to discuss this aspect and to decide among themselves. During the early stages of the professional develop-ment model, the process of "problem solving" was selected as the shared focal point of all of the lesson planning and implementation – a choice well supported by the TIPS4RM resource, as well as in keeping with the overall spirit of the Ontario mathematics curriculum documents and with NCTM's *Principles and Standards for School Mathematics* (2000). The former coordinator describes the advantages of the "choice" element:

RICK: I think that one thing that we did that was kind of smart ... was to give them some kind of choice. We had a meeting with them prior to the thing really rolling, and outlined what we were thinking about, and why we were thinking about it, and what some of the options were ... Particularly what kind of content they might explore and how they might set it up. So, I think then, that once we started, that they had some kind of buy-in or some kind of sense of what was going on. That's just good management generally.

The move towards an increased use of problem-based learning methods (Jarvis, 2008), at both the elementary and secondary levels, was perceived as a welcomed change by the coordinator:

CAROLE: When you've got a teacher that's taught for 10 or 15 years that's never used a manipulative or a hands-on approach and they're saying, "I might try that next week." – I think that makes a big impact ... You can do the chalk-and-talk if it's working, but if you've got a failure rate of 30%, it's not working, and you need to look at another way of doing it. I'm hearing teachers say they're doing more problem solving and letting the kids struggle and work through it. Hopefully the more we do that ... you're going to see the kids talking more and figuring things out – they're going to retain that, and that's going to make them more successful, rather than ... a teacher saying, "Memorize this." ... I do think you're going to start to see more activities, more problem solving, more collaborative work in the classroom because the teachers are beginning to see the benefit of it.

An elementary school teacher provides a similar positive perspective on the benefits of a PBL focus:

ALEX: Whenever you're learning more about a topic, it's automatically going to make its way into your teaching, whether you're doing it consciously or unconsciously. I brought some of the activities into my class and they've gone over well – some of them not so well as others, and it always depends on the group of students you have ... Some of the people that were newer teachers that were involved, I think that they saw that problem solving was a very valuable way that they could be teaching some of the math concepts ... You give them the question and let them struggle with it, then teach some concepts, and go back to that question again.

The secondary school teacher in the study expands the definition of "manipulatives" since the Grade 9 mathematics program at his particular school is uniquely tied to an "integrated technologies" course, providing students with direct "real-world" application of the mathematics being studied.

ROB: We don't use many traditional manipulatives, to be honest with you ... My definition of manipulatives is different from what they are [using] in elementary school ... Well, it could include a calculator, but we are tied to the Integrated Technologies course, so when we're talking about perimeter, and area, and scale diagrams, and so forth, to me the manipulatives there are that they're actually doing drafting and so forth – they're doing construction ... One is actually foods – cooking and with the math we've actually got an activity where they've got to use proportions in order to figure out what they're going to need for making lasagne for 450 people, or something like that ... One of the things that we do is conversions from metric to Imperial, and vice versa. Its reality, and it's also something that they have to do in the wood shop, so construction technology is in there as well and design. We do scale diagrams ... and there is an activity where they get a blueprint of a room andthey've got to figure out, "OK, the scale is 1 to 200 – how big is the room in real life?" ... Well, it's still math, you know. The one thing I don't get as much as I used to is, "Where am I going to use this?"

Finally, one of the most significant benefits afforded by the "family of schools" PD model used in this particular board was the implementation of lesson study and classroom observations.

CLASSROOM-BASED LESSON STUDY WITH
CROSS-PANEL OBSERVATIONS

Professional development initiatives that are practice-based, or classroom-embedded, have been shown to be particularly effective in terms of teacher engagement and growth (Smith, 2001). The notion of "Lesson Study," whether experienced as an individual or as part of a teacher team, has also become a popular approach to professional development for mathematics teachers in North America (Rock & Wilson, 2005; Stigler & Hiebert, 1999). The "family of schools" approach being highlighted in this case study involved both of these powerful aspects: classroom-based lesson implementation and reflection as part of the ongoing professional development schedule, as well as focused lesson study wherein teacher teams co-planned, implemented, and reflected on multigrade versions of key math lessons, and were also afforded the rich (and expensive, in terms of release time) opportunity to observe lessons being taught in the "other panel":

CAROLE: We brought back ... students' work, and then you presented to the group – the Grade 8 and 9 teachers got to see how the Grade 7 teacher taught it, what kind of work the students were producing, the anticipated responses, where the problems were, and they got to see all three grades ... That was really key, getting to see each level ... Depending on the group, three of the families of schools went in and saw [another] teacher teach … In two of the families of schools, one of the teachers volunteered to video-tape their class. So, on a follow-up day, [other] teachers got to see them … teach in their classrooms.

These cross-panel lesson planning and observation cycles were not only highly informative and engaging for the teachers involved, but they also provided incentive and built-in *accountability*:

CAROLE: Having teachers come [to a] meeting and then go off and never have any accountability – that type of stuff isn't working, or at least we don't feel that it's working. Teachers just go back and often throw the handouts in a box somewhere. There always had to be a follow-up, so if you did an afternoon or something there had to be a homework assignment, you might say. You had to go out and do something … it had to be practical, it had to be relevant to what they were doing and then bring back and share.

Further, an elementary school teacher corroborated the importance of classroom implementation of the lessons, which often featured class-room observation by peers as part of the PD process:

ALEX: Certainly with the problem-solving activities – going out and trying some of these with the students, and then when we came back a lot of teachers were saying that we saw all the answers we expected to see. One student doing it this method, another student doing it this method, and then it was always, "But then I saw a student doing it this way …" which may or may not have been mathematically correct, but at least it was something that we had thought of, and that we could discuss.

Cross-panel observations also led to an increased awareness of the dif-ficulties and challenges experienced by colleagues working in the "oth-er" panel of education. The coordinator noted:

RICK: There also came out of that a lot of empathy, I think, for the Grade 8 teachers because – well, university complains that high school doesn't prepare them; high school complains that the senior elementary doesn't prepare them, and it goes on down the line, that everybody feels that they should be doing more. What we found out was that this particular year, the Grade 8 teachers were dealing with multiple-level large classes, so you could have a class of 35 or 34 kids and anywhere from Basic level right up

to gifted within that 35. So, for them to have such a heterogeneous population and such a large group, it's really hard to give individual attention,
remediation, as well as enrichment to the students that need it ... So, that
was the first comment they made when they came here [to secondary] was,
"I can't believe how small the classes are."

The "family of schools" approach provided certain perceived benefits
among participants. The increased communication, content review,
choice of curricular focal point, and cross-panel lesson planning and observations were all viewed as meaningful and enabling aspects of the
overall experience. The inherent accountability function of the classroom
implementation piece was seen as particularly significant by the coordinators, and was corroborated by the teacher participants as well. The PD
was not without its challenges, and it is to these that we now turn.

Perceived Challenges

The two most challenging aspects of the "family of schools" approach,
as shared by participants in the study, were closely related to certain
affordances mentioned above: (1) the facilitation of increased communication among teachers from the two panels and (2) the logistics and
cost involved in organizing the discussion sessions and the classroom
observations.

FACILITATING POSITIVE COMMUNICATION BETWEEN PANELS
As described by the organizing coordinator, some of the mathematical
weaknesses among students in terms of their understanding and
achievement actually begin with conceptual problems that are not well
diagnosed or remediated for, in the earlier K–6 grades. An awareness
that all teachers must share in this responsibility is something that can
be discussed during the cross-panel teacher meetings, even if it is sometimes difficult to begin conversations:

CAROLE: No, it was very good. I don't think that overall there was any, "It's
your fault," kind of thing. I think the teachers were very cognizant to not
do that. The secondary teachers weren't saying, "You guys aren't doing
your job." There was more of an attitude of there's a systemwide problem,
and not just the Grade 7 and 8, but in general, there's a problem with
numeracy. They're recognizing that when you've got a kid in Grade 9 that
says, "I don't know what two times four is," then that's not only a Grade 7

and 8 problem ... It was more about, "We've got a problem, and it starts way before us, and we need to look at the whole system." ... But no, I didn't find that it was a finger pointing – I think it was a very positive thing.

She further notes that elementary school teachers can, by default, feel threatened by their secondary counterparts, particularly in terms of mathematical understanding and mental math flexibility for PBL:

CAROLE: The elementary teachers do ... get a little bit more apprehensive when we do the algebra and jump into it ... We did this cellphone problem – it's just comparing two cellphone [rates], so very typical EQAO and TIPS [Targeted Implementaion and Planning] document type content. Although a lot of the elementary teachers said, "My kids could never do that" ... they were seeing where it would go, and then they were able to understand. You'd see the odd person who didn't understand the equation or the algebra, but someone would work with them and explain a few things, then they would say, "Okay," and they'd start to remember a bit of it. It was good professional development for them, and a refresher for them, but it wasn't super-threatening.

The former coordinator echoes this perspective, noting that he, too, did not notice any negative language, verbal or body, when working with the various teacher teams. He stresses the informal, student-centred conversations that took place, and also underscores the lack of confidence surrounding the mathematical content that was expressed by elementary school teachers at times.

RICK: Certainly the secondary folks never said, "We do all kinds of problem solving and how come you don't do any?" Secondary people seem to be relatively aware, most of them, of not coming across too strong ... "If you would just teach them integers, we could teach them the real math," I don't recall any of that ... They would see the same students, so when you say, "This is the kind of thing that's going on in my class." They would say, "Oh, yes, I had him two years ago," or, "Just wait until you get him." So, I think they seemed to have more of a feeling that they were in the same boat. There certainly were, though, elementary teachers who made a point of saying that they didn't know as much as the secondary teachers, and one of the things about problem solving is the sophistication of the approaches used ... So, there were times when, I think, the Grade 7 and 8 teachers may have felt that they were out of their depth.

The secondary school teacher underscored the positive aspect of just knowing who other teachers are:

ROB: I think that dialogue has begun. I don't want to say that these meetings have overcome that … We've been meeting for a couple of years now. These people know me now and I know them. Before, that wasn't the case – you weren't too sure. A teacher's name was a name on a report card in some cases. You didn't know who they were.

Not everyone felt that communication at the meetings was completely positive. One elementary school teacher described how she felt that certain secondary school teachers did not understand the realities of the elementary context:

LINDA: I would say that our sense was that maybe the high school teachers didn't understand the broad spectrum of what we're teaching … Part of the problem is the reporting. We have to report ten times throughout the year, on the five different strands. So each strand has to be covered twice. You're trying to make sure you're covering all of this, whereas I think their work has a little narrower focus. That was a bit of a problem. I don't think they really understood that. Instead of doing one math mark, you're doing ten marks throughout the year … and often with bigger classes and with mixed ability.

Perhaps one of the biggest barriers to an increased and positive communication among teachers from the two panels is the misconceptions, or popularly held stereotypes concerning teachers from the opposite panel. An example of this would be the elementary school teachers' perception of what kind of mathematics learning is happening regularly in secondary classrooms in the twenty-first century. Although traditional methods of teacher-directed learning may, indeed, still be happening in many Ontario secondary school mathematics classrooms, there are also many Grade 9 and Grade 10 teachers who have moved towards a more reform-oriented, problem-based approach. Rick describes this misconception in some detail, and then Alex provides us with a clear case in point.

RICK: So, I think it's valuable, especially for those folks, to see what high school teachers are really doing … I would say in Grade 7 and 8 there's less hands-on stuff, less manipulatives, less investigations, and more direct teaching ... [O]ne of the factors is that they think that's what [students are] going to get in high school, so they better be ready for it.

ALEX: Admittedly I wanted to do more problem solving this year with our [Grade 8] group, but we had basically an Applied level class this year, so we're trying to focus more on some of the skills they'll need for next year.

To summarize, communication between panels is particularly difficult to facilitate owing to the sense of inferiority that elementary school teachers sometimes feel in discussing mathematics content (or the perceived superiority of secondary school teachers, or both), the lack of awareness of each others' context and challenges, and the persistence of certain stereotypes regarding teachers and the teaching of mathematics in the opposite panel.

LOGISTICS AND THE HIGH COSTS OF PARTICIPATION

The second set of major challenges for cross-panel initiatives were those of logistics, particularly in a large geographical board, and different associated costs such as financial (release time funding) and human (the effects of time-out-of-classrooms on teachers and their students). In the case of the seven lead teachers, these costs were, of course, even more substantial in nature:

CAROLE: The five days was a big commitment for the principals to have the [lead] teachers out for training – a whole week. Then they were out a half-day – that was all I pulled them out for the organizational meeting. Then they were out the full 3 days just like every other teacher, so it wasn't any different ... Unfortunately what happens is that these are the same people that volunteered to be the literacy person, or to be the "healthy schools" person. So, you have this one person that is out of the school for two or three projects that are going on. It takes them out a lot. I don't know how to fix that because you want those key, keen people, especially as facilitators.

Alex, an elementary school teacher, describes his perspective as someone missing many days for the PD initiative: "Certainly time out of the classroom was difficult. When you leave your class behind, that's when things tend to go awry. In the last few years, we've had some challenging students and when the regular teacher is gone from the classroom it tends to cause a problem."

The time spent out of one's classroom must, of course, be balanced with the overall benefits of being involved with the program, as emphasized by Rob, the secondary school teacher: "As teachers ... we don't feel we can leave our classroom all that often – that it's very disruptive to be pulled out for a day ... [but] I don't think it's all that valid because you can give the kids something to do that's just fine without having to be there." When asked if this high level of commitment could lead to adverse affects in one's own classroom, he noted: "It doesn't necessarily negatively impact your classroom."

Beyond the high financial costs of providing release time for participating teachers, a more intangible and human cost – i.e., the willingness of individuals to become, and to stay involved in such learning communities – represents an even more formidable challenge. As Rick noted, creative administrators could become key players in facilitating scheduled teacher involvement:

RICK: I would imagine a situation where you could free somebody up throughout that time – say three times to go see [someone] else ... You could maybe organize enough of that on people's discretionary time. I think if people see where the other folks work, and what they're working with, and how they work with the problems, that it would engage them even better. Then the other thing that's being talked up ... if we could make these families of schools groupings self-sustaining. We've done some facilitator training with folks in those groups, but do they really have enough ownership of the thing to do it on their own, or as soon as the money for release dries up – how do you really set it up so that folks will want to do it, and be prepared to do it without a lot of external prodding or involvement?

With the advent of new communication technologies, an increasing amount of professional development is now occurring via the Internet with software packages such as Adobe Connect, Skype, Elluminate, Go-To-Meeting, etc. Notwithstanding, participants in the study, when asked about these digital alternatives, still maintained that face-to-face interaction was preferable, at least in part. The former coordinator describes his perception of on-line versus on-site interaction:

RICK: I think the ideal is face-to-face, so real conversation, with real people, around real things. I've been involved in all kinds of at-a-distance kinds of meetings, that are very valuable, but when we're talking about our practice or doing professional development, those tools are still pretty quirky. If we were talking about how to use [software] to do something, then I think I can demonstrate that to you and field questions and have somebody working away at it. But if I'm really talking to you about how my classroom runs, and what's important to me, and those kinds of things, I think that the technology can probably help with records of practice and help with those ongoing arrangements of details of things that come up in your mind, but I don't think they can really forge a professional learning community easily.

Although one of the elementary school teachers indicated that he, too, prefers face-to-face interaction, he also infers that once face-to-face contact has been established, digital communication can allow for the quick and effective seeking of advice from well-informed, secondary-level peers:

ALEX: This is just a personal preference, but I would always prefer face-to-face. You get to meet these people. You get to see these people and it's different. You make connections and it's not a big deal if you have a question. At home you'd think, "I wonder how they do this topic in Grade 9." It's not a big deal to pick up the phone anymore or send them an email because you know these people. You know who – let's say we've got five high school teachers – I know who would be the best person to ask the specific question to. So, I think that the networking aspect of face-to-face is key.

Challenges involving costs and communication are real and complex, yet they can be overcome by creative administrators, coordinators, and ministry-level policy makers if these kinds of ongoing, classroom-based professional development initiatives were deemed highly effective and doable.

Discussion and Conclusions

Obviously, one of the limitations of the case study being presented here is the relatively small number of participants. It would have been more informative to interview other participating teachers, sponsoring administrators, and perhaps even students from within the classrooms represented. That being said, the five participants in the study provided the researcher with a wealth of information pertaining to the cross-panel, "family of schools" professional development approach. Participation of the researcher in the final, full-day "celebration" event, wherein all teacher teams took part and shared their students' work, findings, and personal reflections, was also very beneficial, as it provided additional insight into the overall nature and scope of the ongoing board initiative. This final day of sharing was described as being critical in terms of the empathy, closure, and synergetic interaction that it afforded (and perhaps also forecasted):

CAROLE: It was a very positive time as you'll see from the exit cards. It reinforced that we're all in the same boat together ... when the teachers got to see who the secondary [teachers were] and the secondary got to see the elementary, and recognizing that they kind of have the same problems and the same kids. The grass always looks greener on the other side – everybody is dealing with the same things, and that really pulled us together as a group more. Having a district meeting helps with cohesiveness and a sense of community. We're a large board geographically, so it's a worthwhile investment. People tend to work a little harder and feel better about what they're doing if they feel like they belong and that they're [valued].

In the remainder of the chapter, we will discuss the related and complex issue of student streaming, and then conclude by analysing this particular professional development model in terms of key characteristics and participant recommendations.

Grade 9 Student-Level Placements

One of the unintended, yet beneficial, consequences of the cross-panel, "family of schools" approach to professional development was an increased and shared understanding of Grade 9 student placement issues. In fact, teachers would often discuss their students' past performance and/or real, or forecasted, achievement with teachers from the opposite panel. These informal discussions happened spontaneously, and they often led to meaningful communication between teachers, with the actual students providing the linking element. Part of following up on a past student, or helping a current student prepare for future mathematics education, was found in discussing the difficult issue of Grade 9 student placement in terms of the levels and options available in the Ontario school system (i.e., Academic,[4] Applied, or Locally Developed "Essential" level Grade 9 courses available in most secondary schools). The coordinator explains:

CAROLE: Teachers really feel where the students need to be with the Applied, but it all [comes] down to the [parents] wanting the Academic [level for their children], no matter what ... There's this perception [among elementary teachers] of, "You guys have it good because at the secondary level they're already all streamed." The reality of it is that [while] they're streamed, they're really not. You've got all kinds of kids that should be in Applied that are in Academic, or should be in the Essential that are in Applied.

One somewhat controversial approach to addressing this difficult decision (i.e., streaming level for Grade 9 entry) is to begin the streaming earlier on in the elementary panel at Grade 7 or Grade 8, as is done in certain European countries. The secondary school teacher argues in favour of this direction:

ROB: One of the suggestions we started saying ... was that our Grade 7/8 schools need to start streaming, and I think there is talk about doing that. So, we started as a group of teachers commenting on how administration should be structuring things to benefit math, and the fact that you have multiple levels – you're not serving the needs of the individual student, but streaming would – I know that there are negative connotations to streaming, but there is a realism that you've got to get remediation for the kids that need it, and enrichment to the kids that need it.

Indeed, some would argue that streaming already exists in the elementary panel insofar as specialized programming such as French Immersion in Ontario schools often involves grouping the brightest students for the total Immersion experience, including mathematics instruction.

During the interview, the secondary school teacher described a unique system that his school had adopted in order to deal head-on with the perennial issue of Grade 9 mathematics "misplacement." Although the secondary school is run on a semester system like the majority of schools in Ontario (i.e., two semesters per year with exams in January and June for different courses taken), the school administration had decided to schedule the Grade 9 Mathematics as a full-year course, attended every second day by students. At the halfway mark, students are encouraged, along with the corresponding permission from parents/guardians, to "reshuffle" course levels according to the students' achievement to date, in order to address student learning needs and to try to ultimately avoid course failures.

ROB: It starts off as Applied and Academic, and the advantage is that if students are struggling – because they're coming in from different schools

– if they are misplaced amid the shuffle, internally, without re-timetabling the students, we can actually – this year we ended up with, I believe, seven or eight students that were moved to the Locally Developed course from the Applied, and 24 students that were in Academic and moved to the Applied. It works out fairly well because out of a 140 students, only five students did not receive their credit. So, the failure rate in the Grade 9 course, which is typically a high failure course, is very low ... We shuffle them usually around November, but mostly the big switches occur in January after the first midterm examination ... and then we have a better read on what they understood from the first semester ... In October we have our first parent/teacher interviews and sometimes we plant the seed there. We've already been in touch with the parents, previously, that this [class level switch] might be occurring. Sometimes we shuffle the classes internally so that they are ability-grouped, and then after awhile if the remediation isn't working, then we suggest that the parents look at having them switched [to a different level].

It is not uncommon for secondary school teachers to be sent out to local, elementary "feeder schools" as the academic year winds down to do a presentation for Grade 8 teachers, students, and parents/guardians regarding the Academic/Applied placement options and details. One of the elementary school teachers described the benefits of the cross-panel meetings in this regard:

LINDA: They would come to the school and do a presentation to the students, but there wasn't as much interaction ... I know there were some problems for a while where they were saying, "The kids are not picking appropriate courses." So, they were finding some difficulty there – kids were [finding it] either too hard or too easy. I think in that way they would say we've gotten better at streaming the kids and saying to the kids, "This is where you should be." Some of that has been the result of having a cross-panel meeting.

The cross-panel meetings allowed teachers to become familiar with one another – to open up vital lines of communication for many issues, including the complex topic of Grade 9 placement.

Choice, Voice, and Ongoing Support

Professional development models that allow for teacher *choice* (selection from among various options), *voice* (active participation in PD design and implementation), and *ongoing support* (meetings spread out over the school year, and perhaps even available in summer months) hold much promise in terms of teacher engagement and overall effectiveness (Jarvis, 2006). The cross-panel teacher team approach, organized by a family of schools (secondary school teachers grouped with local feeder school teachers), focusing on problem-based learning (self-selected), and which involved a form of lesson study with classroom observations featured all three of the above-mentioned elements. Teachers selected the focal point for the planned meetings, choosing neither a particular mathematics topic or strand in this instance, but rather a mathematical process expectation, that is, problem solving. Much of the time spent during the release half-days focused on teacher discussions regarding co-created lessons, collected students' work, and reflections on the observations made in actual elementary and secondary school classrooms. These events involved inherent accountability in terms of the shared classroom viewing and subsequent lesson analysis and revision stages. They were also spread out over the course of the school year (particularly for the lead teacher facilitators), providing time for deeper and more meaningful new learning.

The researcher asked each candidate towards the end of the interview what kind of advice they would give to other school boards contemplating a move towards a "family of schools," cross-panel PD model. They each stressed different (sometimes overlapping) aspects, most of which have already been discussed to some extent within this chapter. The coordinator emphasized the importance of selecting the team leaders from among both panels, and of choosing these individuals very carefully. She also stressed the critical need for administrative support in order for the initiative to be successful, particularly in terms of a multiyear cycle of events:

CAROLE: I think you have to pick your facilitators really well. It's got to be someone who wants the job and is interested in it and who can work with the other staff ... I think for perception that balance [elementary/secondary teacher leaders] was important so it doesn't look like it's being secondary-led ... This was a board initiative that helped everybody. You need the support of administration which is not always easy ... to get the administrators to see the value of it ... We're changing a culture. It's not going to change overnight and hopefully you can get administrators who are on board and who will support it.

The former coordinator also underscored the need for leadership within each teacher team, as well as emphasizing the critical nature of accountability through shared, classroom observations:

RICK: I think that you can't expect groups to function without people with a stake in it, and whether they're people who ostensibly lead it, or the people that just drive it and make sure it happens. It doesn't necessarily need to be the same people, but even whenever you're going to meet next – if it just gets left to, "See you next time," – who cares enough to make sure there is a next time … The part that I really valued was the accountability piece. I don't really believe that those teachers took anything to heart until they knew somebody was coming to watch … They did seem to need some kind of push to actually give it a whirl in their classroom. I'm not even sure if collecting students' work would have had the same impact … I think change is hard, and I think change without some ongoing push is really hard.

Both of the elementary school teachers highlighted the student-centred benefits surrounding the elementary/secondary transition that were made possible through this PD initiative – Alex emphasizing the teacher-teacher relationships, and Linda the student-teacher communication:

ALEX: I would certainly encourage going that route – using the family of schools. Number one, because you're dealing with the same students. Eventually the majority of them are going to make their way into that secondary school … You're going to be able to work with your colleagues in secondary, and they can be working with us at the elementary. I know we have a lot of focus on transition because we seem to lose a lot when we go from Grade 8 to Grade 9. So this is a good way to help the students, because really that should be our focus.

LINDA: I think it's beneficial for us to be able to say to the kids, "When you're in math you may be getting so and so," so we have some names and faces to connect to. Even though we're very close in proximity, we seldom ever see them, so it's nice to put a name to a face. It helps the kids. That's a real benefit. It helps us to make that transition, and gets the kids thinking about the high school math.

The secondary school teacher stressed the perceived importance of the participatory classroom observations, and the unique feedback from colleagues that was thereby made possible.

ROB: You've got to get the teachers into the other classrooms … to talk about it is one thing, but to see it, and to be a part of what they're doing … I think you could do a combination of video and live observations … So, to get me to report on what's going on in my classes [to other teachers] is very one-dimensional, whereas if you come in and talk to the students in my class, you may get a better idea of things – for better or for worse sometimes – but I think it gives them a better perspective ... I think it has be ongoing and become part of the school structure.

Perhaps one of the most significant aspects of a PD approach that encourages direct communication between teachers from different school panels is that of a consistent teaching and assessment program within an educational jurisdiction or region. A lack of clear communication and informed classroom practice may not only lead to an inferior delivery of the curriculum, but it may also ultimately affect student achievement. If classroom activities, teacher expectations, and related assessment do not coincide – sometimes not even vaguely – with the experiences of other mathematics classrooms within the same school, let alone with those from the school(s) from the opposite panel located down the street or across town, one would not be surprised to find that student achievement would suffer as a result of mixed messages, varying definitions of success, and widely different classroom activities. One teacher describes this type of awkward situation in detail:

TEACHER: I do think it affects student learning because just think about yourself every time you went to a new class or a new course, you were always trying to figure out, "How am I going to be tested?," if it was always a new situation. Whereas, if we start to have common expectations all the way through, then we're emphasizing the same major components or expectations of what we're looking for in them as students, then those expectations are clear. If you stress one thing at one school, and then something completely different in another, then that's very confusing for the student. I've seen it before where I'll say, "Well, you have to do it like this." They'll say, "Well, this was good enough last year."

A lack of curricular alignment pertaining to teaching, learning, and assessment practices can only intensify the already difficult transition for students from Grade 8 to Grade 9 schooling. As mentioned in the Elliott-Johns chapter, a move towards "balanced instructional programming" in language/literacy education reflects a change in beliefs among teachers that has direct and significant influence on student transitions among panels. It appears to likewise be the case within mathematics education reform. As mathematics teachers (i.e., math specialists), and teachers of mathematics (i.e., non-specialists in math), continue to develop their mastery of mathematical content, their effectiveness with teaching resources, their awareness of "math knowledge for teaching," and their ability to balance instructional programming, they will no doubt draw strength and much-needed support from professional development models such as the cross-panel, "family of schools" approach described herein – the kind of support that permeates practice and that serves to benefit all students and teachers in transition.

NOTES

1 To ensure confidentiality, the five names used for participants in this case study are selected pseudonyms.
2 In Ontario, mathematics is usually offered at three different levels in Grades 9 and 10: Academic, Applied, and Locally Developed (i.e., "essential level") courses.
3 The Education Quality and Accountability Office (EQAO) is an arm's-length organization contracted by the Ontario Ministry of Education to conduct assessments and research on student achievement in publicly funded schools. Standardized language and mathematics assessment takes place at Grade 3, 6, and 9; a Grade 10 assessment of literacy is also conducted.
4 In the revised Ontario Mathematics Curriculum (2005b, p. 6), the two main options for Grade 9 course delivery are defined as follows: Academic courses develop students' knowledge and skills through the study of theory and abstract problems. These courses focus on the essential concepts of a subject and explore related concepts as well. They incorporate practical applications as appropriate. Applied courses focus on the essential concepts of a subject and develop students' knowledge and skills through practical applications and concrete examples. Familiar situations are used to illustrate ideas, and students are given more opportunities to experience hands-on applications of the concepts and theories they study. Locally Developed, or "Essential" focused on level courses are open to coordinator/teacher input and are usually more focused on "basic skills."

REFERENCES

Ball, D.L., & Bass, H. (2000). Interweaving content and pedagogy in teaching and learning to teach: Knowing and using mathematics. In J. Boaler (Ed.), *Multiple perspectives on mathematics teaching and learning* (pp. 83–104). Westport, CT: Ablex.

DuFour, R. (2004). What is a "Professional Learning Community"? *Educational Leadership, 61*(8), 6–11.

Hufferd-Ackles, K., Fuson, K.C., & Sherin, M.G. (2004). Describing levels and components of a math-talk learning community. *Journal for Research in Mathematics Education, 35*(2), 81–116. http://dx.doi.org/10.2307/30034933

Jarvis, D.H. (2006). *Tracking the TIPS mathematics document: Curriculum negotiation and professional development models* (Unpublished doctoral dissertation). University of Western Ontario, London, Ontario.

Jarvis, D.H. (2008). Thinking outside the rectangular prism: Fostering problem-based mathematics learning. *Ontario Mathematics Gazette, 47*(2), 23–28.

Jarvis, D.H. (2009). *Parametric creativity: Curriculum negotiation and professional development models in mathematics education.* Cologne, Germany: LAP Lambert.

Loucks-Horsley, S., Hewson, P., Love, H., & Stiles, K. (1998). *Designing professional development for teachers of science and mathematics.* Thousand Oaks, CA: Corwin Press.

McGraw, R., Arbaugh, F., Lynch, K., & Brown, C. (2003). Mathematics teacher professional development as the development of communities of practice, *Navigating between theory and practice: Proceedings of the 27th Annual Conference of the International Group for the Psychology of Mathematics Education* (Vol. 3, p. 269). University of Hawai'i, Honolulu.

National Council of Teachers of Mathematics (NCTM). (2000). *Principles and standards for school mathematics.* Reston, VA: Author.

Ontario Ministry of Education (OMoE). (2005a). *The Ontario curriculum, Grades 1–8: Mathematics, Revised.* Toronto: Queen's Printer.

Ontario Ministry of Education (OMoE). (2005b). *The Ontario curriculum, Grades 9 and 10: Mathematics, Revised.* Toronto: Queen's Printer.

Ontario Ministry of Education (OMoE). (2007). *The Ontario curriculum, Grades 11 and 12: Mathematics, Revised.* Toronto: Queen's Printer.

Rock, T.C., & Wilson, C. (2005). Improving teaching through lesson study. *Teacher Education Quarterly, 32*(1), 77–92.

Smith, M.S. (2001). *Practice-based professional development for teachers of mathematics.* Reston, VA: National Council of Teachers of Mathematics.

Stein, M.K., Smith, M.S., Henningsen, M.A., & Silver, E.A. (2000). *Implementing standards-based mathematics instruction: A casebook for professional development.* New York: Teachers College Press.

Stigler, J., & Hiebert, J. (1999). *The teaching gap: Best ideas from the world's teachers for improving education in the classroom.* New York: Free Press.

Suurtamm, C., & Graves, B. (2007). *Curriculum Implementation in Intermediate Math Research Report: Executive summary.* Ottawa: University of Ottawa.

Thames, M.H., & Ball, D.L. (2010). What math knowledge does teaching require? *Teaching Children Mathematics, 17*(4), 220–229.

14 The Visual Turn: Transitioning into Visual Approaches to Literacy Education

MAUREEN KENDRICK AND JENNIFER ROWSELL

Over the past two-and-a-half decades, conceptions of literacy and what it means to be literate have expanded considerably (e.g., Heath, 1983; Kress, 1997; Lankshear & Knobel, 2003; New London Group [NLG], 2000; Street, 1984). There is now recognition that there is a qualitative difference in how we communicate through modalities such as the visual, audio, spatial, and linguistic (Kress, 2000, 2003; NLG, 2000; Stein, 2008) and that different modalities are combined in complex ways to make meaning (Jewitt & Kress, 2003; Snyder, 2001). New literacy practices require the ability to "read" and "write" texts comprised of these multiple modes; however, pedagogical designs have not yet elaborated a robust theoretical and practical account of how a range of modalities might contribute to literacy learning alongside and interrelated with, *rather than subordinate to*, language.

Our contention is that for students to reach their educational potential, their full range of meaning-making practices must be taken seriously rather than simply as incidental background to their linguistic practices. As literacy educators and researchers, we are particularly interested in the potential of visual methods to create radically new avenues for students to access educationally privileged knowledge and to discursively reposition themselves and re/imagine not only their local and global communities, but also their futures. In this chapter, we argue that twenty-first century literacy requires a transition from the dominance of the linguistic to teaching and learning with visual texts.

The visual in everyday communication has become ubiquitous. In social science research, visual methods have proven to be an important means of documenting the practices and lives of individuals, groups, and cultures (e.g., Banks & Morphy, 1997; Collier, 2001; Kendrick &

McKay, 2005; Kress & van Leeuwen, 1996; Mutonyi & Kendrick, 2011; Rowsell, 2010). Yet, what images are and how to interpret them as representations of experience, ideas, and knowledge is not fully understood. Collier (2001) proposes that images are "complex reflections of a relationship between maker and subject in which both play roles in shaping their character and content" (p. 35). As such, he asserts that the challenge of interpretation "is to responsibly address the many aspects of images, recognizing that the search for meaning and significance does not end in singular facts or truths, but rather produces one or more viewpoints on human experience/circumstances" (pp. 35–36). We take as a starting point the idea that "all images give birth to stories" (Collier, 2001, p. 46). They are complex constructs of signs with considerable pedagogical potential, yet they are often neglected in language and literacy learning.

Barriers and Obstacles to Visual Transitions

Before illustrating ways of understanding the visual, we present barriers and obstacles to opening up literacy education to more visual approaches to teaching and learning. To illustrate a word bias, we look no further than curriculum, policy, and testing regimes in provincial language arts/English policy documents. In education writ large, and literacy education more centrally, there is and has been a privileging of the written word. Students exist within a time-warp: trying to master the five-paragraph essay when all they really want to do is watch YouTube videos, update their Facebook page, or play an app on their smartphones. What this chapter tackles in a collection on transitions in education is the question: how can we possibly transition into the visual when the word is so firmly rooted in our pedagogical, curricular, and assessment psyche? How do we begin? How do we free ourselves from words?

To begin with, a barrier and obstacle to freeing us from linguistic mindsets starts with the central tenets of Canadian provincial curriculum and policy documents. Within Canada, and actually Canada is quite innovative in its literacy policies compared with the United States and other Western countries, there is a strong resolve in policy and curriculum for mastering words. Take our two contexts as examples, British Columbia and Ontario: within their respective provincial curricula there are performance standards for writing and writing traits. The discourse within such documents signals a clear and determined focus on the written word as shaping our thinking and communicating with language (see Table 14.1).

Table 14.1 Comparison of British Columbia and Ontario Language Arts Objectives (Grade 8)

B.C. Performance Standards for Writing (2007) Grade 8	Ontario Writing Achievement Standards (2006) Grade 8
Meaning • Ideas and understanding • Use of detail • Creating a variety of personal, informational, and imaginative texts • Creating thoughtful personal responses, evaluating ideas, and synthesizing and extending thinking • Using elements of style and form appropriate to purpose and audience • Using conventions of language that enhance meaning and artistry	Knowledge and Understanding • Knowledge of content (e.g., forms of text; strategies associated with reading, writing, speaking, and listening; elements of style; terminology; conventions) • Understanding of content (e.g., concepts, ideas, opinions, relationships among facts, ideas, concepts, themes)
Ideas • Details, development, focus • Write meaningful personal texts that explore ideas and information to experiment, express self, make connections, reflect and respond, remember and recall • Write purposeful information texts that express ideas and information to explore and respond, record and describe, analyse and explain, persuade • Write effective imaginative texts to explore ideas and information to make connections and develop insights • Explore literary forms and techniques, experiment with language and style, engage and entertain • Create thoughtful representations that communicate ideas and information to explore and respond, record and describe, explain and persuade, engage	Thinking • Use of planning skills (e.g., generating ideas, gathering information, focusing research, organizing information) • Use of processing skills (e.g., making inferences, interpreting, analysing, detecting bias, synthesizing, evaluating, forming conclusions) • Use of critical/creative thinking processes (e.g., reading process, writing process, oral discourse, research, critical/creative analysis, critical literacy, metacognition, invention)

Table 14.1 Comparison of British Columbia and Ontario Language Arts Objectives (Grade 8) (*Continued*)

B.C. Performance Standards for Writing (2007) Grade 8	Ontario Writing Achievement Standards (2006) Grade 8
Style • Clarity • Variety • Impact of language Word Choice • Precise language and phrasing Sentence Fluency • Correctness, rhythm, and cadence Voice • Tone, style, purpose, and audience Form • Opening, organization and sequence, and conclusion • Write and represent to explain and support personal responses to texts, by making connections with prior knowledge and experiences describing reactions and emotions generating thoughtful questions, developing opinions, using evidence • Write and represent to interpret and analyse ideas and information from texts, by making and supporting judgments, examining and comparing ideas and elements within and among texts, identifying points of view, identifying bias and contradictions • Write and represent to synthesize and extend thinking, by personalizing ideas and information, explaining relationships among ideas and information, applying new ideas and information Conventions • Mechanical correctness • Syntax and sentence fluency, diction, point of view, literary devices, visual/artistic devices • Grammar and usage, punctuation, capitalization, and Canadian spelling • Copyright and citation of references • Presentation/layout	Communication • Expression and organization of ideas and information (e.g., clear expression, logical organization) in oral, visual, and written forms, including media forms • Communication for different audiences and purposes (e.g., use of appropriate style, voice, point of view, tone) in oral, visual, and written forms, including media forms • Use of conventions (e.g., grammar, spelling, punctuation, usage), vocabulary, and terminology of the discipline in oral, visual, and written forms, including media forms

Table 14.1 Comparison of British Columbia and Ontario Language Arts Objectives (Grade 8) (*Continued*)

B.C. Performance Standards for Writing (2007) Grade 8	Ontario Writing Achievement Standards (2006) Grade 8
Presentation • The way the message appears	Application • Application of knowledge and skills (e.g., concepts, strategies, processes) in familiar contexts • Transfer of knowledge and skills (e.g., concepts, strategies, processes) to new contexts • Making connections within and between various contexts (e.g., between the text and personal knowledge or experience, other texts, and the world outside the school; between disciplines)
SUMMATIVE EVALUATION • Foundational Skills Assessment (FSA)	SUMMATIVE EVALUATIONS • Education Quality and Accountability Office (EQAO) Literacy Assessments in elementary and secondary education

Although both documents, particularly the British Columbia document, make reference to representation and literacies and even different modes of representation, the fact remains that they are premised on word logic. Words are still important, but our curricular, policy mindset and attendant discourses need to transition into multimodal, visual logics. Other terms can be applied to a use and understanding of other modes such as visual, audio, and spatial. Other provincial curricula share similar turns of phrases and policy discourses; however, they are more forward looking compared with British Columbia (see B.C. Ministry of Education [BCMoE], 2006) and Ontario (especially Ontario). The *Saskatchewan Language Arts Curriculum* (Saskatchewan Ministry of Education [SMoE], 2010), for instance, adopts terminology from new literacies and multimodality such as "developing literacies" and underscores the importance of viewing and analysing different media and what they do. The Atlantic Provinces are particularly strong in making a transition from monomodal curriculum and assessment to multimodal curriculum and assessment with phrases such as "writing and other ways of representing" and creating photo stories and digital stories. Yet, with these strides, we are still haunted by conservative curriculum and policy.

Policy documents and standardized tests talk about learning vocabulary, editing your writing, clarity and syntax, and writing across genres. Occasionally, such documents talk about viewing and representing or communicating across media, but these words, this discourse does not quite cover the transition that we need to make for students to migrate from an exclusive focus on words, to a focus on words *plus* visuals (e.g., photos, art, drawing, moving images), *plus* audio (e.g., podcasts, rants), *plus* spatial and performative modes (e.g., drama, gaming).

Testing and assessment are significant challenges for educators because we do not have guidelines and deeper understandings about how we assess visual texts or sound-based texts or moving image texts that are fundamentally premised on notions such as design and visual frameworks. In the next section, we take account of visual methodologies as a way forward to transitioning into multimodal curricula and pedagogy.

Visual Methodologies

Over the past decade, through our various research projects, we have become keenly aware of the complexity and multilayered nature of visual texts. This richness and complexity, in combination with forms ranging from moving to still images, presents inherent methodological and analytical challenges for both researchers and classroom teachers. What is most productive in making sense of these texts? Rose (2001) points out that although there is substantial academic work on "things visual" being published in the social sciences, "there are remarkably few guides to possible methods of interpretation and even fewer explanations of how to do those methods" (p. 2). Many educational researchers have turned to visual grammar frameworks developed within the broad domain of Western contemporary visual culture (e.g., Baldry & Thibault, 2005; Kress & van Leeuwen, 1996). As researchers working in culturally and linguistically diverse contexts, including Canadian and East African classrooms, we have sought alternative means of analysing visual texts that allow us to move beyond Western visual culture.

In Becker's (2007) insightful writing about ways of "telling about society," he argues that reports on society, visual or otherwise, "make most sense when you see them in organizational context, as activities, as ways some people tell what they think they know to other people who want to know it, as organized activities shaped by the joint efforts of everyone involved" (p. 15). In other words, he contends that we need to see the visual as social and cultural artefacts, as the "frozen remains of collective action, brought to life whenever someone uses them" (p. 15). Interpreting visual texts as artefacts of a particular place and space requires an interdisciplinary approach. As Siegel and Panofsky (2009) articulate, researchers working with multimodal texts need to draw on a range of theoretical frameworks relevant to their research interests, purposes, and questions. They need to create a hybrid approach – "a blend or 'mash-up' of theories" (p. 99). Similarly, Pahl and Rowsell (2006) assert that accessing the underlying meanings of visual and other multimodal practices, "we need not only to account for the materiality of the texts, that is, the way they look, sound, and feel, but also have an understanding of who made the text, why, where, and when" (p. 2).

We view all meaning making as situated social practice, thus our approach to visual analysis requires both a focus on product (the image itself) and process (the practices/activities surrounding the production and viewing of the image). In our evolving understanding of how to use visual texts with students, and ultimately how to approach the analysis of these diverse texts, we have turned to Rose's (2001) visual methodologies as a productive way forward. Rose, like Becker (2007), emphasizes that "images are made and used in all sorts of ways by different people for different reasons, and these makings and uses are crucial to the meanings an image carries" (p. 14). Moreover, because both images and audiences may be sites of "resistance and recalcitrance" (p. 15), a critical approach to visual images is required, one that takes seriously the agency of the image, the social practices/activities and effects around viewing, and the specific nature of viewing by various audiences. According to Rose, a critical methodology requires careful consideration of the intersections and relationships across three modalities (technological, compositional, and social) and three sites of meaning making (production, image, and audiencing/viewing). In terms of modalities, *technological* defines any apparatus designed to be looked at (e.g., oil paintings) or to enhance normal vision (e.g., the Internet). *Compositional* refers to formal strategies of composing such as content, colour, and spatial organization, among others. *Social* is the range of institutions, practices, and relations (economic, social, and political) that provide context for an image and through which it is understood and used. The three sites of meaning making progress from understanding the particular circumstances under which an image is produced (Site 1), to focusing on the image itself as a bounded unit (Site 2), to carefully considering how an image is looked at by various audiences in relation to the ways of seeing and the kinds of knowledges they bring to the viewing (Site 3). Although presented as distinct sites, Rose emphasizes that there is considerable overlap across the sites of production, image, and viewing given that process and product are inextricably linked.

Many of the theoretical disagreements about visual analysis across disciplines relate to disputes over which sites of meaning making are most important and why (Rose, 2001). We find it most productive to place equal emphasis on each of the three sites, seeing them as inextricably connected and recursively relational to each other. Moreover, we take her core methodology as a constructive space for the integration of other visual methodologies (see e.g., Kendrick & Jones, 2008; Mutonyi & Kendrick, 2011). In other words, Rose's framework allows for the creation of hybrid or mixed theories and methods that give access to the accretive layers of visual texts.

Case Studies of Visual Transitioning

In this section, we provide case study examples of the power of visual texts in classrooms using Rose's sites of meaning making as a framework for the analysis. Pseudonyms for students and schools are used throughout.

Case Study 1: Carl

INTRODUCTION AND CONTEXT
Carl is a 12-year-old Chinese Canadian boy who attends Garneau School in Vancouver's Downtown Eastside. Along with 24 other students in his Grade 6/7 class, Carl participated in a research project with Maureen that used Ewald's *Literacy through Photography* approach (see Ewald & Lightfoot, 2002) to engage students in taking still photos and writing narratives in relation to four themes: self, school, community, and dreams. The project was a response to a Canadian documentary program that featured Garneau School as part of a series on inner-city education. The documentary portrayed the "dark side" of this community, directing viewers' attention to images that related to "drugs, gangs, and prostitution," in conjunction with social issues labelled "illiteracy," "poverty," and "family dysfunction." The school project was intended

to provide an opportunity for students to speak back to the media by producing their own visual narratives about their school, their community, and ultimately, themselves. It was immediately apparent that students' perceptions of their lifeworlds differed markedly from those portrayed in the media, as evident in Carl's photographs below.

SITE OF PRODUCTION

At the outset of the project, all students received training in photographic methods during a language arts workshop with a university-based photographer/art educator. Students were then provided with disposable cameras and, following a series of discussions about possible images and ideas, they were encouraged to produce a collection of 24 photographs across the contexts of home, school, and community. Once the photographs were developed, the students wrote in a journal about what their images reveal. Students had the opportunity to display their photographs and narratives in a variety of combinations (e.g., as single images, images and text, image sequences, slide-show with audio) and contexts (e.g., in class, with caregivers and friends, with the larger community, including media personnel). These multiple readings allowed students to explore their own identities and the multiple ways that identity can be constructed through visual images and text. For Carl, these exercises provided a means for him to show how he sees himself both now and in the future, and how this sharply contrasts with the media's portrayal of the students in his school and the community in which he lives.

IMAGE

Carl created a series of images where he is the subject. In this first image, he is sitting at his desk in his bedroom "on the weekend" (see Figure 14.1).

He is dressed casually in a t-shirt and jeans. On the right corner of the desk is a stack of books, an English dictionary is set on top; on the left, there is a collection of small plants. As he explained in his journal: "This picture shows how hard I work." He juxtaposed this image with a second photograph of himself, similarly seated at a desk in his home (see Figure 14.2).

This second image offers a view to Carl's future: he is dressed in a collared shirt and a tie working at a computer. As he described in his journal: "A business guy siting on [at] a computer all day long trying to be Bill Gates ... I think this is what I will be when I grow up."

Figure 14.1. Carl working hard.

Figure 14.2. Carl trying to be Bill Gates.

SITE OF VIEWING

The producers of the documentary featuring his school were the intended audience for the images Carl created in his photographs. His images offer a very different portrayal of this inner-city community, which is consistently portrayed in the media by a series of negative images. Carl shows himself as a hard-working student, the backdrop for his imagined future identity as Bill Gates. His photography reveals the hope of children living in this community who imagine future identities that transcend the identities of drug dealers, gangs, and sex-trade workers made available in the media. Carl further explained in his journal:

> I don't think it was very nice to say our school is poor and everything. We are kids and it discourages us to say that we are poor ... It hurts us to hear that we are one of the poorest communities ... it is filled with drug dealers, prostitutes and homeless people. But our school has tried to make us feel safe ... don't judge us by this community. We are just kids and we do not deserve to hear bad things about us at this age.

The images that Carl created are powerful and revelatory in the way they interpolate his own subjectivities, interests, and intentions.

KEY POINTS

Both art and language provide a means to encode experience, whether real or imagined (Baron, 1984). Yet, as Kress (2000) argues, the two modes are "embedded in distinct ways of conceptualizing, thinking, and communicating" (p. 195). Unlike language alone, photography allowed Carl to "speak back" to the media by showing his unique conceptual understanding of his own lifeworld. Photography also allowed him to engage in a dialogue using the visual modality of the news media. He was able to reposition his own identity to make visible who *he* imagines he is allowed to become in this society. His compositional choices in the photographs constitute what Willis (1977) refers to as "the organization of self in relation to the future" (p. 172). The meanings reflect reality as imagined by the sign maker and influenced by his beliefs, values, and biases. Norton (2000) contends that students' imagined identities and communities provide a key to understanding how and why they engage or do not engage with particular literacy practices. We argue that these visual texts reflect these identities in important and compelling ways while simultaneously engaging students in authentic and meaningful literacy practices.

Case Study 2: Dustin[1]

INTRODUCTION AND CONTEXT

Dustin is a 10-year-old Canadian student who lives on the rural periphery of a western Canadian city. He participated in a research study with Maureen in which students visually depicted their conceptualizations of literacy. The school where the study was conducted is located in a middle-class neighbourhood.

The procedure we followed in soliciting drawings of literacy included group discussions and individual interviews (see Kendrick & McKay, 2002, 2004; Kendrick & Jones, 2008, for full description of method). Specifically, the participating students met in groups with both of the researchers for 60 minutes to discuss and draw pictures of their ideas about literacy in their lives in school, outside school, and in the future. The groups ranged in size from 4 to 21 children, with the average group size being 17 children. Dustin's drawing of literacy illuminates how visual representations can reveal complex narratives that may not be readily evident.

SITE OF PRODUCTION

Students were provided with blank white paper, markers, crayons, and pencils. Although Dustin began drawing quickly, he kept his work under a shroud of secrecy. He showed his first drawing, a gopher being shot, to only a few select boys, who proceeded to make comments in hushed tones. Dustin eventually crumpled this drawing into a ball, obscuring it from our view. His second attempt at completing the assignment, equally mysterious, included cryptic queries such as, "Can we draw anything we want about reading and writing?" and, "Does our teacher get to see it?" Once reassured that he was free to draw what he chose, and that his teacher would not see the drawing without his permission, he set to work with quiet determination.

IMAGE

Dustin wrote the following on the front of his drawing: "I shot my first buck with a doble [sic] barel shotgut [sic]. It is at my grapernts [sic] farm. My dad helped me." As the text indicates, his drawing was of a freshly killed buck, hanging upside down, blood dripping from its neck (see Figure 14.3).

Dustin, rifle in hand, is drawn beside the buck. He is engaging directly with the viewer through eye contact. His facial expression and bodily stance beside the buck communicate visible pride in his accomplishment.

Figure 14.3. Dustin and freshly killed buck.

SITE OF VIEWING

The original audience for this assignment was us as educational/litera-
cy researchers trying to better understand what students' visual depictions of literacy might reveal about the literacy narratives they bring to
school and use to make sense of reading and writing. It would have
been easy to overlook Dustin's drawing or assess its content based on
low achievement or a disinterest in reading and writing. By carefully
considering his drawing, as he interpreted it within the context of his
life both inside and outside the classroom, we were able to tap into his
perception of the multiple layers of meaning embedded in the image.
We suspected from his secrecy that guns and hunting were not topics
that he thought would meet his language arts teacher's approval; they
were topics that, according to him, constituted "violence," something
he was "not allowed to write about." An interview with Dustin's teacher confirmed that guns, blood, and dismemberment were banned from
classroom drawing, writing, and reading as part of the school's "zero
tolerance" policy on violence. We also speculated that his teacher and
family had very diverse perspectives on the practice of hunting.

In many ways, Dustin was also keenly aware of a possible second
audience, his peers, as his drawing represents a small act of rebellion
against his perception of his teacher's policy on violence. This rebellion
is what Goffman (1961) referred to as an "underlife," an individual's

attempt to "keep some distance, some elbow room, between himself and that with which others assume he should be identified" (p. 319). Resistance of this nature may be especially attractive to boys like Dustin who may see "good studenthood" as "acquiescent, unmasculine, a denial of who they are and want to be" (Newkirk, 2000, p. 299). Indeed, many boys attempt to distance themselves from the "school" behaviours and language practices they perceive as threatening and feminine while trying to maintain their status as sons and peers. Dustin's graphic drawing of the buck he shot provided an alternative way for him to express his own positioning in relation to the school's policy. He was simultaneously able to position himself as a rebel among his peers, who clearly had some awareness that the drawing would not be acceptable to their teacher. In fact, the content of the drawing became playground legend and within a few days, we had a small entourage of students inquiring, "Did Dustin really draw a gopher with his head being shot off?" and "Did Dustin draw a buck with blood dripping from its head?"

KEY POINTS

Dustin's drawing is a powerful message about what he was not allowed to write about in his classroom. His position on his school's policy was also evident in his blank journal: when he was told on the Monday mornings following his weekend hunting trips with his father and grandfather to write about his weekend, he sat in silent resistance. As he further elaborated in an interview, "She [the teacher] just wants us to write about sunny days and stuff like that." His visual narrative offers a window on how he sees himself as a writer. It provided a safety zone for him to both bring into the classroom life experiences that may not meet with his teacher's approval and for him to take a stand on his school's no violence policy. In Dustin's case, schooled notions of what counts as literacy ignored his potential as a writer and failed to validate his life experience and the identity he was constructing within his family.

Case Study 3: Winston

INTRODUCTION AND CONTEXT

Jennifer first met Winston[2] in his Grade 9 support English class. Winston lives and goes to school in a U.S. university town. He moved to the United States from Haiti when he was small and although "home" to him is the United States, he feels strong ties to Haiti and to his Haitian roots. All of the students in his English support class struggle with reading and writing, yet most of them engage in creativity and meaning making outside of the English classroom. Some are avid gamers, some compose music, some design tattoos. Winston, one of our focal students, takes photographs.

SITE OF PRODUCTION AND IMAGE

When assigned a multimodal project, Winston asked his teacher and Jennifer if he could take photographs "of his world." The multimodal project was one of several projects that encouraged students to broaden their use, appreciation, and understanding of other modes of representation and expression. For an assignment on visual expression, Winston opted for a collage of photographs.

The photograph in Figure 14.4 was taken in a park behind Winston's house on a Sunday afternoon.

Winston described to his friend how he wanted the photograph taken, and then they took photographs from different angles. What he liked about this photograph in particular are the shadows, the movements from light to dark, silhouettes and shadows. He felt that the photograph was layered and contemplative; he described it as "more complicated than his other photographs."

SITE OF VIEWING

Jennifer first saw Winston's photograph at a celebration event of our multimodal project at the end of the school year, when students in his Grade 9 class presented their multimodal portfolios. Jennifer saw Winston's photographs over his shoulder as he presented them to his principal. This particular photograph stood out for Jennifer, as well, so she asked Winston if he could share it with her and he agreed. Knowing Winston and keeping in contact with him to this day (he is now in university), Jennifer views the photograph and photo context in a certain way. But, what does a broader audience see? In the photograph, Winston is not the focal point, in fact, he is in the shadows of the trees. What stands out are the silhouettes and shadows and the trees, the light and dark, the leaning figure in the centre of the photograph. It is more of a landscape photograph than it is a portrait of Winston. During the celebration event, Winston described these effects to his principal.

KEY POINTS

The key point of the photo in relation to the other case studies is that it is so entirely motivated by the interests and convictions of the producer.

Figure 14.4. Winston's Sunday afternoon.

Admittedly, Winston did not actually take the photograph, but he was specific, explicit to the photographer about how the photograph should be taken, and he was clear about the mood, ethos, and effects that he wanted to achieve. Winston had not shown such motivation before in our class, and it was the visual that gave him a voice.

Case Study 4: Andre

INTRODUCTION AND CONTEXT

Andre was in a different year, but took the same class that Winston took. Andre lives in the same university town. Although an active participant in the class, he resisted writing. In fact, he frequently talked about his different interests, but he seldom wrote about these experiences. As part of an in-class activity during the school year, Jennifer and the English teacher asked students to choose a photograph or image and write a narrative to accompany what the image makes them think of. Andre exhibited creativity and strong writing abilities, but he simply did not seem motivated by reading and writing. Given his variety of interests in fantasy, war, wrestling, and the list goes on, Andre was a "Renaissance man," and he frequently spoke about his different interests during class time. What Jennifer noted is that Andre preferred assignments and activities that combined words with visuals and he preferred real-world, authentic texts overly literary texts.

SITE OF PRODUCTION AND IMAGE

The site of production of the text is during class time, and Andre found the visual on a website of stock photographs. Where Winston's photograph evokes an atmosphere and mood through lighting and landscape, Andre's image (see Figure 14.5) and accompanying written narrative triggered an epiphany about visual interpretations. The written narrative is indecipherable in the figure; however, it says the following: "This picture reminds me of the third world. These are actually shacks, separated by walls, and instead of a front door, there is a mailbox nailed to the door with weeds growing out of stepping stones."

Now, Andre did not spend half as much time on the reflection and narrative as Winston did thinking through his photograph, but during our student conference he spoke at length about what the image analysis did for his thinking. The assignment tied to this image was to write a narrative that depicts the mood of an image. Andre chose this image as depicting poverty – specifically, poverty in developing countries.

SITE OF VIEWING AND KEY POINTS

Andre shared his image and reflection with Jennifer. Andre and Jennifer sat down for a conference, and like Winston, Andre described why he chose the image and the complexities of his reading of the text. Andre was dismissive of his written narrative, but he did insist that it was the best image that he could find and that the image made him think. An epiphany he had after writing and thinking about the site of the photographs is that, actually, he had imposed his own view of poverty and that people who lived in these "shacks" had constructed them based on their local conditions and their own needs and desires. Taken on an island in the West Indies, the image and the choices made to focus on elements of the image could be read in different ways. Andre liked the idea of multiple, sometimes antithetical readings of the same image. The key point of the image and accompanying narrative is that it serves as a contested image because, initially, he viewed the image as typifying poverty,

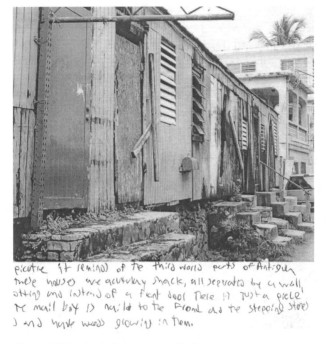

picture it reminds of the third world parts of Antigua
these houses are actually shack, all separated by a wall
sitting instead of a front door there is just a piece
the mail box is nailed to the front and the stepping stones
and have weeds growing in them.

Figure 14.5. Andre's image analysis.

yet through discussion, he ended up viewing from a more nuanced lens. The implication of this case study for literacy teaching is that the visual opened the door for multiple readings of the visual.

Case Study 5: Flimbar

INTRODUCTION AND CONTEXT

In a different year of the Artifactual English Project, Jennifer met Flimbar (self-selected pseudonym). Flimbar was in Grade 9 and in the support English class because he had difficulty organizing his work and keeping up with deadlines. Like Winston and Andre, Flimbar showed remarkable creativity and was known for his vivid illustrations. For the same assignment featured above with Andre's image analysis, Flimbar offered an illustration that he created on-the-fly during a science class earlier that week.

The illustration (see Figure 14.6) depicts a day in his life. Provided below is the original (and transcribed) text juxtaposed against the illustration (see Figure 14.7).

Transcription: Flimbar – I can't remember which day it was but I think it was a Thursday. I went outside and the air was warm and the sun was shining. I walked out without shoes so I could feel the cool grass between my toes. I picked up a knobbled stick that resembles a club and climbed the tree in front of my house. I climbed about feeling like Tarzan. I then dropped my club to the ground and climbed on a branch like a sloth upside-down. I did a half-flip to land on my all fours. I put some long sticks in the ground 20 feet away. I think I gripped my mace tight, narrowed my eyes to the stick enemies. I charged singing a battle cry, as I close the space between me and my enemies, I swing and swing broken sticks flying as I fight through them in a fluid motion. (March 2010)

The site of the illustration is a drawing made in the midst of daily, school routine. Flimbar drew the picture when he finished his work during science class. The subsequent written narrative was produced reflecting on the meaning of the image. There is interest and motivation behind the illustration from the menacing expression, the knobbled stick, the crouching stance, the battle cry – there is attention to details, an adept choice of the right kind of adjectives and words to depict the scene. The site of the image is Flimbar's front yard and the site of Jennifer's viewing of Flimbar's illustration is in his classroom at his high school.

The interesting thing is that Jennifer saw the illustration among miscellaneous pieces of paper, some crumpled, on his desk as Flimbar cleaned his knapsack. Once prompted by Jennifer, Flimbar wrote a narrative about the illustration. In this instance, although a viewer can certainly see Flimbar's menacing look, the illustration is not as powerful as the written text. The difference is Flimbar's pathway (Kress, 1997) into the written text emerged from the illustration. The explicit nature and return to that particular Thursday and the events that unfolded in his written narrative would not have been as powerful if he did not have his illustration that captured the moment.

Figure 14.6. Flimbar's Sunday afternoon (image).

KEY POINTS
The key point of this case study lies in how Flimbar arrived at his written narrative – directly through the visual. Flimbar's other written texts for assignments and activities do not carry the precision and fluency of thought that this written assignment has. Flimbar could often be seen doodling during class, and it was the teacher who noted that he is far more of a visual learner than he is a writer. Invoking an illustration made in the corner of his day, Flimbar was able to find fluency in his writing voice.

Implications of Transitioning into the Visual

In considering implications, we look across the five case studies with a specific focus on literacy pedagogy and the potential of visual texts to contribute to students' learning. The NLG (2000) argues that for literacy

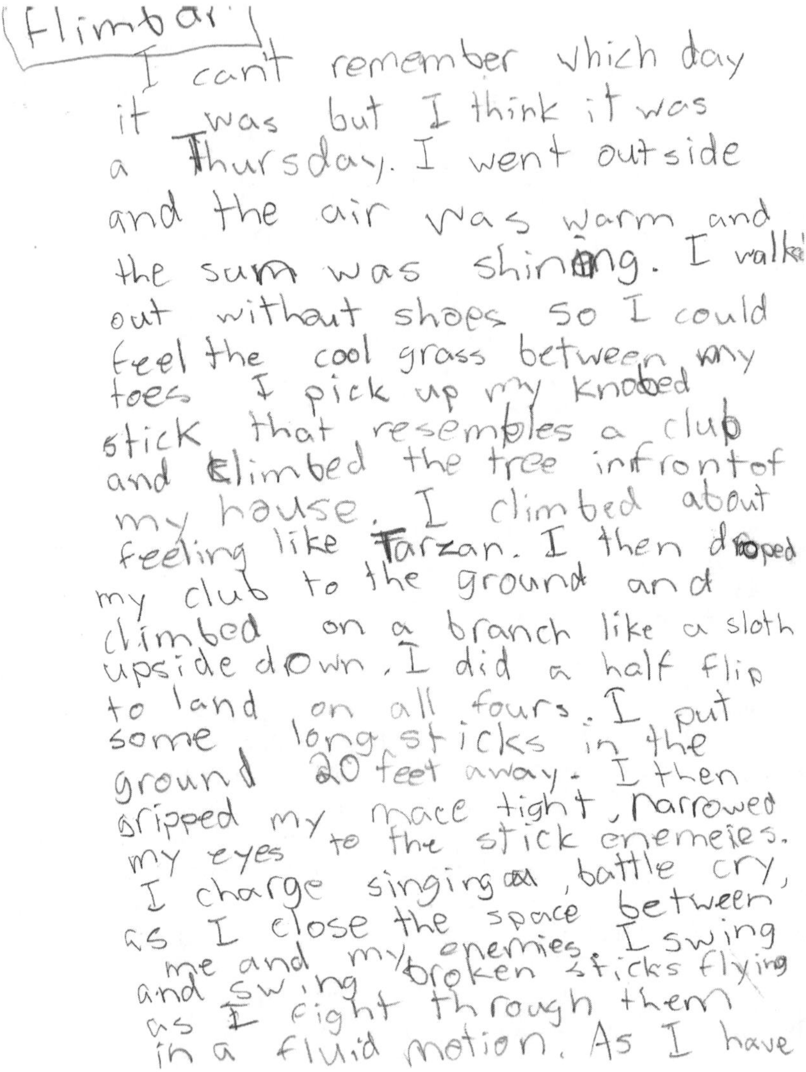

Flimbar
I can't remember which day
it was but I think it was
a Thursday. I went outside
and the air was warm and
the sum was shining. I walked
out without shoes so I could
feel the cool grass between my
toes I pick up my knobed
stick that resembles a club
and climbed the tree infrontof
my house. I climbed about
feeling like Tarzan. I then droped
my club to the ground and
climbed on a branch like a sloth
upside down. I did a half flip
to land on all fours. I put
some long sticks in the
ground 20 feet away. I then
gripped my mace tight, narrowed
my eyes to the stick enemeies.
I charge singingod, battle cry,
as I close the space between
me and my enemies. I swing
and swing broken sticks flying
as I fight through them
in a fluid motion. As I have

Figure 14.7. Flimbar's Sunday afternoon (text).

pedagogy to be truly relevant to students' lives, it needs to "recruit, rather than attempt to ignore and erase, the different subjectivities, interests, intentions, commitments, and purposes that students bring to learning" (p. 18). In the case studies spotlighted in this chapter, there are clear pedagogical patterns in how the visual serves to recruit students' passions and preoccupations through its ability to (1) promote student agency, (2) reveal hidden pathways to learning, (3) create opportunities for both construction and critique on society, and (4) evoke the dialogic (i.e., a stronger sense of audience and purpose). Finally, we also comment on the gendered nature of our case studies.

Promoting Agency

One clear pattern is the degree of agency that the visual gave each learner. Carl could foreground his dreams and his frustrations with the media through the visual. Although Carl could certainly talk about stereotypes that the media built about his community and the people who inhabit his community, the material world that he exudes in his Bill Gates photo collage permits him to visualize self in subtle, layered ways. Similarly, Winston, a self-professed class clown, displayed his capacity for creativity and artistic expression through his series of photographs. Flimbar, regarded as an illustrator by his friends and teacher, visualizes his life all of the time, in stolen moments during class or at home as he watches television. Flimbar's agentive meaning making is at its most powerful when he creates visuals.

Revealing Hidden Pathways

An intriguing finding that arises from all five of the case studies is the hidden and purloined literacies that became visible through the visual. Using linguistic modes alone, Maureen and Jennifer would not have acquired a window onto each learner's worlds without some orchestrating, nudging, even coercing. The students' common interest and inspiration from the visual would have remained silent if teaching and learning did not transition from words to images. It certainly makes us wonder how many other students have hidden visuals in their knapsacks, homes, and cubbies that would provide a valuable window into their dispositions for creativity and their overall pathways into learning.

Constructing and Critiquing

A subtheme for some of the case studies is the visual as subversive and polemical. For Carl, Dustin, and Andre, visuals can be contested, layered, and at times not appropriate, yet these visuals still speak to their experiences, ruling passions, and interests. Such is the case for Dustin who has a passion for hunting and, as an intergenerational practice carried over from his grandfather to his father and to him, an important part of his masculine identity and his family history. Similarly, for Carl to make a statement about his neighbourhood as a site of promise and dreams, he stages visual depictions of his dreams and how they too can be fulfilled in an area often viewed as on the margins. Andre needed to interrogate his visual in order to challenge his own stereotypes about poverty.

Evoking the Dialogic

One of the key factors in motivation and engagement in classroom language arts activities is students' sense of audience and purpose. Inherent in the production of these visual texts is a dialogic (Bakhtin, 1986), a heightened sense of audience and intertextuality that is often absent in assignments that require students to express their ideas solely through language-dominant modes. Indeed, for many students, the perceived audience for classroom writing assignments is exclusively their teachers as part of assessment-based purposes. In our case studies, each student's image was part of a dialogic. Carl's image speaks back to the media about their misrepresentations of his home community. Dustin's visual text unmasks a writer's voice that had been silenced in his language arts classroom. Winston did not want to depict his everyday in a literal way; he wanted to make his everyday artistic and laden with mood and expression. When he discussed his photograph with his principal, he talked about the light and dark expressing light and dark in life – using nature as a pathetic fallacy to express emotions. Similarly, Andre chose the image that he did for its specific material qualities such as grass and weeds growing through the steps, the rusty old mailbox all expressing poverty and what he regarded as third world conditions. Flimbar's voice is very much informed by the visual, and he infused movement, adventure, and intrigue through character stance, facial expressions, and gaze.

As a final point in this section on implications, we speculate that it may not be a coincidence that all five of our case studies feature boys. Across our various visual projects involving numerous students in elementary and secondary schools, our most salient examples of the power of visual texts place boys in the spotlight. Four of the boys we describe here had been labelled "reluctant writers" by their classroom teachers, yet each brought important ideas, knowledge, and purposes to the creation of images. As Newkirk (2000) argues, this reluctance to engage in more traditional curricular writing may be a kind of resistance to particular language practices that are perceived as feminine and associated with "school" behaviour, and that threaten the status of some boys among their family and peers. Monomodal writing practices may also lack the action-oriented possibilities of the visual, in both production and form, integral to the meaning-making practices of many boys.

Conclusion

From a pedagogical and research perspective, Rose's (2001) visual analysis framework allowed us to consider the unique narratives that emerge from the images produced by the boys featured in our case studies. It also helped us to raise important and unexamined questions about these students as meaning makers and the related educational possibilities. It is our strong contention that visual texts have the potential to recruit students' subjectivities, identities, experiences, and knowledge in important ways that allow for participation in social, economic, and political activities in their societies in unprecedented ways. What interests us as literacy researchers and educators is not only the nature and materiality of the visuals but also the sites of production – most of them being homes and private spaces. The visual tends to be relegated to a private, almost hidden enterprise not often invoked in the classroom. If visuals do appear at school, it tends to be during personal time or outside of formal instruction.

Clearly, words still loom large in communication, especially within formal schooling. What our modest study of the visual and its function in the lives of five young boys does is it imbues learning with more agency and fluency of thought. We live in a visual culture and students' everyday lives pivot on visual texts. Transitioning and harnessing teaching to the visual in literacy education might begin with engaging students in critical readings of visual texts; honouring and displaying students' visual texts and artefacts; modelling and organizing teaching around the visual; explicitly and overtly teaching visual techniques; and using visuals as a pathway into written narratives. Relegating the visual to early childhood classrooms or private past-times fails to acknowledge the critical role that the visual plays in helping students reach their educational and human potential.

NOTES

1 An extended version of this case study was published in Kendrick and McKay (2002).
2 Winston is featured in a co-written book, *Literacy and Education* (2nd ed.).

REFERENCES

Bakhtin, M.M. (1986). *Speech genres and other late essays*. Austin, TX: University of Texas.

Baldry, A., & Thibault, P. (2005). *Multimodal transcription and text analysis: A multimedia toolkit and coursebook*. London: Equinox.

Banks, M., & Morphy, H. (1997). *Rethinking visual anthropology*. New Haven, CT: Yale University Press.

Baron, N.S. (1984). Speech, sight, and signs: The role of iconicity in language and art. *Semiotica, 52–53*, 197–211.

Becker, H.S. (2007). *Telling about society*. Chicago: University of Chicago Press.

B.C. Ministry of Education (BCMoE). (2006). *British Columbia Language Arts Curriculum*. Retrieved from http://www.bced.gov.bc.ca/irp/subject. php?lang=en&subject=English_Language_Arts

Collier, M. (2001). Approaches to analysis in visual anthropology. In T. van Leeuwen & C. Jewitt (Eds.), *Handbook of visual analysis* (pp. 35–60). London: Sage.

Ewald, W., & Lightfoot, A. (2002). *I wanna take me a picture: Teaching photography and writing to children*. Boston: Beacon Press.

Goffman, E. (1961). *Asylums: Essays on social situations of mental patients and other inmates*. New York: Anchor.

Heath, S.B. (1983). *Ways with words: Language, life, and work in communities and classroom*. Cambridge: Cambridge University Press.

Jewitt, C., & Kress, G. (2003). A multimodal approach to research in education. In S. Goodman, T. Lillis, J. Maybin, & N. Mercer (Eds.), *Language, literacy, and education: A reader* (pp. 277–292). Stoke on Trent, UK: Trentham Books in association with the Open University.

Kendrick, M., & McKay, R. (2002). Uncovering literacy narratives through children's drawings: An illustrative example. *Canadian Journal of Education, 27*(1), 45–60.

Kendrick, M., & McKay, R. (2004). Drawing as an alternative way of understanding young children's constructions of literacy. *Journal of Early Childhood Literacy, 4*(1), 109–128.

Kendrick, M., & Jones, S. (2008). Girls' visual representations of literacy in a rural Ugandan community. *Canadian Journal of Education, 31,* 371–402.

Kress, G. (1997). *Before writing: Rethinking the paths to literacy.* London: Routledge.

Kress, G. (2000). Multimodality. In A. Apple (Ed.), *Multiliteracies: Literacy learning and the design of social futures* (pp. 182–202). London: Routledge.

Kress, G. (2003). Literacy and multimodality: A theoretical framework. In A. Apple (Ed.), *Literacy in the new media age* (pp. 35–60). London: Routledge. http://dx.doi.org/10.4324/9780203164754

Kress, G., & van Leeuwen, T. (1996). *Reading images: The grammar of visual design.* London: Routledge.

Lankshear, C., & Knobel, M. (2003). *New literacies: Changing knowledge and classroom learning.* Buckingham: Open University Press.

Mutonyi, H., & Kendrick, M. (2011). Cartoon drawing as a means of accessing what students know about HIV/AIDS: An alternative method. *Visual Communication Journal, 10*(2), 231–249.

New London Group (NLG). (2000). A pedagogy of multiliteracies: Designing social futures. In B. Cope & M. Kalantzis (Eds.), *Multiliteracies: Learning and the design of social futures* (pp. 9–37). London: Routledge.

Newkirk, T. (2000). Misreading masculinity: Speculations on the great gender gap in writing. *Language Arts, 77,* 294–300.

Norton, B. (2000). *Identity and language learning: Gender, ethnicity, and educational change.* London: Pearson Education.

Pahl, K., & Rowsell, J. (2006). Introduction. In K. Pahl & J. Rowsell (Eds.), *Travel notes from the New Literacy Studies: Instances of practice* (pp. 1–15). Clevedon, UK: Multilingual Matters.

Rose, G. (2001). *Visual methodologies.* London: Sage.

Rowsell, J. (2010). In-character: Inhabiting literary worlds through Facebook. *Balanced Reading Instruction Journal, 13,* 4–20.

Saskatchewan Ministry of Education (SMoE). (2010). *Saskatchewan Language Arts Curriculum.* Retrieved from http://www.education.gov.sk.ca/adx/aspx/adxGetMedia.aspx?DocID=6823

Siegel, M., & Panofsky, C.P. (2009). Designs for multimodality in literacy studies: Explorations in analysis. In K. Leander, D.W. Rowe, D. Dickinson, R. Jimenez, M. Hundley, & V. Risko (Eds.), *58th National Reading Conference Yearbook* (pp. 99–111). Oak Creek, WI: National Reading Conference.

Snyder, I. (2001). A new communication order: Researching literacy practices in the network society. *Language & Education: An International Journal*, *15*(2–3), 117–131.

Stein, P. (2008). Multimodal instructional practices. In J. Coiro, M. Knobel, C. Lankshear, & D. Leu (Eds.), *Handbook of research on New Literacies* (pp. 871–898). New York: Lawrence Erlbaum.

Street, B. (1984). *Literacy in theory and practice.* Cambridge: Cambridge University Press.

Willis, P. (1977). *Learning to labour.* London: Gower.

15 Transitioning to Being Bilingual: Examining the Linguistic and Non-linguistic Effects of Brief Bilingual Exchanges

CALLIE MADY

The concept of transition is most often applied to major life changes. In applying the idea to education, transition is often related to substantial educational changes as indicated by previous chapters: transitioning to school, transitioning from one school to another, as examples. In addition to such evident periods of change, Schlossberg (1981) proposes a definition of transition that can also account for more subtle changes: a transition can be said to occur if an event or non-event results in a change in assumptions about oneself and the world and thus requires a corresponding change in one's behaviour and relationships (p. 5). Schlossberg's broad definition and accompanying framework provide a basis with which bilingual exchanges can be analysed, in that bilingual exchanges that demand a change in language and culture are known to elicit changes in the perceptions of the participants.

Non-linguistic Changes as a Result of Study Abroad Programs

Research in the broader arena of study abroad programs, where participants live in the target culture without necessarily having to host someone in return, shows that participants often change as a result of their participation. One focus of the studies is the examination of the non-linguistic effects of studying abroad – on student personalities (e.g., Harrison & Voelker, 2008; Van Hoof & Verbeeten, 2005) and motivation (e.g., Allen, 2010). Over the past several years, research findings have shown that language learning in a study abroad experience can influence learners' personalities. Dwyer (2004), for example, in her retrospective survey of over 3,500 study abroad participants, found that study abroad participants had increased confidence in their linguistic abilities and were apt to set goals to later participate in an internship, field study, or take a university course – the longer the experience abroad, the greater the increase. Also of positive note, it has been shown that students who took part in study abroad opportunities reported an increase in feelings of independence and success (e.g., Bond, 2009). In addition to greater independence, the focus group participants representing eight postsecondary institutions in Bond's study reported being transformed with greater self-confidence. Similar to the research on transitions, not all research into the non-linguistic effects of study abroad opportunities reports solely positive outcomes. Pellegrino (1998), for example, in her extensive review of students' experiences and perceptions of language learning in study abroad situations, found that a high degree of personal and social risk was involved when learners try to communicate and establish relationships using their second language (L2). As a result of these communicative experiences, learners sometimes felt embarrassed, discouraged, or unmotivated to pursue interactions (ibid.).

There is little doubt among researchers that motivation plays an influential role in L2 learning and that it has an effect on learning outcomes and academic performance (Allen, 2010). Of positive note, for example, in his study of a short-term abroad experience of 17 university students, Ingram (2005) found that, following the experience, the participants were not only more motivated to continue their study of French but also more apt to seek further experiences. However, although some existing research shows that students' motivation to continue to study the L2 is enhanced after taking part in a short-term study abroad program (e.g., Lewis & Niesenbaum, 2005), some researchers argue that students' motivation to L2 study does not change after such an experience (Allen, 2010). In their examination of motivation, as measured pre- and post-study abroad experience, Allen and Herron (2003) found no change in their 25 participants' integrative motivation as a result of their participation.

Impact of Study Abroad Programs on L2 Acquisition

Similar to other periods of transition (Lenz, 2001), study abroad programs require participants to develop new skills. In addition to the non-linguistic impacts of study abroad experiences, opportunities for communication with a target language community are often seen as advantageous for L2 acquisition (Masuda, 2011; Davidson, 2007). Since

Carroll (1967), who examined the relationship between language proficiency of students majoring in an L2 and their study abroad experiences, found that study abroad was one of the strongest variables in predicting language proficiency, numerous studies have been conducted to explore the effect of the study abroad experience on language proficiency (e.g., Anderson, Lawton, Rexeisen, & Hubbard, 2006; Kinginger, 2010; Tanaka & Ellis, 2003). Kinginger (2008), for example, in her comparison of French test results pre- and post-study abroad found that participants made linguistic gains after one semester abroad. More specifically, Freed (1990) discovered that students with a lower level of proficiency in a target language benefit from social and oral interaction, although students with a high level of proficiency benefit from involvement with a variety of media. Further, she discovered that proficient language students, studying French abroad in a 6-week program, benefited linguistically from non-interactive contact (i.e., reading a newspaper, watching television) with the language. However, the belief that simply being abroad will result in meaningful learning or result in great linguistic change for students has come under investigation in the past decade or so (e.g., Davidson, 2007; Freed, 1995; Hess, 1997; Stephenson, 1999; Wilkinson, 1998). Wilkinson (2000), in her case study of seven university students studying abroad in France for the summer, revealed that linguistic progress was not a given result, but influenced by the participants and the study abroad circumstances. Similarly, Tanaka and Ellis (2003) strongly conclude that the "extent to which learners gain from a study-abroad experience will depend to a considerable extent on the nature of the program" (p. 81). Although study abroad programs are thought to be experiential in nature, Lutterman-Aguilar and Gingerich (2002) advise that programs need to put into practice the principles of experiential education rather than simply assuming they are experiential. Kaufmann, Martin, Weaver, and Weaver (1992) argue that the "design of the program and the selection of participants can also make a significant difference in a program's outcome" (p. 3).

Effects of Intracountry Exchanges

When narrowing the focus of bilingual programs to intracountry bilingual exchanges of short duration where the participants spend time in each other's communities, such programs have been shown to elicit positive non-linguistic (Rose & Bylander, 2007; Allameh, 1996) and linguistic (Mady, 2011a) outcomes. Specifically, as it relates to this study's context, Canadian exchanges with a home-stay component have been shown to offer both linguistic and non-linguistic benefits. In regard to non-linguistic outcomes, research (MacFarlane, 2001, 1997; Mady, 2011b) has shown positive gains in confidence and intergroup attitudes. Through her survey and case study of anglophone and francophone youth participating in a 2-week exchange, MacFarlane (2001) found that most participants indicated more self-confidence post-exchange. They also indicated a desire to continue their L2 studies and to use their L2 outside of the classroom in the future. Likewise, Arnott and Mady (2012) revealed that participants in a 10-day volunteer exchange made gains in confidence and motivation as revealed through data gathered from interviews and pre- and post-exchange questionnaires.

As it pertains to linguistic outcomes, in her examination of anglophone and francophone youth participating in a 2-week bilingual exchange in Canada, Mady (2011a) found linguistic gains for both groups, as shown by self-assessments of the pre- and post-exchange experience. Similarly, MacFarlane (1997) found that almost all of the youth participants, anglophone and francophone alike, indicated an improvement in listening and speaking skills after having spent one week in their target language community.

The potential for intracountry bilingual exchanges to offer linguistic and non-linguistic benefits is recognized by the Canadian government (Office of the Commissioner of Official Languages [OCOL], 2009). Linguistically, the government (p. 51) has supported exchanges as a means to facilitate transition to bilingualism, to increase the proportion of official language bilingual Canadians. Commissioner Graham Fraser (p. 45) recommends that all "young Canadians have the opportunity to practise and master their second official language within the other linguistic community." Beyond the potential linguistic results of an exchange, the federal government also recognizes the possible positive non-linguistic outcomes such as motivating young people to learn the other official language (p. 46).

The Society for Educational Visits and Exchanges in Canada (SEVEC) is a Canadian charity that provides bilingual experiential learning opportunities through home-stay program opportunities to youth across Canada with the goal to have youth gain respect and understanding for Canadian diversity (SEVEC, 2008, 2006). A SEVEC-organized 2-week bilingual exchange, of which one week is spent in the target language community, provides the context and the funding for this study.

Given the above research that highlights exchanges as periods of transition, Schlossberg's transition theory can provide a framework through which the exchange experience can be examined. Although originally conceptualized with adults in mind, Schlossberg, Lynch, and Chickering (1989) acknowledge the applicability of the framework to adolescent learners to assess their learning experiences. To examine the transition process within the context of a bilingual exchange, I explore the three components of transition: *moving in, moving through, and moving on*. In the first stage, *moving in*, I explore the exchange participants' perceptions prior to their exchange experience. The second stage, *moving through*, corresponds to the actual exchange experience focusing, in particular, on the one week in the target community. In the third stage, *moving on*, I study the participants' post-exchange perceptions and plans.

Research Questions

The above-cited L2 literature forms the foundation for this study, in general, and for the research questions, in particular. Thus, with a continued focus on the potential linguistic and non-linguistic effects of exchanges, this study sought to examine the following questions:

• How do short-term exchange participants' attitudes towards L2 learning and culture compare pre- and post-exchange?
• How do the assessed linguistic and non-linguistic outcomes compare across the two participant groups – anglophone and francophone?

Method

The broader study, on which this chapter is based, used a mixed methods design to explore the linguistic and non-linguistic effects of a brief bilingual exchange on anglophone and francophone youth. This chapter reports on the analysis of exchange participants' journal entries to explore (1) attitudes of exchange participants as they pertain to L2 learning and communities; (2) participants' confidence, motivation, willingness to communicate and goal setting; (3) participants' self-assessment of their L2 skills and strategy use pre and post-exchange; and (4) comparisons between the participant groups.

Participants

The exchange students participated in a 2-week exchange where they spent one week in the target language community living with a host family and participating in activities as organized by the host school. The other week the students received their exchange partner and offered a similar experience as the host community. The anglophone participants hosted in their home province, one of four Canadian provinces (Alberta, British Columbia, Ontario, or Saskatchewan) and the francophone participants all received their partners to their home province of Quebec. Of the 243 exchange participants, 153 returned their journals for analysis having completed all three sections: 81 were received from the francophone participants, 72 from anglophone participants. Although teachers were committed to returning the completed journals at the beginning of the project, teachers expressed difficulty collecting the journals from the students and organizing their mailing to SEVEC with the accompanying duties that the end of a school year brings. Due to time and budgetary considerations, a subsample of 80 of the journals received at the time of analysis was analysed (39 anglophone, 41 francophone). The subsample was chosen using purposive sampling (Patton, 1990). In particular, given that age (MacIntyre, Baker, Clément, & Donovan, 2003) and gender (Baker & MacIntyre, 2003) have been shown to have an impact on language learning, a representative subsample was analysed accounting for age and gender (see Table 15.1).

Instrument

JOURNALS
The participants kept a journal for the duration of the exchange. The journal included questions created for the purpose of this study, to be completed while *moving in, through, and on from the exchange experience.* Each question was printed on the same page of the exchange journal in English and French. The majority of both groups responded in their dominant language. The questions probed the participants' cultural knowledge, feelings associated with speaking their L2, and plans for future use. There were three *moving in* questions completed with the classroom teacher just prior to departure to the host community:

1 Are you planning on speaking another language while on exchange? How do you feel about that?

Table 15.1 Description of Journal Participants

Participant groups	Named journals received (n)	Journals, by age (n)	Journals, by gender (n)	Journals analysed (n)	Journals analysed, by age (n)	Journals analysed, by gender (n)
Anglophone	72	15 yrs. (8) 14 yrs. (24) 13 yrs. (32) 12 yrs. (8)	Female (48) Male (24)	39	15 yrs. (4) 14 yrs. (13) 13 yrs. (17) 12 yrs. (5)	Female (27) Male (12)
Francophone	81	14 yrs. (41) 13 yrs. (29) 12 yrs. (7) 11 yrs. (4)	Female (57) Male (24)	40	14 yrs. (19) 13 yrs. (14) 12 yrs. (4) 11 yrs. (3)	Female (28) Male (12)

2 What three things do you know about your twin community and its people (its history, its geography, its traditions)?
3 What three things do you want to visit the most when you travel to your twin community?

The journal included the following four *moving through* questions completed during the exchange:

1 How do you feel about living with a different family for a week? What are you looking forward to? Any concerns?
2 What did you do today? How did it go? How does it feel to be here?
3 What was the highlight of the day?
4 What has been the highlight of your trip so far?

The following five questions served as the *moving on* questions/ prompts and were completed directly on return to the home community:

1 What new things have you learned about your twin community, its people, and their culture?
2 What is the most important thing you learned about yourself in taking part in this exchange?

3 Describe how your feelings about your twin community and its people have been affected by this exchange.
4 How have you used French/English since your exchange experience? What was it like?
5 Have you made plans to improve your French or English? Why or why not?

Procedure

The journals were collected by the teacher organizer and forwarded to SEVEC, who then made them available for analysis. Journal entries were inputted according to the questions posed, and divided by group: anglophone and francophone. Responses to questions were also manually enumerated by tracking each time that a word was used by the participants to describe a feeling or event. In addition to identification by participant groups, the entries were also identified by gender and age. Once entered, the data were examined across groups for consistencies and differences as they related to language learning. The data were also coded across questions in search of themes and patterns.

Findings

Summary of Quantitative Findings

The focus of this chapter is the qualitative findings; I present a summary of the quantitative findings here so as to add context to the qualitative analysis. The questionnaire included two sections that served as the pre- and post-exchange questionnaire. The first Likert-scale section sought to gather information on participant attitudes towards L2 learning and cultures, their confidence, motivation, and willingness to communicate in L2 and goal setting for future L2 use. The second Likert-scale section serves as a self-assessment of L2 skills and strategy use. Analysis of the pre-exchange questionnaire showed both the francophone and anglophone groups have positive L2 attitudes and L2 self-assessment. Both groups maintained but did not increase their L2 attitudes post-exchange. In regard to linguistic gains, the anglophone group reported an improvement in ease of speaking, while the francophone group reported a marked increase in ease with all linguistic scales: listening, speaking, reading, and writing, including that of strategy use post-exchange.

Journal Findings

The journal consisted of three *moving in* questions in response to which both language groups voiced their L2 desire to communicate during the exchange.[1] Although the participants were willing to communicate in their L2, the most common responses of both groups used opposing adjectives to describe their desire; the most common description for both groups revealed nervousness/stress mitigated by excitement/fun:[2]

> Yes, I do plan on speaking as much French as I can while there. I'm nervous because my French isn't perfect and I'm afraid to embarrass myself there. I'm excited though to test out my French skills on actual francophone people. (Anglophone, female participant 14a)
>
> I'm very excited to practise my French with my twin and my host family, and also in real life situations. I am also a little nervous for understanding my host family and twin. They can talk so fast that I can't understand, but I will try my best. I really want to improve my French speaking skills. (Anglophone, female participant 15f)
>
> I have been planning to speak English with my twin and I don't know how to feel about that. Shy or excited. I think both. (Francophone, female participant 14i)
>
> I think that is a great experience for all of us. I feel good but a little bit stressed. (Francophone, female participant 14d)

In addition to the accompanying feelings, many of both groups of respondents linked the exchange to an opportunity to improve their L2 skills. In fact, they related the opportunity of being in an L2 community as a means of improving their language:

> I am very excited to speak another language because it is an excellent opportunity to become more fluent. By speaking French in a community where it is spoken through the day I am hoping to improve and am very excited. (Anglophone, female participant 14k)
>
> I'm really excited to go to a French community. I can't wait to learn new words and practice eight years worth of French. I hope I'll improve at least a little bit. (Anglophone, female participant 13h)
>
> Sa va être un peu difficile parce que je ne connait pas beaucoup. Je vais parler la français parce que je pense que sa va fait l'expérience plus amusante, et que sa va m'aider de apprendre des nouveau mots. Je suis

heureuse de aller quellle que place qui parle ma deuxième langue. [It is going to be a little difficult because I don't know a lot. I am going to speak French because I think it will make the experience more fun, and it will help me learn new words. I am happy to go to some place that speaks my second language.] (Anglophone, female participant 13p)

Je pense que ce voyage sera une bonne opportunité pour moi d'améliorer mon anglais parce que tout le monde autour de moi durant les activités et dans ma famille où je serais accueillie vont parler cette langue. Je pense que d'être entouré par des personnes qui parlent fréquemment l'anglais m'inciterais à faire de même. [I think this trip will be a good opportunity for me to improve my English because during the activities everyone around me and my host family will speak this language. I think that being surrounded by people who frequently speak English will encourage me to do the same.] (Francophone, male participant 13g)

When asked about their knowledge of the twin community, its people, and their desires while visiting the community, the majority of respondents in both groups were able to cite facts regarding the history and geography of their host community and attractions they would like to visit. Such knowledge is likely indicative of advanced preparation as guided by the teacher. A minority of respondents, more anglophones than francophones, linked the exchange to their desire to learn more about their L2 and the L2 culture:

I think it is going to be really interesting to see how people do things and how they act because it's not in English and how everything is going to be in French. (Anglophone, female participant 14e)

I would like to learn more French than I already know. (Anglophone, female participant 12a)

I want to see the Chinatown because there's a different culture and we will learn about it. (Francophone, female participant 14d)

During the exchange, the journal participants were asked to respond to four *moving through* questions. The pre-exchange feelings of nervousness accompanied by excitement were reiterated as the most common responses from both groups on the first day of the exchange. In elaborating on their desires and concerns in relation to living with another family, the participants offered a variety of responses. The most common Anglophone responses included references to language and culture:

I am really looking forward to improving my French a lot and doing everything like watching TV in French or just hanging out speaking in French. (Anglophone, female participant 15d)
I am pretty excited to be able to live with a French family for a week. I am looking forward to improving my French by living in a French community for a week. (Anglophone, female participant 14f)

They also indicated looking forward to differences in culture and language with the following comments:

Je pense que sa va être une expérience très spécial et intéresants. Il y a beaucoup de chose qui m'enthouse. J'aime beaucoup essayer des nouvelles choses, alors essayer la nourriture va être très awesome. Et de voir si les maisons don différentes et comment ils vivent différentes que nous. [I think it will be a special and interesting experience. There are a lot of things that make me excited. I like to try new things a lot, so trying new food is going to be awesome. And to see different houses and how they live differently from us.] (Anglophone, female participant 13p)
I'm looking forward seeing their home, what they eat how they speak French differently from us. (Anglophone, female participant 14a)
It's a great opportunity to live with people who only speak French. Je suis contente de voir tout les different choises qu'il y a. [I am happy to see all the different things there are.] (Anglophone, female participant 13d)

Although a variety of concerns were expressed, the most common response among the anglophone group included concerns about language:

My only concerns are they will speak English to me so I won't improve my French or that they will speak French too quickly and I will always be asking them to repeat it slower. (Anglophone, female participant 15d)
I'm concerned that I won't be able to understand while they are speaking French to me. (Anglophone, male participant 13b)

Although the francophones' responses were equally balanced between nervousness and excitement, only one of the francophones expressed a concern in relation to language:

I was stressed and afraid because I was alone and they don't understand French so I have to speak in English all the time. (Francophone, female participant 14k)

Where no francophones made a connection between their feelings and their learning of English, a minority of anglophones connected their positive feelings to learning French:

> It is really fun to be here and think and talk in French. (Anglophone, female participant 14h)
> J'aime beaucoup être ici en Québec la culture est si différent et interessant et j'ai hate d'apprendre plus. [I like being here in Quebec a lot the culture is different and interesting. I can't wait to learn more.] (Anglophone, female participant 15d)

Five *moving on* questions were analysed for this study. In their description of what they had learned about their twins' community, people, and culture, the majority of both groups' responses (85% of the anglophones, 75% of the francophones) related to culture. Most commonly, both groups acknowledged similarities between their cultures:

> They have different cultures from us but at the same time so much alike. (Anglophone, female participant 14i)
> That French people aren't as different from English people. (Anglophone, female participant 13o)
> Finalement, ces gens ne sont pas si différent de nous. [In the end, the people aren't that different from us.] (Francophone, female participant 13c)
> Il n'y a pas beaucoup de différences sur leur culture comparée à la notre, d'après ce que j'avais pensé. [According to what I thought, there are not a lot of differences between their culture and ours.] (Francophone, female participant 14c)

A minority remarked on the differences:

> I learned that nearly everything is different and they appreciate everything. (Anglophone, female participant 14d)
> The culture is different but just a little bit! (Francophone, female participant 14j)

It is interesting to note that both groups made comments associated with language. Although many anglophones commented on the presence of English in their twin communities in Quebec:

J'ai apprendre que plusieurs personne là parle l'anglais et français. [I learned that several people there speak English and French.] (Anglophone, female participant 13p)

I have learned that there are a lot of people that do speak English and French. I was really surprised at the high number of English-speaking people I talked to. (Anglophone, female participant 15f)

Some of the francophones took the opportunity to comment on their English progress:

De plus, cette échange m'a permis de mieux m'étriser mon anglais. [What's more, this exchange allowed me to better master my English.] (Francophone, female participant 11a)

J'ai apris beaucoup de mots ou de phrases en anglais. [I learned a lot of English words or phrases.] (Francophone, male participant 13h)

In responding to the question regarding the most important thing they learned about themselves as a result of the exchange, the anglophone journal participants most commonly mentioned the relationships they established. The second most common response for the anglophone group, and first for the francophone respondents, was regarding their perception of their L2:

[I learned] that I can improve my French just by speaking it. (Anglophone, female participant 14d)

How good it is that I can speak two languages. (Anglophone, female participant 14f)

[I learned] that I'm almost good in English and I have faith in me. (Francophone, female participant 14c)

I saw that I'm good in English and I'm proud of myself. (Francophone, female participant 14f)

When asked, post-exchange, how they felt about their twin community and its people, all of the responses from both groups were positive. The most common response from both groups was a reference to culture:

Best decision I have ever made doing this exchange, I am so glad I got to go to Quebec and experience a new language and culture ... love Quebec, love the people, love the culture. (Anglophone, female participant 14h)

I loved seeing a different way of living and another culture. It has inspired me to learn about new cultures around the world and visit other countries and meet new people. (Anglophone, female participant 15e)

J'adore les gens qui vivent là. Je ne connaissais rien sur leur culture et maintenant j'en connais beaucoup. Ce sont des personnes très attentive aux gens de leur communauté. [I love the people who live there. I didn't know anything about their culture and now I know a lot. They are people very mindful of the people in their community.] (Francophone, female participant 14a)

Cette échange m'a permis de vraiment comprendre leur façon de vivre et de la partager avec eux. Avoir seulement été touriste, j'aurais découvert leur ville mais gardé mes habitudes. Je n'aurais pas pu vivre comme eux pendant tout ce temps et ça a été très enrichissant pour moi. [This exchange allowed me to really understand their way of life and to share that with them. If I had only been a tourist, I would have discovered their city but kept my way of doing things. I couldn't have lived like them all this time and it was very enriching for me.] (Francophone, female participant 14b)

The fourth *moving on* exchange question asked participants to describe their use of their L2 post-experience. All of the anglophone participants and the vast majority of the francophone participants (92%) had used their L2 post exchange and all of those expressed improvement in their skills:

Mon français a améliorer beaucoup er je peux maintenant parler un peu slang avec les québécois quand je parle oralement. [My French improved a lot and I can now use a bit of slang with Quebeckers when I speak.] (Anglophone, female participant 15d)

My French is a lot better and my vocabulary has expanded. (Anglophone, female participant 14d)

Je crois que je me suis améliorée. [I think I improved.] (Francophone, female participant 14b)

Ca vas mieux, J'utilise plus de mot courant et mes phrase sont plus naturel. [It is better, I use more common words and my sentences are more natural.] (Francophone, male participant 13e)

The final question of the journal asked the participants if they had plans to improve their L2. The vast majority of the anglophones and francophones, 95% and 90% respectively, claimed to have plans to improve their L2. However, their motivations to continue to improve their L2 were different. In explaining their motivation to do so, the anglophone group expressed the desire to travel and continue with their French studies as their most common answers.

> This trip has inspired me to keep speaking French, keep more opportunities open to visit French-speaking countries. (Anglophone, female participant 15d)
>
> Because I want to improve and return to Quebec on vacation. (Anglophone, female participant 14a)
>
> I will continue to take French courses throughout high school. (Anglophone, female participant 15e)
>
> I am staying in French Immersion for the rest of school and am going to Quebec in the summertime. (Anglophone, female participant 14e)

The most common motivation expressed by the francophone group was the desire to improve their English followed by recognition of its general importance:

> Because it's never perfect but I want to be very good to realize my dreams. (Francophone, female participant 14j)
>
> Pcq c'est important. [Because it is important.] (Francophone, female participant 13a)
>
> Car je veux améliorer mon anglais, car c'est important. [Because I want to improve my English, because it is important.] (Francophone, female participant 13b)

These journal findings describe the participants' view of an exchange as an opportunity that is different from school, to improve their L2 skills and cultural awareness. The journal analysis showed the participant groups to be anxious about their L2 abilities, while at the same time looking forward to using their L2 both pre- and during-exchange. Post-exchange, the participants noted similarities between their twin culture and that of their own and their improved L2 skills which at times were acknowledged with pride. Although the vast majority of both participant groups were planning on continuing to improve their L2, they acknowledged different motives in doing so: the anglophone group connected their plans with the desire to travel and study in French, whereas the francophones wanted to improve their English attributing a general importance to doing so.

Discussion

Transitions can be anticipated or unanticipated (Goodman, Schlossberg, & Anderson, 2006). The anticipated transition of this exchange provided the participants the opportunity to contemplate the potential associated changes in advance. In turn, such contemplations may have eased the participants' into the exchange experience. The *moving in*, or pre-exchange, qualitative data from both groups of participants show the participants' intent to go on exchange with the goal of improving L2 skills and participants who believed themselves capable of obtaining those consequences. Explanation of the participants' *moving in* attitudes can be found in Brammer's (1991) conceptualization of transition, where he acknowledges the courage required to take the risks associated with transitions and the accompanying ability to cope with the connected fear. Lewin's (1951) field theory provides additional support as it reveals that driving forces (belief in positive consequences) in transitions may outweigh existing restraining forces (e.g., nervousness) and thus result in risk taking. In responding to the *moving in* questions, both groups of participants most frequently responded with a balance of feelings corresponding to nervousness and excitement. The participants' driving forces (e.g., fun) outweighed their restraining forces (e.g., nervousness) as evidenced in their participation in the exchange.

Similarly, Ajzen and Fishbein's (Ajzen, 1988; Ajzen & Fishbein, 1980) theory of reasoned action offers a complementary explanation for the high degree of positive pre-exchange attitudes. The theory proposes that behaviour is determined by the intention to act with two influencing factors: attitude and evaluation of the future situation. The students volunteered to go on exchange (behaviour) as they judged the exchange (situation) as a means to gaining enhanced language proficiency as based on their self-assessed ability to do so (attitudes).

Another explication of the participants' positive attitudes pre-exchange in spite of their concerns may be found in the participants' distinction between L2 use inside the classroom and outside the classroom (MacIntyre et al., 2003; Yashima, Zenuk-Nishide, & Shimzu, 2004).

Such a distinction supports the concept that the participants viewed the situation (the exchange) as beneficial, perhaps even necessary, to their language development. The perceived value of the exchange as different from the in-class L2 learning supports the benefits of providing exchange opportunities to intact L2 classes (MacFarlane, 1997).

Lazarus and Folkman (1984) suggest that during the *moving through* period of transitions individuals reassess their pre-experience notions. Given the pre-exchange participants' positive evaluation of the exchange opportunity and its potential results (L2 improvement) in the *moving in* period, it is not surprising that many journal entries focused on language use as the participants *moved through* the exchange. It is during this period that there were differences noted between the anglophone and francophone groups. The anglophone participants expressed concerns specific to comprehension, whereas the francophones more often expressed confidence and focused on production. Goodman et al. (2006) confirm that examination of context as a factor in transitioning is pertinent. The anglophones' concerns are reflective of MacFarlane's (1997) exchange research that found the anglophones' comprehension of French challenged by accent, speed, and the use of idiomatic expressions. The status afforded to English in Canada also offers a possible explication for such intergroup differences. The dominant value placed on English in Canada may have provided the francophones with more exposure to anglophone communities and thus greater confidence. Support for grounding an explanation of the above between-group difference in linguistic status is also supported by this study's post-exchange qualitative data, as the journal data show the participants to be differentially motivated to continue to improve their L2. Although the anglophones stated that the desire to continue to learn French was grounded in their studies and hope for travel, the francophone group connected their motivation to improve their English on their judgment that English was a language of general importance. A connection between intergroup attitudes and goal setting for the francophone group is also supported by research (MacIntyre, 2007) that suggests that intergroup attitudes include goal setting.

Finally, the *moving on* component of transition includes a focus on looking ahead to next steps. The majority of exchange participants in this stage of transition, post-exchange, made plans to improve their L2. Such goal setting at this stage is consistent with Schlossberg's transition theory (1981), where consideration is given to what comes next. Likewise, it corresponds to Brammer's (1991) concept of transition, in which he positions the setting of goals as renewal where one period of transition ends provides for a new beginning. As applied to the exchange experience, the end of the exchange may result in goal setting that could lead to the pursuit of other language-learning opportunities resulting in increased proficiency. In conjunction with previous research on bilingual exchanges, this study boasts the potential for brief periods of transition into the target language and culture as a positive step in the larger transition to official language bilingualism.

Limitations

Given that the participants completed the pre-exchange questionnaire after having volunteered to participate in the exchange, it is unclear from this study whether the anticipated exchange contributed to the positive attitudes pre-exchange or whether it was influenced by the classroom environment or by a combination thereof. For future research, it would be important to determine attitude-related factors a priori to the exchange. It would also be worth verifying the data with observations pre-, during, and post-exchange.

Conclusion

This study highlights the advantages of providing L2 learners an opportunity for authentic L2 use in the L2 community. One advantage revealed by the participants in this study is the occasion for authentic language use, which they judged as being different than classroom use. The participants viewed the exchange opportunity as a means of testing their L2 abilities and judged themselves successful post-exchange. The desirability of spending time in an authentic L2 environment accompanied by the perceived linguistic gains suggest that it would be advantageous to provide bilingual exchange opportunities to all L2 students. The fact that the exchange resulted in such gains and that the vast majority of participants then set goals for further language improvement gives credence to a possible positive cycle by which students participate in exchanges, improve their L2, and therefore, seek further exchange opportunities to further their progress and thus achieve their stated goal of language learning.

NOTES

1 The findings are presented in the language used by the participants, where French was used an approximate translation is provided by the author; a minority of both groups wrote in their L2.
2 The entries are reproduced as written by the participants.

REFERENCES

Ajzen, I. (1988). *Attitudes, personality, and behavior.* Chicago: Dorsey Press.

Ajzen, I., & Fishbein, M. (1980). *Understanding attitudes and predicting social behavior.* Englewood-Cliffs, NJ: Prentice Hall.

Allameh, J. (1996). Interactive exchanges: American and international students at an IEP. *Paper presented at Teacher of English to Speakers of Other Languages.* Chicago, 26–30.

Allen, H.W. (2010). Language-learning motivation during short-term study abroad: An activity theory perspective. *Foreign Language Annals, 43*(1), 27–49.

Allen, H.W., & Herron, C. (2003). A mixed-methodology investigation of the linguistic and affective outcomes of summer study abroad. *Foreign Language Annals, 36*(3), 370–385.

Anderson, P.H., Lawton, L., Rexeisen, R.J., & Hubbard, A.C. (2006). Short-term study abroad and intercultural sensitivity: A pilot study. *International Journal of Intercultural Relations, 30*(4), 457–469.

Arnott, S., & Mady, C. (2012). Volunteer exchange experiences and willingness to communicate (WTC): An English language learner (ELL) perspective. *Contact, 38*(2), 40–48.

Baker, S., & MacIntyre, P. (2003). The role of gender and immersion in communication and second language orientations. *Language Learning, 53*(S2), 65–96.

Bond, S. (2009). *World of learning: Canadian postsecondary students and the study abroad experience.* Ottawa: Canadian Bureau for International Education.

Brammer, L. (1991). *How to cope with life transitions: The challenge of personal change.* New York: Hemisphere.

Carroll, J. (1967). Foreign language proficiency levels attained by language majors near graduation from college. *Foreign Language Annals, 1*(2), 131–151.

Davidson, D.E. (2007). Study abroad and outcomes measurements: The case of Russian. *Modern Language Journal, 91*(2), 276–280.

Desrochers, A., & Gardner, R.C. (1981). *Second langage acquisition: An investigation of a bicultural excursion experience.* Quebec: International Centre for Research on Bilingualism, Laval University.

Dwyer, M.M. (2004). More is better: The impact of study abroad program duration. *Frontiers: The Interdisciplinary Journal of Study Abroad, 10,* 151–164.

Freed, B.F. (1990). Language learning in a study abroad context: The effects of interactive and non-interactive out-of-class contact on grammatical achievement and oral proficiency. In J. Alatis (Ed.), *Linguistics, language teaching and language acquisition: The interdependence of theory, practice and research. Georgetown round table on linguistics* (pp. 459–577). Washington, DC: Georgetown University Press.

Freed, B. (1995). *Second language acquisition in a study abroad context.* Philadelphia: John Benjamins.

Goodman, J., Schlossberg, N.K., & Anderson, M.L. (2006). *Counseling adults in transition: Linking practice with theory* (3rd ed.). New York: Springer.

Harrison, J., & Voelker, E. (2008). Two personality variables and the cross-cultural adjustment of study abroad students. *Frontiers: The Interdiscliplinary Journal of Study Abroad, 17,* 69–87.

Hess, J.D. (1997). *Studying abroad–learning abroad: An abridged edition of the whole world guide to culture learning.* Yarmouth, ME: Intercultural Press.

Ingram, M. (2005). Recasting the foreign language requirement through study abroad: A cultural immersion program in Avignon. *Foreign Language Annals, 38*(2), 211–222. http://dx.doi.org/10.1111/j.1944-9720.2005. tb02486.x

Kaufmann, N.L., Martin, J.N., Weaver, H.D., & Weaver, J. (1992). *Students abroad: Strangers at home. Education for a global society.* Yarmouth, ME: Intercultural Press.

Kinginger, C. (2008). Language learning in study abroad: Case histories of Americans in France. [Monograph.]. *Modern Language Journal, 92*(S1), 1–124.

Kinginger, C. (2010). American students abroad: Negotiation of difference? *Language Teaching, 43*(2), 216–227.

Lazarus, R., & Folkman, S. (1984). *Stress, appraisal and coping.* New York: Springer.

Lenz, B. (2001, Dec.). The transition from adolescence to young adulthood: A theoretical perspective. *Journal of School Nursing, 17*(6), 300–306.

Lewin, K. (1951). *Field theory in the social sciences: Selected theoretical papers.* New York: Harper.

Lewis, T.L., & Niesenbaum, R.A. (2005). Extending the stay: Using community-based research and service learning to enhance short-term study abroad. *Journal of Studies in International Education, 9*(3), 251–264.

Lutterman-Aguilar, A., & Gingerich, O. (2002). Experiential pedagogy for study abroad: Educating for global citizenship. *Frontiers: The Interdisciplinary Journal of Study Abroad, 8,* 41–82.

MacFarlane, A. (1997). *Linguistic and attitudinal aspects of school year group exchanges: Immediate and long-term outcomes for participants* (Unpublished doctoral dissertation). University of Ottawa.

MacFarlane, A. (2001). Are brief contact experiences and classroom language learning complementary? *Canadian Modern Language Review, 58*(1), 64–83.

MacIntyre, P. (2007). Willingness to communicate in the second language: Understanding the decision to speak as a volitional process. *Modern Language Journal, 91*(4), 564–576.

MacIntyre, P.D., Baker, S.C., Clément, R., & Donovan, L.A. (2003). Talking in order to learn: Willingness to communicate and intensive language programs. *Canadian Modern Language Review, 59*(4), 589–605.

Mady, C. (2011a). The chicken or the egg: Examining the impacts of a brief bilingual exchange on willingness to communicate. *Babel, 46*(1), 22–29.

Mady, C. (2011b). The results of short-term bilingual exchanges keep on ticking: Long-term impacts of brief bilingual exchanges. *Foreign Language Annals, 44*(4), 712–726.

Masuda, K. (2011). Acquiring Interactional Competence in a Study Abroad Context: Japanese Language Learners' Use of the Interactional Particle "ne." *Modern Language Journal, 95*(4), 519–540.

Office of the Commissioner of Official Languages (OCOL). (2009). *Annual Report 2008–2009.* Ottawa: Queen's Printer.

Patton, M. (1990). *Qualitative evaluation and research methods* (2nd ed.). Newbury Park, CA: Sage.

Pellegrino, V.A. (1998). Student perspectives on language learning in a study abroad context. *Frontiers: The Interdisciplinary Journal of Study Abroad, 4,* 91–120.

Rose, S., & Bylander, J. (2007). Border crossings: Engaging students in diversity work and intergroup relations. *Innovative Higher Education, 31*(5), 251–264.

Schlossberg, N. (1981). A model for analysing human adaptation to transition. *Counseling Psychologist, 9*(2), 2–18.

Schlossberg, N., Lynch, A., & Chickering, A. (1989). *Improving Higher Eduction Environments for Adults.* San Francisco: Jossey-Bass.

Society for Educational Visits and Exchanges in Canada (SEVEC). (2006). *A report to the board of directors on educational exchanges.* Ottawa: Impact Consulting Group.

Society for Educational Visits and Exchanges in Canada (SEVEC). (2008). *Additional funds allow more Canadian youth to take part in life changing exchanges.* Press Release 2 June 2008.

Stephenson, S. (1999). Study abroad as a transformational experience and its effects on study abroad students and host nationals in Santiago, Chile. *Frontiers: The Interdisciplinary Journal of Study Abroad, 5,* 1–38.

Tanaka, K., & Ellis, R. (2003). Study-abroad, language proficiency, and learner beliefs about language learning. *JALT Journal, 25*(1), 63–85.

Van Hoof, H.B., & Verbeeten, M.J. (2005). Wine is for drinking, water is for washing: Student opinions about international exchange programs. *Journal of Studies in International Education*, 9(1), 42–61.

Wilkinson, S. (1998). Study abroad from the participants' perspective: A challenge to common beliefs. *Foreign Language Annals*, 31(1), 23–39.

Wilkinson, S. (2000). Emerging questions about study abroad. *ADFL Bulletin*, 32(1), 36–41.

Yashima, T., Zenuk-Nishide, L., & Shimizu, K. (2004). The influence of attitudes and affect on willingness to communicate and second language communication. *Language Learning*, 54(1), 119–152.

16 Aboriginal Education: A Transition of World Views

CHRIS HACHKOWSKI

In her article, "Assimilation and Oppression: The Northern Experience," Susan Chisholm (1994), describes the acculturating affects on Aboriginal students who are forced to leave their home communities to attend secondary schools in large, urban centres. She illustrates the challenges and pathways of three fictional characters, based on the experiences of real individuals. First, there is Ellen, who has left her small community for the first time. Within the first month at her new school, she is becoming uncomfortable with the speed and activity of the school, classes, and students. She feels anxious and alone and decides to leave the school during the day to spend time elsewhere. Richard, a young man whose entire community came to support him at his departure from the airport, is experiencing culture shock in his new environment. He is unsure of his ability to remember his boarding school's rules and consequences, which results in diminished confidence in his overall abilities. Lastly, there is Christine, an older student who takes care of her infant child with the support of her boarding home's owners. Through the article, Chisholm argues that the transitions for most Aboriginal students in these situations are frustrating, confusing, and sometimes traumatic. For these characters, the constant emotional stress they undergo can result in substance abuse, constant absenteeism, or criminal behaviour. The article concludes with a short narrative of how these characters coped with their situations. Richard becomes a substance abuser, resulting in his untimely death. Ellen quits school and returns to her home community. The single mother, Christine, receives academic rewards at her high school graduation ceremony and is determined to continue her success by enrolling in the local community college to ensure stability for herself and her child.

For many Aboriginal students in Canada, the pseudo-fictional stories described above are similar to the experiences they may encounter when leaving their community to attend school in larger, urban cities across the country. According to Statistics Canada (2006a), approximately 40% of First Nations peoples live on reserve, totalling close to 280,000 individuals. Approximately 34% of these individuals are between the ages of 0 to 14 years (Statistics Canada, 2006b), representing close to 100,000 First Nations children. Approximately 60% of all on-reserve Aboriginal children attend one of the 550 elementary schools located in First Nations communities across Canada (Mendelson, 2008). Due to the very limited number of First Nations communities that can deliver a full secondary school program, the vast majority of Aboriginal youth attend high school outside their community. Overall, the result is that one out of six Aboriginal children receive their education in a First Nations school, while the other five receive education from their respective provincial departments of education (Richards, 2008).

Historically, the formal educational and school experiences for Aboriginal peoples in Canada have been synonymous with trauma, discrimination, and tragedy. For almost the entirety of the twentieth century, the primary means by which the Canadian government provided formal education to Aboriginal children was through church-sponsored residential schools. Aboriginal children were pulled from their homes and communities and brought to these culturally foreign institutions where the Aboriginal student population did not know the customs, culture, or language of the dominant society. These schools offered minimal education, teaching children the barest skills needed to survive in the dominant non-Aboriginal[1] world (Barman, Hebert, & McCaskill, 1986). In addition, acts of physical, mental, and sexual abuse of the children were common in this demeaning education system resulting in Aboriginal students losing touch with the traditions, languages, and identification with their own culture (Stout & Kipling, 2003; Van Hamme, 1995). To compound the effects of losing their cultural traditions and heritage, residential schools failed to properly provide students with the skills to successfully live in non-Aboriginal communities. The multiple generations of victims from the residential school system transformed into individuals who existed between two worlds, neither belonging to their traditional Aboriginal culture nor the dominant, Euro-Western culture. The survivors and their descendants have lived with the effects of residential schools through reduced capacity to continue pursuing an education because of suspicion of formal educational institutions.

In 1972, the National Indian Brotherhood (NIB) released their policy paper entitled, *Indian Control of Indian Education*. The policy outlined the philosophy, goals, principles, and directions that Native education needed to follow to ensure that their children would gain the "knowledge to understand and be proud of themselves" (p. 1). The paper clearly stated that only through parental responsibility and local control of education would their desires and goals be realized. Parents would set the goals to reinforce their children's sense of their Aboriginal identity. Administrative control at the local level of the educational needs of the community would ensure that programs and curriculum would teach their children their rich cultural heritage through culturally appropriate pedagogy: "The lessons he learns in school, his whole school experience, should reinforce and contribute to the image he has of himself as an Indian" (p. 9). By the early 1980s, 450 of Canada's 577 First Nations communities were involved in some or all aspects of the administration of their local schools, and by 1984, 187 bands were operating their own schools (Barman, Hebert, & McCaskill, 1987). With the increase in First Nations schools, the expectation was that more Aboriginal peoples would experience academic success and be proud of their Aboriginal ancestry.

However, the educational attainment rate for Aboriginal peoples in Canada continues to be significantly lower than for non-Aboriginal peoples. According to the statistics available through the Canadian government, the secondary school completion rates for Aboriginal students compared with non-Aboriginal Canadians in 2006, were 56.3% and 76.9% for individuals 15 years of age and older, respectively (Community Foundation of Canada, 2009). However, for students living on reserves, the statistics indicate a far worse situation. Between the years 1996 and 2006, the high school completion rate for individuals between 20 and 24 years old, living on-reserve, decreased from 19% to 14% (Mendelson, 2008).

In recognition of these historically lower academic achievement rates, provincial and territorial departments of education across Canada have invested resources and considerable funds to improve the quality of education for Aboriginal students in their public schools. The Ontario Ministry of Education has increased its funding for its First Nations, Metis, and Inuit supplement from $10.5 million in 2007–08 (OMoE, 2008) to $37.1 million in 2011–12 (OMoE, 2011). These funds are designated specifically for Native language and Native studies programming, and other resources and activities designed at the local school board level. The government of British Columbia has increased its funding for Aboriginal education from $52.6 million to $61.5 million in 2010–11 (British Columbia Ministry of Education [BCMoE], 2011). This type of financial commitment has seen completion rates modestly increase from 48% to 51% for self-identified Aboriginal students in the province's schools between the years 2005 and 2010 (BCMoE, 2010). However, with the increased financial and political commitments to improving educational success rates among Aboriginal students, the question remains: why do educational attainment rates still remain significantly lower for Aboriginal than for non-Aboriginal peoples in Canada?

Numerous studies have analysed factors that contribute to the lower rates of academic success and the reasons for leaving school among Aboriginal students across North America. Dehyle (1992) interviewed Ute and Navajo youth and found that their principle reason for early leaving was that school had no priority in their lives. In a study done in Montana (Coladarci, 1983), Native American students identified the irrelevance of school in general as their main reason for dropping out. A report from the B.C. Ministry of Education (BCMoE, 2000) identified social and economic levels of children's families, avoidance of negative aspects of schooling, and decreased fluency rates as some of the reasons for Aboriginal youth leaving school. One Navajo youth indicated that it was the teacher's indifference to Native American peoples that was his sole reason for leaving school:

> The way I see it seems like the whites don't want to get involved with the Indians. They think we are bad. We drink. Our families drink. Dirty. Ugly. And the teachers don't want to help us. They say, 'Oh no, there is another Indian asking a question because they don't understand. So we stopped asking questions.' (Dehyle, 1992, p. 24)

The larger implications of this irrelevance and the unfounded stereotypes directed at Aboriginal students in schools where the majority of students are non-Aboriginal has led to lower expectations of Aboriginal students' abilities from teachers and administrators (Kleinfield & McDiarmid, 1987). This has caused a disproportionate number of students to be placed in lower academic levels in their schools (Common & Frost, 1994; Riley & Ungerleider, 2008).

Other studies have indicated that cultural differences between Aboriginal students and the dominant culture of the school that they attend are motivating factors towards the decision for Aboriginal students to drop out. Cultural differences within schools take on many forms. For example, there is a lack of culturally relevant curricula being taught in schools (BCMoE, 2000; Dehyle, 1992; Dehyle & Swisher, 1994; Reyhner, 1994) and teaching styles utilized by teachers are often culturally biased and are not conducive to Aboriginal learning (Ledoux, 2006; Reyhner, 1994). Others continue to face personal and systemic racism by non-Aboriginal students and teachers (Hare & Pidgeon, 2011). For others, the lack of personal connections and relationships lead to dissociation with their schools (Iverson, 2007). On their own, the above issues, obstacles, and challenges can prove difficult for most Aboriginal students to overcome, as demonstrated in recent statistics. However, the transitioning of Aboriginal students from the relative familiarity and safety of their communities' on-reserve school to the unfamiliar, foreign learning environment of the provincial public school system may compound the detrimental influences of these factors.

Transitions

For any student, the transition from middle school to high school can be an anxious, disheartening experience. Cohen and Smerdon (2009) reviewed the developmental and contextual issues that pertain to transitioning from middle school to high school. Typical for adolescents at this time, high school students undergo physical changes usually through experiencing puberty, which cause greater anxiety because of hormone fluctuations. Contextually, students gain newer autonomy when entering high school, but lose emotional and personal ties with teachers and peers resulting in higher absenteeism and course failures. In a study by Barber and Olsen (2004), students transitioning to Grade 9 located in different schools, found that the

> ninth graders reported less liking of school, higher perceived need of school organization, lower support from teachers, lower support from principals and assistant principals, less monitoring from teachers, lower classroom autonomy, less involvement in school activities, lower self-esteem, and higher depression. (p. 18)

The transitional experience of students who transfer from on-reserve schools to off-reserve public secondary schools presents additional challenges to the successful transition of Aboriginal students. For

Aboriginal students who live on reserves that are located in southern parts of Canada and that are considered accessible by road all year, the journey between their home and their off-reserve high school may mean a school bus ride that lasts from 30 minutes to 2 hours, in one direction. For the thousands of Aboriginal students who either live in communities that are far from larger urban centres or in fly-in communities, a high school education may mean leaving home, travelling hundreds of kilometres, and living with extended family members or friends in larger, more urbanized communities. Other students may live on their own, either in boarding homes or in rental properties with extended families and friends. This situation can lead to less permanency in residences for Aboriginal students. On a national level, Aboriginal peoples have a greater chance of moving within their census area and are more likely to have moved from a different community than is the case for non-Aboriginal peoples (Statistics Canada, 2008a), typically in accommodations that are more crowded and in need of more repair than typical housing of non-Aboriginal peoples (Statistics Canada, 2008b). Because of the transiency of some Aboriginal students, this mobility is inherently problematic for academic success. In British Columbia, in nearly every high school provincewide, mobile Aboriginal students had poorer school completion outcomes than their non-mobile Aboriginal peers in the same high school (Aman, 2008). The study also showed that less than one-third of a cohort of students did not experience a change in secondary schools, resulting in the remaining nearly two-thirds of students changing schools at least once, contributing to a less coherent and sustained learning environment after transitioning to secondary school.

On average, the Aboriginal student begins secondary school academically less prepared than the non-Aboriginal student. Although no national statistics are available on the specific content/subject achievement rates for Aboriginal students in Canada, one may extrapolate provincial findings to provide a measure of how Aboriginal students compare with non-Aboriginal students. An analysis of core learning indicators (reading, writing, and mathematics) of self-declared Aboriginal students in Saskatchewan indicated a performance achievement below the standards achieved by the broader student population at all grade levels. This was demonstrated in all grade levels tested, for all indicators of core learning, and at both levels of achievement (adequate and above, and proficient) (Steeves, Carr-Stewart, & Marshall, 2010). In British Columbia (Aman, 2009), Aboriginal students who identified with a

First Nations band showed that only 14% of students in Grade 4 did not achieve at their grade level. This percentage dramatically increased to 31% of students in Grade 10, with female students more likely not to be at grade level compared with their male counterparts. The situation is similar south of the Canadian border. The U.S. Department of Education compiles statistics of the academic achievement levels of American Indian/Alaskan Native (AI/AN) students and recent statistics indicate that AI/AN students score 17 points lower on a national assessment of reading than non-AI/AN students in Grade 4 and 13 points lower in Grade 8 (Grigg, Moran, & Kuang, 2010). In the same study, AI/AN students who attended public schools performed better in reading and mathematics than AI/AN students who attended Bureau of Indian Affairs schools. The lower level of academic skills of Aboriginal students is problematic for lower-achieving students, especially during transitions, as one of the greatest affects on achievement when transitioning to high school is inadequate preparation (Neild, 2009).

As previously described, five of six on-reserve Aboriginal students attend public schools administered by provincial governments with the vast majority of this ratio attending public secondary schools. Often, the students from an Aboriginal community arrive as a single cohort to the one easily accessible high school. In other cases, especially in Canada, depending on the location of the Aboriginal community, students may have a choice between attending schools administered by different school boards (i.e., separate, French, public), thus splitting their small cohort into smaller networks of peers. In addition, on-reserve schools have smaller enrolment than urban, public schools, resulting in single grade cohorts from Kindergarten and to Grade 8. In some cases, multiple grades share one classroom and teacher. As most First Nations communities in Canada are considerably smaller in population, and would be labelled "rural communities," the First Nations schools in these communities would share some characteristics of other rural schools. The advantages of rural schools include higher levels of participation rates in extracurricular activities and more one-on-one attention; however, the negative effects are the lack of privacy among a small cohort of students that moves through each grade together (Patton Kennard, 2009). In summary, the elementary educational experience of the Aboriginal student is one in which an on-reserve student enters Kindergarten with a cohort of peers and moves through each grade with this cohort, developing both positive and negative personal relationships with friends and extended family members.

That network of peer support may not, however, assist in an Aboriginal student's successful transition into a public secondary school. Langenkamp (2010) analysed how middle school social relationships and the student's school district policies of secondary school enrolment affected a middle school student's transition to high school. The study found that the school districts that mixed their students from various feeder schools appeared to provide low-achieving students with protection against failure compared with school districts where students arriving at their secondary school were from one middle school. It was suggested that the higher protection against failure in mixed schools could be attributed to increased opportunities for students to develop more social interactions. Within this context, it would suggest that Aboriginal students transferring from on-reserve schools would be protected from underachieving, as on-reserve Aboriginal students would feed into a public secondary school together with public middle school students for whom the secondary school was originally intended. Concurrently, on-reserve Aboriginal students supposedly arrive from their community school with a supportive network of friends and established relationships. Langekamp's study also demonstrated that students who had either bonded with their middle school teachers or who were more popular among middle school classmates were less likely to fail courses in their first year of high school.

Low-achieving students do not, however, have the same protection against failure that is associated with having more friends as average or high-achieving students. As previously noted, a greater percentage of Aboriginal students enter secondary school with lower than average levels of academic achievement, thus negating the effects of arriving at school with established friendships. Concurrently, the high turnover rate of teachers in First Nations schools (Anderson, Horton, & Orwick, 2004; Kavanagh, 2006) makes bonding with middle school teachers difficult, further reducing the protection against academic underachievement. As a result, Aboriginal students enter public secondary schools without the advantages that originate from a supportive network of friends and peers that one would expect coming from a single First Nations school cohort.

How Do We Start Assisting Aboriginal Students?

The transition to secondary school can affect any student, whether Aboriginal or non-Aboriginal. To counter the negative affects of this transition, programs and other supports have been developed and administered at the school or local level. These programs, typically, involve the implementation of transitional supports and activities that build a greater sense of community for students or an increase in parental involvement (Akos & Galassi, 2004; Gentle-Genitty, 2009; Smith, 1997). However, as successful as specific programs may be, it is important to recognize the inflexibility of some programs to meet the individual needs of all students. As Cohen and Smerdon (2009) state, "One-size-fits-all solutions are unlikely to be successful in the long term because the middle to high school transition is a personal and deeply nuanced process, and students drop out of high school for different reasons" (p. 181). As such, it is within this context, and because of other extraneous factors, that schools and educators must be cognizant of when interpreting the transitional pathways of Aboriginal students entering their school system.

In a report prepared for the Ontario Native Education Counselling Association, Toulouse (2010, p. 23) compiled a list of factors that assist in the successful transition of Aboriginal students from elementary to secondary school based on surveys administered to members of the association throughout Ontario. These factors include the following:

- Visits to the high school and tours, as well as meet the staff over a meal
- Mentorship and buddy programs with current high school students (go to them and they come to the elementary level) to discuss high school courses, challenges, and options (Ruttan, 2000)
- Relationship with the full-time Native education counsellor that offers social, cultural, mental, and academic programming in a designated space
- Parental and community involvement with events that celebrate the transitions (graduation and incentives and events)
- Orientation to high school extracurricular activities (social, physical, academic) and organized shared events between elementary and secondary schools
- Career guidance plans at elementary schools that drive course selection in secondary schools
- Assist students with course selection at secondary school and take to high school in August to locate classes before the school year begins.

Bazylak (2002) identified factors that contributed to the success of Aboriginal female students at the students' public secondary school. These factors included supportive families, friends, and teachers; having Aboriginal teachers on staff; setting personal goals: an engaging curriculum; and additional support programs. Baydala, Rasmussen, Birch, et al. (2009) surmised that students who had created friendships in a school environment that developed social skills and culturally appropriate interventions provided the resources for Aboriginal students to achieve academically.

To assist classroom teachers and other educators in their responsibilities in limiting the negative effects of transitioning to the secondary level, research has identified tangible behaviours, understandings, and actions that speak to the learning characteristics of the Aboriginal student in the classroom. Castagno and Brayboy's (2008) extensive literature review of learning styles of Indigenous youth cite the most common styles as "visual, hands-on, connecting to real-life, direct experience, participating in real-world activities, global, seeing the overall picture before the details, creative, holistic, reflective, collaborative, circular, imaginal, concrete, simultaneous processing, observation precedes performance, and naturalistic" (p. 954). Pewawardy (2002) identified that Indigenous peoples are field-dependent learners, meaning Aboriginal peoples prefer not to separate themselves from the environment when attempting to understand the meaning of the learning experience to a global picture. The reviewers emphasize that these styles are not necessarily comprehensive to all Aboriginal students and that there will be variation among individuals.

Gilliland (1999, p. 63) identified different ways to adapt teaching practices to match the generally accepted learning styles of Aboriginal children. Although there is some overlap in categories and definitions, some methods are summarized here:

1 Recognize, encourage, and use alternative ways of learning: Use less Eurocentric modes of teaching (lecturing, sequencing, building from detail) and use a teaching method that allows students to watch, image, and reflect.
2 Learn about the children's early training: Traditionally, the child learns through observation and direct experience and active participation in applicative activities. This allows children to learn "through their strengths."

3 Use family instructional techniques: Demonstration, observation, and imitation: Modelling of behaviours and skills were used rather than verbal instructions. Aboriginal students perform better than non-Aboriginal students on skills that require observation, visual discrimination, and spatial configuration.

4 Let children learn from children: Traditionally, new skills are learned from extended family members and companions. The skills are learned as part of a group, and the success of the skill was dependent on the individual's success.

5 Lower the stress of over-verbalization: Most Aboriginal children learn the value of silence as a time for reflection. As well, young children are taught not to interrupt adults when they speak. As such, students may not engage in immediate discussion about content until after reflection.

6 Teach listening skills: Indigenous peoples value careful listening. It is important to provide a focus for students on what they should listen for.

7 Advance holistic intuitive learning: As global thinkers, Aboriginal children prefer large overviews of subjects, rather than approaching content from small components that have no apparent relation to each other.

8 Emphasize application of the information in students' daily lives: Because of the practicality of Indigenous knowledge, allow students the opportunity to reflect on how new knowledge is applicative to their lives or how it relates to previously taught information.

9 Employ active learning strategies: Most Aboriginal children learn more easily through multisensory, active, and relevant instructional techniques. Active learning also provides opportunities for students to have freedom of choice content, organization, and time limits.

10 Teach through stories and legends: Most Aboriginal values are taught through listening carefully and quietly to stories told by Elders. In some cultural groups, the whole winter season was dedicated to the sharing of stories and legends for the purpose of teaching values and lessons. As well, morals of stories were not overtly obvious to all learners, and it required repetitive listening to stories and time for reflection for learners to understand the lessons contained therein.

The lists of actions presented provide a basic embarkation point for educators who desire to assist the Aboriginal student in the public classroom. However, these teaching strategies only address the symptoms of student disengagement in secondary years. Instead, one must look deeper into the cultural contexts of our education system and begin to address the fundamental reason for the disconnection that Aboriginal students face in this foreign system.

Culture, Identity, and School

It has been the focus of every policy paper from the Indian Control of Indian Education policy document (NIB, 1972) to the Royal Commission on Aboriginal Peoples (Department of Indian and Northern Affairs [DINA], 1996) to employ education to reinforce Aboriginal cultural identity with Aboriginal youth. With greater cultural identity, an Aboriginal student feels more confident in herself and gains more self-esteem, resulting in a benefit to every aspect of her life.

Gotowiec (1999) examined the connections between ethnic identity and self-esteem among Aboriginal adolescents. This study found that Native youth had lower self-esteem than non-Aboriginal youth in the many aspects of esteem. The largest differences between the two groups occurred within academic self-concepts with Aboriginal youth having the lower scores. In addition, as Aboriginal identification increased, associations between group esteem and self-esteem became weaker, meaning those students who more readily identified themselves as Aboriginal had lower self-esteem scores. A recent study of American Indian high school students showed that self-esteem was strongly related to academic success, however both of these factors had no significant relationship with American Indian identity (Whitesell, Mitchell, & Spicer, 2009). The researchers stipulate that perhaps their measures of academic success were grounded in "mainstream U.S. cultural values, including high grades, outperforming peers, liking school, and planning for higher education" (p. 47), which conflict with some cultural values. Regardless, these studies demonstrate that Aboriginal youth who identify themselves as Aboriginal have lower self-esteem, and if their self-esteem or academic success increases, there is a greater chance that they will not identify themselves as Aboriginal.

One reason for this is the problem associated with belonging to a minority culture in public schools. In most cases, this "cultural conflict has given rise to a variety of emotional and social problems" (Cajete, 1999,

p. 137). It has also been described as the "Crossover Phenomenon" (Common & Frost, 1994) in reference to the "psychological turmoil of adolescents compounded with cultural value conflict in the school" (p. 142). Others describe this as "cultural discontinuity" (St. Germaine, 1995):

> Minority children, having been initially raised in a distinctive culture of their own, are often thrust into a school system that promotes the values of the majority culture – not those of their own. If the resulting clash of cultures continues, the minority child may feel forced to choose one culture at the expense of the other. (Cultural Discontinuity section, para. 1)

Hawthorn (as cited in Witt, 1998) defined culture as the "totality of behaviour, values, attitudes of a given group" (p. 261). This includes factors such as the organization of a person's life, the relationships the person forms with others and his or her environment, the methods for learning, and how discipline is implemented. As societies have distinct cultures, their schools perpetuate their cultural norms and assimilate their youth through its education system: "To put it differently, if we view culture as a system of knowledge, beliefs, values, attitudes, artifacts and institutions, then we may regard education as the intentional attempt to pass on such a complex whole from one generation to another" (Pai & Adler, 2001, p. 4). For Aboriginal students, cultural discontinuity occurs because their cultural, or world views, differ from the dominant culture permeating through the public school system. For educators, the necessity of recognizing students' cultural foundations is integral to the educators' ability to effectively teach to every child. Without this understanding, and its implications in lesson planning, it can produce student disinterest or alienation from the curriculum and the class, resulting in possible lower academic levels (Parhar & Sensoy, 2011). As Battiste (2002) indicates, "Canadian schools teach a silent curriculum of Eurocentric knowledge by the way teachers behave and the manner in which they transmit information" (p. 30).

The terms Euro-Western, Western, or European world views are used to describe the mainstream, non-Indigenous ontology, of how the world is perceived and defined, with the individual placed at its centre. Gonzales (2008) defines this perspective as a world in which "life moves around material needs; innovation is protected by individual property rights; truth is only possible through science; only what is tangible is real; materialism is the only thing that matters; spirituality is irrelevant;

and nature is an endless source of resources" (p. 299). In contrast, Indigenous knowledge is "a refusal to divide and compartmentalize in any reductionist way" and "is accompanied by adherence to recognizing all things existing in relation to one another" (Haig-Brown, 2008, p. 13).

In describing the epistemology of Indigenous knowledge, Castellano (2000) describes three sources of knowledge: traditional, knowledge that has been handed down from generation to generation; empirical, knowledge that has been gained from careful observation of the world around; and revealed, knowledge that is acquired through dreams and visions. These sources contain similar characteristics, in that the knowledge is "said to be personal, oral, experiential, holistic and conveyed in narrative or metaphorical language" (p. 25). Wilson (2008) states that "[Indigenous knowledge] is seen as belonging to the cosmos of which we are a part and where researchers are only interpreters of this knowledge" (p. 38). This cosmological aspect of knowledge can be described as an energy that is inherent in all of existence that provides animacy to all things in the universe: "If everything is animate, then everything has spirit and knowledge. If everything has spirit and knowledge, then all are like me. If all are like me, then all are my relations" (Little Bear, 2000, p. 78). Within these contexts, then everything in the universe, animate and inanimate, has inherent capacities for knowledge acquired through personal reflections and interpretations of ones' relationship to everything around oneself.

This relational construct may be construed as the basis of understanding an Aboriginal world view:

> In an Indigenous ontology, there may be multiple realities, as in the constructivist research paradigm. The difference is that, rather than the truth being something that is "out there" or external, reality is in the relationship that one has with the truth. Thus an object or thing is not as important as one's relationship to it. This idea could be further expanded to say that reality is relationships or sets of relationships. Thus there is no one definite reality but rather different sets of relationships that make up an Indigenous ontology. Therefore reality is not an object but a process of relationships, and an Indigenous ontology is actually the equivalent of an Indigenous epistemology. (Wilson, 2008, p. 73)

This concept can be summarized in simpler terms by an Elder, testifying at hearings to consider an injunction to stop the first James Bay hydroelectric power development in Quebec, "I can't promise to tell you the truth; I can only tell you what I know" (Castellano, 2000, p. 25).

The Elder's knowledge, his reality, is based on his interconnected relationships with his environment, developed over decades of empirical observation and inner reflection.

What is also important to understand about Aboriginal knowledge is that it is diverse, as diverse as the Nations that exist in the land. This is because each Nation developed a knowledge based on the unique ecosystems of its living environment, and that the Nation is "but one strand in the web of life" (Henderson, 2000, p. 259). As each ecosystem has its own unique properties, so will the "knowledge" that is learned from the people who live in it. Therefore, we must remember that there is not just Indigenous knowledge, but rather Indigenous "knowledges."

For practical and tangible purposes for educators, Hammersmith (2007, p. 4) summarizes common characteristics that notable Aboriginal scholars describe as Indigenous knowledge. They are the following:

- Practical common sense based on the teachings and experiences passed on from generation to generation.
- Knowing its home country. Indigenous knowledge covers knowledge of the environment – snow, ice, weather, resources – and the relationships among things.
- Holistic. It cannot be compartmentalized and cannot be separated from the people. It is rooted in the spiritual health, culture, and language of the people. It is a way of life.
- A traditional authority system. It sets out the rules governing the use of resources – including respect and an obligation to share. It is dynamic, cumulative, and stable. It is truth.
- A way of life – wisdom in using traditional knowledge in "good" ways. It means using the heart and the head together. It survives because it comes from the spirit.
- Giving credibility to people.
- Serving community needs and interests first.
- Having the potential to realize that the real contributions of local and traditional knowledge incorporate knowledge of the ecosystem.
- Relationships and a code of ethics govern the appropriate use of the environment.
- Recognizing that this code of ethics includes rules and conventions promoting desirable ecosystem relations, human-animal interactions, and even social relationships.
- Enabling traditional knowledge to articulate with non-traditional knowledge to form a rich and distinctive understanding of life and the world.

Gregory Cajete (1999) summarizes the core cultural values of Indigenous cultures across North America. They include the values of patience, open work ethic, mutualism, holistic orientation, time orientation, and practicality. These core values influence the cognitive processes that are prevalent in Indigenous students that influence how Aboriginal students learn.

The Canadian Council on Learning (2007) identifies a number of key attributes of Aboriginal learning, recognizing that this compartmentalization of the attributes is counterintuitive to the holistic nature of knowledge and learning from an Aboriginal world view. The attributes were listed as: holistic; a lifelong process; experiential in nature; rooted in Aboriginal languages and culture; spiritually oriented; a communal activity, involving family, community, and Elders; and an integration of Aboriginal and Western knowledge. A Western definition of learning focuses on changes in behaviour, or the potential of behaviour that is the result of life experiences (Hergenhan & Olson, 2005). From an Aboriginal perspective, learning was directly connected to relevance for individuals and their community. Its focus was on mastering context-specific skills (Klug & Whitfield, 2003), which contrasts starkly with Western educational environments that tend to teach through abstract, context-free concepts that are then expected to be applied to varying situations.

These differences in purposes of learning are reflected in how cultures view knowledge. David Peat (2002) describes knowledge for non-Indigenous peoples as a commodity that can be accumulated. For Indigenous peoples, knowledge must be gained through the activity of "coming-to-knowing" (p. 55), as knowledge is a living thing, with spirit and energy. To come to know knowledge, one must enter a relationship with it, so that "he or she is not only transformed by it but must also assume responsibility for it" (p. 65). Entering a relationship requires personal reflection and introspection, an ability to comprehend how the individual being will be affected and cause effect.

Integrating Aboriginal Perspectives and Knowledge

In a comprehensive review of factors that contributed to tangible progress for Aboriginal students, a number of First Nations schools in Canada were examined by analysing and comparing various factors to determine their influence on this success (Bell, 2004; Fulford, Raham, Stevenson, & Wade, 2007). Two of these factors included respecting Aboriginal culture and traditions to make learning relevant and secure and exceptional language and cultural programming. The transmission of culture through language is a traditional component of Aboriginal communities and tribal groups. As Marie Battiste (2000) writes, "Aboriginal languages are the basic media for the transmission and survival of Aboriginal consciousness, cultures, literatures, histories, religions, political institutions, and values" (p. 199). The Kativik School Board (2001), in Nunavut, designed and implemented a bilingual school program that was consistent with the school board's mandate of maintaining the Inuit language and culture. The result of this program showed that students who were instructed in their native language of Inuttitut had "significant academic and linguistic advantages" (p. 11) over students who did not participate in the program. In Rock Point, Arizona, schools taught all subjects in the Navajo language, so designed as to reinforce the culture and linguistic abilities of the students. Evaluations of this program by Dehyle and Swisher (as cited in Lipka, 2002) indicate that those students in the language program scored consistently higher than other Native students from the same reservations in reading, language, and math achievement tests. These examples clearly demonstrate the importance of including Native language within a school's curricula; however, the implementation and delivery of Native language immersion programs can be difficult and expensive for public schools.

Teacher Transformation

Even the integration of Aboriginal perspectives, issues, and culture into school curricula can be problematic for teachers with little or no understanding of these identified concepts. Kanu (2011) analysed the situations where Aboriginal culture was introduced in the school curriculum through James Banks' typology of teachers' engagement of inclusion towards multicultural perspectives (Banks, 2008). Banks identifies four approaches to inclusion beginning with the contributions approach which focuses on holidays and other discrete cultural elements; the additive approach, where content and issues are added to a non-modified curriculum; the transformational approach, where the structure of the curriculum is viewed from multiple perspectives; and the social action approach, where students make decisions towards solving social issues. Banks indicates that neither the contributions nor the additive approaches challenge "the basic structure or canon of the curriculum" (p. 47), although the last two stages are representative of the transformation approach that "changes the canon, paradigms, and basic assumptions of the curriculum and enables students to view concepts, issues, themes, and problems from different perspectives and points of view (p. 49).

In Kanu's (2011) research, the dominant-culture teachers used the additive approach when integrating Aboriginal issues, which "unwittingly contributed to this process of assimilation by allowing the curriculum topics, not Aboriginal issues/perspectives to remain at the centre of their teaching" (p. 173). It was the Aboriginal teachers who exemplified the transformational approach. As one Aboriginal teacher stated, "I am Aboriginal … I include my culture in everything I teach" (p. 172). The research also identified that in addition to a lack of knowledge, some teachers were not confident in their ability to introduce these subjects, or had little or no resources that addressed the topics. The teachers acknowledged the existing resources and activities within the school (i.e., pow-wows, Aboriginal student liaison worker) but most teachers strongly felt that more needed to be done to strengthen "what they called *teachers' professional efficacy*" (p. 191) to properly and effectively integrate Aboriginal perspectives into their classrooms.

To counter the diminished capacity of non-Aboriginal teachers to effectively integrate other cultural perspectives into their classroom, active strategies are available for educators who are prepared for a measure of introspection and self-reflection. Ladson-Billings (1995) coined the term "culturally relevant pedagogy" to distance itself from the pervading approach of cultural deficits as explanations for lower academic performance by minorities in North America. Culturally relevant pedagogy addresses the issue of student achievement but also allows students to confirm their cultural identity through the development of critical analyses of the obstacles and challenges that minorities face in schools. During the development of this positive pedagogical approach, Ladson-Billings observed broadly defined areas that exemplified educators who demonstrated behaviours connected with culturally relevant pedagogy. These teachers committed themselves to ensuring that all students succeeded academically and that they involved themselves within the student's community to instil community pride. They created "equitable and reciprocal" (p. 480) relationships with students to create a collaborative community of learners. These teachers recognized that knowledge was not static but was shared, viewed critically, and that their assessment of knowledge must be as varied as the manners in which students demonstrated their understanding and action towards knowledge.

During interviews with teachers who believed they practised cultur-ally relevant pedagogy (Parhar & Sensoy, 2011), some teachers experi-enced discomfort and challenges to their desired practice. When beginning the process, initial discomfort was perceived during ongoing critical self-reflection of the individual teachers' biases and prejudices. In addition, participants shared their challenges in implementing the practice of collaborative learning strategies either through their indi-vidual lack of knowledge of the strategy or the difficulty of its imple-mentation due to the physical space of the classroom and large class sizes. As well, participants discussed the constraints of the formal cur-riculum and the individualistic and competitive nature of assessment practices. Other challenges were the perception of an overall domi-nance of Euro-Western ideologies in the curriculum and its related re-sources, and direct and indirect resistance by administration to allow teachers the freedom to explore culturally relevant pedagogy.

Klug and Whitfield (2003) understood that to successfully address the lower academic achievement rates of American Indian children in schools, teachers must begin to recognize the importance of transform-ing personal pedagogy. They prescribe that teachers must become bi-cultural to ensure representation of both Aboriginal and Western cultures and values in the classroom. Using a model of cross-cultural interactions (Cushner, McLelland, & Safford, 1996), the original model incorporated three intercultural stages of (1) emotional arousal, (2) un-derstanding unfamiliar behaviour, and (3) personal adjustment. How-ever, based on the personal experiences of the authors working in Aboriginal communities, additional steps were included.

Concurrently, Klug and Whitfield's (2003) model conforms to a circu-lar process, different than the original linear process. The circular mod-el permits the educator to repeat the bicultural transformative process, to develop more thorough knowledge of Aboriginal culture. This recur-sive process forces the educator to re-examine previous learning in a continuous cycle. The stages are summarized as follows:

1 Learning stereotypes and prejudices of Native peoples. Individuals
  must understand that our current perceptions were developed
  during early childhood experiences, mostly influenced by parents.
  The young child would mimic these negative attitudes and ideas
  and his perceptions were not challenged until faced with a genuine
  opportunity to meet and interact with individuals from different
  ethnic groups.

2 Confronting our prejudices. As we begin to experience the other culture, there is a choice to abandon or retain existing preconceptions. A "fight-or-flight" response from the individual can result, based on confusion or anxiety when confronted by these new experiences. This response is driven by our need to protect ourselves in new environments.

3 Redefining our perceptions of Native American cultures. Educators begin to question their preconceptions realizing that these previous experiences were based on limited parameters. Teachers become empowered to find new resources and understand specific pedagogy that works with Aboriginal students.

4 Opening ourselves to new experiences. The educator begins to attend social events in the community to observe and experience Aboriginal cultural life outside the classroom and school. This process builds trust between the educator, the students and their families, and other members of the community.

5 Adjusting and reshaping our cultural identities. The educator examines the world from multiple perspectives and is able to "blend categories of information to explain behaviours and cultural norms" (p. 22). The teacher is no longer fearful to take risks, and has "learned to 'walk in someone else's moccasins'" (p. 22).

6 Our transformation as bicultural teachers. The educator has demonstrated genuine interest and willingness to work with each student and the Aboriginal community. The teacher becomes an advocate for all Aboriginal students inside and outside the classroom and has adjusted her teaching styles in recognition of cultural traditions of the community.

Another manner in which teachers can engage Aboriginal students is to partake in border crossing between the shifting, imaginary point between the counter-viewpoints and beliefs, between the colonized and the colonizer. We must recognize that our current education systems are derived from a Euro-Western perspective with its assumptions, narrative, and dynamics that allow power and privilege to reside outside the "other," those individuals whose ontologies and epistemologies run counter to the dominant paradigm. Henri Giroux (1992) introduces and describes border pedagogy as a recognition of the pedagogical, cultural, and social differences that define the "structure of history, power and difference" that speaks to a "need to create pedagogical conditions in which students become border crossers in order to understand otherness in its own terms, and to further create borderlands in which diverse cultural resources allows for the fashioning of new identities within existing configurations of power" (p. 28). Border crossing parallels Banks' (2008) engagement typology of both the transformation and social action stages. In these stages, the teacher provides the student with the freedom to learn about "the other" and is given the opportunity to act on the new knowledge in a manner of personal meaning. In these situations, the teacher becomes a culture broker. Aikenhead (2001) describes this process in relation to science education:

> A culture-brokering science teacher makes border crossings explicit for Aboriginal students by acknowledging students' personal preconceptions and Aboriginal worldviews that have a purpose in, or connection to, students' everyday culture. A culture broker identifies the culture in which students' personal ideas are contextualized, and then introduces another cultural point of view, that is, the culture of Western science, *in the context of Aboriginal knowledge.* (p. 340)

In this method, the Aboriginal context is the starting point in which concepts are introduced. The placement of Aboriginal knowledge as a foundation counters the standard educational practice of ignoring or minimizing Aboriginal students' cultural connections with the curricula.

Conclusion

The transition from a First Nations school to the public school system will be difficult for most Aboriginal students, filled with challenges and obstacles. However, it is the essential translocation of Indigenous knowledge from the sidelines of our curricula to a more central role that will allow Aboriginal students to see themselves as part of the school mosaic instead of as peripheral members. In this context, the emphasis is directly placed on the shoulders of educators to review and assess their practices and motivations to ensure the academic success of their Aboriginal students. The transformational journey will be full of obstacles, but no different from or more difficult than the challenges that the transitioning Aboriginal student faces when entering our classrooms. As Marie Battiste (2002) explains:

> To affect reform, educators need to make a conscious decision to nurture Indigenous knowledge, dignity, identity, and integrity by making a direct

change in school philosophy, pedagogy, and practice. They need to develop missions and purposes that carve out time and space to connect with the wisdom and traditions of Indigenous knowledge. They need to teach holistic and humanistic connections to local and collective relationships. They need to generate educational space that allows them to be challenging, caring, inspiring, and alert to their students' intellectual travails and attuned to their inner conditions. They need to make educational opportunities for students to come together in community with people who bring out their holistic better selves. Only when these changes in thought and behavior are made can we create an educational system that is a place of connectedness and caring, a place that honours the heritage, knowledge, and spirit of every First Nations student. (p. 30)

Through this journey, the educator will not only facilitate the successful transition of her Aboriginal students, but will also undergo a similar transitional experience. In this case, the educator will transition from maintaining a singular world view to celebrating and respecting the richness and value of Aboriginal world views.

NOTE

1   The word "Aboriginal" is used to describe the Indigenous peoples of North America. In Canada, the word Aboriginal collectively describes the original peoples of Canada that include First Nations, Metis, and Inuit. When known, the exact cultural group will be identified (e.g., Anishnaabe, Ute, etc.).

REFERENCES

Aikenhead, G. (2001). Integrating western and Aboriginal sciences: Cross-cultural science teaching. *Research in Science Education, 31*(3), 337–355.

Akos, P.P., & Galassi, J.P. (2004). Gender and race as variables in psychosocial adjustment to middle and high school. *Journal of Educational Research, 98*(2), 102–108.

Aman, C. (2008). Aboriginal students and school mobility in British Columbia public schools. *Alberta Journal of Educational Research, 54*(4), 365–377.

Aman, C. (2009). Gender differences and academic outcomes in British Columbia's K–12 aboriginal population. *Canadian Issues,* 45–51. Retrieved from http://search.proquest.com/docview/208674732?accountid=12792

Anderson, D., Horton, L., & Orwick, S. (2004). *Aboriginal teacher education: Issues for First Nations communities.* Retrieved from http://www.chiefs-of-ontario. org/sites/default/files/files/Aboriginal%20Teacher%20Education.pdf

Banks, J.A. (2008). *An introduction to multicultural education.* Toronto: Pearson Education.

Barber, B.K., & Olsen, J.A. (2004). Assessing the transitions to middle and high school. *Journal of Adolescent Research, 19*(1), 3–30.

Barman, J., Hebert, Y., & McCaskill, D. (1986). The legacy of the past: An overview. In J. Barman, Y.M. Hebert, & D. McCaskill (Eds.), *Indian education in Canada: The legacy* (Vol. 1, pp. 1–19). Vancouver: UBC Press.

Barman, J., Hebert, Y., & McCaskill, D. (1987). The challenge of Indian education: An overview. In J. Barman, Y.M. Hebert, & D. McCaskill (Eds.), *Indian education in Canada: The challenge* (Vol. 2, pp. 1–21). Vancouver: UBC Press.

Battiste, M. (2002). *Indigenous knowledge and pedagogy in First Nations education: A literature review with recommendations – A report to the Minister's National Working Group on Education.* Retrieved from Assembly of First Nations website: http://www.afn.ca/uploads/files/education/24._2002_oct _marie_battiste_indigenousknowledgeandpedagogy_lit_review_for_min _working_group.pdf

Battiste, M. (2000). Maintaining Aboriginal identity, language, and culture in modern society. In M. Battiste (Ed.), *Reclaiming Indigenous voice and vision* (pp. 192–208). Vancouver: UBC Press.

Baydala, L., Rasmussen, C., Birch, J., Sherman, J., Wikman, E., Charchun, J., …, & Bisanz, J. (2009). Self-beliefs and behavioural development as related to academic achievement in Canadian Aboriginal children. *Canadian Journal of School Psychology, 24*(1), 19–33.

Bazylak, D. (2002). Journeys to success: Perceptions of five female Aboriginal high school graduates. *Canadian Journal of Native Education, 26*(2), 134–151.

Bell, D. (2004). Sharing our success: Ten case studies in Aboriginal schooling. Retrieved from the Society for the Advancement of Excellence in Education website: http://dspace.hil.unb.ca:8080/xmlui/bitstream/han- dle/1882/8733/SOS2004.pdf?sequence=1

British Columbia Ministry of Education (BCMoE). (2000). *Aboriginal education: Improving school success for First Nations students.* Retrieved from http:// www.bced.gov.bc.ca/abed/

British Columbia Ministry of Education (BCMoE). (2010). *Aboriginal Report, 2005/06–2009/10, How Are We Doing?* Retrieved from http://www.bced.gov .bc.ca/abed/perf2010.pdf

British Columbia Ministry of Education (BCMoE). (2011). *Aboriginal Education: K–12 Funding.* Retrieved from http://www.bced.gov.bc.ca/abed/

Cajete, G.A. (1999). *The native American learner and bicultural science education.* (Report No. RC 021 798). Washington, DC. (ED 427 908).

Canadian Council on Learning. (2007). *Redefining how success is measured in First Nations, Inuit and Métis learning, Report on learning in Canada 2007.* Retrieved from the Canadian Council on Learning website: http://www.ccl-cca.ca/pdfs/RedefiningSuccess/Redefining_How _Success_Is_Measured_EN.pdf

Castagno, A.E., & Brayboy, B.M.J. (2008). Culturally responsive schooling for Indigenous youth: A review of the literature. *Review of Educational Research, 78*(4), 941–993.

Castellano, M.B. (2000). Updating Aboriginal traditions of knowledge. In B.L. Hall, G.J. Sefa Dei, & D. Goldin Rosenberg (Eds.), *Indigenous knowledges in global contexts: Multiple readings of our world* (pp. 21–36). Toronto: University of Toronto Press.

Chisholm, S. (1994). Assimilation and oppression: The northern experience. *Education Canada, 34*(4), 28–34.

Cohen, J.S., & Smerdon, B.A. (2009). Tightening the dropout tourniquet: Easing the transition from middle to high school. *Preventing School Failure, 53*(3), 177–184.

Coladarci, T. (1983). High-school dropout among Native Americans. *Journal of American Indian Education, 23*(1), 15–22.

Common, R., & Frost, L. (1994). A case study of Native and non-Native student progress in a public school system. In R. Common & L. Frost (Eds.), *Teaching wigwams: A modern vision of Native education* (pp. 137–165). Muncey, ON: Anishnaabe Kendaaswin Publishing.

Community Foundation of Canada. (2009). *Canada vital signs 2009: Research findings.* Retrieved from http://www.vitalsignscanada.ca/pdf/VitalSigns _Research_Findings_2009.pdf

Cushner, K., McClelland, A., & Safford, P. (1996). *Human diversity in education: An integrative approach* (2nd ed.). New York: McGraw-Hill.

Dehyle, D. (1992). Constructing failure and maintaining cultural identity: Navajo and Ute school leavers. *Journal of American Indian Education, 31*(2), 24–47.

Dehyle, D., & Swisher, K. (1994). Adapting instruction to culture. In J. Reyhner (Ed.), *Teaching American Indian students* (pp. 81–95). Norman, OK: University of Oklahoma Press.

Department of Indian and Northern Affairs (DINA). (1996). *Royal Commission on Aboriginal Peoples.* Retrieved from http://www.collectionscanada.gc.ca/ webarchives/20071115053257/http://www.ainc-inac.gc.ca/ch/rcap/sg/ sgmm_e.html

Fulford, G., Raham, H., Stevenson, B., & Wade, T. (2007). Sharing our success: More case studies in Aboriginal schooling – A companion report. Kelowna, BC: Society for the Advancement of Excellence in Education.

Gentle-Genitty, C. (2009). Best practice program for low-income African American students transitioning from middle to high school. *Children & Schools, 31*(2), 109–117.

Gilliland, H. (1999). *Teaching the Native American* (4th ed). Dubuque, IO: Kendall/Hunt.

Giroux, H. (1992). *Border crossings: Cultural workers and the politics of education.* New York: Routledge, Chapman and Hall.

Gonzales, T. (2008). Re-nativization in North and South American. In M.K. Nelson (Ed.), *Original instructions: Indigenous teachings for a sustainable future* (pp. 298–303). Vermont, VT: Bear and Company.

Gotowiec, A.P. (2000). Ethnic identity and self-esteem in Native adolescents [Abstract]. *Dissertation Abstracts International, 60*(9B), 4928.

Grigg, W., Moran, R., & Kuang, M. (2010). National Indian Education Study – Part I: Performance of American Indian and Alaska Native students at grades 4 and 8 on NAEP 2009 reading and mathematics assessments (NCES 2010–462). Retrieved from http://nces.ed.gov/nationsreportcard/pubs/studies/2010462.asp

Haig-Brown, C. (2008). Taking Indigenous thought seriously: A rant on globalization with some cautionary notes. *Journal of the Canadian Association for Curriculum Studies, 6*(2), 8–24.

Hammersmith, J.A. (2007). *Converging indigenous and western knowledge systems: Implications for tertiary education* (Unpublished doctoral thesis). University of South Africa, East London.

Hare, J., & Pidgeon, M. (2011). The way of the warrior: Indigenous youth navigating the challenges of schooling. *Canadian Journal of Education, 34*(2), 93–111.

Henderson, J.Y. (2000). Ayukpachi: Empowering Aboriginal thought. In M. Battiste (Ed.), *Reclaiming indigenous voice and vision* (pp. 248–278). Vancouver: UBC Press.

Hergenhan, B.R., & Olson, M.H. (2005). *An introduction to theories of learning* (7th ed.). Upper Saddle River, NJ: Pearson Education.

Iverson, M.K. (2007). The role of connectedness in American Native school success. *International Journal on School Disaffection, 5*(1), 16–21.

Kanu, Y. (2011). *Integrating Aboriginal perspectives into the school curriculum: Purposes, possibilities, and challenges.* Toronto: University of Toronto Press.

Kativik School Board. (2001). Kativik initiated research: *The basis for informed decision making.* Retrieved from http://www.kativik.qc.ca/sites/kativik.qc.ca/files/documents/11/KSBIR_e.pdf

Kavanagh, B. (2006). *Teaching in a First Nations school: An information handbook for teachers new to First Nations schools.* Retrieved from http://www.fnesc .ca/wordpress/wp-content/uploads/2011/05/Teaching%20in%20a%20 FN%20School.pdf

Kleinfeld, J., & McDiarmid, G.W. (1987). Teacher expectations as a political issue in rural Alaska schools. *Research in Rural Education, 4*(1), 9–12.

Klug, B., & Whitfield, P.T. (2003). *Widening the circle: Culturally relevant pedagogy for American Indian children.* New York: Routledge Falmer.

Ladson-Billings, G. (1995). Toward a theory of culturally relevant pedagogy. *American Educational Research Journal, 32*(3), 465–491.

Langenkamp, A.G. (2010). Academic vulnerability and resilience during the transition to high school: The role of social relationships and district context. *Sociology of Education, 83*(1), 1–19.

Ledoux, J. (2006). Integrating Aboriginal perspectives into curricula: A literature review. *Canadian Journal of Native Studies, 26*(2), 265–288.

Lipka, J. (2002, Jan.). Schooling for self-determination: Research on the effects of including Native language and culture in the schools. (Report No. EDO-RD-01–12). Retrieved from http://www.indianeduresearch.net/ edorc01-12.htm.

Little Bear, L. (2000). Jagged worldviews colliding. In M. Battiste (Ed.), *Reclaiming indigenous voice and vision* (pp. 77–85). Vancouver: UBC Press.

Mendelson, M. (2008). *Improving education on reserves: A First Nations education authority act.* Retrieved from http://www.caledoninst.org/Publications/ PDF/684ENG.pdf

National Indian Brotherhood (NIA). (1972). *Indian control of Indian education: Policy paper presented to the Minister of Indian Affairs and Northern Development.* Ottawa, ON: Author.

Neild, R.C. (2009, Spring). Falling off track during the transition to high school: What we know and what can be done. *Future of Children, 19*(1), 53–76.

Ontario Ministry of Education (OMoE). (2008). *Technical paper.* Retrieved from http://www.edu.gov.on.ca/eng/funding/0708/technical.pdf

Ontario Ministry of Education (OMoE). (2011). *Technical paper.* Retrieved from http://www.edu.gov.on.ca/eng/funding/1112/technical11.pdf

Pai, Y., & Adler, S.A. (2001). *Cultural foundations of education* (3rd ed.). Upper Saddle River, NJ: Prentice-Hall.

Parhar, N., & Sensoy, Ö. (2011). Culturally relevant pedagogy redux: Canadian teachers' conceptions of their work and its challenges. *Canadian Journal of Education, 34*(2), 189–218. Retrieved from http://search.proquest.com/ docview/881643998?accountid=12792

Patton Kennard, H. (2009). *Perceptions of school from students in a rural school environment*. Mississippi State University. Retrieved from http://search .proquest.com/docview/304941566?accountid=12792

Peat, F.D. (2005). *Blackfoot physics: A journey into the North American universe.* Boston: Weiser Books.

Pewawardy, C. (2002). Learning styles of American Indian/Alaska Native students: A review of the literature and implications for practice. *Journal of American Indian Education, 41*(3), 22–56. Retrieved from http://jaie.asu.edu/ v41/V41I3A2.pdf

Reyhner, J. (1994). Adapting curriculum to culture. In J. Reyhner (Ed.), *Teaching American Indian students* (pp. 96–103). Norman, OK: University of Oklahoma Press.

Reyhner, J. (1994). *American Indian/Alaska Native education.* (Report No. RC-019–552). Bloomington, IN: Phi Delta Kappa Educational Foundation. (ED369585)

Richards, J. (2008). *Closing the Aboriginal/Non-Aboriginal education gaps.* C.D. Howe Institute Backgrounder, No. 116. Retrieved from http://www. cdhowe.org/pdf/Backgrounder_116.pdf

Riley, T., & Ungerleider, C. (2008). Preservice teachers' discriminatory judgements. *Alberta Journal of Educational Research, 54*(4), 378–387.

Smith, J.B. (1997). Effects of eighth-grade transition programs on high school retention and experiences. *Journal of Educational Research, 90*(3), 144–152.

Statistics Canada. (2006a). *Aboriginal peoples in Canada in 2006: Inuit, Métis and First Nations, 2006 Census: First Nations people.* Retrieved from http://www12 .statcan.gc.ca/census-recensement/2006/as-sa/97-558/p16-eng.cfm

Statistics Canada. (2006b). *Aboriginal peoples in Canada in 2006: Inuit, Métis and First Nations, 2006 Census: First Nations people.* Retrieved from http:// www12.statcan.gc.ca/census-recensement/2006/as-sa/97-558/table/ t19-eng.cfm

Statistics Canada. (2008a). *Aboriginal peoples in Canada in 2006: Inuit, Métis and First Nations, 2006 Census.* (Catalogue no. 97–558-XIE). Retrieved from http://www12.statcan.ca/census-recensement/2006/as-sa/97-558/ pdf/97-558-XIE2006001.pdf

Statistics Canada. (2008b). *Aboriginal Peoples in Canada in 2006: Inuit, Métis and First Nations, 2006 Census.* (Catalogue no. 97–558-XIE). Retrieved from http://www12.statcan.ca/census-recensement/2006/as-sa/97-558/ pdf/97-558-XIE2006001.pdf

Steeves, L., Carr-Stewart, S., & Marshall, J. (2010). Aboriginal student educational attainment: A Saskatchewan perspective. *EAF Journal, 21*(2), 19–31. Retrieved from http://search.proquest.com/docview/896272331?account id=12792

Stout, D.M., & Kipling, G. (2003). Aboriginal people, resilience and the residential school legacy. Aboriginal Healing Foundation, Ottawa. Retrieved from http://www.ahf.ca/downloads/resilience.pdf

St. Germaine, R. (1995). *Drop-out rates among American Indian and Alaska native students: Beyond cultural discontinuity.* (Report No. EDO-RC-96-1). (ED388492).

Toulouse, P. (2010). *Walk in our moccasins: A comprehensive study of Aboriginal education counsellors in Ontario 2010.* Retrieved from http://www.oneca .com/oneca-resources-and-articles.shtml

Van Hamme, L. (1995). American Indian cultures and the classroom. *Journal of American Indian Education, 35*(2), 21–36.

Whitesell, N.R., Mitchell, C.M., & Spicer, P. (2009, Jan.). A longitudinal study of self-esteem, cultural identity, and academic success among American Indian adolescents. *Cultural Diversity & Ethnic Minority Psychology, 15*(1), 38–50.

Wilson, S. (2008). *Research is ceremony: Indigenous research methods.* Halifax, NS: Fernwood.

Witt, N. (1998). Promoting self-esteem, defining culture. *Canadian Journal of Native Education, 22*(2), 260–273.

PART IV

Secondary (Grades 9–12) to Postsecondary (College/University)

17 Secondary to Postsecondary Transitions

MICHAEL FOWLER AND GAYE LUNA

Researcher Susan Goldberger (2007) found that 48% of all students in the United States who begin at a 4-year college fail to earn a degree. Equally bleak are the statistics regarding high school preparedness for college; Green and Forster (2003) found that 70% of the freshmen enrolled in college in 2001 were high school graduates; however, only 32% of all students leave high school academically qualified to succeed at a 4-year college. The figures are even lower for specific ethnic groups: Only 51% of all Black students and 52% of all Hispanic students graduate from high school, and only 20% of all Black students and 16% of Hispanic students graduate from high school academically qualified to complete college work. These authors also reported that more than half of the students who manage to graduate from high school have not completed the minimal requirements needed to secure admission to a 4-year college or university.

Credit-based transition programs have gained attention as a means of facilitating high school success and college access (Bailey & Karp, 2003). Recent studies provide evidence that credit-based transition programs are very beneficial for high school students personally and educationally (Peterson, Anjewierden, & Corser, 2001; Puyear, Thor, & Mills, 2001), because from their inception these programs have focused on easing the transition and accelerating the passage of students through the education system into college. Although ease and acceleration are certainly important, of greater importance is the fact that preliminary evidence suggests that the credit-based transition strategy improves college preparation by motivating students to take a more rigorous high school program (Bailey & Karp, 2003; Boswell, 2001a; Puyear et al., 2001; Wilbur & Lambert, 1995). The literature (Adelman,

2006; Black, 1997; Gomez, 2001) provides favourable indications of high school students participating in credit-based transition programs.

High School and Higher Education Curricular Movement

Throughout the history of American education there have been many changes within the system that prepare students for college entrance and connect secondary and postsecondary education. The original pattern of the English school system is evident in the diverse American education system. The University of Oxford in England had no predetermined age for students to start university classes (Whitlock, 1978). In 1784, the New York Board of Regents specified that students would be admitted into classes based on previous knowledge, thus allowing early entry for some students. Concurrent enrolment of high school students in college courses in America was widespread in the nineteenth and early part of the twentieth century (Boughton, 1987).

In 1828, the Yale Report (see Lane, 1987) addressed the need for a classical high school curriculum to achieve college admission. The authors of the report, Yale President Jeremiah Day and Professor James L. Kingsley, felt that in spite of economic and social changes in the nineteenth century there was still a need to maintain a classical high school curriculum. Classical languages were central to this idea and thought of as an effective way to stimulate the intellect of an individual (ibid.). Up until the mid-nineteenth century, high school curriculum focused on an understanding of the classics, math, and science. A classical curriculum remained the main course of study in colleges until the turn of the twentieth century (ibid.).

Dr. Charles W. Eliot, President of Harvard University, during 1888 felt that the division of school into primary, grammar, and high school was artificial and hindered the individual student. Eliot believed that "the whole school life should be one unbroken flow from one fresh interest and one new delight to another and the rate of the flow ought to be different for each individual child" (Boughton, 1987, p. 10). To improve college admission, Dr. Eliot later led the Committee of Ten into proposing changes to the high school curriculum.

In 1894, Dr. Eliot published the overall findings of the Committee of Ten, who proposed to the National Council on Education a sequence of studies for high school students (Zelenski, 1988). The committee recommended the following subjects: Latin, Greek, mathematics, English, foreign languages, natural history, physical science, geography, history, civil government, and political economy (U.S. Department of Education

[USDoE], High School Leadership Summit, 2004). The Committee of Ten stated that the main purpose of secondary school was to prepare students for life and that college preparation was a less important goal; however, the proposed high school coursework also served as a recommendation for prerequisites for college admissions (ibid.).

American Junior College Concept

The original concept of the junior college is closely aligned with some of the ideas of credit-based transition programs. The goal of the early American junior college was to integrate the first two years of general college education with the completion of secondary education. Joliet Junior College, established in 1901, is the first junior college in America and the result of an arrangement between Joliet High School and the University of Chicago (Gutek, 1991). Similarly, the University of California at Berkeley was instrumental in the decisions of high school boards to start junior colleges in Fresno in 1911 and Bakersfield in 1913. These pioneering junior colleges were part of the secondary system; they met on high school campuses sharing facilities, staff, and students (Koos, 1946).

In 1918, *The Cardinal Principles of Secondary Education* (Department of the Interior/National Education Association) was issued by the Commission on the Reorganization of Secondary Education. The commission stated that the main purpose of high schools was to focus on health, citizenship, and commendable home membership, secondary to this focus was a command of fundamental processes (USDoE, High School Leadership Summit, 2004). Also, during the first half of the twentieth century, sizeable immigration impacted the schools as large numbers of school-aged children from immigrant parents entered the school system. Consequently, at this time in American history, a general studies curriculum was considered adequate for high school students and was designed to assimilate these new citizens into American society. The focus on general studies in high school pushed out the academic and career/technical disciplines (ibid.). The general studies model did not hamper the few college-bound elite students who were noticeably absent from the public high schools, choosing instead, to attend college preparation schools.

6-4-4 System: Linking High School and College

To meet the demand for a general studies model, public high schools began to improve articulation with the junior college. The "6-4-4 Plan" includes attendance for 6 years at an elementary school, attendance in a second unit of four grades at what is usually called a "junior high school," and then attendance in a third unit of 4 years at what is called the "junior college." The purpose of the 6-4-4 system was to link the last 2 years of high school with the first 2 general education years of college (Boughton, 1987). In 1931, Dr. William Proctor from Stanford University evaluated the 6-4-4 system operating at Pasadena Junior College (California) and found the academic programs to be similar to those offered by other institutions, except the programs covered a 4-year span avoiding duplication. He concluded that the students completing courses at Pasadena Junior College were adequately prepared to enter a 4-year college or university. Pasadena Junior College became the first middle college in America offering Grades 11 through 14. Later, Simon's Rock College in Massachusetts pioneered the idea of students taking college classes in an isolated setting away from regular high school and college students (Lieberman, 1976). Pasadena and Simon's Rock junior colleges helped set the stage for future special programs for high school students.

Postwar Boom in Education

Following the Second World War, college education became available to a much larger pool of students. Included in the benefits to veterans was the GI Bill of Rights that provided grants for college education. Attending college, once an opportunity restricted to the elite (wealthy, White, or gifted), became an option for a larger number of middle-class students and students with moderate abilities. New occupations that were a result of industrial expansion created a demand and increase in formal college training and a specialized and knowledgeable workforce. In addition, scientific research at the universities created hundreds of new special occupations. As a result, student populations increased in junior colleges as well as in graduate schools at this time (Pulliam & Van Patten, 2004).

Political Change, Education Movements, and New Mandates

The political landscape in America was changing because of three major happenings in education: Sputnik, the National Defense Education Act, and the Civil Rights Act. The Soviets launched a series of satellites called Sputnik in 1957, and this event stimulated a great deal of emphasis on the education of scientists and engineers in the United States (Rhoton, 2001). The National Defense Education Act of 1958 provided student loans for higher education, as well as support for curriculum improvement in secondary education. The Civil Rights Act of 1964 greatly influenced education by authorizing federal action against segregation in public accommodations, facilities, and employment (Strouse, 1997). The Civil Rights Act greatly improved opportunities for ethnic minorities, women, and the disabled. Research studies have pointed out that credit-based transition programs responded to learners of diverse backgrounds, ethnicities, and ages (ibid.).

High School Curriculum Change

In 1959, Dr. James B. Conant, the president of Harvard University, suggested a different curriculum for high schools. In his book entitled *The American High School*, Conant suggested the following curriculum for high schools: (1) 4 years of English, (2) three or four units of social studies (including 2 years of history and one of American social problems or American government), (3) one year of mathematics, algebra, or general mathematics, and (4) at least one year of science (biology or general physical science; cited in Zelenski, 1988). Later, in *The Comprehensive High School*, Conant (1967) expressed his belief that in order for students to study calculus and 4 years of a modern language, schedules should be arranged so that students could study in any one year English, mathematics, science, a foreign language, social studies, physical education, art and music, and one or more advanced placement courses (Zelenski, 1988). Recommendations, actions, and legislation by influential individuals, committees, commissions, and government set the stage for quality education and educational transitions.

Title I and Disadvantaged Students

The Elementary Secondary Education Act (ESEA) of 1965, initially endorsed by President Lyndon Johnson as part of his War on Poverty, was designed to concentrate federal funding on disadvantaged students. Title I was aimed at improving education for low-achieving students in poor schools and continues to be the focus of ESEA. The impact of Title I remains positive – millions of America's less fortunate students have raised their academic achievement as a result of this important federal funding (Jorgensen & Hoffman, 2003).

A Nation at Risk Report and Standards-Based Education

On 26 April 1983, the release of *A Nation at Risk* brought national attention to the major issues facing the education system in America. This national report highlighted disturbing indicators that placed American student achievement well below students of other industrialized nations (Gordon, 2003). In addition, *A Nation at Risk* showed that American students lacked higher-level thinking skills. Nearly 40% of students could not draw inferences from written material; only one-fifth could write a persuasive essay; and only one-third could solve mathematics problems requiring several steps (Gordon, 2003).

A Nation at Risk outlined solutions to the issues, specifically focusing on the high school curriculum. The National Commission on Excellence, author of *A Nation at Risk*, recommended that high school graduation requirements be strengthened. The following courses were recommended: 4 years of English, 3 years of mathematics, 3 years of science, 3 years of social studies, and one-half year of computer science. In addition, those students seeking college admission were strongly encouraged to also take 2 years of a foreign language (Gordon, 2003). This report greatly influenced society's view of the education system in the United States, and local school districts began to make changes.

The national curriculum movement is currently demanding more than the basic core of courses recommended in *A Nation at Risk*, to help improve academic preparation of college-bound students. The literature clearly supports the belief that students who enrol in rigorous high school courses improved their academic preparation (Adelman, 2006; Zelenski, 1988). In an article entitled "High School Academic Curriculum and the Persistence Path through College: Persistence and Transfer Behavior of Undergraduates 3 Years after Entering 4-Year Institutions," it was reported that the level of college students' high school curricula was strongly related to their persistence in postsecondary education (Horn & Kojaku, 2001). In another study, "Bridging the Gap: Academic Preparation and Postsecondary Success of First-Generation Students," it was discovered that among first-generation students who took rigorous high school courses or scored in the top quartile on their college entrance exam, their GPAs in their first year of college and remedial course-taking patterns were not significantly different from their non–first-generation peers (Warburton, Bugarin, & Nunez, 2001). Both studies showed that students who did succeed beyond high school academically took a more rigorous curriculum than the new basic core emphasized in *A Nation at Risk*.

Students should consider a rigorous curriculum to increase their chances of academic success. A rigorous curriculum includes 4 years of English, 3 years of a foreign language, 3 years of social studies, 4 years of mathematics (including pre-calculus or higher), 3 years of science (including biology, chemistry, and physics), and at least one Advanced Placement course or test taken (Horn & Kojaku, 2001).

A movement towards standards-based education began with *A Nation at Risk*; it became a national movement when the Improving America's Schools Act (IASA) was passed in 1994. IASA and the Goals 2000: Educate America Act I (1994) for the first time directed the focus onto the needs of all students, not just at-risk students. The IASA had three requirements for the states: (1) content and performance standards, (2) standards aligned by grade with assessments, and (3) an accountability system to identify school achievement based on the standard (Jorgensen & Hoffman, 2003).

In the mid-1990s, K–12 institutions shifted towards high-stakes standards-based assessments. During this time, most states established content standards and performance standards for all K–12 schools. Schools were now measured through the use of a secure testing system that gathered annual data for comparison. The development of standards-based assessment was evident by 2000 – 48 states received approval from the Department of Education for their content-standards development processes (Jorgensen & Hoffman, 2003).

No Child Left Behind Mandate

President George W. Bush signed into law the No Child Left Behind Act (NCLB) in 2001, which reauthorized the ESEA in striking ways. This new law certainly accentuated the impact of assessment in the lives of key stakeholders in the American education system. NCLB brought focus to the value, use, and significance of achievement testing for students in the K–12 system. With NCLB, a new era of accountability began. Local control, parental involvement, and an improved funding system all became cornerstones of the nation's education system (Jorgensen & Hoffman, 2003).

NCLB mandated that every state establish reading and mathematics minimum proficiency standards that every high school student was expected to reach by the 2013–14 school year and school districts were to submit annual reports on progress (Hess & Kendrick, 2008). NCLB standards required educators to evaluate expectations, organizations, administration, curriculum, instruction, and support services needed to meet required levels of proficiency (USDoE, 2004).

The standards and testing portion of NCLB comprised two-thirds of the federal accountability system. In addition, NCLB connected the test results to a varying degree of penalties for schools and school districts. Schools that did not achieve adequate yearly progress (AYP), according to NCLB, were subject to a progressive set of remedies, sanctions, and interventions to improve schools and to provide other options to parents of children who were in failing schools. A school that failed to make AYP in 2 consecutive years entered into "improvement" status. Improvement status required district and school officials to develop a school improvement plan as well provide students the opportunity to transfer to another school district. Schools that failed for 3 consecutive years had to provide free tutoring for students. Four years of failure initiated corrective action, which could range from curriculum reform to the extension of the school day. Finally, if a school failed to make AYP for 5 consecutive years, the district was required to reconstitute the entire school. District sanctions for not making AYP were similar in intent to those for individual schools, but eventually, failing school districts were subject to restructuring, including the option of a state takeover (Hess & Kendrick, 2008).

Another far-reaching development imposed by NCLB was the new mandate that all students be taught by a "highly qualified teacher." The highly qualified rule applied to core academic subjects. To be considered highly qualified, a teacher must have earned a bachelor's degree, received a valid teaching certificate, passed the state teacher examination, and possess a record of demonstrated subject knowledge. The law allowed individual states to determine how these parameters were to be met; consequently, many states exploited the "highly qualified" loophole and implemented these requirements differently (Hess & Kendrick, 2008).

No Child Left Behind was debated extensively and drew criticism across the political field. There were the following three major criticisms: (1) NCLB was founded on an idealistic and misdirected accountability system – one with uncertain expectations, an unclear identification process, and incentives and sanctions insufficiently connected to individuals; (2) school districts were not prepared to administer the complicated accountability system that NCLB mandated; and (3) highly qualified teacher provisions of NCLB were not effective and actually hampered the accountability system (Hess & Kendrick, 2008).

Funding of NCLB was an ongoing issue, although funding for the education programs in NCLB did increase after the law's passage, with the largest impact in the area of Title I funding. The most significant increase in Title I funding was from 2001 to 2006 when monies almost doubled; however, many states argued that the actions necessitated by NCLB cost billions more and created an unfunded federal mandate. Criticisms and funding concerns of NCLB have shifted the focus from a school student's performance to a new growth model that considers how much individual students are improving. State interest in these new growth models is motivated by the concerns from many schools that serve disadvantaged populations that have been labelled "improvement" status under NCLB (Hess & Kendrick, 2008).

Although No Child Left Behind focused on the K–12 system, it had an impact on the entire education landscape by focusing attention on achievement and on racial and economic achievement gaps while nationalizing the education debate to an unprecedented degree. In the process, it has upended traditional education politics and created new federal-state tensions. This federal-state tension has led to the latest development in the national curricular movement for K–12 education: the development of the Common Core State Standards (CCSS).

Core Standards Movement

The CCSS symbolizes a major improvement in the standards for mathematics and English language arts. These standards have been established based on research about what it takes for high school graduates to be ready for college and careers and utilizes state and international standards. CCSS helps to provide a clear and focused progression of learning for K–12 that provides all educational stakeholders the information they need for student success. The National Governors Association and the Council of Chief School Officers led the states in this voluntary effort. The CCSS provides a new opportunity for states to positively impact education polices and practices and to ultimately benefit all students with schoolwide reform (Achieve, 2010).

An important aspect of the CCSS is that the new standards are set at the college- and career-ready level: "They set a clear bar and communicate a shared set of expectations across the system: All students, ready for college and careers, by end of high school" (Achieve, 2010, p. 3). The CCSS emphasis on excellence increases outcomes and opportunities for all students and provides a foundation for a new broader system within college- and career-ready reforms. In addition, CCSS helps direct course requirements, assessments, data, and accountability (Achieve, 2010).

Community Colleges and Change

Community colleges have worked hard to meet the new demands of a changing society and were originally established to meet the following three needs: (1) offer a postsecondary option, (2) become the initial access point for postsecondary education, and (3) educate or service greater numbers of community college freshman and sophomore students preparing to attend colleges or universities (Cohen & Brawer, 2008). As one example of change, students attend community colleges for 2 additional years of training to acquire occupational skills not offered in high school. In addition, remedial education has become a focus at community colleges to assist with basic academic skills (Herr & Cramer, 2006). Community colleges have also become a means of improving one's position in society; students after attending a community college transfer to a 4-year college or university to gain skills for higher-paying professions.

Barriers and Obstacles to Transition

There continues to be a number of factors within society that impact a student's transition from high school to college. The next section of this chapter will examine high school completion, the high school senior slump, articulation between educational institutions, the Carnegie Commission on Higher Education Changes, and age-appropriate academics in schools.

High School Completion

Even though there have been recent curriculum changes and increases in students earning high school diplomas, many students are still not academically prepared for college. A 1998 study revealed weak areas in the high school curriculum. Two of the most striking findings were that 43% of the California State University freshmen failed the English placement test, and 27% of traditionally aged college freshmen in Ohio were enrolled in remedial courses (Breneman, Haarlow, Costrell, Ponitz, & Steinberg, 1998).

In addition, in 2000, the National Center for Education Statistics (NCES) reported a startling fact: Only one-third of college students who enrol in remedial reading in college earn either a 2- or 4-year degree, compared with more than half of the students who do not take any remedial courses to graduate. These data are a major factor signifying the need for more academically rigorous courses for college-bound high school students (NCES, 2000). Horn and Kojaku (2001) reported in "High School Academic Curriculum and the Persistence Path through College" that the distribution of beginning students enrolled in 4-year institutions across three levels of course taking included approximately one-third (31%) completing coursework no higher than core curricula, one-half (50%) completing mid-level curricula, and the remaining (one-fifth, 19%) completing rigorous curricula.

Because of the perceived benefits of a better life and financial success through obtaining a college degree, the increase in student pursuits for college has led to the development of the comprehensive high school. The main purpose of the comprehensive high school is to address a myriad of educational needs for students by reorganizing and teaching students according to their perceived intellectual abilities and college or vocational plans (Rubenstein, 2001). High schools are challenged to meet two divergent educational needs: college curriculum preparation and entry-level employment. Rubenstein suggested that these conflicting needs impact high school students who are preparing to enter college, because the high schools in balancing the two needs are deficient in their academic offerings for the college-bound students. As a result, and even though the high school diploma remains a prerequisite for college admission, most students who graduate have no guarantee that they are prepared for college-level work (ibid.). The literature suggests that often the content and structure of the college preparatory classes and assessment tests fail to prepare students for analytical writing and problem-solving skills (ibid.).

Senior Slump Factor and Impact

Students who take a rigorous high school curriculum are much better prepared for college; however, the absence of academic rigour in many high school programs is often exacerbated during the senior year, contributing to what is called the "senior slump" (Kirst, 2001). The senior slump affects senior students by lowering student motivation to complete high school with their best efforts. A review of high school graduation requirements in several states revealed that only five states required students to take more than 3 years of courses in any subject area other than English (ibid.). Once students reached their senior year, many had successfully completed all but one of the requirements for graduation. This important empirical finding becomes a major issue when thorough analysis reveals that often high schools have few other course offerings for students except weak academic electives. In *The Toolbox Revisited: Paths to Degree Completion from High School through College*, Adelman (2006) found that the strongest predictors of completion for a bachelor's degree are the intensity and quality of students' high school curriculum.

Research findings reveal that high school students are gaining admission to college much earlier; for some students, admission is gained even prior to their senior year (Kirst, 2001). For many other students, their academic performance in their senior year has little or no impact on their admission to colleges and universities. As a result, there is an increase in student apathy in their senior year, and many choose to slack off instead of gearing up for the rigours of more challenging college work. The message to students may be that the high school senior year is a time to relax and not take school seriously. According to the National Center for Education Statistics (1997) (as cited in McCarthy, 1999), only 43% of high school seniors reported themselves to be in demanding academic programs, compared with 45% in general education and 12% in career and technical education programs.

The following is a summary of recommendations by the National Commission on High School Senior Year (2000) (as cited in Conley, 2001, p. 29): (1) direct a shift in high school from just preparing students for college or work to preparing all students to live and prosper in an increasing complex interdependent world; (2) help students develop a learning plan that includes education, work, and service experiences to reach their goals; (3) guide students to develop strong connections with at least one adult who can assist with career explorations; (4) improve the collaboration between K–12 and postsecondary institutions; (5) develop a structured student-focused, quality work-based learning environment (including community service programs and internships); and (6) gather key stakeholders of U.S. high schools (e.g., parents, students, school leaders, postsecondary institutions, employers, and the military) to design and allocate responsibilities for Grade 12 improvement (ibid.).

David Conley (2007b) further developed a set of standards that identified university-level expectations regarding the knowledge and skills that high school students need to be successful in college. He identified the following four essentials for college success: (1) the cognitive strategies emphasized in entry-level college courses, such as analysis, reasoning, argumentation, and interpretation; (2) the content knowledge necessary to understand the structure of each academic discipline, such as the specific knowledge and skills developed by studying English, math, or science; (3) academic behaviours that enable students to cope with the academic demands of college, such as self-monitoring and study skills; and (4) the college knowledge necessary to understand how the postsecondary system operates, including an understanding of the process of college admissions, financial aid, and successful functioning in college.

Articulation between High School and College

Although the education system has been developing credit-based transition options and progress has been made, some problems still exist. There continues to be a disconnection of curricula and services between high schools and colleges. As early as the 1880s, the Massachusetts Teacher Association documented a lack of continuity between high school and college programs. As a result, a national panel was established to standardize the high school curriculum to coordinate secondary and postsecondary education (Stoel, 1988). Three significant factors have narrowed the gap between secondary and postsecondary education: (1) implementation of the College Board examinations, (2) standardization of admission policies for colleges and universities, and (3) reorganization of college entry status by the number of academic units earned in high school (Boughton, 1987).

The literature in the 1940s and 1950s provides extensive research that examined the lack of cooperation between high schools and colleges. Leonard V. Koos (1946), in his book titled *Integrating High School and College*, discussed curriculum change and a 6-4-4 Plan. The 6-4-4 Plan, discussed earlier, includes a 6-year elementary school; a second unit of four grades, usually called "junior high school"; and a third unit of 4 years called the "junior college." In addition to College Board examinations, standardization of admission policies, and reorganization of academic units earned in high school, reorganization of the junior high school and the advent of the junior college were two other movements behind the 6-4-4 Plan. Koos's research expands the history of these changes and movements flowing back to the early 1900s.

Koos (1946) cited research conducted in 1944 by Ralph W. Tyler, at the University of Chicago. Tyler found that different studies of mental abilities of students aged 15 and 16 showed that they are capable of performing college-level work (ibid.). Tyler concluded that there is little evidence to justify the proposition that students 15, 16, and 17 are too young to undergo the intellectual work of college. Finally, in the Chicago study, Tyler suggested that many high school students are mature enough to complete college work and are mature enough to receive rigorous mental stimulation (ibid.).

In the study *General Education in School and College* (as cited in Boughton, 1987), published in 1952 by members of the faculties of Andover, Exeter, Lawrenceville, Harvard, Princeton, and Yale, curriculum redundancy between the last 2 years of high school and the first 2 years of college was noted. Important research findings revealed (1) time and resources were lost as a result of academic redundancy between high school and colleges and (2) both high schools and colleges failed to instil in students a love for learning and to show students the value of education.

The Carnegie Commission and Restructuring Education

The Carnegie Commission on Higher Educationsuggested the need for structural changes in the American system of higher education. The commission suggested omitting one of the high school or college years, creating a 3-year bachelor's program, and awarding college credit for senior high school work. In 1971, the commission issued a report entitled, *Continuity and Discontinuity*, in which it criticized both age segregation and physical separation of junior colleges and high schools. The report recommended five common interests that needed improved articulation (Carnegie Commission, 1971, p. 81):

1 Making equal educational opportunities a reality
2 Developing non-overlapping curricula
3 Gaining public approval
4 Maximizing limited financial resources
5 Improving the welfare of education.

Such reports emphasize the need for partnerships that would provide for less repetition and a smoother transition from high school to college as well as promote educational reform and student success (Boswell, 2001a; see also, Helfgot, 2001; Orr, 1999).

The excessive overlap of material in high school and college has been noted as wasteful in terms of time and money. From Osborn (1928) to Blanchard (1971) to Greenberg (1991), duplication, overlap, and redundancy of curriculum between the last 2 years of high school and the first 2 years of college have been lamented. Critics have called for high schools and colleges to re-evaluate the curriculum and services that bridge the gap between high school and college (Boyer, 1987; Kleiman, 2001; Parnell, 1985).

In recent years, articulation agreements have begun to bridge the gap between colleges and high schools, focusing on the two issues of curriculum redundancy and the changing demographics of students. Research findings suggest that with college tuition increasing annually the opportunity to take college courses in high school, usually at little or no expense, is an economic advantage for students and parents (College Board, 2005a). Declining community college enrolment, low achievement test scores, high secondary school dropout rates, and an ill-prepared workforce have been contributing factors in the past for colleges to create and coordinate improved articulation with high schools (Mabry, 1988).

Some initiatives developed as a result of the findings that students could handle more intellectually challenging academic work in their later years of high school. Simon's Rock College, located in western Massachusetts, pioneered the idea of students taking college classes in an isolated setting away from regular high school and college students (Lieberman, 1976). Simon's Rock College emphasized that college is not for an elite group but for academically capable, motivated, and reasonably mature 16-year-olds (Goldberger, 1980). Both Pasadena Junior College (mentioned earlier) and Simon's Rock Junior College helped set the stage for future special programs for high school students.

Age-Appropriate Academics

Other strategies, suggested by studies addressing the issue of age-appropriate academics, are to provide opportunities for academically motivated students to enrol in college courses for credit before they finish high school and for high schools to offer dual-credit courses on their campuses through cooperative agreements with postsecondary institutions. Bailey, Hughes, and Karp (2002) suggested that dual enrolment can increase the intensity and rigour of the high school curricula and that by challenging high school students through these programs improved levels of college success could be achieved. This initiative to link secondary education to postsecondary education is a more recent phenomenon that shows some promise (ibid.).

Recommendations and Conditions for Successful Transition

Credit-based transition programs have grown substantially in the past 10 years (Bailey & Karp, 2003). Currently, 38 states have implemented credit-based transition programs (Boswell, 2001b) that are designed by community colleges and high schools to meet students' needs (Gomez, 2001), with the expectation that these programs would increase college enrolment and student success (Bailey & Karp, 2003). From their inception, credit-based transition programs have focused on easing the transitions and accelerating the passage of students through the education system into college. Educators hope that successful implementation of these programs will achieve the following five goals: (1) provide challenging educational opportunities, (2) improve college preparation, (3) promote a trained competitive workforce, (4) accelerate educational progress with significant financial savings, and (5) foster collaboration among high schools and colleges (Boswell, 2001a). The next section will examine the history of credit-based transition programs, credit-based transition models, and benefits of programs.

History of Credit-Based Transition Programs

It is difficult to date the beginning of credit-based transition programs because of the inadequate documentation and lack of studies regarding the early development of such programs. One study suggested that the original concept of eliminating the repetitive curriculum by awarding joint high school and college credit for a single, jointly recognized course be attributed to J.W. Osborn in 1928 (Puyear et al., 2001). The earliest actual credit-based transition program that can be documented is Project Advance at Syracuse University, developed when local high school principals and superintendents collaborated with the university staff to challenge high school seniors, many of whom had completed the requirements for graduation by the end of the eleventh grade. Project Advance has served as a model for similar programs in the following years (Syracuse University, 2005).

Although there are other colleges and universities that claim that credit-based transition programs originated with their faculty and staff, no documentation is available to support their claim. Educators in the state of Connecticut boast of credit-based transition programs that began as early as 1955 (Puyear et al., 2001). Also, Saint Louis University indicated that in 1959 they responded to pleas from the Saint Louis University High School to address the redundancy in curriculum between the last year of high school and the freshman year of college (ibid.).

These cooperative programs, known as credit-based transition programs, enable high school students to take college courses and earn college credit while still in high school (Bailey & Karp, 2003, p. 1). Supporters explained that properly designed and supervised credit-based transition programs could reduce senior-year boredom and even motivate senior students by maintaining their enthusiasm for learning. Wilber and LaFray (1978) suggested that cooperative programs would have the following four impacts: (1) eliminate unnecessary course duplication and college course remediation; (2) give students a taste of college before large financial or time commitment to college were made; (3) enable high schools and colleges to adjust their curricula to ensure a smooth transition between the two education systems; and (4) allow seniors the opportunity to earn college credit while still in high school (pp. 22–23).

Community colleges were originally established to meet similar student needs, although the literature shows no direct links between the community college system and the early creation of credit-based transition programs. The community college system continues to serve multiple missions that include career development of learners, improving students' basic skills, enhancing students' positions in society, and transferring to 4-year colleges and universities (see, e.g., Pluviose, 2008).

Credit-Based Transition Models

Credit-based transition programs diverge extensively in terms of content, location, the earning and granting of college credit, and student characteristics (Chapman, 2001; Robertson, Chapman, & Gaskin, 2001; Wilbur & Lambert, 1995). The literature separates credit-based transition programs into three broad categories of concentration: (1) singleton programs, which are separate college-level courses; (2) comprehensive programs that include most students' academic experiences; and (3) enhanced comprehensive programs that offer college courses to high school students as well as a support system to ensure success in postsecondary education (Bailey & Karp, 2003).

Singleton Programs

Singleton programs usually offer college-level courses to high school students as electives. The main objective of this type of program is enrichment of the high school curriculum, although a "secondary goal is to provide students with the opportunity for them to earn college credits so they may start their postsecondary education providing a 'head start' towards graduation" (Bailey & Karp, 2003, p. 13). Advanced Placement (AP) classes are the most frequent type of a singleton program (College Board, 2005a), and many dual-credit programs also follow the AP model (Bailey & Karp, 2003; Galloway, 1994).

Advanced Placement courses and examinations, developed in 1955, were the first organized national effort to aid students in the transition from high school to college. Advanced Placement courses and examinations use standardized tests to determine a student's proficiency in certain subject areas. Students scoring a 4 or 5 out of 5 on the AP exam earn credit for introductory college courses; currently, a score of 3 is considered a passing score by some postsecondary institutions where college credit is offered in specific subjects (Alliance for Excellent Education, 2008; College Board, 2005a).

For the American high school class of 2007, about 25% (or more than 2.8 million students) took at least one AP exam, with over 15% scoring a 3 or higher on at least one AP exam (College Board, 2008). As the College Board noted, "Over the years, schools with diverse populations have become increasingly involved in the Advanced Placement Program. From 1994 to 2004, there was a 222 percent increase in the number of AP Exam grades of 3 or higher among traditional underserved minority students" (2005b, para. 10).

Comprehensive Programs

Comprehensive programs usually require that "students take many, if not all, of their courses, usually during the last year or two of high school, under its auspices, either as an articulated series of courses spanning many semesters or as their entire curriculum" (Bailey & Karp, 2003, p. 15). There are several well-recognized comprehensive programs within the literature.

The International Baccalaureate (IB) program, offered by a non-profit organization, provides courses of study for high school students around the world. The IB program was originally organized in 1968, only shortly after the Advanced Placement program, and it has continued to offer a more comprehensive curriculum than the AP program. The IB is based on flexible and positive concepts of education, where students and teachers are motivated to participate in international cooperative projects that ultimately result in being evaluated against international competition (Peterson, 2003). For highly motivated students, the IB provides an academically challenging program of study. They take exams in specific subject areas and earn credit, at the discretion of the college, based on a cut-off score (International Baccalaureate Organization [IBO], 2004). As stated on their organizational website, the International Baccalaureate Foundation coordinates with 2,384 schools in 129 countries to offer the three IB programs to approximately 646,000 students (IBO, 2008).

Project Advance from Syracuse University was the first university to offer a credit-based transition program (Edmonds, Mercurio, & Bonesteel, 1998, as cited in Puyear et al., 2001). Project Advance originated in 1972, when local high school principals and superintendents collaborated with the Syracuse University staff to develop the program for high school seniors who had completed graduation requirement and wanted additional coursework (Syracuse University, 2005). Project Advance is offered in New York, New Jersey, Maine, Michigan, and Massachusetts, and it reaches approximately 8,000 students in 170 high schools. Syracuse University (2008) promotes their Project Advance program by stating:

> Students seeking a bachelor's (or four-year) degree who have taken SU courses through Project Advance typically complete their program within four years, as compared to the average of over five years for all students. This can result in less expense for students and their families. Some students can even complete their degree in less than four years. (para. 5)

The Postsecondary Enrollment Options (PSEO) Program, located in Minnesota, allows high school students to enrol in postsecondary education courses either on a part-time or a full-time basis and to earn both high school and college credit. In 2005, almost 19,000 students enrolled in college-level courses offered by the Minnesota State Colleges and Universities (2008). An audit of the program reported the following five findings: (1) ease of access to college is the most significant indicator of a school's participation rate; (2) most colleges have tougher admission requirements for PSEO students than for the regular college program;

(3) PSEO students receive higher course grades than other students; (4) most students enrol to earn college credit; and (5) high schools found problems with the program because of budgeting and scheduling difficulties (Minnesota Legislative Auditor, 1996). A follow-up study focused on PSEO program participants 5 to 10 years after graduation and their successes (Nathan, Accomando, & Fitzpatrick, 2005).

The Running Start Program, created by the Washington state legislature in 1990, is a comprehensive program in which public funding allows qualified juniors and seniors to take college classes and earn both high school and college credit. The program provides a challenging atmosphere for academically gifted students but also aims to provide for underachieving students who feel constrained by their high school's often-rigid structure (Running Start Program, 2008.). The State of Washington reported significant financial savings resulting from the Running Start Program (Gomez, 2001) as well as student academic success and favourable college graduation rates (Running Start Program, 2008).

The reauthorization of the Carl D. Perkins Vocational and Technical Education Act of 1990 helped to create additional credit-based transition programs. These programs, commonly called Tech Prep, were founded on coordination between high school and college courses in technical or occupational areas. The Tech Prep program of study is organized so that students take their first 2 years in a vocational program in high school and then complete their higher-level coursework in 2 more years in college (Bailey & Karp, 2003; Bragg, 2001). Tech Prep is targeted for students who might desire some college but are not likely to pursue a bachelor's degree.

Tech Prep's planned sequencing of technical courses came about through the Carl D. Perkins Vocational and Applied Technology Act of 1990, which was later amended in the School to Work Opportunities Act of 1994 (USDoE, 2008). A New York study reported that Tech Prep students were more likely to graduate from high school in 4 years than those students not enrolled in Tech-Prep programs (Brodsky, Newman, Arroyo, & Fabozzi, 1997).

Enhanced Comprehensive Programs

The most comprehensive of all credit-based transition programs are based at the college campus and focus on preparing low- or middle-achieving students for postsecondary education through academic rigour and support programs. This extensive support system, which delineates this credit-based transition program from others, includes counselling, application assistance, and mentoring for students. One type of enhanced comprehensive program is the Middle College High School, developed for underserved and underprepared students (Bailey & Karp, 2003; see also, Middle College National Consortium, 2008). One example of a Middle College High School is the College Now Program in New York that includes enrichment and remediation courses (Kleiman, 2001; see also, Middle College National Consortium, 2008). Also in New York, the LaGuardia Middle College High School has a program entitled "Excel," where most of those admitted are ethnically diverse students from low-income, single-parent households who begin a specialized curriculum in the eleventh grade. Terry Born (2006) reported that students apply to the program for three reasons: (1) the ability to save money and time, (2) increased flexibility in course requirements, and (3) more one-on-one contact with the personnel.

The Early College High School Initiative (ECHSI) is yet another example of a comprehensive program. This program is offered in 24 states and the District of Columbia, with a goal of opening 250 small schools to serve over 100,000 students annually (ECHSI, 2008; see also, Trevino & Mayes, 2006). The Bill and Melinda Gates Foundation and other philanthropic groups support an ECHSI objective of challenging and engaging high school students to graduate and advance to postsecondary education institutions (ECHSI, 2007).

The Maricopa County Community College District, in Arizona, initiated Achieving a College Education (ACE), a collaborative program designed to reduce dropouts and improve student transitions into college. This enhanced comprehensive program was first offered at South Mountain Community College; and a few years later, the same program, entitled ACE Plus, initiated a partnership between Glendale Community College and the Glendale Union High School District (Achieving A College Education, 2006). Student retention, student graduation, and postsecondary enrolment data were significantly higher for ACE Plus students compared with similar students who did not participate in the partnership program (Luna & Fowler, 2011).

Credit-Based Transition Benefits

Studies that empirically assess credit-based transition programs have become more frequently reported, and numerous qualitative studies have discussed reasons for adopting these programs at various educational levels, with themes of cost effectiveness, retention, and graduation most prevalent. Arthur Greenberg (1989) who has done extensive research on credit-based transition programs claims that there are benefits not only to the students participating in these programs but also to parents, to the high schools, colleges, and to society in general.

Cost Effectiveness

Boswell (2001b) highlighted key benefits of credit-based transition programs, emphasizing how they ensure that students are prepared for postsecondary education and how they also limit duplicative courses, resources, and time. This yields a savings not only for institutions but also for students and parents, as well.

Four additional financially related advantages for students include the following: (1) earning college credit prior to entering the university, (2) completing university at an accelerated rate, (3) providing financial benefits by taking college-level courses that are offered at a much lower rate through the high school, and (4) helping students graduate early from their university (Greenburg, 1989).

There is a notable savings in tuition costs for students who take part in credit-based transition programs (Greenberg, 1989). Parents can evaluate their children's abilities to do college-level work prior to making commitments of time and money (ibid.). Then, too, taxpayer dollars may be saved through fewer tax-supported remediation programs, particularly at the community-college level (see, e.g., Education Commission of the States, 2000).

Retention of Students

Educational retention refers to students' continued study until successful completion of a degree. Burr, Burr, and Novak (1999) described proactive efforts and strategies to anticipate and identify student needs and provide a seamless transition. Secondary schools constantly strive to retain their high school students, and as argued, "if the students who dropped out of the class of 2008 [in all states] had graduated, the nations economy would have benefited from an additional $319 billion in income over their lifetimes" (Alliance for Excellent Education, 2008, para. 3). Studies noted some credit-based transition programs with successful retention efforts that could be easily adopted for academically motivated high school students.

In 1985, about 20% of all colleges supported federally funded programs, such as Upward Bound, for disadvantaged students who lacked resources such as money and an accessible location to take classes (Cornett, 1986). The Upward Bound Program at North Texas State University focused on rural students in north Texas who were economically disadvantaged and had the potential to do college-level work; moreover, this program provided inspiration for students to study and learn, and thus students remained in high school (ibid.).

Bridge programs can also increase options for potential college-bound students, as well as help improve students' study habits and general academic readiness (Black, 1999). The first bridge program for students at risk was the Fenway Middle College High School at Bunker Hill Community College in Massachusetts. Fenway MCHS focused on personalized attention and care for students as individuals (Assar, 1991). In New York State, the Clarkson School Bridge Program required high school seniors to undergo an intensive 5-day orientation session before starting the program. The orientation encompassed a full experience that included students living on campus in their own dormitory under a strict set of rules. The Clarkson School Bridge Program was designed to give high school students access to a solid college math and science curriculum, and after completing the first year of the program, students could return to their own high schools. Kelly (1984) described the important benefits of increased retention and improved study skills when the students attended a 5-day orientation session.

Like Bunker Hill and Clarkson, the La Guardia Middle College High School program in New York offered bridge programs on their inner-city college campuses. The La Guardia College's program was designed to reduce the high school dropout rate, reduce the need for course remediation at the college level, and encourage more high school students to enter higher education. The purpose of offering the program on college campuses was so that the high school students had regular college students as role models. Both colleges focused on minority students who were at risk of becoming dropouts, with the attrition rate from semester to semester averaging between 1% and 8% (Cullen & Moed, 1999; Greenberg, 1989).

Graduation of Students

The literature suggests that students benefit academically from a more challenging learning environment. The LaGuardia Middle College

High School Program in New York reported that 95% of the students graduate from high school, and 90% go on to college (Kleiman, 2001). LaGuardia's success is especially impressive when you consider that at-risk minority students were the focus of the program. Clarkson School Bridge Program, with its orientation program and focus on college math and science, provided data indicating significant improvements in high school graduation rates (Bruno, 1990).

Researchers comparatively analysed 3.4 million student records in Texas, including five multigrade Tech Prep cohorts of totalling 247,778 students (Brown, 2000). Results for the comparison of the three subgroups of tenth through twelfth grade students involved in Tech Prep (mentioned earlier), showed these students were retained in high school more so than either of the non–Tech Prep groups, and Tech Prep students were more likely to graduate from high school (ibid.).

Additional studies indicate increased graduation rates and college attendance for high school students participating in credit-based transition programs. The Phoenix Think Tank reported huge differences between student success: 90% of credit-based transition students graduated from high school as compared with only 45% of similar students not in the program (Finch, 1997). Peterson et al. (2001) in a study connected with Salt Lake Community Colleges found 45% of credit-based transition students planned to attend college, and 56% of the students stated credit-based transition classes positively affected their decision to attend college. Stewart (2002) reported a significantly higher rate of college persistence by former credit-based transition students, almost 20% of concurrently enrolled high school seniors matriculated as regular college students following high school graduation. Then, too, other researchers indicated that high school students experienced the richness of college life by enrolling in credit-based transition programs (Bailey & Karp, 2003; Lords, 2000; McCarthy, 1999). Arriving on a college campus equipped with knowledge of what it takes to succeed in college seems to improve the likelihood of graduating from college.

Discussion

High schools continue to be challenged with how best to prepare all students for postsecondary education or vocational training. Stakeholders share a vested interest in meeting this current challenge and enabling students. Benefits for each individual are evident: College graduates earn more money, have better careers, engage in greater civic activities, and have an over all higher quality of life (Osterman, 2008).

The contrasted advantages of a college degree compared with high school diplomas only have widened over the past 60 years. U.S. Census Bureau (2009) statistics provide the following average yearly income comparisons based on educational attainment: (1) high school diploma, $30,303; (2) associate's degree, $42,163; and (3) bachelor's degree, $54,091. Extrapolating these same numbers over an average working career, the total income numbers are staggering: $1.2 million for high school education, $1.68 million for 2 years of college, and $2.2 million for someone with a 4-year college degree.

Credit-Based Transition Programs and Student Success

Studies have revealed that credit-based transition programs help high school students make a successful transition to college. These programs can serve to bridge the gap between high school and college by ensuring that students do not repeat high school coursework during their first year of college, and they can prepare students for the rigours of college-level work by providing challenging educational opportunities. Studies have argued that transition policies help high school students use their senior year more productively (see, e.g., Southern Regional Education Board, 2002), and the majority of students in credit-based transition programs have indicated that participation had a positive influence on both their decision (Burns & Lewis, 2000; Hudson Valley Community College, 1998; Peterson et al., 2001) and motivation to attend college (Allen, 1999; Bruno, 1990; Southern Regional Education Board, 2002).

Boswell (2001a) further noted that credit-based transition programs promoted a trained competitive workforce, accelerated educational progress with significant financial savings, and fostered collaboration among high schools and colleges. These programs are popular today. Results of a 2008 survey conducted by Phi Delta Kappa and the Gallup polling organization indicated that Americans agree that high school students should have the opportunity to receive college credit while in high school (PDK/Gallup Polls, 2008).

Research findings denote benefits to colleges in relation to student retention (Johnson, 1997; Levin & Levin, 1991), persistence in pursuing courses of study and staying in school (Horn & Kojaku, 2001), and improvement in graduation rates (ACE, 2006; Bruno, 1990; Kleiman, 2001) for those students who participate in credit-based transition programs. Other favourable impacts of credit-based transition programs include the potential impact on the senior slump. The participation in a credit-based transition program can serve to decrease senior students' apathy and assist them in gearing up for the academic rigours of more challenging college work. The inclusion of college coursework provided intellectual stimulation during the high school senior year and better prepares seniors for college (Greenberg, 1989).

A recent phenomenon is an articulation agreement that bridges the gap between college and high school. The opportunity to take college courses in high school provides an economic advantage for students and parents. Bailey et al. (2002) suggested that dual enrolment can increase the intensity and rigour of the high school curricula and that the challenge of these programs could lead to improved levels of college success for students.

College Readiness

Researcher David Conley (2007a) suggested that one of the major reasons that students fail in college is the gap between their high school experiences and college expectations. Many other issues exist including some fundamental differences between high schools and colleges in terms of courses, instructor expectations, and the accelerated pace of learning (Chait & Venezia, 2009). This is a complicated issue with respect to academic preparation, and there are numerous other factors that are not explored in this chapter, including peer and parental influences and social and emotional issues that relate to secondary to postsecondary transitions.

Four recommendations for closing this gap and improving college readiness are the following: (1) aligning high school curriculum and instruction with college expectations, (2) developing high-quality syllabi in all courses (high school and college), (3) implementing senior seminars (seminars increase the pace of work, provide student direct feedback, and require higher-level thinking to create a collegelike experience for high school students), and (4) adding the missing content to high school courses (Conley, 2007a).

Secondary schools and postsecondary institutions need to engage in a methodical process of preparing students to be ready for college. They should work collaboratively towards this goal through the following five activities: (1) adopting college-readiness standards and assessments, (2) increasing rigorous graduation requirements, (3) providing academic support, (4) ensuring course quality, and (5) effectively using credit-based transition programs (Chait & Venezia, 2009).

This chapter did leave open some areas for further investigation. First, although there are likely advantages and disadvantages to individuals in each type of credit-based transition program, a comparative analysis could provide key insight in finding the best program fit for a student, such as a singleton, comprehensive, or advanced comprehensive program. Second, the benefits that are highlighted in credit-based transition programs are no longer presumed but quantifiable, which will help encourage similar replicated studies in the areas examined: cost benefits, retention, and graduation. Although, numerous examples of successful credit-based transition programs were highlighted in this chapter, there is still a need for quantitative research studies to examine successful credit-based transition programs. Finally, it is hoped that this chapter will encourage a deeper and richer examination of all credit-based transition options.

Conclusion

Secondary education leaders can take an active role in the school improvement process by encouraging cultural change for their campuses through two key initiatives: (1) promoting a rigorous curriculum by encouraging more students to take Advanced Placement and/or dual-enrolment classes and (2) entering into credit-based transition agreements with local colleges to help academically motivated and prepared students to successfully transition to postsecondary institutions. Both initiatives allow educational stakeholders to positively impact the entire school community and very likely decrease high school dropout rates. In the final analysis, everyone gains from having students take a more rigorous course of study, graduate from high school, and successfully enter postsecondary education.

Credit-based transition programs for high school students are a valuable option, and evidence supports their use as a method to strengthen the quality and rigour of secondary curricula. No doubt the goals of increased high school graduation and college enrolment will remain prominent as administrators and teachers try to motivate and encourage high school students to remain in school and make a successful transition to college. Educational stakeholders make an investment in the success of individuals when transition programs are offered.

REFERENCES

Achieving a College Education (ACE). (2006). *Maricopa Colleges ACE program honored with national award*. Retrieved from http://www.maricopa.edu/news/index.php?story=79

Achieve. (2010, Aug.). *On the road to implementation: Achieving the promise of the common core state standards.* Retrieved from http://achieve.org

Adelman, C. (2006). *The toolbox revisited: Paths to degree completion from high school through college.* Washington, DC: U.S. Department of Education.

Allen, D. (1999). Desire to finish college: An empirical link between motivation and persistence. *Research in Higher Education, 40*(4), 461–485.

Alliance for Excellent Education. (2008, June 17). *The high cost of high school dropouts: What the nation pays for inadequate high schools* (Issue Brief). Washington, DC: Author.

Assar, K. (1991, Apr.). *Dimension of diversity: The Fenway Middle College High School comes to Bunker Hill Community College.* Paper presented at the Annual Convention of the American Association of Community and Junior Colleges, Kansas City, MO.

Bailey, T.R., Hughes, K.L., & Karp, M.M. (2002). *What role can dual enrollment programs play in easing the transition between high school and postsecondary education?* Washington, DC: U.S. Department of Education, Office of Vocational and Adult Education.

Bailey, T.R., & Karp, M.M. (2003). *Promoting college access and success: A review of credit-based transition programs.* Washington, DC: U.S. Department of Education, Office of Vocational and Adult Education.

Black, W.A. (1997). *Program assessment of the success of high school students concurrently in college courses* (Unpublished doctoral dissertation). Available from ProQuest Dissertations and Theses database. (UMI No. 972899)

Blanchard, B.E. (1971). *National survey of curriculum articulation between the college of liberal arts and the secondary school (Second Interim Report).* Chicago: DePaul University, School of Education.

Born, T. (2006). Middle and early college high schools-providing multilevel support and accelerated learning. *New Directions for Community Colleges,* no. 135, 49–58. http://dx.doi.org/10.1002/cc.247

Boswell, K. (2001a). Dual enrollment programs: Accessing the American dream. *Update on Research and Leadership, 13*(1), 1–3.

Boswell, K. (2001b). State policy and postsecondary enrollment options. *New Directions for Community Colleges,* no. 113, 7–14. http://dx.doi.org/10.1002/cc.3

Boughton, R.W. (1987). *The Minnesota 11th and 12th grade postsecondary enrollment options program: Is it changing the traditional structure of postsecondary schools?* Austin, MN: Council of North Central Community and Junior Colleges. (ERIC Document Reproduction Services No. ED282600).

Boyer, E.L. (1987). *College: The undergraduate experience in America.* New York: Harper & Row.

Bragg, D.D. (2001). *Promising outcomes for Tech Prep participants in eight local consortia: A summary of initial results.* St. Paul, MN: National Research Center for Career and Technical Education.

Breneman, D.W., Haarlow, W.N., Costrell, R.M., Ponitz, D.H., & Steinberg, L. (1998). *Remediation in higher education.* Washington, DC: Thomas B. Fordham Foundation.

Brodsky, S.M., Newman, D.L., Arroyo, C.G., & Fabozzi, J.M. (1997). *Evaluation of tech prep in New York state: Final report.* New York State Department of Education. Retrieved from http://web.gc.cuny.edu/dept/case/tech/EXECSUM.htm

Brown, C.H. (2000). A comparison of selected outcomes of secondary tech prep participants and non-participants in Texas. *Journal of Vocational Education Research, 25*(3), 273–295.

Bruno, E.M. (1990). *Follow-up study on guidance 7, college success students at Columbia College, 1989–90.* Lanham, MD: Educational Research Information Center. (ERIC Document Reproduction Service No. ED332743).

Burns, H., & Lewis, B. (2000). Dual-enrolled students' perceptions on the effect of classroom environment on education experience [On-line serial]. *Qualitative Report, 4*(1–2), 31 paragraphs. Retrieved from http://www.nova.edu/ssss/QR/QR4-1/burns.html

Burr, P., Burr, R., & Novak, L. (1999). Student retention is more complicated than merely keeping the students you have today: Toward a "seamless retention theory." *Journal of College Student Retention, 1*(3), 239–253.

Carnegie Commission. (1971). *Continuity and discontinuity.* New York: McGraw-Hill.

Catron, R.K. (2001). *Dual credit English: Program history, review and recommendation* (Unpublished doctoral dissertation). Available from ProQuest Dissertations and Theses database. (UMI No. 972899).

Chait, R., & Venezia, A. (2009, Jan.). *Improving academic preparation for college: What we know and how state and federal policy can help.* Washington DC: Center for American Progress. Retrieved from http://www.americanprogress.org

Chapman, B. (2001). A model for implementing a concurrent enrollment program. *New Directions for Community Colleges,* no. 113, 15–22.

Cohen, A.M., & Brawer, F.B. (2008). *The American community college* (5th ed.). San Francisco, CA: Jossey-Bass.

College Board. (2005a). *AP program materials.* Retrieved from http://www.collegeboard.org/

College Board. (2005b). *Increase of 15 percent the number of independent schools participating in the College Board's Advance Placement Program* (Press Release). Retrieved from http://www.collegeboard.org/

College Board. (2008). *The fourth annual APA Report to the Nation*. Washington, DC: Author.

Conant, J.B. (1967). *The comprehensive high school*. New York. McGraw-Hill.

Conant, J.B. (1959). *The American high school today*. New York. McGraw-Hill.

Conley, D.T. (2001). Rethinking the senior year. *National Association of Secondary School Principals Bulletin*, *85*(625), 26–41.

Conley, D.T. (2007a). The challenge of college readiness. *Educational Leadership*, *64*(7), 23–29.

Conley, D.T. (2007b). *Towards a more comprehensive concept of college readiness*. Eugene, OR: Education Policy Improvement Center.

Cornett, L.M. (1986). *Improving student preparation: Higher education and the schools working together*. Atlanta, GA: Southern Regional Education Board.

Cullen, C., & Moed, M.G. (1988). Serving high risk adolescents. *New Directions for Community Colleges*, *63*, 37–49. http://dx.doi.org/10.1002/cc.36819886306

Department of the Interior/National Education Association. (1918). *Cardinal principles of secondary education. A report of the Commission on the reorganization of secondary education*. Bureau of Education. Bulletin No. 35. Washington, DC: US Government Printing Office. Retrieved from http://tmh.floonet.net/articles/cardprin.html

Early College High School Initiative (ECHSI). (2007). *Overview and FQA*. Retrieved from http://www.earlycolleges.org/

Early College High School Initiative (ECHSI). (2008). [Home web site]. Retrieved from http://www.earlycolleges.org

Edmonds, G.S., Mercurio, J., & Bonesteel, M. (1998). *Syracuse University project advance and the advanced program: Comparing two national models for curricular articulation and academic challenges*. Syracuse, NY: Syracuse University.

Education Commission of the States. (2000, Nov.). *State funding for community colleges: A 50-state survey*. Denver, CO: Author.

Finch, P. (1997). *Intervention assessment: The status of concurrent/dual enrollment*. Phoenix, AZ: Phoenix Think Tank.

Galloway, J. (1994). Dual enrollment gets students where they want to go only faster. *Vocational Education Journal*, *69*(4), 13.

Goldberger, N. (1980). Simon's Rock: Meeting the developmental needs of the early college student. *New Directions for Higher Education*, (29), 37–46.

Goldberger, S. (2007). Doing the math, what it means to double the number of low-income college graduates. In N. Hoffman, J. Vargas, A. Venezia, & M.S. Miller (Eds.), *Minding the gap* (pp. 1–33). Cambridge, MA: Harvard Education Press.

Gomez, G.G. (2001). Sources and information: Creating effective collaborations between high school and community colleges. *New Directions for Community Colleges*, (113), 81–86.

Gordon, D.T. (Ed.). (2003). *A nation reformed? American education 20 years after A Nation at Risk.* Cambridge, MA: Harvard Education Press.

Green, J.P., & Forster, G. (2003, Sept.). *Public high school graduation and college readiness rates in the United States.* (Center for Civic Innovation-Education working paper). New York: Manhattan Institute for Policy Research.

Greenberg, A.R. (1989). *Concurrent enrollment programs: College credit for high school students.* Bloomington, IN: Phi Delta Kappa Educational Foundation.

Greenberg, A.R. (1991). ASHE-ERIC Higher Education Report (Vol. 5). *High school-college partnerships: Conceptual models, programs, and issues students.* Washington, DC: George Washington University, School of Education and Human Development.

Gutek, G.L. (1991). *An historical introduction to American education* (2nd ed.). Prospect Heights, IL: Waveland Press.

Helfgot, S.R. (2001). Concurrent enrollment and more: Elements of a successful partnership. *New Directions for Community Colleges,* (113), 43–49. http://dx.doi.org/10.1002/cc.7

Herr, E.L., & Cramer, S.H. (2006). *Career guidance and counseling through the lifespan* (6th ed.). Buffalo, NY: HarperCollins College.

Hess, F.M., & Kendrick, R.H. (2008). *No child left behind: Trends and issues.* The Book of the States 2008. Retrieved from http://knowledgecenter.csg.org/drupal/system/files/hess.pdf

Hoffman, N. (2003, July/Aug.). College credit in high school: Increasing college attainment rates for underrepresented students. *Change, 35*(4), 43–48.

Hoffman, N. (2005, Apr.). *Add and subtract: Dual enrollment as a state strategy to increase postsecondary success for underrepresented students.* Boston, MA: Jobs for the Future.

Horn, L., & Kojaku, L.F. (2001). High school academic curriculum and the persistence path through college: Persistence and transfer behavior of undergraduates 3 years after entering 4-year institutions. *Educational Statistics Quarterly, 3*(3). Retrieved from http://nces.ed.gov/pubs2001/2001163.pdf

Hudson Valley Community College. (1998). *College in high school evaluation report.* Troy, NY: Author.

International Baccalaureate Organization (IBO). (2004). [Program materials]. Retrieved from http://www.ibo.org

International Baccalaureate Organization (IBO). (2008). *Who we are.* Retrieved from http://www.ibo.org/

Johnson, J. (1997). Commuter college students: What factors determine who will persist and who will drop out? *College Student Journal, 31*(3), 323–333.

Jorgensen, M., & Hoffman, J. (2003, Aug.). *History of the no child left behind act of 2001 (NCLB)* (Assessment Report). New York: Pearson Education.

Kelly, G. (1985). The Clarkson School: Talented students entering college early. *Phi Delta Kappan, 67*(2), 291–294.

Kirst, M.W. (2001, May). Overcoming the high school senior slump: New education policies. In *Perspectives in public policy: Connecting higher education and the public schools* (pp. 1–35). San Jose, CA: Institute for Educational Leadership, National Center for Public Policy and Higher Education.

Kleiman, N.S. (2001, 12 June). *Building a highway to higher education: How collaboration efforts are changing education in America.* New York: Center for an Urban Future. Retrieved from http://www.ecs.org/html/offsite. asp?document=http://www.nycfuture.org/content/reports/report_view .cfmrepkey=10

Koos, L.V. (1946). *Integrating high school and college: The six-four-four plan at work.* New York: Harper.

Lane, J.C. (1987). The Yale Report of 1928 and liberal education: A neorepublican manifesto. *History of Education Quarterly, 27*(3), 325–338. http://dx.doi .org/10.2307/368631

Levin, M., & Levin, J. (1991). A critical examination of academic retention programs for at-risk minority college students. *Journal of Counseling Psychology, 31*(3), 356–362.

Lieberman, J.E. (1976). *Report on articulated programs coordinating secondary and post secondary institutional funds for the improvement of post secondary education.* Washington, DC: U.S. Department of Health, Education, & Welfare. (ERIC Document Reproduction Service No. ED139468).

Lords, E. (2000). New efforts at community college focus on under achieving teens. *Chronicle of Higher Education, 46*(43), 45–47.

Luna, G., & Fowler, M. (2011). Evaluation of Achieving a College Education Plus: A credit-based transition program. *Community College Journal of Research and Practice, 35*(9), 673–688.

Mabry, T. (1988). The high school/community college connection: An ERIC review. *Community College Review, 16*(3), 48–55.

McCarthy, C.R. (1999). Dual enrollment programs: Legislation helps high school students enroll in college courses. *Journal of Secondary Gifted Education, 11*(1), 24–33.

Middle College National Consortium. (2008). [Home web site]. Retrieved from http://www.mcnc.us/

Minnesota Legislative Auditor. (1996). *Postsecondary Enrollment Options program satisfies participants and needs little change.* St. Paul, MN: Author.

Minnesota State Colleges and Universities. (2008). *Postsecondary Enrollment Options program.* Retrieved from http://www.mnscu.edu/admissions/ pseo/index.html

National Center for Education Statistics (NCES). (2000). *Digest of education statistics, 1996.* Washington, DC: U.S. Department of Education. Retrieved from http://nces.ed.gov/pubs2000/2000031.pdf

National Commission on Excellence in Education. (1983). *A nation at risk: The imperative for educational reform: A report to the Nation and the Secretary of Education.* United States Department of Education. Washington, DC: Author.

Nathan, J., Accomando, L., & Fitzpatrick, D. H. (2005, Dec.). *Stretching minds and resources: 20 years of post secondary enrollment options in Minnesota.* Minneapolis, MN: University of Minnesota, Center for School Change, Hubert Humphrey Institute of Public Affairs.

Orr, M. T. (1999, May). *Community college and secondary school collaboration on workforce development and education reform: A close look at four community colleges.* New York: Columbia University, Teachers College, Community College Research Center. (ERIC Document Reproduction Service No. ED439761).

Osborn, J.W. (1928). *Overlapping and omission in our course of study.* Bloomington, IL: Public School Publishing.

Osterman, P. (2008). *College for all? The labor market for college-educated workers.* Washington, DC: Center for American Progress. Retrieved from http://www.americanprogress.org

Parnell, D. (1985). *The neglected majority.* Washington, DC: Community College Press.

Peterson, A.D.C. (2003). *Schools across frontiers: The story of the international baccalaureate and the united world colleges.* IL, Peru: Open Court Publishing.

Peterson, M.K., Anjewierden, J., & Corser, C. (2001). Designing an effective concurrent program: A focus on quality of instruction and student outcomes. *New Directions for Community Colleges,* (113), 23–31.

PDK/Gallup Polls of the Public's Attitude Towards the Public Schools. (2008). *College courses for high school students.* Retrieved from http://www.pdkpoll.org

Pluviose, D. (2008). More high-achieving students are choosing community college first. *Diverse Issues, 25*(1), 19–21.

Pulliam, J.D., & Van Patten, J.J. (2004). *History of education in America* (8th ed.). Columbus, OH: Merrill.

Puyear, D.E., Thor, L.M., & Mills, K.L. (2001). Credit-based transition in Arizona: Encouraging success in high school. *New Directions for Community Colleges,* no. 29, 33–41. http://dx.doi.org/10.1002/cc.6

Robertson, P.F., Chapman, B.G., & Gaskin, F. (Eds.). (2001). *Systems for offering concurrent enrollment at high schools and community colleges: New Directions for Community Colleges,* no. 113. San Francisco, CA: Jossey-Bass.

Rhoton, J. (2001). School science reform: An overview and implications for secondary school principals. *National Association of Secondary School Principals Bulletin, 85*(623), 10–23.

Rubenstein, M.C. (2001). *Transforming the senior year of high school.* Conceptual Framework. Retrieved from http://www.commissiononthesenioryear.org/Suggested_Reading/transforming.html

Running Start Program. (2008). *Running Star/Dual Credit Programs* [Office of Superintendent of Public Instruction, Washington]. Retrieved from http://www.k12.wa.us/SecondaryEducation/CareerCollegeReadiness/DualCredit/CollegeEnrollment.aspx

Southern Regional Education Board. (2002). *High schools to college and careers: Aligning state polices (College Readiness Series).* Atlanta, GA: Author.

Stewart, J.J. (2002). Concurrent high school enrollment program: Tracking subsequent college matriculation and persistence. *iJournal: Insight into Student Services.* Retrieved from http://ijournalccc.com/articles/

Stoel, C.F. (1998). *Programs offering college-level instruction to pre-college students.* Washington, DC: American Association for Higher Education, National Directory of School-College Partnerships.

Strouse, J.H. (1997). *Exploring socio-cultural themes in education.* Upper Saddle River, NJ: Merrill-Prentice-Hall.

Syracuse University. (2005). [Home web site for Syracuse University Project Advance]. Retrieved from http://supa.syr.edu

Syracuse University. (2008). *About us.* [Home web site for Syracuse University Project Advance]. Retrieved from http://supa.syr.edu/about/index/php

Trevino, A., & Mayes, C. (2006). Creating a bridge from high school to college for Hispanic students. *Multicultural Education, 12*(2), 74–77.

U.S. Census Bureau. (2009). *Historical income tables.* Retrieved from http://www.census.gov/hhes/www/income/data/historical/people/index.html

U.S. Department of Education (USDoE). (2008). *Tech Prep.* Retrieved from http://www2.ed.gov/programs/techprep/index.html

U.S. Department of Education (USDoE), High School Leadership Summit. (2004). *From there to here: The road to reform of American high schools* [Issue Paper]. Retrieved from http://www2.ed.gov/about/offices/list/ovae/pi/hsinit/papers/history.pdf

Warburton, E.C., Bugarin, R., & Nunez, A.M. (2001). Bridging the gap: Academic preparation and postsecondary success of first-generation students. *Education Statistics Quarterly, 3*(3). Retrieved from http://nces.ed.gov/pubs2001/2001153.pdf

Wilber, F.P., & LaFray, J.W. (1978). The transferability of college credit earned during high school: An update. *College and University, 54*, 21–34.

Wilbur, F.P., & Lambert, L.M. (1995). *Linking America's schools and college: Guide to partnership and national directory.* Washington, DC: Banker.

Whitlock, B.W. (1978). *Don't hold them back: A critique guide to new high school college articulation models.* New York, NY: College Board Publication.

Zelenski, J.F. (1988). Articulation between colleges and high schools: Something old or something new? A historical perspective 1828–1987. *Community College Review, 16*(1), 34–38.

18 Student Transitions from Secondary to College Mathematics

TRISH BYERS

Ontario college students have struggled with poor mathematics performance for as long as most faculty can recall. Colleges have responded by introducing assessment tests for placement and remediation strategies for incoming students, foundation mathematics courses, and pre-college programs (e.g., pre-technology and pre-business programs), to name a few. Many faculty anecdotally report high failure rates on college mathematics tests, primarily because of a lack of basic mathematics skills and high attrition and failure rates. The key factors cited as contributing to student difficulties in first-semester mathematics courses are (1) a lack of preparation for college studies and (2) an inability to transfer mathematics knowledge learned in secondary school.

In fall 2004, research results from the College Mathematics Project (CMP[1]) confirmed concerns for students who took a specific sequence of secondary mathematics courses to prepare for college technology programs: 65% of these students were considered "at risk," scoring a "D" or "F" or withdrawing from first-semester college mathematics (Sinclair, Schollen, & Orpwood, 2007, p. 34). However, less than one-quarter of this same cohort took a secondary course sequence developed to prepare students for college technology and achieved good grades, scoring "A," "B," or "C" (p. 34). These results verified college faculty concerns; in addition, the research demonstrated that college student achievement is dependent on particular secondary course sequences, that is, the curriculum between secondary and college mathematics needs alignment.

The Need for Skilled Postsecondary Workers

A critical examination of Ontario's workforce and educational trends reveals significant shifts to technology sector occupations. According to a report released by Colleges Ontario, future employment will require skills in technology "not yet invented," and new jobs will be influenced by "higher engineering and production standards, e-commerce, communications and quality, safety and environmental regulation" (2007a, p. 2). In 2004–05, 18% of all Ontario college graduates were from the engineering technology program sector (p. 2). There were 10,717 graduates from programs such as automotive, chemical/biological, aviation maintenance and flight, and power. Of these graduates, 3,931 were from electronic and civil programs alone, representing approximately 37% of the total number of technology graduates (p. 2). These occupational shifts are placing greater demands on colleges to educate individuals for roles requiring a high degree of technical expertise, the ability to work independently while applying critical-thinking and decision-making skills, and the ability to adapt to the changing workplace.

The College Mathematics Student

Interest in college mathematics achievement in the past 10 years is demonstrated in studies conducted nationally and provincially in Canada. The results of these studies identified a strong relationship between secondary school mathematics achievement and first-year pass rates (Association of Community Colleges of Canada [ACCC], 2007; King, 2003; Orpwood, Schollen, Marinelli-Henriques, & Assiri, 2010; Schollen, Orpwood, Byers, Sinclair, & Assiri, 2008; Schollen, Orpwood, Sinclair, & Assiri, 2009). These studies found many students who failed in college lacked adequate mathematics preparation. In general, these studies describe a diverse student population with a multiplicity of needs that colleges attempt to support. The research also highlighted the importance of bringing sound secondary school numeracy skills into college programs where strong mathematics and problem-solving skills are required.

The Association of Community Colleges of Canada conducted a survey in conjunction with Human Resources and Social Development Canada, in 2005, to identify the characteristics of first-semester postsecondary students, and describe their experience. In this survey, students were asked to self-report on academic skills typical of college success; they identified seven skills that would help them succeed in college (ACCC, 2007, p. 26): comprehension of language of instruction, writing ability, reading ability, mathematical ability, time management, note/test taking, and study skills. In general, this survey revealed that relatively low percentages of first-year college students viewed themselves proficient in such fundamental skills as reading (44%), writing (33%), and mathematics (25%). In sum, over one-third of Canadian college students do not consider themselves to have good mathematics skills, nor do they perceive college studies help to improve these skills (p. 45).

Additional research on college students illustrates the demographic, academic, cultural, and economic diversity of Ontario's college student body (Colleges Ontario, 2007b, p. 2). For example, almost two-thirds of all college applicants come from the workforce or other postsecondary institutions. Ten percent had at least one previous college credential, and 9% held university degrees. Culturally, 17% of the students were not born in Canada and 4% identified themselves as Aboriginal. In addition, 12% used "Special Needs/Disability Services" (ibid.).

Additional data describing the college applicant pool comes from the *Double Cohort Study* commissioned by the Ontario Ministry of Education (OMoE) through a series of four research reports: Phase 1 (2001), Phase 2 (2002), Phase 3 (2003; revised in January 2004), and Phase 4 (2005). Key findings from the Phase 3 report included a focus on characteristics and postsecondary direction of college-bound students from data collected via student interviews. First, in the double-cohort year 2003, fewer than 15% of college-bound students were "slightly less likely to meet college admission requirements" (King, 2003, p. 21) than in the previous year, 2002. In fact, "there was no clearly defined college/tech group of students" (p. 39). Finally, the report noted that 27% of graduates were taking a year off between secondary school and college studies (p. 56) for socio-economic reasons or to take time off from studies (p. 57).

These studies describe a student group with mixed educational backgrounds. Some students arrive at college directly out of secondary school, while others are admitted with work and life skills experiences, diplomas, and/or degrees. They are often challenged by a fast-paced curriculum, traditional teaching styles, a new social milieu, adjustments of living on one's own for the first time, and more (Pascarella & Terenzini, 2005). An increasing number of foreign students are being admitted to college programs. A significant proportion of students are not necessarily prepared for college studies, particularly in the technology area. In general, students are not perceived to be academically strong for college programs, and they may not be mathematically prepared to succeed in their program of studies. A disrupted student transition often results in failure or departure from a chosen career path. Only recently have issues related to student transitioning from secondary to college mathematics classrooms been investigated in Ontario (Byers, 2010; Orpwood et al., 2009; Orpwood et al., 2010; Schollen et al., 2008).

Mathematical Transitions

Many educators discuss the transition that students make between secondary and college mathematics; however, few have a working definition of mathematical transitions. To arrive at such a definition, mathematics knowledge and skills from secondary school need to be recognized as *continuities* that ease the student's understanding and learning of college mathematics. Research has identified potential *dis*continuities between traditional versus reform mathematics curricula at the university level leading to several significant barriers to student learning (Smith & Star, 2007). To explore the issues and strategies impacting college student learning, this chapter adopted the definitions suggested by Smith and Star (2000, p. 3):

- *Mathematical discontinuities*: differences between students' prior notions of what it means to think and act mathematically and how they are expected to think and act in their current classroom
- *Mathematical transition*: students' conscious experience of and responses to these discontinuities.

College Student Adjustments to Mathematical Transitions

The college classroom differs from the secondary classroom on a variety of levels; for example, language use, appropriate behaviour, values, and customs interconnect the student with the learning experience. As a result, students accommodate to differences in a college education through a variety of cognitive and social behaviours. Adjustments to these new demands account for the difficulties students encounter when learning first-semester mathematics; their resolutions are fundamental to student achievement. If student transition is not successful, failing or dropping out from a chosen career path is often predicted.

To understand a student's ability to transition into the first semester of college, the student's ability to learn and the classroom dynamics that contribute and/or stifle mathematics learning need to be unpacked. The components are revealed through student psychological and behavioural responses as the college experience unfolds (Pascarella &

Terenzini, 2005). This transitional process recognizes that students may be challenged as they follow the mathematics trajectory from one educational sector to another particularly when there is a mismatch in curriculum between educational panels (Smith & Star, 2007). These difficulties complicate learning, particularly when a student's career path evolves to require more complex levels of mathematical thinking.

Students entering college take on the role of a college mathematics learner and learn the skills and roles of a new vocation. Teaching styles, classroom norms, and faculty expectations challenge students' previous understandings of what a mathematics classroom and mathematics learning should be.

To apply problem-solving skills in contexts not previously encountered requires the use of heuristics, for example, the tenacity to learn, to avoid "giving up" quickly on a mathematics problem and self-regulated learning. There is little or no time available for college students to complete homework in class, and much work is completed outside the classroom. Students are expected to seek out assistance from the various supports that colleges put into place. Discussions with faculty suggest students lack these heuristics, and they seek out the available resources that provide the tools to succeed in mathematics learning.

In sum, the student is expected to read and understand the problem, identify the resources required to solve the problem, assess his or her own knowledge level and determine which resources are lacking, seek out those resources and learn them, apply them to the problem, and determine their success. If the problem is not solved, the process is repeated. Ultimately, this inability to employ these skills in a systematic manner, compromises a student's ability to transition to college mathematics learning.

Successful transitioning reflects students' acceptance of the college experience, advancement through the program of choice, and identification with the chosen career. It can also mean students makes personal choices about the direction taken in their academic career while remaining in the postsecondary education stream. This may involve switching courses and/or programs to find the right career fit.

Current research into mathematical transitions suggests the move from a secondary to a college mathematics environment may be difficult for students on a number of fronts. These issues are examined in the context of the research and strategies focusing on minimizing or eliminating these issues to reduce this gap.

Supporting Student Transition

As discussed, research conducted within the past 10 years on student transitions uncovers issues facing incoming college mathematics students. Once aware of these issues, educators, administrators, and students can strategize how to support the transition between secondary and college mathematics learning and implement these strategies for student success. Analysis of this interplay of issues and strategies can be examined as an integrated continuum as conceptualized and shown in Figure 18.1.

Some issues impacting college student mathematics success arise at the secondary level, some are the result of practices implemented at the college level, and others are the result of gaps and differences in curriculum content and frameworks related to each educational panel (Byers, 2010; Orpwood et al., 2009; Smith & Star, 2007). There are four major issues students may encounter when taking a first-semester mathematics course:

1 There may be a curriculum mismatch between secondary and college mathematics resulting in a curriculum model gap.
2 Students may be unprepared for college success due to taking a secondary pathway[2] or course sequence that does not prepare the student for mathematics learning in a particular college program – leading to a curriculum mismatch between secondary and college mathematics.
3 There may be discrepancies and omissions in representations – symbolic (e.g., language and notation), geometrical, graphical, and algebraic in secondary and college mathematics courses.
4 College assessment for placement could put potential demands on students.

Figure 18.1 also depicts strategies that focus on reducing or eliminating these issues for students. Again, some of these strategies lie in the realm of the secondary sector, some are the responsibilities of colleges, but most need to be implemented through secondary–tertiary collaborations where educators from each classroom learn of the other's content and practices. If these strategies are implemented in a coordinated way, they have the potential to reduce the issues impacting student transitions:

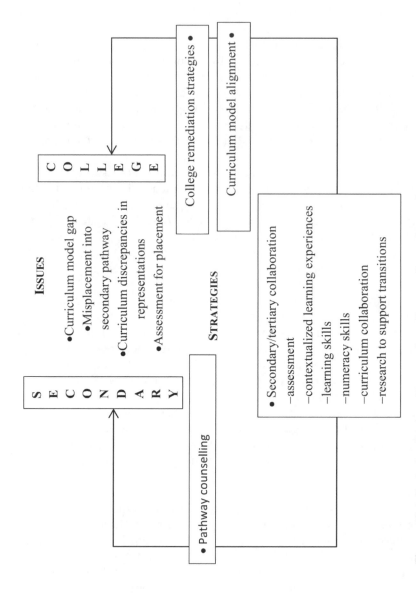

Figure 18.1. Reducing the transition gap for college mathematics students.

1 Secondary schools counselling can help students select the pathway needed for college program success.

2 College remediation strategies can support incoming students, and refocus curriculum and pedagogy to bring it in line with secondary classroom teaching.

3 Secondary schools and colleges can collaborate to help students prepare for the assessment for placement test; learn using contextualized learning experiences in secondary and college classrooms; learn mathematics learning skills; reinforce their numeracy skills; learn representations (e.g., language, symbols) used in college classrooms; and make a successful transition to college mathematics learning as the result of effective practices learned through research formulated with this goal in mind.

As these strategies are implemented, the distance between secondary and college mathematics learning decreases, resulting in a seamless transition for college students.

Transition Issues Impacting College Students

The Gap between Reform-Based and Traditional Mathematics Classrooms

Transitioning from a reform to a traditional mathematics environment may be difficult for students as evidenced by research conducted by Smith and Star (2007). This research examined calculus students transitioning among the following four curriculum panels: (1) secondary reform to university reform, (2) secondary reform to university traditional, (3) secondary traditional to university reform, and (4) secondary traditional to university traditional. The researchers found that the university reform classroom demanded that students come to the postsecondary classroom with strong skills in geometry and algebra, have a sense of "number," and be able to communicate mathematics through the use of tables of values, graphs, equations, and diagrams. Students were also expected to transfer learned representations of mathematical concepts to the university classroom to build on and extend their ability to think mathematically.

Analysis of the reform-based calculus course contrasted with the description of the traditional model, which had an emphasis on algebra alone. This emphasis on calculations increased for students since their knowledge base needed to be more comprehensive mathematically, extending beyond algebra. In the reform classroom, students needed to demonstrate an ability to work with mathematics on many dimensions. The results of this research described a curriculum mismatch, where students moved from a traditional algebraic-based curriculum to a reform curriculum that emphasized solving real-world, contextualized problems, and vice versa, as a source of student difficulties. Further examination revealed that student learning is potentially disrupted less when transitioning from a reform-based secondary school to a reform-based college curriculum (Smith & Star, 2007).

Current practices in the Ontario secondary classroom, implemented in 1999, were founded on research of the mathematics curriculum. This curriculum model provided students with broader access to all forms of mathematics, learning tasks that are complex, open-ended, and rich in real-life contexts, and opportunities to construct mathematical ideas through discovery and the use of mathematical tools (e.g., manipulatives, calculators, software) (Ross, McDougall, Hogaboam-Gray, & LeSage, 2003). In this model, the teacher creates a mathematics learning community and is a co-learner encouraging student-student interaction and discourse (ibid.).

However, college programs offer mathematics as a service course, which focuses on content acquisition. In this way, mathematics courses are developed to fulfil one of the following three goals:

1 Students are provided with a specific skill set required in other courses within the program; e.g., trigonometry taught in first semester will be used in other courses related to mechanical engineering, specifically drafting.
2 A mathematics course may be entirely application driven where few new concepts are taught but are applied in contexts related to a specific program area; e.g., knowledge of decimals, fractions, percentages, and exponents may be applied in a business program when studying annuities.
3 Goals are blended – students are taught specific mathematical concepts and apply these concepts to pertinent applications; e.g., students in a technical mathematics course learn and apply trigonometric concepts using vectors and vector addition.

As the engineering, computer, and business professions evolve, changes in the service mathematics curricula are warranted. However, as suggested earlier, there is enough evidence indicating that students are not prepared to handle a traditional service curriculum even though it is a major trend in postsecondary education.

Secondary Mathematics Pathway: Impact on College Students

IMPACT ON ACHIEVEMENT

In the first 3 years of CMP, preliminary analyses validated the concerns expressed by many college faculties about student mathematics performance, attrition, and failure rates. For example, in 2005–06, CMP research reported by the end of the first semester that 69% of the secondary school course MAP4C) (Foundations for College Mathematics, Grade 12) group was considered "at risk," compared with only 31% of the MCT4C (Mathematics for College Technology, Grade 12) group. Unfortunately, a low proportion (25%) of students had taken MCT4C, which was listed as a prerequisite to college technical mathematics, while more than half of the the incoming students took a course not recommended for college technical mathematics studies. Hence, students who took the secondary Grade 12 college technology (MCT4C) course in preparation for a college technical mathematics course were in a better position for success (Sinclair et al., 2007, p. 34).

By 2009, CMP was able to report on data analysed from all 24 colleges and 1,179 programs that had a first-semester mathematics course. In addition, CMP could compare data results from six colleges over a 3-year period and 11 colleges over a 2-year period. In general, student scores at these colleges did improve; however, improvement was small (Orpwood et al., 2010, p. 28). CMP results are demonstrating student achievement is improving since 2007. The proportions of students who earned an A, B, or C in mathematics during their first semester in college by year are:

- 2007, 64.6%
- 2008, 67.0%
- 2009, 68.6% (ibid., p. 23)
- 2010, 68.6% (Leclaire, 2011; YSIMSTE College Mathematics Project News, 2011).

The research results from the *College Mathematics Project 2009: Final Report* included the following information related to gender: female college students outperformed male students by 2:1 in all age groups even though there were fewer females taking college mathematics courses (Orpwood et al., 2010, p. 6). In addition, the research continued to demonstrate that taking a prescribed secondary mathematics course sequence and high achievement in these courses led to college "good grades." For example, 78% of students scoring over 80% in MAP4C obtained good grades in college (p. 32). In addition, students taking Grade 11 university/college (MCF3M: Functions and Applications) and MCT4C courses led to 70% of college students who had recently earned an Ontario Secondary School Diploma (OSSD) achieving good grades (p. 34). Students taking Grade 11 college (MBF3C: Foundations for College Mathematics) and MAP4C led to 55% of these students achieving good grades in college (p. 34). A positive outcome of the years of research was that more students were taking the Grade 12 mathematics for college technology course than in the past, and a revised mathematics curriculum in 2005 opened up a course sequence for students between Grade 10 applied and Grade 11 university/college mathematics courses with the outcome that a higher proportion of students taking this course were achieving good grades (66%) in college (p. 6).

Curriculum Discrepancies in Representations

Many educators would presume that the representations and language used when learning and doing mathematics are consistent, regardless of the educational arena and that secondary school prepares students for college studies through teaching the language, symbols, and representations that are used in the others' classroom. However, this is not always the case.

Motivated by the need to uncover possible curricular issues as potential sources of difficulties for students transitioning between education panels, Byers (2010) tracked and compared trigonometric representations from textbooks used in different Ontario secondary school course sequences with those used in the textbooks for many college programs. Textbooks are fundamental resources in teaching mathematics, according to Cirillo, Drake, and Herbel-Eisenmann (2009). Representations could be symbolic (e.g., language and notation), geometrical, graphical, and algebraic, and used to denote, suggest, or stand for something else (Byers, para. 16).

The research identified inconsistencies and gaps in representations between textbooks. For example, textbooks used in the secondary sequence that resulted in poor student achievement (e.g., MAP4C, as noted in CMP research results) used the following:

- The right triangle and primary trigonometric ratio representations
- Only one set of notational symbols
- Angles measured in degrees only.

Textbooks used in the secondary sequence that facilitated higher achievement in college mathematics (e.g., MCT4C, as noted in CMP research results) used the following:

- Many representations such as the right triangle
- Trigonometric ratios and functions
- The unit circle to develop the sinusoidal waveforms.

The standard form of the right triangle was not used extensively in textbooks from either course sequence.

The college textbook used the following (Byers, 2010, para. 28–30):

- Multiple representations such as vectors, primary and secondary trigonometric functions, and sinusoidal waveforms
- Radian measure
- The standard form of the right triangle extensively to teach trigonometric concepts
- Numerous symbols to identify sides and angles of triangles (e.g., Greek letters, subscripts, and prime notation).

The study also revealed that some representations, such as the unit circle, were omitted from the college textbook development of the sinusoidal waveform; yet, this development was evident in secondary textbooks (Byers, para. 31). Rather, the college textbook relied heavily on the vector representation at all levels of developing trigonometric concepts but the secondary textbooks did not (ibid.). In these ways, and others, there were "gaps and omissions in a coherent pathway for students learning trigonometry between secondary school and college" (para. 38). As a result, students learning trigonometry at college would find discrepancies, inconsistencies, and gaps between representations whether they were symbolic, geometric, tabular, or algebraic. With the number of discrepancies found between textbooks from different educational panels, the question exists: What other gaps or omissions in other curricular concepts exist between secondary and college?

When there are disparities in the representations, language, and symbols between secondary and college learning, students may encounter *cognitive conflicts, learning obstacles* (epistemological, cognitive, or didactic), and *semiotic conflicts*. As students advance their mathematical thinking, cognitive conflicts arise when they choose, often unconsciously, between previously held ideas and newly acquired ones (Tall, 1992, p. 495). This is particularly true when students are presented with a different language, or use of symbols or representations in college from those used in secondary school. Students may bring very different representations, notations, and symbols into the college classroom, and they may not be able to redefine them into the college contexts. The result may be a view of a particular representation and its application that conflicts with the instructor's.

Epistemological obstacles arise from the complexity of mathematics knowledge. For example, college students who have few representations in their mathematical toolkit would lack the resources needed to solve complex problems presented at college compared with those students who learned more representations in a particular course sequence.

Cognitive obstacles are caused by an ability to conceptualize or apply the mathematics. Once again, inconsistencies in resources learned in secondary school put students at a disadvantage for higher-level thinking at college. For example, the student who learns functions in secondary school is in a better position to conceptualize notions associated with trigonometric functions and sinusoidal waveforms.

Didactic obstacles are student misconceptions or misinterpretations of a mathematical concept that may result when teaching practices have not provided opportunities for or have impeded learning (Selden & Selden, 2001, pp. 240–241). Opportunities for success in learning and applying advanced trigonometric concepts in college are hampered if students are presented with too many discrepancies in representations. Unless teachers know what is in the others' classrooms, neither can prepare the student for college mathematics success. Each obstacle complicates learning, particularly when a student's career path evolves to require more complex levels of mathematical thinking.

Semiotic conflicts occur when students experience a "discordance, disparity or mismatch between the meanings attributed to the same expression" (Godino, Batanero, & Roa, 2005, p. 7). The secondary mathematics classroom may not provide the written and oral language and the symbols that students need to participate in the college mathematics classroom. When students arrive at college, many faculty spend little time teaching students specific mathematical terms, symbols, and representations, particularly in the contexts that are required of these mathematical tools. De Abreu, Bishop, and Presmeg (2002) confirm this: "Schools do not enter a process of negotiation which helps the learner to construct chains of signification, where concepts and mathematical objects can acquire multiple meanings, legitimated by the contexts in which they are used" (p. 10).

Representations and the symbols and language used in representations are dependent on a shared language with specialized syntax and semantic structure. Without this shared language, students are unable to internalize the external representations being taught and thus to develop the cognitive structures needed to learn a concept. They are also unable to take their own representations, translate them using mathematical language, and communicate them to the classroom community. Learning the language of mathematics is akin to learning the spoken language of a community with all its words, intonations, idioms, and gestures. According to Presmeg, "Even if a physical move is part of the experience, the major components of all transitions are mental ones by virtue of the need to construct new meanings" (2002, p. 213). Students who lack fluency in mathematical language at college face another barrier to learning new mathematical concepts, concept applications, and problem-solving activities. These can be subtle, hidden issues facing students as they transition into the college classroom.

College Assessment for Placement

Assessment testing for placement is a response to concerns by faculty that college incoming students lack fundamental mathematics skills (e.g., order of operations; the ability to move between fractions, decimals, and percents) needed to perform the complex tasks expected of college programs. To this end, many Ontario colleges adopted, or created, and administer mathematics assessment instruments as a means to determine whether a student has the requisite skills needed for the demands of a college program. Applicants, or those with admission acceptance, take this test before classes begin or within the first week of class. Test items may represent fundamental arithmetic competencies such as working with decimals, fractions, percentages, order of operations, scientific notation, ratio and proportion, complex fractions, radicals, and exponents. Other questions may represent fundamental algebraic concepts such as working with positive and negative exponents, simplifying expressions, algebraic fractions, isolating variables, factoring, and solving a two-by-two system of linear equations. Each institution would identify its own competency level or parameter for a passing grade.

The Ontario Colleges Mathematics Association (OCMA) developed three assessment instruments for college use in the early 1990s to respond to the particular mathematics needs of college programs: general, business, and technology. Many colleges were pre-testing incoming students, but the test instruments and procedures in use at the time varied considerably. The OCMA's goal was to design an assessment tool that could be customized to the needs of individual colleges. Funding shortfalls impeded progress in this venture and interest dissipated.

At the January 2006 meeting of the heads of mathematics (HoM), an informal survey identified many colleges using versions of the OCMA tools developed in the mid-1990s. With recent changes in the secondary school mathematics curriculum, there has been renewed interest in instituting the OCMA Assessment Test or other assessment platforms provincewide. For example, colleges are developing their own assessments and administering them on student admission or collaborating with school boards to assess students' level of mathematics competencies (Orpwood et al., 2010, pp. 44–46).

Many incoming students view taking this test with trepidation. They may or may not realize that progress through their selected program of study is impacted. If the student does not pass this test, she may be placed into a mathematics course to "hone" basic numeracy skills. However, this test and the subsequent placement into a remedial mathematics course can be an issue for students as they transition into first semester.

In many cases, this process is taken at the student's expense, both in time and money. It is a high-stakes venture for the student; it is also high stakes for the college. If the student cannot meet the challenge of a mathematics placement test, the college invests additional time, financial resources, and academic resources to support academic success. Placement testing, in all its myriad formats, represents an additional cost that colleges are reluctant to take on, particularly when millions of education dollars are spent in the elementary and secondary school systems to prepare students for postsecondary studies. Colleges are ill-prepared to spend these funds while operating in an environment where they are chronically strapped for cash.

Placement into a foundation or remedial mathematics course also impacts students socially; it does not guarantee that the student will be with other students from the selected program. In this way, a student may be considered marginalized from a peer group, hindering the development of and integration into a support group. Separated from colleagues, this same student may be expected to "catch up" in the next semester while the rest of the program cohort moves on in its studies, stigmatizing him or her as being less competent. Even if the test is not used for placement, poor test scores can impact the student psychologically. The message is clear: skills learned in high school are insufficient to succeed in college even though the criteria for college admission were met. Female students in programs such as engineering technology may have the perception of being less competent by a predominantly male peer group. Opportunities to mesh with colleagues become limited.

Strategies Supporting Student Transitions

Pathway Counselling for Successful Transitions

The Ontario Ministry of Education suggests pathways for students to take to prepare for the workplace, university, or college. The secondary school course sequences for college mathematics studies include two Grade 12 courses: MAP4C and MCT4C (developed specifically for admission into college technology programs). Unfortunately, some school boards are unable to offer MCT4C because of low student enrolments, for example. For this reason and others, some colleges accept students into technology programs with any Grade 12 mathematics course. CMP research initially identified only 25% of students entering technology programs with MCT4C, yet 69% of these students had "good grades" (Sinclair et al., 2007, p. 34). This proportion has gradually increased over the years as awareness regarding the success of students taking this course has increased (Orpwood et al., 2010, p. 6). However, many school boards still are unable to offer numerous mathematics courses to prepare students for multiple postsecondary options. The School College Work Intitiative [SCWI]–Eastern Ontario Regional Planning Team (2009) noted, "Given that approximately 67% of secondary students go to a destination other than university, it is critical that teachers are prepared to speak knowledgeably about the variety of secondary and postsecondary opportunities including college and apprenticeship programs."

To support successful transitioning, students need guidance to select the Grade 11 and Grade 12 mathematics course sequence that provides them with the greatest opportunities for success in college programs. This issue was discussed at the CMP deliberative forums, and the following recommendations were made (Orpwood et al., 2010, p. 18):

1 Colleges need to communicate to secondary school boards their admission requirements and those courses leading to success in specific program areas.
2 Secondary school boards need to increase the availability of mathematics courses, such as Mathematics for College Technology, to students via multiple formats.
3 Secondary school counsellors need to utilize CMP data when counselling students regarding the best mathematics course sequence required for success in specific college programs.
4 The Grade 11 and Grade 12 mathematics course sequences should be revised and simplified to enhance student choice and preparation for college studies.

College Remediation Strategies

College instructors have found students taking first-semester mathematics courses ill-prepared for the demands expected of them. As discussed earlier, many colleges have incoming students take an assessment course for placement into a specific first-semester course. Some colleges have introduced a one-year foundation program, which provides students an introduction into college studies. Informal surveys, formal research studies such as the CMP, and anecdotal evidence of poor mathematics achievement have shown that students who are weak in mathematics are also weak in communications skills. A pre-college program facilitates the transition that students need to make into college life while, at the same time, providing them with the academic requirements needed to be successful in their program. This program could also serve as an orientation for students to a chosen vocation giving them the opportunity to ascertain whether they are bested suited to their program of choice. In these ways, the transitional experience through first semester is supported.

Curriculum Model Alignment

College educational research supports instructional approaches based on psychosocial, cognitive-structural, and sociological learning theories (Pascarella & Terenzini, 2005). As a result of this research, institutions of higher education are taking up the challenge of mathematics reform: "Colleges have either added mathematics requirements for the first time or eliminated basic algebra courses from the core in favor of new classes focusing on mathematical modeling and problem-solving" (Wilson, 2000). In a similar way, Ontario colleges, collectively or individually, need to examine their mathematics courses in light of mathematics reform and alignment with the secondary mathematics courses to reduce curricular discrepancies. Discussion on mathematics reform and its implications for college mathematics is needed whether through learning communities, peer review literature, or professional organizations; and whether by individuals, departments, or colleges. For example, learning communities or study groups could be established among college faculty to develop curricula based on situated learning principles.

Review of activity in the United States, where curriculum reform at the postsecondary level has taken place, would provide a viable start in developing local awareness of mathematics curriculum reform. Support for curriculum reform can be found from the American Mathematical Association for Two-Year Colleges (AMATYC).[3]

Secondary–Tertiary Collaborations

Student transition issues may be reduced if the secondary and college sectors coordinate to support curriculum alignment. In particular, research by Smith and Star (2007) found student learning potentially to be less disrupted when transitioning from a reform-based secondary school to a reform-based college curriculum. In addition, curriculum change at the tertiary level is enhanced through secondary and college collaborations. According to Wood (2001), "As secondary school curricula change, reflecting increased use of technology as well as alternate pedagogical approaches, such as group activities, we need to listen to what the high school teachers have to say" (p. 96).

The formation of local consortia of high schools, colleges, and universities enables mathematics faculty at all levels to work in concert to improve mathematics education (AMATYC, 1995, p. 57). These liaisons between colleges and local secondary schools are critical to identifying issues related to mathematics education and sharing expertise. These liaisons can be instrumental in providing insights for teachers in both sectors regarding the college programs, the role of mathematics at the college level, expectations of college mathematics teachers, and the resources available for student assistance at college. College personnel would gain additional awareness of the dynamics of the secondary school classroom, current teaching methodologies, use of technology in the classroom, and implementation of the revised curriculum. Dialogue between the partnering groups would provide a forum to discuss when students tend to err in mathematics and where knowledge gaps may exist.

In its list of recommendations, CMP advocated for a K-to-career strategy – a "Provincial Roundtable on Secondary/Postsecondary Transitions." In its recommendation, this committee should be established by the Ministry of Education and the Ministry of Training, Colleges and Universities. The mandate of the panel would be able to deliberate issues related to transitioning to college, such as the myriad of admission, curricular, and assessment policies between and among secondary and college mathematics classrooms and recommend policies that would serve to facilitate a successful transition for college students (Orpwood et al., 2010, pp. 54–57). This initiative has been endorsed through letters from the presidents of Colleges Ontario and the Council of Ontario Universities to the Ministry of Education and the Ministry of Training, Colleges and Universities (College Mathematics Project Team [CMPT], 2011).

PROVIDING CONTEXTUALIZED LEARNING EXPERIENCES

Secondary pedagogy discusses the value of providing coaching, scaffolding, and fading; college educators can take the initiative to incorporate these strategies in their classrooms while capitalizing on the sophisticated mathematics skills presented by mathematics reform. Case and Gunstone (2003) found contextualized learning experiences contribute towards deeper meanings of learning in higher education classrooms (p. 57). College teachers can re-examine their curriculum in light of mathematics curriculum reform and situated learning principles to provide experiential learning opportunities for students to achieve a meaningful mathematics learning experience.

The need for secondary and college mathematics teachers to incorporate real-world examples and learning experiences into classroom teaching and assessment strategies was also recommended at the CMP deliberative forums. This goal can be achieved in a variety of ways, such as investing in professional development opportunities, sharing between educational panels examples of college-related mathematics activities to be used in secondary classrooms, and emphasizing college education for potential secondary school educators, to name a few (Orpwood et al., 2010, pp. 48–51).

REFOCUSING ASSESSMENT AND EVALUATION

Students entering college are given practice in secondary school assessments that prepare them to do the following:

- Work through mathematics problems similar to those presented in secondary school
- Use graphing calculators or spreadsheets to model data and extract information to analyse
- Demonstrate a problem-solving approach to a mathematical problem.

These practices are reflective of a non-traditional, reform curriculum model. However, college students are frequently evaluated using de-contextualized multiple-choice questions administered to students on-line or generated from computerized test banks provided by publishing companies. Yet, a higher-order thinking model that includes strategies to solve complex, authentic real-world mathematical problems is truly commensurate with college assessment and evaluation. Moreover, any assessment should evaluate how students think through the solution to a mathematical problem. According to Ollerton (2001), "assessment techniques must enable students to demonstrate not only *what* they have learnt but also *how* they learnt it" (p. 134, original emphasis).

The Ministry of Education published *Growing Success: Assessment, Evaluation and Reporting in Ontario Schools* (OMoE, 2010). This document describes policies and procedures to be implemented in Ontario's elementary and secondary schools pertaining to assessment and evaluation, and how this information is to be reported. The implementation of this policy provides an opportunity for colleges to consider assessment and evaluation policies at their institution.

For example, colleges could ease student transition into college by examining assessments and revising them to reflect the secondary curriculum and pedagogy. Colleges could share examples of college placement tests with secondary school boards for one of the two following purposes: (1) students could practice in preparation for the college test, or (2) students could take the test in secondary school with the results made available to colleges.

Fundamentally, colleges need to ask: Do the assessment and evaluation tools used in classrooms align with secondary practices? And, how will colleges interpret the revised assessment, evaluation, and reporting guidelines implemented by the Ministry of Education? Answers to these questions and others may help college educators determine whether the assessment and evaluation practices they use are accurate predictors of student achievement.

TEACHING LEARNING SKILLS

According to a recommendation from the CMP deliberative forums, secondary and college mathematics classrooms should incorporate learning skills, such as "self-discipline, study and time management skills, ability to work independently, and a personal sense of responsibility for learning" (Orpwood et al., 2010, p. 53), to support success in college and as effective learning tools in the workplace.

Effective study skills in mathematics and the development of heuristics in mathematical problem solving need to be reinforced at every grade of the high school curriculum with best practices identified. Strategies to explore how to develop a community of learning should also be examined to encourage students to take advantage of additional supports outside of the classroom. Colleges need to continue with faculty dialogues to develop strategies to assist students within their own departments. Publishers could include study skills sections in mathematics texts that support students' learning in a meaningful way.

REINFORCING NUMERACY SKILLS

College educators need to find a balance between the secondary and the college curricula to reinforce foundation skills while teaching higher-level thinking with rich learning tasks. College teachers may need to spend more time in the classroom teaching basic skills such as order of operations, working with decimals and percentages, ratio and proportion, and algebra. There needs to be a focus on the big ideas in mathematics with dissemination of research results on curriculum and pedagogy (e.g., ratio and proportion) (CMPT, 2011; Orpwood et al., 2010, pp. 51–53).

CURRICULUM COLLABORATION

Secondary school and college educators can collaborate to familiarize themselves with the language, symbols, and representations used in the other's teaching. College teachers can then build on what is familiar to the student, thereby easing the cognitive conflicts and mathematical discontinuities students may be experiencing in the classroom:

> Rather than deal initially with formal definitions that contain elements unfamiliar to the learner, it is preferable to attempt to find an approach

that builds on concepts that have the dual role of being familiar to the students and providing the basis for later mathematical development. (Tall, 1992, p. 497)

Knowledge may be nonsensical for the student if the teacher does not make the connections between a secondary and college mathematics lesson (Tall, p. 496). Educators need to clarify underlying, unspoken assumptions by collaborating with students to identify ideas familiar to students. Faculty need to recognize transitioning as a massive process of cognitive restructuring (p. 508). Acknowledging transitioning involves acknowledging the differences in thought processes expected in secondary school versus college studies.

RESEARCH TO SUPPORT STUDENT TRANSITIONS
Additional studies in the area of college mathematics transitions are warranted. A key area requiring investigation is college students' perceptions of their mathematics learning as they make the transition from the secondary model of learning to a more traditional, college model. Research investigating curricular differences (e.g., Byers, 2010) is needed with the results shared in the educational community; such research will help increase awareness and support curricular change among educators, administrators, and stakeholders. Research involving educational change is needed to investigate and monitor how curriculum reform in mathematics is unfolding in both the secondary school and college sectors. Finally, research is needed to examine student achievement in light of the changes made in each educational sector. Only then will educators know whether these changes are, in fact, providing a seamless transition for college mathematics learning.

Conclusion

Moving from one educational panel to another places students in a transitional space (Wood, 2001). This symbolic space in first-semester college mathematics is a potential source of cognitive conflicts and social adjustments threatening student achievement. The transition period is a time of adjustment when student difficulties in the first semester can limit a mathematics student's academic potential. Unfortunately, poor mathematics achievement, and high failure and attrition rates, are often the outcome of the student's inability to navigate the college mathematics transition gap.

Poor success rates in college mathematics courses are clear indicators for changes in curriculum, pedagogy, and assessment. These issues have been ignored for too long. The College Mathematics Project has made numerous recommendations to educators, administrators, counsellors, and the public in general (e.g., parents and students) to address these issues. However, these recommendations need to be implemented in a consistent and collaborative way. Responding to these changes involves commitment from faculty and support from college administrators. Only then will the gap between secondary and college mathematics teaching and learning be reduced and a seamless transition for college students be achieved.

APPENDIX TO CH. 18: THE COLLEGE
MATHEMATICS PROJECT – AN OVERVIEW[4]

Is there a relationship between student achievement in a selected secondary mathematics course sequence and that student's performance in first-semester college mathematics? Until 2004, there was no proven answer to this question in Ontario. The College Mathematics Project (CMP), in collaboration with the York/Seneca Institute for Mathematics, Science, and Technology Education (YSIMSTE) and Seneca College of Applied Arts and Technology, conducted research to answer this question and others pertaining to first-semester college mathematics achievement. This was the first study in Ontario to examine first-semester college students' scores in general and look for a relationship between these scores and their secondary mathematics course sequence. The research project has continued more formally since 2007 and now includes results from an analysis of all incoming college students and involves all district school boards in Ontario.

Historical Background to CMP

Results of the initial CMP study in 2004 involving students from only one community college prompted interest to expand the research to other colleges. This initiative was supported by the School College Work Initiative (SCWI), an Ontario government initiative. Its mandate is to "assist in creating a seamless transition for students from secondary school to college." With funding from the SCWI in 2005 and 2006, CMP expanded its research from one to six colleges to relate first-semester college technology student achievement with respect to their secondary mathematics courses. These pilot projects focused on developing and refining details of the study and analysis techniques (Orpwood et al., 2010, p. 9). Collaborative forums were also held to bring secondary and college teachers, administrators, guidance counsellors, and other stakeholders together. The goal of these forums was to discuss the research findings, share classroom and student experiences, and share practices designed to improve secondary and college mathematics teaching and learning (p. 9).

In 2007, a full-scale study was initiated with six community colleges and collaborating district school boards; in 2008, 50,000 student records at 11 colleges were analysed; and, in 2009, nearly 80,000 students at 24 colleges and 72 school boards were included in the study (Orpwood et al., 2010, p. 9). Student scores from all college programs and not just technology programs were analysed. Collaborative forums were held in all districts across the province. The latest study, CMP 2011, examined records of almost 95 000 students who were entering college programs in 2010. Since 2008, the CMP research study has been co-funded by the Ontario Ministry of Education and the Ontario Ministry of Colleges, Training and Universities (ibid.). It has support from a steering committee consisting of members from the mathematics education community whose mandate is to provide guidance and direction to the project (p. 10). Emerging trends based on three years of data were identified in this study.

CMP Goals

From its inception, the CMP research study was fulfilling a much-needed role in Ontario's mathematics education sector. No link existed between the Ministry of Education and the Ministry of Training, Colleges, and Universities (Sinclair et al., 2007, p. 33). Therefore, early into the project, it was decided a twofold analysis was required: (1) a quantitative component examining student achievement using a database of student scores and (2) a qualitative component that examined colleges' policies and programs through collaborative forums (ibid.).

The goals of CMP are the following:

- To analyse the mathematics achievement of first-semester college students, particularly in relation to their secondary school mathematics backgrounds

- To deliberate with members of both college and school communities about ways to increase student success in college mathematics. (Orpwood et al., 2012, p. 4)

In addition, CMP has had a third long term goal: "to assemble a longitudinal database on student achievement that will provide evidence of change – hopefully improvement – as schools and colleges work towards the goal of increased student success" (p. 22).

Methodology

In 2007, CMP adopted the *Deliberative Inquiry Model* to address policy research issues by developing a meaningful relationship between practice and research (Schollen et al., 2008, p. 4). The CMP website summarizes this methodology, "Problems of practice drive the research questions; results of research drive the stakeholder deliberations; and stakeholder deliberations drive changes in policy and practice" (CMP, 2011). CMP uses this model in a cyclical manner: (1) student achievement data are collected and analysed in a variety of ways; (2) the research findings are communicated to stakeholders in the project – school and college teachers, counsellors, administrators, and ministry officials – through a forum; (3) these stakeholders deliberate, from their various perspectives, about potential policies and practices to achieve the goal of increasing student success; and (4) research questions arise from the forums to further the following year's study (Schollen et al., p. 10).

Resolving College Grade Scores

Central to the quantitative component of CMP research is the ability to determine the likelihood of student success in a first-semester college mathematics course. However, CMP soon discovered colleges report grades in a variety of ways. Therefore, a key issue in the CMP methodology was the need to resolve the colleges' grading system. The CMP research team adopted the following grade parameters (in percentages) to decide "good grades": A (80–100); B (70–79); C (60–69), and students "at risk": D (50–59); F (less than 50); W (withdrawal) (Orpwood et al., 2010, p. 14). These grade parameters have been used consistently in all research phases.

Student Participation

To investigate the impact of secondary school courses from the revised curriculum had on first-semester college mathematics scores, the methodology required students be divided into one of two categories – (1) recent Ontario graduates (ROGs) and (2) non-recent Ontario graduates (non-ROGs). Generally, the ROG student is less than 23 years of age at the time of data collection and held an Ontario Secondary School Diploma (OSSD); the non-ROG student is not an Ontario secondary graduate. By 2008, a third student category was added: the very recent Ontario graduate (VROG); this category represents ROGs who followed the mathematics program most recently revised in 2005. Their last mathematics mark is recorded since 1 September 2007. These students were included in the 2008 and 2009 studies (Orpwood et al., 2010, p. 19).

College Mathematics Courses

The college mathematics courses were selected based on which college programs had a first-semester mathematics course. The college programs were sorted into one of four clusters: applied arts, business, general, and technology. Within each cluster of programs, subclusters of programs were identified. (For a listing of these clusters and subclusters with examples, see Orpwood et al., 2010, p. 13.) Detailed information about the mathematics courses is obtained from each college; each course is identified as a regular college-level course or a preparatory (remedial) course (ibid.). This sorting of courses permitted detailed analysis of student scores and provides colleges and school boards the opportunity to examine student achievement in finer detail (p. 14).

The Process

CMP reviews student files from participating colleges and sorts them into three categories: ROG, VROG, and non-ROG. The students are grouped by type of first-semester college mathematics course; depending on whether a student is assessed for placement, this course could be a preparatory course, offered by the college with or without credit, or a regular credit course. Through a student's college application, the college files are linked with the student's secondary school transcripts.

Then, CMP analyses the data for a relationship between the students' first-semester college mathematics grade and their secondary mathematics courses (Orpwood et al., 2008, p. 23). All data are blinded and confidentiality is ensured by CMP's policy on the *Protection of Privacy and the Public Reporting of Data* (CMPT, 2011; Orpwood & Schollen, 2010, p. 11).

Web-Based Database

A highlight of the CMP research is the development of a web-based database of all student data. All data is organized by student category (ROG, VROG, and non-ROG), age, gender, secondary mathematics courses, college programs, college mathematics courses (regular and remedial), and college mathematics scores ("good grades" and "at risk"). The database is linked to the research questions determined by CMP with guidance by the Steering Committee and as outcomes of the collaborative forums. The final reports focus on province-wide analysis of the data. However, the flexibility and transparency allows registered members of school boards and secondary schools, and colleges access to their data and the aggregated data. There is no access permitted to data from other school boards or colleges, as determined by CMP's policy on confidentiality and privacy (Orpwood et al., 2010, p. 38).

CMP Deliberative Forums

A key feature of the *Deliberative Inquiry Model* is the CMP collaborative forums. Here, the research findings are discussed and promising practices for secondary and college classrooms shared. The purposes of the forums, as identified on the CMP website, are to:

1 Receive the results of CMP research
2 Share college and school board strategies for student success in relation to mathematics
3 Develop recommendations for policy and practice aimed at increasing student success in mathematics at college level
4 Develop commitment among a wide range of stakeholders ensuring the implementation of the CMP recommendations (CMPT, 2011).

The forums are conducted with a common agenda as determined by CMP (Orpwood et al., 2010, p. 40). This format provides all stakeholders the opportunity to listen to presentations on the research results; promising practices by school and college teachers, and/or counsellors; student panels; and by government representatives. Opportunities are also provided to participate in discussions and contribute to recommendations for CMP and other stakeholders.

In 2009, forums and student panels were held in all nine project regions. Presentations by representatives from school boards and colleges are listed on the CMP website; for example, "Where Mathematics Meets Technology," "Impacts of CMP 2007," "Math Retention Plan," "The Math Drop-in Centre," "E-learning module for delivering the MCT4C1 math course," and "Promising Practices" (CMP, 2011).

At each CMP forum, recommendations are made to the CMP research team to further the research. Recommendations are also made in the spirit of a broader call to action to educators, administrators, counsellors, and government officials. In its most recent final report (CMP, 2011), CMP identified four recommendations as a result of these conversations and the presentation of promising practices. Evidence for these recommendations come from comments made by students in the forum panels, others from analysing the data, such as the higher scores obtained by mature college students over younger ones (Orpwood et al., 2010, p. 25) and yet other comments from college faculty sharing their classroom experiences. In general, these recommendations speak to the professional evolution of the project and their potential impact on educational change on behalf of college mathematics achievement (ibid., pp. 50–51).

Summary

The results of the College Mathematics Project were listed as follows:

- Demonstrated college student mathematics achievement is improving for some students;
- Provided a wealth of student information related to achievement in secondary and college mathematics studies to school boards, secondary schools, and colleges through a web-based database;
- Influenced secondary curricular changes;
- Increased provincial awareness of the need to address the issue of student transition into first-semester college mathematics; and
- Conducted province-wide forums as a venue for collaboration and deliberation by stakeholders.

CMP conducted a qualitative analysis of regular and remedial courses in relation to elementary and secondary school curricula. It recently
developed a position paper supporting a re-examination of secondary
mathematics courses with the goal to increase course relevance for college students. It continues to advocate for secondary-college collaborations through presentations at conferences for mathematics groups
such as the Ontario Association of Mathematics Educators (OAME), the
Ontario Colleges Mathematics Association (OCMA), the Ontario Colleges Mathematics Council (OCMC), the heads of technology (HoT),
the heads of business (HoB), the Ontario Colleges Mathematics Association (OCMA), and other provincial organizations (CMPT, 2011). It
continues to lobby government for a provincial roundtable committee
that explores and discusses transition issues for students, and recommends policies to support student success. In these ways and others,
CMP continues to be a change agent and research leader in the realm
of college mathematics transition and student achievement. However,
CMP obtains funding on an annual basis and funding sources have
shifted over the years. Both issues make its existence tenuous at a time
when an effective mechanism for policy change in college mathematics
transitions is critical.

NOTES

1 See Appendix to Chapter 18: The College Mathematics Project – An
   Overview.
2 In this chapter, a secondary school pathway is defined as a progression
   of secondary school mathematics courses that prepare students for college
   programs.
3 For additional information, see http://www.amatyc.org.
4 For additional information, CMP provides documents and reports
   of the research results and forum outcomes at its website:
   http://collegemathproject.senecac.on.ca/cmp/.

REFERENCES

de Abreu, G., Bishop, A., & Presmeg, N. (2002). Mathematics learners in
   transitions. In G. de Abreu, A. Bishop, & N. Presmeg (Eds.), *Transitions
   between Contexts of Mathematical Practices* (pp. 7–21). London: Kluwer
   Academic.

American Mathematical Association of Two-Year Colleges (AMATYC). (1995). *Crossroads in mathematics: Standards for introductory college mathematics before calculus*. Memphis, TN: Author.

Association of Community Colleges of Canada (ACCC). (2007). Report 1: Student characteristics and the college experience. *Pan-Canadian study of first-year college students*. Gatineau, QC: Author. Retrieved from http://css.oise.utoronto.ca/UserFiles/File/200708StudentStudy.pdf

Byers, P. (2010). Investigating trigonometric representations in the transition to college mathematics. *College Quarterly, 13*(2). Retrieved from http://www.collegequarterly.ca/2010-vol13-num02-spring/byers.html

Case, J., & Gunstone, R. (2003). Going deeper than deep and surface approaches: A study of students' perceptions of time. *Teaching in Higher Education, 8*(1), 55–69.

Cirillo, M., Drake, C., & Herbel-Eisenmann, B. (2009). Curriculum vision and coherence: Adapting curriculum to focus on authentic mathematics. *Mathematics Teacher, 103*(10), 70–75.

College Mathematics Project (CMP). (2011). Retrieved from the Seneca College Website: http://collegemathproject.senecac.on.ca/cmp/en/publications.php

College Mathematics Project Team (CMPT). (2011). The College Mathematics Project – Research, Recommendations, and Action! *Presentation at the meeting of the Ontario Colleges Mathematics Association (OCMA)*, Orillia, ON. Retrieved from http://collegemathproject.senecac.on.ca/cmp/en/publications.php

College Mathematics Project Final Report. (2011). Retrieved from the Seneca College Website: http://collegemathproject.senecac.on.ca/cmp/en/publications.php

Colleges Ontario. (2007a). *Ontario college technology graduates and the economy*. Retrieved from http://www.collegesontario.org/news/fact-sheets/CO_FACTSHEET _04.pdf

Colleges Ontario. (2007b). *Ontario's colleges: An overview*. Retrieved from http://www.collegesontario.org/news/fact-sheets/fact-sheet-overview.pdf

Godino, J.D., Batanero, C., & Roa, R. (2005). An onto-semiotic analysis of combinatorial problems and the solving processes by university students. *Educational Studies in Mathematics, 60*(1), 3–36. http://dx.doi.org/10.1007/s10649-005-5893-3

King, A. (2003). *Double cohort study: Phase 3*. Toronto: Ministry of Education.

Leclaire, R. (2011, 29 Mar.). Seneca College's Math Project Shows Higher Grades in Ontario. *Study Magazine*. Retrieved from http://studymagazine.com/2011/03/29/seneca-colleges-math-project-shows-higher-grades/

Ollerton, M. (2002). Redesigning success and failure. In M. Peelo & T. Wareham (Eds.), *Failing students in higher education* (pp. 124–136). Philadelphia, PA: The Society for Research into Higher Education & Open University Press.

Ontario Ministry of Education (OMoE). (2010). *Growing success: Assessment, evaluation, and reporting in Ontario schools.* Retrieved from http://www.edu .gov.on.ca/eng/policyfunding/growsuccess.pdf

Orpwood, G., Schollen, L., Marinelli-Henriques, P., & Assiri, H. (2010). *College mathematics project 2009: Final report.* Retrieved from http:// collegemathproject.senecac.on.ca/cmp/en/publications.php

Orpwood, G., Sinclair, M., & Schollen, L. (2008, June). College Mathematics Project 2007. *OAME-AOMÉ Gazette, 47*(4), 23–24.

Pascarella, E., & Terenzini, P. (2005). *How college affects students: A third decade of research.* San Francisco, CA: Jossey-Bass.

Presmeg, N. (2002). Shifts in meaning during transitions. In G. de Abreu, A.J. Bishop, & N.C. Presmeg (Eds.), *Transitions between contexts of mathematical practices* (pp. 213–228). London: Kluwer Academic.

Ross, J., McDougall, D., Hogaboam-Gray, A., & LeSage, A. (2003). A survey measuring elementary teachers' implementation of standards-based mathematics teaching. *Journal for Research in Mathematics Education, 34*(4), 344–363.

Schollen, L., Orpwood, G., Byers, P., Sinclair, M., & Assiri, H. (2008). *College mathematics project 2007: Final report.* Retrieved from http:// collegemathproject.senecac.on.ca/cmp/en/publications.php

Schollen, L., Orpwood, G., Sinclair, M., & Assiri, H. (2009). *College mathematics project 2008: Final report.* Retrieved from http://collegemathproject.senecac .on.ca/cmp/en/publications.php

School College Work Initiative [SCWI]–Eastern Ontario Regional Planning Team. (2009). *Partnering to Achieve Student Success (PASS), Why is SCWI important?* Retrieved from http://wordpress.passpathways.on.ca/?page_ id=77

Selden, A., & Selden, J. (2001). Tertiary mathematics education research and its future. In D. Holton (Ed.), *The teaching and learning of mathematics at university level: An ICMI Study* (pp. 237–254). London: Kluwer Academic.

Sinclair, M., Schollen, L., & Orpwood, G. (2007). The College Mathematics Project. *OAME–AOMÉ Gazette, 45*(4), 33–34.

Smith, J., & Star, J. (2000, Sept.). Understanding "reform" at the collegiate level: Exploring students' experiences in reform calculus. *Paper presented at the meeting of Research on Undergraduate Mathematics Education (RUME),* Chicago.

Smith, J., & Star, J. (2007). Expanding the notion of impact of K–12 standards-based mathematics and reform calculus programs. *Journal for Research in Mathematics Education*, *38*, 3–34.

Tall, D. (1992). The transition to advanced mathematical thinking: Functions, limits, infinity, and proof. In D. Grouws (Ed.), *Handbook of research on mathematics teaching and learning* (pp. 495–511). New York: Macmillan.

Wilson, R. (2000). The remaking of math. *Chronicle of Higher Education, 46*(18), A14–A16.

Wood, L. (2001). The secondary-tertiary interface. In D. Holton (Ed.), *The teaching and learning of mathematics at the university level: An ICMI Study* (pp. 87–98). Dordrecht: Kluwer Academic.

YSMISTE College Mathematics Project News. (2011, Mar.). *Release of CMP 2011 Report.* 2(1). Retrieved from http://collegemathproject.senecac.on.ca/cmp/en/pdf/CMP-Publications/CMP-News-Letter/2011/CMP%20News%20 2.1%20Final%202011.pdf

19 Inspirational Transitions: Cultivating the Capacity to Embrace Technology-Enhanced Learning and Teaching

ROB GRAHAM

Moving from classroom teacher to university professor has been an interesting transition. Five years into the career change, I have started to notice a feeling that I can best label as a professional disconnect with the public school teaching culture of which I was so many years a part. Recently, my feeling of disconnect was brought to a higher, almost uncomfortable level, when a student in my pre-service teacher Educational Technology Leadership class asked, "Professor Graham, how did the kids respond to the clickers [wireless response system] that we are investigating when you used it with them?" At that moment, I paused and confessed, "I actually never had a chance to use these devices with my students in my classrooms." Later, back in my office, that response continued to disturb me and led me to begin reading a paper to which I was referred by one of my tutors for my doctoral studies at Lancaster University. It was by Somekh (1995) on the topic of action research. From that paper, I identified a passage that framed my feelings at the time and also offered some insights into my situation:

> Action research is a good example of 'situated learning' in contrast to learning away from the context of practice in which an additional layer of difficulty arises from the need to imagine practical applications for what is being learnt, or alternatively manipulate the ideas in an abstract from which it may subsequently be difficult to translate into practice. (p. 8)

As clarified for me by Somekh, I was teaching the imagined use of the wireless response system to my students instead of teaching from an experience that had been grounded in a situated context that was at the crux of my feelings of professional disconnect. Put in another way, by

Argyris and Schön (1974), I was experiencing the resulting conflict between espoused theory and theory in use. Confounding the situation is the fact that I am no longer required as a faculty member to supervise my students in action and within the context of a classroom environment. My pre-service teachers may have a situated learning experience with these devices while on their practice teaching placements, complete with all of the tacit aspects of learning that are off-loaded onto the very contextualized environment in which they will be teaching. The explanation by Somekh helped to clarify my feelings and my situation, but it also offered me action research as a vehicle to use for my research endeavours, however, not comfortably. Although the AR approach would allow me the opportunity to reconnect with the classroom, it would also require me to unpack some of the uncomfortable realities that may be impeding the use of educational technology in teaching practice. It would require me to view them through a critical lens that sees and magnifies change (Kemmis, 2006). This reflective research process has provided me with a level of inspiration that has helped inform and invigorate subsequent explorations and discussions of clicker technology use with my current classes of pre-service teachers. It also provided me with a first-hand experience of a research a vehicle I now advocate for with my students as I feel they can travel in it with a level of efficiency that can inform their educational practice at the onset of their journey as educators or at any point during it.

The Foundational Question: Do You Desire to Inspire?

My transformation from classroom teacher to university professor continues. Today, however, it is my role to help the pre-service teacher candidates I teach, at Nipissing University in the Schulich School of Education, transition their use and understanding of technology. They have primarily used technology in an egocentric manner in their undergraduate courses, and it is my job to help them create a heightened awareness of its potential to connect and vitalize the learning and teaching in the classrooms that they will visit during their practicums and, ultimately, their careers. My aim is to expand their vision for learning and teaching beyond the traditionally accepted chalk and talk pedagogy to a learning framework that values diversity, promotes inquiry, and attempts to connect with the experiences and passions of the students. A fundamental question that is posed early in my course to my pre-service teacher candidates, and one that is pivotal to the pedagogy that I believe provides the impetus for effective technology integration in teaching, comes in the form of a simple, yet direct, question: "Do you desire to inspire?" It is largely on this foundational challenge that I attempt to build some structure and understanding around what my students will experience in practice while also providing them with some of the pedagogy that will guide their use of technology for what I believe can be some of the glue that may allow the learning to stick. It has always been my conviction that if you sincerely have the desire to inspire as an educator, you must be able to find a crevice in the curriculum where students and teachers can create higher levels of engagement. The challenge confronting many of my students is the uneven and jagged technology landscape that they will be required to traverse with regards to the use of technology in Ontario public schools.

Removing Transitional Barriers

Essential to understanding my approach to transitioning undergraduate students into a professional program and, ultimately, into a contemporary classroom in the role of teacher is understanding my personal epistemology and ontology. It reveals the foundation on which I continue to build my approach to learning and teaching. This foundation continues to be strengthened as my knowledge and vision of the twenty-first century lifelong learner continues to evolve. Schuetze and Slowey (2000) suggest today's view of a lifelong learner has been shaped by the impact of technology, advances in educational theory such as social-constructivism, and changing workplace requirements that demand constant upgrading. The implication is that learners should not be encumbered by the traditional modes of teaching, time, and mobility (ibid.).

There are also essential affordances offered by networked learning environments that have implications for how knowledge is produced and how learning takes place. Mode 2 knowledge production is a conception offered by Gibbons et al. (1994). This form of knowledge production is categorized as being flexible, transdiciplinary, collaborative, and involving a wide range of partners to develop. Opposing a traditional notion of knowledge creation that exists in many educational institutions whereby localized teams of experts in a given discipline generally produce the knowledge and are also the gatekeepers of it, today's on-line-networked learning environments enable Mode 2 knowledge production. One-way transmission of knowledge on site in the context of a lecture represents an impoverished notion of learning in the minds of some researchers. Hedge and Hayward (2004) caution that this form of teaching and learning has little do with self-actualization. Laterally transferring the pedagogy that is embedded within the notion of an on-line Mode 2 form of knowledge to a traditional or non-virtual classroom seems natural and logical. Isolating terms such as *open*, *flexible*, *collaborative*, and *self-actualizing* gives important hints at how opportunities for learning can be constructed within these learning environments. Furthermore, the inherent understanding that students are not tabula rasa or empty vessels to be filled up with knowledge is an essential understanding in helping my students make the transition to contemporary teacher.

Knowledge can be collaboratively constructed and built on. In order for this to happen, there must be teachers who desire to connect the curriculum to the interests of the students. One key source of pedagogy that is used in my course for establishing a framework for understanding the types of skills, attitudes, and pedagogy a twenty-first century teacher should be entering the classroom with comes from the International Society of Technology Educators (ISTE). As an organization, based in the United States, ISTE has developed a set of technology-enhanced learning standards for teachers, students, and administrators.

In Ontario, some school districts have also started to loosely embrace these standards given the fact that no such standards are provided by the Ministry of Education. As benchmarks, they are well articulated and capture the hallmarks of what many regard could, and should, be happening intwenty-first century schools. For my students, the ISTE standards are posed as a challenge and are offered as guidance for their professional development and annual personal growth plans. The ISTE criteria for teachers are also incorporated into a self-evaluation that is completed by my students after they teach a lesson integrating some level of technology during one of their placements. The opportunity for this integrated technology teaching experience and the concurrent opportunity for a guided and grounded self-reflection is a hallmark of the education technology course that I collaboratively teach with a colleague.

The following are the five benchmarks offered by the International Society for Technology in Education (ISTE, 2012). Notable is that they specifically address the enhanced learning needs of the twenty-first century student that are largely the result of enhanced on-line information, communication technologies, and the processes of globalization.

1 *Facilitate and Inspire Student Learning and Creativity*

Teachers use their knowledge of subject matter, teaching and learning, and technology to facilitate experiences that advance student learning, creativity, and innovation in both face-to-face and virtual environments. Teachers:

- Promote, support, and model creative and innovative thinking and inventiveness
- Engage students in exploring real-world issues and solving authentic problems using digital tools and resources
- Promote student reflection using collaborative tools to reveal and clarify students' conceptual understanding and thinking, planning, and creative processes
- Model collaborative knowledge construction by engaging in learning with students, colleagues, and others in face-to-face and virtual environments.

2 *Design and Develop Digital-Age Learning Experiences and Assessments*

Teachers design, develop, and evaluate authentic learning experiences and assessments incorporating contemporary tools and resources to maximize content learning in context and to develop the knowledge, skills, and attitudes identified in the NETS•S. Teachers:

- Design or adapt relevant learning experiences that incorporate digital tools and resources to promote student learning and creativity
- Develop technology-enriched learning environments that enable all students to pursue their individual curiosities and become active participants in setting their own educational goals, managing their own learning, and assessing their own progress
- Customize and personalize learning activities to address students' diverse learning styles, working strategies, and abilities using digital tools and resources
- Provide students with multiple and varied formative and summative assessments aligned with content and technology standards and use resulting data to inform learning and teaching.

3 Model Digital-Age Work and Learning

Teachers exhibit knowledge, skills, and work processes representative of an innovative professional in a global and digital society. Teachers:

- Demonstrate fluency in technology systems and the transfer of current knowledge to new technologies and situations
- Collaborate with students, peers, parents, and community members using digital tools and resources to support student success and innovation
- Communicate relevant information and ideas effectively to students, parents, and peers using a variety of digital-age media and formats
- Model and facilitate effective use of current and emerging digital tools to locate, analyse, evaluate, and use information resources to support research and learning.

4 Promote and Model Digital Citizenship and Responsibility

Teachers understand local and global societal issues and responsibilities in an evolving digital culture and exhibit legal and ethical behaviour in their professional practices. Teachers:

- Advocate, model, and teach safe, legal, and ethical use of digital information and technology, including respect for copyright, intellectual property, and the appropriate documentation of sources
- Address the diverse needs of all learners by using learner-centred strategies and providing equitable access to appropriate digital tools and resources
- Promote and model digital etiquette and responsible social interactions related to the use of technology and information
- Develop and model cultural understanding and global awareness by engaging with colleagues and students of other cultures using digital-age communication and collaboration tools.

5 Engage in Professional Growth and Leadership

Teachers continuously improve their professional practice, model lifelong learning, and exhibit leadership in their school and professional community by promoting and demonstrating the effective use of digital tools and resources. Teachers:

- Participate in local and global learning communities to explore creative applications of technology to improve student learning
- Exhibit leadership by demonstrating a vision of technology infusion, participating in shared decision making and community building, and developing the leadership and technology skills of others
- Evaluate and reflect on current research and professional practice on a regular basis to make effective use of existing and emerging digital tools and resources in support of student learning
- Contribute to the effectiveness, vitality, and self-renewal of the teaching profession and of their school and community.

From Barriers to Bridges: Cultivating Techno-Resilience

In the wake of forces such as a revitalized Mode 2 understanding of knowledge production, innovative and rapidly emerging information and communication technologies (ICTs), and the post-industrialization learning and teaching paradigm shift (Wellman, Koku, & Hunsinger, 2006), developing an appropriate technological response to the notion of a lifelong learner who expects a more pliable learning schedule with timely access to the resources that are required to support on-demand learning is a challenge for those developing on-line learning environments in higher education. Likewise, challenges are faced by many of the pre-service teachers I teach who attempt to integrate technology in their off-line more traditional teaching modes. Challenged to be guided by the high standards set by ISTE, and teaching largely within environments that may be lacking both resources, and more importantly, the motivation and supports to integrate inspired uses of technology, many I teach struggle to find inclusive and cost-effective solutions in the wake of all the other demands that are placed on them.

A key feature of my teaching and overall transition plan to move my students from pre-service teachers to in-service teachers is to foster a form of what I regard as *techno-resilience* and a capacity for technology leadership that can help hurdle some of the financial and emotional barriers that they will inevitably face when they enter the teaching profession. Much of this is inherently embedded in my philosophy and is revealed in the form of cultivating a mindset that values the need for a connected, relevant, and inspiring curriculum that embraces technology at some level. Notable is that technology does not have to be at the centre of it all, but always in the consciousness.

For example, at the onset of each class, I provide an opportunity to collaboratively explore a cost-effective technology that I have picked up at a second-hand store or on sale; this is called "Rob's Techno Inspirational Moment." The range of technologies explored has included digital voice recorders, digital cameras, USB digital drum pads, iPods, digital photo frames, and a variety of relatively cost-effective USB-driven devises and freeware programs. Not surprising to me, this exercise in group collaboration with a focus on pedagogy and discovery, which challenges the students to reflect on and connect with their recent classroom placements, almost always reveals a myriad of creative cross-curricular ideas for how the given technology can be used across a range of grade levels. The intent is also to demonstrate that technology-enhanced learning goes beyond the use of SMARTBoards (a common misconception that persists with many of my students). This practice also models the type of collaboration and creativity that is required in order for a technology to afford itself; it is part of the teaching process that I have devised for shaping a skills set and the appropriate attitude required for adapting technology within the disparate, jagged, and rocky teaching landscape that currently exists in Ontario schools and is reported by my students specific to technology-enhanced learning.

The goal at the end of my teaching term with the students is to provide them with a package of resources that has the capacity to inspire and enhance learning at a price point of under $200. More specifically, the package this year included the following peripherals: Korg USB controller, Samsung digital picture frame, Panasonic digital voice recorder, and a range of digital video recorders and cameras. These are augmented and supported by a list of freeware titles and on-line resources that are investigated. Without providing much of the specific details highlighting these explorations, the fundamental underlying premise of these investigations is that a twenty-first century teacher must be able to make literate and cost-effective decisions about what types of technologies can enhance learning experiences for students. An inclusive approach towards technology-enhanced learning requires resourcefulness. My personal narrative reinforces this element of my teaching.

The first junior/intermediate computer lab I taught in was, essentially, built by a colleague and me from computers being thrown out and with parts and peripherals that were mostly taken from a dumpster. When pictures of this lab and the old school laser printer, which was salvaged from a dumpster, are shown to my students, the fact that my teaching philosophy has been moulded from a lived teaching experience is reinforced. In the wake of constantly emerging technologies, an element of being techno-resilient, to my mind, is understanding that just because a technology is dated does not mean it has no capacity left to enhance the learning experience. This has served me well in terms of connecting with the stories from the field that the students share.

Pivotal to me is the belief that when I began working with technology in teaching more than 15 years ago, cost was rightfully cited as a key obstacle. Today, given the plethora of freeware and cost-reduced technologies, it is not so much cost that I believe is the barrier; rather, it is the lack of an *open* and *creative mind*. Helping students identify free online resources and cultivating a spirit of resourcefulness is the easy part in my teaching. Perhaps more vital is providing them with the emotional supports and the ongoing inspiration that will undoubtedly be required not just to successfully and creatively integrate technology in teaching, but also to survive the demands of the profession.

In Ontario, the support offered to newly hired teachers has been deficient. As suggested by Glassford and Salinitri (2007), many schools across Canada, with the exception of New Brunswick, should receive a failing grade in this area. According to Reig, Paquette, and Chen (2007), novice teachers continue to be assigned the most challenging teaching assignments and are regularly placed in classrooms late in the fall when the school year has already begun. Reig et al. (2007) identify a lack of confidence due to a lack of experience, unclear perception of status, conflict between advice and expectations, and a lack of coping mechanisms for dealing with stress as being other key stressors. Now more than ever, new teachers entering the profession require more than just access to teaching resources; they require a vital source of inspiration and mentoring.

Recent trends and projections have severely diminished the hopes and possibilities of new graduates finding work in Ontario. As reported by the Ontario College of Teachers in the state of the profession 2007 survey (Browne, 2007), there are 8,000 more new teachers licensed each year in Ontario than the number of teachers retiring from the profession. A result of this trend is that many new teachers entering the profession now find themselves having to spend several years volunteering and taking supply work before actually securing full-time jobs. This represents a key psychological barrier for my students that often enters our classroom conversation.

Recognizing that many of my students may not have full-time jobs on graduating, it is imperative that they take some comfort from the realization that they are not alone. Although much of the focus of my teaching is framed around the notion of technology as a potential source of inspiration and engagement for students, no less vital to my teaching and the transition plan is understanding the inspiration that can come from being part of an on-line community of practice (CoP). As noted by Wenger (2004), the element of inspiration can be cultivated and found within a community of practice. Wenger and Lave (1999) explain that the social theory of learning, by which a CoP is framed, sees individuals actively engaging in and contributing to the practices of their communities. For an on-line CoP, it implies that learning means the ongoing refinement of practice and the assurance of new generations of members (Wenger & Lave, 1999). Although Wenger (2004) proposes that CoPs are all around us, many in the field of education are largely unaware or confused by the concept. Cox (2005) suggests the concept of a CoP is very diverse in terms of its usage and understanding. The result is ambiguity. In this sense, the important aspect is leading the students to some of the on-line communities that may offer the required inspiration, motivation, and support.

How Will I Know I Have Arrived?

During a recent class, I was asked the following question, "How will you know that you have developed an open and willing mind for embracing technology as a teacher?" I responded, "because you will not be able to look at advertisements in the newspaper for technological devices in the same way again or be able to walk through stores like Future Shop or Best Buy without constantly asking yourself, 'I wonder how I can use that piece of technology to engage learning in my classroom!' You will also find yourself asking for technology-related presents that many of your relatives may find peculiar!" This response was inspired by a quote from the distinguished sociologist Peter Berger (1963) who wrote, "People who feel no temptation before closed doors, who have no curiosity about human beings, who are content to admire scenery without wondering about the people who live in the houses on the other side of that river, should probably stay away from sociology" (p. 24).

Likewise, I feel it is important for my students who will be transitioning into the profession of teaching to have a similar curiosity about technology and learning. Anderson and Dron (2011) suggest "the technology sets the beat and creates the music, while the pedagogy defines the moves" (para. 4). A teacher who aspires to make effective and inspirational use of technology will also be able to better interpret the music and the dance that ensues by harmonizing pedagogy and technology. In their work, Anderson and Dron specifically map three generations of distance education pedagogies; however, their work can be more broadly extrapolated to more traditional learning environments. In my own work and research about on-line learning, I have become aware of the changing face of learning and teaching.

Essentially, the focus on on-line learning and the process of globalization has resulted in a challenge to our thinking about what learning is. This pivotal question for educators is one that, in my opinion, has largely been taken for granted. In this sense, I have used the work by Anderson and Dron as a conceptual framework to consolidate some of my past and present classroom-based teaching experiences. As well, their writing has helped shape my understanding of the past, present, and future use of technology in education. As such, it continues to impact my instruction at some level. Their work is clearly distinguished from earlier researchers who have taken a *techno-lustful* slant in that they have been myopically focused on the technologies of the time and have not paid attention to issues of pedagogy (Garrison, 1985; Nipper, 1989).

In this sense, the review by Anderson and Dron fills an important void in the existing research on this topic. Although the historical pedagogical frameworks concerned are specifically related to on-line and distance education, on some level, they mimic the evolution of classroom-based practice. They propose that the cognitive-behaviourist model typifies the first era of individualized distance education. The learning package format that defines cognitive-behaviourist pedagogical models is designed to be self-contained and complete, requiring only teacher-learner interaction for marking and evaluation. Teaching presence is mediated only through text and recorded sound and images. Highlighting this era has maximized access, student freedom, and the ability to service very large numbers of students at significantly lower costs than traditional education. However, these advantages were accompanied by very significant reductions in teaching, social interaction, and formal models of cognitive presence. A pedagogical limitation of this era was the lack of recognition of the richness and complexity of human learning. It was also marred by a view of people entering the learning experience as blank slates. Such a conception clearly negates the understanding that people bring prior learning, rich and contextualized experiences, and models to the learning experience.

The Changing Face of Learning

The second era proposed by Anderson and Dron (2011) is the social-constructivist pedagogy of distance education. Highlighting this era was an evolved understanding of the learner as no more than a mere vessel in need of being filled with knowledge. This pedagogy also views learning as an active process with a need for the learning environment to be learner centred with a high level of metacognitive involvement. An emphasis on the importance of multiple perspectives was also a hallmark. This era moved distance education learning beyond a narrowly conceived notion of packaged knowledge and one-way transmission of it to a form of human communications-based learning that was able to operate via synchronous and asynchronous media types. This era was supported by and evolved simultaneously with the emergence of many-to-many technologies.

As opposed to the previous era, however, the focus on human interaction placed limits on accessibility and tended to produce more costly models of distance education. This insight is interesting given the fact that many in higher education tend to view the move to on-line learning as being a cost-effective strategy able to teach and reach much larger numbers of students at a lower per student cost. Many higher education administrators commonly cite these as key justifications (Kirkwood, 1998). Surprisingly, a social-constructivist model of distance education shares some of the affordances and liabilities of campus-based education. The potential for a teacher-dominated approach, passive lecture delivery, and restrictions on geographical and temporal access persist.

The third era that these researchers propose is the connectivist pedagogy of distance education. This recently emerging pedagogy argues that learning is the process of building networks of information, contacts, and resources that are applied to real problems. A key assumption is that ubiquitous access to networked technologies exists. The need to build and maintain flexible networked connections is vital, as is the need to access vast amounts of information. In this respect, this era is closely aligned with and determined by the existence of a particular technology. Importantly, social-connectivism assumes that the learner's role is not to memorize or even understand much of the information but, more importantly, to have the competence to find and apply information where needed. It also builds on the existence of a social-constructivist framework.

Although this third generation of distance education pedagogy outlined by Anderson and Dron (2011) is in its conceptual infancy, it seems to assume too much and is too greatly hindered by existing network capabilities, at this point in time, to offer any real functional and immediate opportunity for those in distance higher education and, most certainly, within the context of the teaching environments that my students will be transitioning into. There is a dispersed nature and intrinsic uncertainty of goals, beginnings, and endings implied by a social-connectivist approach that represents too radical a shift within an education system using more formal and traditional courses designed with a social-constructivist and/or a cognitive-behaviourist model. Perhaps, what the connectivist pedagogy offers my students and me is a heightened sensitivity to the types of skills and training required by the twenty-first century, lifelong learner. As well, it may offer a glimpse into the future of education.

The Need to Capitalize

Based on the history of distance education pedagogy, it is evident that it is closely aligned with the technologies of the time. As new technological affordances avail themselves to educators, it becomes possible to explore and capitalize on different aspects of the learning process (Anderson & Dron, 2011). However, a key assumption is that educators today have the capacity, willingness, and creativity to reveal the key educational learning benefits and affordances of these technologies. Fostering in my students a willingness to investigate and integrate technology in inspirational and engaging ways is a hallmark of what I try to do.

This comes back to my foundational question, "Do you have the desire to inspire learning?" Answering "yes" to this question calls for a higher level of curiosity, creativity, resilience, and investigation into what some of the technological affordances of a technology may be. For each mode of engagement, different types of knowledge, learning, and contexts must be applied, and distance educators and students must be skilled and informed in order to select the best mix of pedagogy and technology to enhance learning and teaching (Anderson & Dron, 2011).

Ideally, teachers need to capitalize simultaneously on the technology and the pedagogy of the time while continuing to respect issues of access and equality. This is a complex and difficult to manage task. Attempting to merely capitalize on the technology without a guiding pedagogy can come with risks. This type of *techno-lustful* approach is ill advised by Bassi, Buchanan, and Cheney (1997). The image by Anderson and Dron (2011) of a choreographed dance between the technology and the pedagogy once again emerges. The technology is the beating drum and the music; the pedagogy must find creative dances with which to respond. There is little doubt that the beat and the music being set by the technology today is fast moving and requires considerable stamina and creativity in order to effectively respond to it.

Developing the required mental stamina and capacity within the pre-service teachers that I work with is, in part, supported by what Nipissing University's Shulich School of Education has framed and promoted as the Iteach Laptop Learning Program. The specific details of the program can be found on the university website. In essence, the requirement is that all students in the program must have a laptop that meets a set of minimum requirements. Another facet of the program is the inclusion of regular workshops that highlight creative and functional uses of existing software all framed within the pedagogy of learning and teaching. In addition, the inclusion of student technology assistants (STAs) who act as key mentors and trouble-shooting agents for students in the various sections and divisions is notable. The intention is that by providing these students the opportunity to be technology mentors, supporters, and collaborators at this stage of their career, they will continue to use and share these skills as full-time teachers. The STAs also help equalize some of the extra burden placed on professors in the program who may not have the capacity to support student needs specific to hardware and software issues. Acting as a vital source of support for professors and students alike, within a program that requires a laptop as a prerequisite for acceptance, STAs are a key facet of the Iteach Laptop Learning model. The use of STAs also replicates and reinforces the need for a supportive and collegial teaching practice.

ICT: Technolust or Promise of Hope?

In my Educational Technology Leadership classes, I often begin by stating, "If you truly believe the educational technology that we are going to explore today does not have the potential to inspire and lead to higher levels of classroom engagement and learning, find another tool that does." Underscoring all of our technology-enhanced learning investigations is a discussion of the pedagogical underpinnings for a particular technology's use. A critical, complex, and often misunderstood relationship exists among the use of information and communication technology, the practice of teaching, and the affiliated act of learning.

As argued by Kirkwood and Price (2006), ICT merely offer tools to help students and teachers attain educational outcomes. Although not a new message, central to their argument is the idea that, although technology can enable new forms of teaching and learning, ICT alone will not somehow magically afford itself to educators; it must be driven by educational purposes. The problem of "putting the *"T"(echnology)* before the *"P"(edagogy)*," Lin (2007) views as having some inherent and serious ethical issues. According to Lin, the key ethical issue is that the technology often takes precedence over the learning needs, "or each new technology is used as a replacement for all existing learning methodologies" (p. 416).

The process and practice of knowingly adopting or recommending ICT that is unnecessary is "technolust" (Bassi et al., 1997, as cited in Lin, 2007, p. 416). Unfortunately, it is a practice that continues to perpetuate itself in education, both in public school education environments and now in higher education. The remedy may appear straightforward: determine the learning needs and analyse the technology to find the ones that best address those needs (Lin, 2007). The fact remains that having the opportunity for an experiential and pedagogical exploration of a technology prior to its purchase in a school would be the Rolls Royce version of what Lin has suggested should take place more regularly. The action research investigation on the SMART Response clickers I conducted was partly based on the understanding and lamenting expressed by Lin over the lack of critical performance and pedagogical analysis of a given technology prior to its purchase. The opportunity to regularly explore and examine emerging technologies with my students represents my attempt to offset the deficiency that Lin highlights and that my students are likely to experience in practice.

My pre-service students are quick to report a pattern of putting technology before the pedagogy in the Ontario schools where they are placed. This discovery is accelerated by a key assignment that is used by my teaching colleague Professor Ken Waller and me entitled, "What Is Out There? Taking Inventory of the ICT in Your School." In essence, students are required to speak with key teachers and administrators within their school to find out what educational technology is currently being used and available. The data gathered from this process become a central focus for classroom discussion. The data also provide a platform for discovery that inevitably reveals the uneven and rocky teaching landscape in terms of educational technology use and availability of resources that currently exists within Ontario schools. If my students are going to have any chance of traversing this teaching landscape, they will require a twenty-first century skills set that demands perseverance, creativity, problem-solving skills, the ability to self-direct, a willingness to collaborate, and the ability to communicate effectively. Each lesson in my teaching is a step towards recognizing and achieving this skills set.

The Need for Revitalization

Despite the call for imagined and creative uses of existing technologies, the fact remains that many educators and students that I will work with to transition into practice will continue to be mired in a teaching tradition that has many inherent instructional deficits. Namely, it is a tradition that remains pedagogically grounded in a one-way, transmissive, and impersonal style of teaching that fails to capture the attention and imagination of many students. This is in contrast to a vision of a teaching profession and learning environment that values a more active and inquiry-based philosophy. Within this practice, attempts to provide for a less abstract and more contextualized learning experience for students are the priority. We cannot separate what is learned from how it is learned. In this sense, there is a need to bridge the breach between the *know what* and the *know how* (Brown, Collins, & Duguid, 1989).

Of course, no amount of technology in teaching is going to solve this deep-rooted problem in education; however, Draper (1998) suggests a technology is worth using only if it can effectively enhance a specific instructional deficit. Challenging the pre-service teachers in my classes to consider what technologies may have the potential to ameliorate some of the traditional instructional deficits is vital to an understanding of technology-enhanced learning and aiding in their transition into the profession. According to some researchers, several educators and institutions have adopted technologies such as the clickers I explored in my investigation in the hope of reducing attrition rates and creating a learning environment that is more engaging, less impersonal, and more active in nature (Burnstein & Lederman, 2001).

The communicative and collaborative possibilities that recent technologies offer provide hope for learning enriched by engagement with others (Conole & Dyke, 2004). Much of the focus of the research on clicker technology has been in large higher education classes where the challenges of nurturing the interpersonal and interactive classroom dynamic are greater. There exists a presumed, more passive environment that is associated with the lecture form of instruction and that dominates higher education learning environments (Duncan, 2006). As observed by Duncan, "the regular use of clickers can transform a class in a very positive way. Students become active participants, not merely passive listeners to a lecture" (p. 2). A notable discrepancy in the existing literature about clicker use seems to be the lack of attention and investigation devoted to their use in smaller-sized elementary and secondary classroom environments where the need to inspire, engage, and provide a more active learning experience is no less vital. Extrapolating from this research, and my action research on the use of clicker technology in teaching, I can conclude that the pre-service teacher candidates I teach must be open to the possibilities that a technology affords. They must also be aware of, and willing to embrace, a humanistic pedagogy of learning and teaching that has at its heart a desire to offer a connected, compelling, and engaging curriculum. In my opinion, having the desire and the capacity to make the process of learning more engaging with the integration of technology is a necessary part of being a twenty-first century teacher. Giving the students in my program the opportunity to experience what this may *feel* like while they are seated as students in my class is always at the heart of my teaching.

Where to Go from Here?

Based on this experiential review of my approach to teaching educational technology to pre-service teachers in the Schulich School of Education at Nipissing University, I offer the following as summary points and key recommendations:

1 Attempts to teach specific skills related to educational technology in pre-service teacher programs would do well to emphasize the supporting pedagogy and rationale for a particular technology's use. Allowing for inquiry- and discovery-based explorations and discussions of a given technology that are connected to the lived practicum experiences of the students can aid in modelling the type of explorations that should be more regularly taking place in schools. Beware of advocating for a technolustful use of technology in teaching. A focus on pedagogy before the technology is vital. It is a focus that is largely missing in many educational settings.

2 Preparing and transitioning pre-service teachers into the role of full-time teacher must consider the current state of teaching where jobs are scarce and the technology landscape in many schools is jagged and uneven. Recognizing the differential technology and hiring experiences that students are likely to experience calls for a teaching program that fosters a form of techno-resilience and overall perseverance. Introducing students to the notion of on-line communities of practice is one way to foster some of the much-needed inspiration and support that is required.

3 Understanding the needs of the twenty-first century learner can come with an investigation of the impact that globalization and on-line forms of learning are having on education. With the process of globalization and the rush to capitalize on the on-line learning market, there has been a renewed focus on the question, how do students learn? The revitalized notion of learning that is emerging in the research and the discussion of this topic should be an integral part of transitioning pre-service teachers' understanding of how and why students learn. Recognizing that there will likely be a disconnect between the twenty-first century notion of inquiry- and discovery-based learning and the one-way transmissive type of teaching and learning that many of the pre-service teachers I teach have been regularly schooled in is vital.

Using the technology standards developed by the International Society for Technology in Education offers twenty-first century teaching benchmarks that can become important aspects of lifelong professional development and personal growth plans.

REFERENCES

Anderson, T., & Dron, J. (2011). Connectivism: Design and delivery of social networked learning – Three generations of distance education pedagogy [Special Issue]. *International Review of Research in Open and Distance Learning*, *12*(3).

Argyris, C., & Schön, D.A. (1974). *Theory in practice: Increasing professional effectiveness*. San Francisco, CA: Jossey-Bass.

Bassi, L., Buchanan, L., & Cheney, S. (1997). *Trends that affect learning and performance improvement: A report on the members of the ASTD benchmarking forum*. Alexandria, VA: American Society for Training and Development.

Berger, P. (1963). *Invitation to sociology: A humanistic perspective.* New York, NY: Anchor Books.

Brown, J.S., Collins, A., & Duguid, P. (1989). Situated cognition and the culture of learning. *Educational Researcher, 18*(1), 32–42.

Browne, L. (2007). State of the teaching profession 2007. *Professionally Speaking,* 50–58.

Burnstein, R.A., & Lederman, L.M. (2001). Using wireless keypads in lecture classes. *The Physics Teacher, 39*(1), 8–11.

Conole, G., & Dyke, M. (2004). What are the affordances of information and communication technologies? *ALT-J: Research in Learning Technology, 12*(2), 113–124.

Cox, A. (2005). What are communities of practice? A comparative review of four seminal works. *Journal of Information Science, 31*(6), 527–540.

Draper, S.W. (1998). Niche-based success in CAL. *Computers & Education, 30*(1–2), 5–8.

Duncan, D. (2006). Clickers: A new teaching aid with exceptional promise. *Astronomy Education Review, 5*(1), 70–88.

Garrison, D.R. (1985). Three generations of technological innovations in distance education. *Distance Education, 6*(2), 235–241.

Gibbons, M., Limoges, C., Nowotny, H., Schwartzman, S., Scott, P., & Trow, M. (1994). *The new production of knowledge.* London: Sage.

Glassford, L., & Salinitri, G. (2007). Designing a successful new teacher induction program: An assessment of the Ontario experience, 2003–2006. *Canadian Journal of Educational Administration and Policy, 60,* 1–34.

Hedge, N., & Hayward, L. (2004). Redefining roles: University distance education contributing to lifelong learning in the networked world. In D. Murphy, R. Carr, J. Taylor, & W. Tat-meng (Eds.), *Distance education and technology: Issues and practice* (pp. 111–128). Hong Kong: Open University of Hong Kong Press.

International Society for Technology in Education (ISTE). (2012). NETS for Teachers. Retrieved from http://www.iste.org/standards

Kemmis, S. (2006). Participatory action research and the public sphere. *Educational Action Research, 14*(4), 459–476.

Kirkwood, A. (1998). New media mania: Can information and communication technologies enhance the quality of open and distance learning? *Distance Education, 19*(2), 228–241.

Kirkwood, A., & Price, L. (2006). Adaptation for a changing environment: Developing learning and teaching with information and communication technologies. *International Review of Research in Open and Distance Learning, 7*(2), 1–14.

Lin, H. (2007). The ethics of instructional technology: Issues and coping strategies experienced by professional technologists in design and training situations in higher education. *Educational Technology Research and Development, 55*(5), 411–437.

Nipper, S. (1989). Third generation distance learning and computer conferencing. In R. Mason & A. Kaye (Eds.), *Mindweave: Communication, computers and distance education* (pp. 63–73). Oxford: Pergamon.

Reig, S., Paquette, K., & Chen, Y. (2007). Coping with stress: An investigation of novice teachers' stressors in the elementary classroom. *Education, 128*(2), 211–226.

Schuetze, H.G., & Slowey, M. (2000). *Higher education and lifelong learners: International perspectives on change.* London: Routledge Falmer.

Somekh, B. (1995). The contribution of action research to development in social endeavours: A position paper on action research methodology. *British Educational Research Journal, 21*(3), 339–355.

Wellman, B., Koku, E., & Hunsinger, J. (2006). Networked scholarship. In J. Weiss, J. Nolan, & J. Hunsinger (Eds.), *The international handbook on virtual learning environments* (Vol. 2, pp. 1429–1447). Dordrecht: Springer.

Wenger, E. (2004). *Communities of practice: A brief introduction* [Electronic version]. Retrieved from http://www.ewenger.com/theory/index.htm

Wenger, E., & Lave, J. (1999). *Situated learning: Legitimate peripheral participation.* Cambridge: Cambridge University Press.

Coda: Supporting Students and Teachers within and across Transitional Spaces

SUSAN E. ELLIOTT-JOHNS AND DANIEL H. JARVIS

A major catalyst for this collaborative project was the realization of a considerable overlap in our respective research interests regarding transitions in schooling and instructional practices, specifically relating to literacy and mathematics education. Later, discussions around a working paper that presented major perspectives in research on early childhood transitions (Vogler, Crivello, & Woodhead, 2008) revealed prominent areas in need of attention in both research and practice, and the value of using a variety of conceptual and methodological tools to better understand childhood transitions. The work by Vogler and Woodhead also prompted the question, "Who is actually doing the research in the multi-faceted area of 'transitions'?" This text was, therefore, a result of our efforts to begin to formulate an answer to that question. Furthermore, the role of multidisciplinary collaboration, and the need to broaden and diversify perspectives on transitions in both schooling and instructional practices, became increasingly evident.

Subsequent exploration of the voices of the invited contributors to this volume focused our attention on the critical relationship between transitions in schooling and instructional practice. The combined work of the featured authors around "transitions" presents a landscape that is highly complex, and one that, ultimately, requires integrated, contextualized frameworks and programs in order to facilitate successful transitions at all levels of formal education. Although some of the issues described may not seem particularly surprising or "new" (e.g., the benefits of *consistency* in approaches to student/teacher transitions, *collaborative* efforts between various stakeholders, and highly effective *communication* systems), the insights shared within the text allow us to reflect on these common themes from some very different vantage points, or perspectives.

We contend that three pervasive themes emerged from the previous 19 chapters as a whole: Academic achievement within social learning contexts; the changing nature of teaching and learning in twenty-first century schools and classrooms; and effective structures and processes for facilitating transitions. These three themes are discussed in more detail, followed by a specific set of recommendations for further research and practice.

Academic Achievement within Social Learning Contexts

Academic achievement and the development of the intellect is, of course, a central goal of education and schooling at all levels. Holistic approaches to student success also include other crucial aspects of learning (e.g., social, emotional, and physical), as well as intellectual, thus promoting and enhancing success in progressive transitions *beyond* academics alone. The integrated nature of transitions *across* "organized" schooling, that is, across grades, divisions, panels, disciplines, and co-curricular activities (Hauser et al., Ch. 11), sometimes makes it difficult to pinpoint exactly what is needed, and who is responsible for making it happen. Teachers, counsellors, students, parents, school administrators, and government officials all have important roles to play in successful student transitions. However, in many jurisdictions, it appears that there is often no one particular individual or group specifically charged with the responsibility for overseeing these complex transition processes.

This is unfortunate, given the research-based importance of transition episodes within the academic and social journeys of all students within formal schooling, and in light of the clear connection between positive transition experiences and the ultimate achievement of school graduation, as well as the lifelong goals that may hinge on that significant event. Increased academic achievement is, in general, regarded to be a natural ripple effect of successful transitions (Hauser et al., Ch. 11, and many of the other contributors to this volume). That said, pertinent discussions of potentially long-lasting negative effects on all aspects of academic achievement, should transitions be unsuccessful (Jackson & Cartmel, Ch. 3; Hauser et al., Ch. 11, & Hachkowski, Ch. 16), strongly suggest that these transitions are far too important to be left to chance.

Changing Nature of Teaching and Learning
in Schools and Classrooms in the Twenty-First Century

The changing nature of teaching and learning relates directly to considerations of the work of students and teachers in contemporary classrooms (e.g., students' abilities, learning styles, special needs, English
Language Learners, French as a Second Language, "funds of knowledge," attitudes/values, and aspirations/expectations). The needs of
students not only make it increasingly essential for educators to "keep
pace" with changes in the broader educational landscape, but also to be
adept at successfully navigating transitions in their own professional
learning, and the development of effective instructional practices over
time (Elliott-Johns, Ch. 6; Sharratt, Ch. 7; Small, Ch. 8; Jordan, Ch. 9).
Cross-panel teams and sustained professional dialogue in structured,
ongoing learning communities (Helling, Ch. 12; Jarvis, Ch. 13) offer additional examples of successful programs in this regard.

Considerable expansion in the conceptions of literacy for twenty-first
century learning (Kendrick & Rowsell, Ch. 14) clearly resonate with notions of educators as "lifelong learners" in the realm of transitions in
instructional practices. The refining of professional knowledge (e.g.,
curriculum, pedagogy, and assessment) over time, in order to engage
students in learning (academic skills, learning skills, behaviours, self-
regulated learning, Buzza, Ch. 10) is suggested as having the potential
to ease and enhance transitions at all ages and stages – from preschool
to postsecondary. The kind of transition frameworks that assist in student understanding (e.g., "moving in, moving through, and moving
on," in Mady, Ch. 15) across and through transitional spaces (Byers,
citing Wood, Ch. 17) may also reduce "stresses in the system" (Small,
Ch. 8). The increasing influence of globalization, on-line forms of learning, and an ever-expanding array of technological advancements and
applications (Yeo, Ch. 2; Graham, Ch. 19) further underscore the complex factors that influence success – the inescapable reality of students
as teachers, and vice versa.

A visual representation of the four main student transitions in formal
schooling, beginning in the early years through postsecondary levels, is
presented here in Figure C.1. In the model, S represents students, T is
for teachers, A stands for administrators, F means family members
(parent/guardian), and C represents other community members. The
four large arrows map the student transitions between the various levels. Dotted lines represent clusters of communication and activities

shared across panels by teachers and students alike (e.g., cross-panel teacher professional development initiatives; older students pairing up with younger students for projects in the same K–8 elementary school; college/university faculty speaking at local high school information nights). Administrators, family, and other community members all play a significant role in each of the major transitions in schooling, as we have clearly seen throughout the various chapters of this book. Note also how both the students and teachers are shown to be experiencing personal changes, as represented by the proximal duplication of each letter (e.g., S > S and T > T).

In the case of each teacher, in particular, this motion can be viewed as a continuous cycle of new learning and changing practice – a process of perennial knowing and growing. As these teacher transitions (e.g., teachers implementing new board-level or provincial initiatives, preparing for a new grade level assignment, or adopting a new technology in the classroom) are regularly modelled and observed in classrooms, students learn much about what it is to continually learn throughout one's lifetime. In other words, coping with often radical changes in school location/environments and with differing teacher expectations is somehow made more manageable for students who are in transition, knowing that their role models (i.e., teachers/professors) are also negotiating multiple ongoing changes, and that these transitions are often no less stressful and challenging for the teacher/professor. From this perspective, transitions in schooling and instructional practice can be viewed as parallel and shared.

Effective Structures and Processes for Facilitating Transitions

Calls for the increased identification of effective strategies to both promote and support successful transitions are woven throughout the chapters in this collection. A consistent emphasis is also placed on increased understandings about the complexity of transitions, and the central importance of successful transitions in the lives of both students and teachers. Many different stakeholders are described as being engaged in concerted efforts to work towards the common goal of success for all students (Jackson & Cartmel, Ch. 3; Binstadt, Ch. 4; Jordan, Ch. 9). Reported successes include supporting transitions through strategic planning, collaboration, shared goals, recognition of areas for improvement, and, implementing "action plans" (Akos & Felton, Ch. 5). These successes clearly indicate instances where, "Educational stakeholders

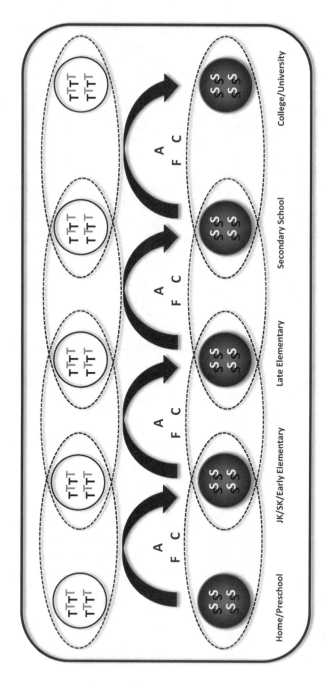

Figure C.1. Transitions in schooling and instructional practice.

make an investment in the success of individuals when transition programs are offered." Furthermore, at all levels of formal education, authors' insights on the topic under study suggest that frequent barriers to effective transitions are socio-economic issues, insufficient time, a lack of funds, the need for more effective communications between stakeholders, and a lack of skilled articulation between institutions (e.g., Fowler & Luna, Ch. 17).

Recommendations

We conclude by presenting recommendations related to four specific areas that we regard as integral to effective transitions in schooling and instructional practice: professional learning and leadership, attention to the affective domain, formalizing structures, and the need for further research in this area.

Professional Learning and Leadership

The importance of effective leadership surfaces over and again in discussions of successful transitions. The critical role of professional learning for teachers, principals, and school system leaders is central to facilitating successful transitions within and across panels (e.g., Cantalini-Williams & Telfer, Ch. 1; Sharratt, Ch. 7; Fowler & Luna, Ch. 17). A strong case can also be made for student leadership opportunities (Helling, Ch. 13); these are opportunities that often result in empowerment, increased student engagement, and a welcome sense of relevance in terms of student-perceived issues and challenges.

Professional knowledge and effective practices in curriculum, pedagogy, and assessment are integral to student success and academic achievement. How well these instructional practices relate or align across panels/levels – at the local, provincial/state/district, and national levels – may bear directly on the total effectiveness of a schooling system (Sharratt, Ch. 7; Small, Ch. 8). In the absence of such cohesiveness, students are often required to invest significant time and energy in interpreting the values, expectations, and assessment practices held by teachers to whom they are assigned throughout their school experience. Although standardized assessments at the regional or national level may represent one (highly controversial) attempt at ensuring consistency in curriculum implementation, many of the chapters in this text also point towards other types of support mechanisms designed to achieve student success (e.g., professional learning communities, more effective use of teacher time/resources, related research).

Attention to the Affective Domain

The many stakeholders involved in supporting successful, "seamless" transitions highlight the need to acknowledge the essentially social nature of learning (Vygotsky, 1934/1986) and that the ability to build relationships that support and promote learning and development is critical. This has important implications for both students and teachers. Learning to establish and sustain friendships cannot be underestimated in the early years of formal schooling (Cartmel & Jackson, Ch. 3), and the fostering of these relationships throughout school life should also be seen as a vital component of successful transitions. Another aspect for consideration is the fostering of teachers' abilities to build relationships and collegial approaches towards learning from each other, both within their own school contexts and, perhaps even more importantly, across schools and/or school panels (Jarvis, Ch. 13) in an effort to better understand the lived experiences (i.e., successes and challenges) of students moving through school and postsecondary systems.

Formalizing Structures

Throughout a number of chapters in this volume, authors draw attention to strategies that support transitions, as well as to the many potential barriers to success. More formalized structures appear to facilitate transitions within and across panels, in terms of both schooling and instructional practice. Recommendations include opportunities for administrators and teachers to work together in their own buildings, and to also work with cross-panel teams to better understand the complexities involved in transitions for students. In organizing for transitions (e.g., productive meetings involving a wide range of stakeholders) and other logistical considerations around "making it happen," the importance of consistency, collaboration, and effective communication across formalized structures for strategic approaches to transitions cannot be underestimated.

Further Research

Finally, further research, specifically research into making more explicit the many and complex factors involved in moving smoothly and successfully within and across transitional spaces, is recommended. It would be especially helpful to know more about the nature and availability of professional learning/support for personnel actively engaged in transitions at various levels of schooling "in the field." Furthermore, little is known about how teachers are prepared (during their initial teacher education) to actively engage in successful transitions in the areas of both schooling and instructional practice (Elliott-Johns, Ch. 6). Studies that have the potential to greatly enhance the work of teachers, administrators, and policy makers would offer increased understandings of (a) the inherent conditions that facilitate and support student transitions at *all* levels of schooling, and in teacher instructional practice, and (b) the reasons why some students (and teachers) navigate transitions more successfully than others.

REFERENCES

Vogler, P., Crivello, G., & Woodhead, M. (2008). *Early childhood transitions research: A review of concepts, theory and practice.* Working Paper No. 48. The Hague: Bernard van Leer Foundation.

Vygotsky, L. (1986). *Thought and language.* Cambridge, MA: MIT Press. (Original work published 1934).

Index